AN EVER-WIDENING SCREEN

AN EVER-WIDENING SCREEN

Peter Malone MSC

Connor Court Publishing

Connor Court Publishing Pty Ltd

Copyright © Peter Malone MSC 2015

ALL RIGHTS RESERVED. This book contains material protected under International and Federal Copyright Laws and Treaties. Any unauthorised reprint or use of this material is prohibited. No part of this book may be reproduced or transmitted in any form or by any means, electronic or mechanical, including photocopying, recording, or by any information storage and retrieval system without express written permission from the publisher.

PO Box 224W
Ballarat VIC 3350
sales@connorcourt.com
www.connorcourt.com

ISBN: 9781925138474 (pbk.)

Cover design by Maria Giordano

Printed in Australia

CONTENTS

PART I

1. How Did You …?	1
2. Catholics, 1940s Style	5
3. Films and Codes	11
4. Sister Mary Philomena	18
5. Nana and Aunty Sheila	25
6. Chevalier College	30
7. The Projection Room	37
8. A Choice	43
9. On the Screen Again	49
10. Wider Horizons: ANU	57
11. High Seas, Studies – and the Vatican Council Shakes the Church	67
12. Diploma: Corso di Filmologia	79
13. Ordained, Then …	86
14. Ecclesiastical Peeping Toms	92
15. 1968 and All That	105
16. Formation, Seminary Work	113
17. A Changing Film Landscape	123
18. Don Chipp and the Censorship Debate	131

19. *The Film*, a Chevalier Book	141
20. Changes, More than Anticipated	151
21. An Academic World	166
22. Meanwhile, Films in the 1970s	180
23. In Melbourne	192
24. The US: a Brief Encounter	202
25. The Way Home	216
26. New Job	224
27. New House and …	237
28. Christ-Figures	246
29. Statesides, Many	255
30. Beyond the Pathology (Ecclesiastical, that is)	265
31. In 42nd Street and in More Salubrious Locations	274

PART II

32. The Phone Call that Changed the Next 20 years	281
34. Some Four Letter Signs	290
34. Family	300
35. The Pacific	308
36. 'I Suppose it Will Entail Some Travel'	319
37. OCIC and Cinema	328
38. The OCIC Experience, 1998-2001	341

39. Merger: OCIC and Unda Become SIGNIS	363
40. The First SIGNIS Years, 2002-2004	382
41. Festivals and Juries	406
42. 2005	422
43. Into Some Controversies	430
44. The SIGNIS Cinema Desk, 2006-2010	459
45. Back Home, 2010-	471
46. 'It's Cancer'	484
47. And …	490
Afterwords: My Mother, Eileen, My Father, Joe	492

PART I

1. HOW DID YOU ...?

MRS. ADDAMS.

Or, 'possibly, Mrs. Addams'.

That's the first answer I'd offer to those questions I've been asked more than frequently over the years, 'How did you become involved with films?'

Perhaps it's the priest/film juxtaposition that some enquirers might find hard to link – both in theory and in practice. Or, and I think this is the case with both religious and non-religious questioners, it is a perceived disjunction, for want of a clearer word, between priest/film. Some devout people consider cinema rather worldly, often too worldly. Some secular people assume that cinema is too worldly for priests or, at least, for their idea of a priest. But, then they make a very irritating assumption about my film work which, in my constant desire to seem, and even be, agreeable, I hope I answer politely. 'So, your job is censoring films?' 'No', or more realistically, 'NO ...' If only I had a dollar for every time the questioner moved on to this conversation refuge!

But, back to Mrs. Addams.

Who, you are probably wondering, is Mrs. Addams? Mrs. Addams – I don't think my brother, Philip or I, ever knew her Christian name – was employed by my father, Joe, when my mother, Eileen, became seriously ill in 1946. I have a vague memory that she was preceded by Mrs. Jones for a short time but that that must not have worked. When my mother died on 23 February 1947, it was Mrs. Adams who was minding us. She took us to stay with one of her 12 (I think) children in Hammondville so that we did not attend the funeral, something I have always regretted, but it was thought in those days that children did not go to funerals. It was our piety, a childlike spirituality of the times, which seemed to overcome our grief and, maybe, what later became known as childhood trauma. We knew that our mother was in heaven and the annual anniversary of her death was her feast day as a saint.

I invite you to read a story I once wrote about Eileen and my memories of memories. You will find it in the postscript to this book.

Well, as mentioned, Mrs. Addams had a good many married children living in and around Sydney and, at times, rather holiday-like, we went to stay with them. The point is, as you might have worked out already, that Mrs. Addams liked 'to go to the pictures'. That's the way we put it then. And off we went and the rest is my personal history.

Actually, I can't remember the first film I saw but a blurred memory lurks of *Bambi* at the Amusu theatre in Anzac Parade, Maroubra Junction. The other picture show in Maroubra Junction (in the sourthern suburbs of Sydney, in case you were wondering) was the Vocalist where I do remember seeing a close-up of a feathered Indian headdress and then Bob Hope's face looking up at us under the feathers, *Paleface* (and 'Buttons and Bows'). I should add that I have never heard of any other cinemas anywhere in Australia or the world called the Amusu or the Vocalist. Have you? (It's 2012 and I have had to add this parenthesis: the word Amusu has leapt out at me from *The Age*: there was another Amusu, in Manildra, near Orange, in New South Wales, built in 1936 and is still functioning. I feel a touch of disappointment and a twinge of dispossession at this news!)

With Mrs. Addams, we went everywhere. For some reason – it must have imprinted itself deeply in my consciousness (conscience?) in 1946, the year of my first confession and communion – I have a memory-image of a close-up of Merle Oberon (in black and white) in a film called *Temptation*, which we saw at the Victory in George Street in town (which is what we called central Sydney in those days). What Mrs. Addams was doing taking us to see *Temptation*, I don't know.

This is probably a good place to offer a warning. People tell me that I remember too much detail, especially of times and places, names and dates. They are (generally) too polite to remark that this detail is all trivial and/or irrelevant. But, I can't help it and I will try to be moderate in telling this story. If I'm not, please feel free to skip a little.

It now seems to me that I was fascinated by the stories. These I could remember and recount fairly fully. I must have responded to the images and their immediate impact though I don't have a memory for the visual detail of a scene even now. Its power, yes, but I usually don't see it again in my mind's eye as other friends and reviewers do. And, I enjoy words. I appreciate solid, clever, intelligent word-power and wordplay. I have a card on my desk, 'A pun is its own reword.' And, with that basis, courtesy of Mrs. Addams and her love of the pictures and her family, I absorbed the films and learnt something of the popular film culture. I have remembered it and, so, have been able to build on this early experience to learn more about world cinema and become more visuate – which is my word for the image equivalent of 'literate'.

One other memory might illustrate my love for films and my lifelong commitment to arriving on time, seeing the whole film (and, ultimately, staying for all the credits). My behaviour in this anecdote is not as edifying as I would like it to have been.

In 1947, after our mother died, Dad invited Colin and Thora Malone (Colin was Dad's first cousin) and their children to move into our house with us. No more need for Mrs. Addams – unfortunately. I have only the vaguest of memories but it was probably not the best of arrangements. In 1948, Philip and I went to boarding school. In 1949, Dad changed his life completely, work and home, and moved to Melbourne. From the end of that year, Philip and I went for term and Christmas holidays to the poorer Paddington end of the fashionable suburb of Woollahra, to live with Dad's mother, Bessie Malone, and his youngest sister, Sheila. Nana was turning 67 when she took us on and Sheila, who never married but stayed with Nana until her death in 1971, was turning 28. Philip and I owe them so much.

Oh, the story! There we were in the Amusu on a Saturday afternoon in 1948, Philip, the young cousins and I. It seems very strange but the main film at that session was *Anna Karenina*, Julien Duvivier's version with Vivien Leigh. Who knows what we were doing there for this picture? But, in one of the tense later scenes, one or other of the children wanted to go to the toilet. On the surface, it might have looked as if I was responsible and democratic and could delegate authority. But, truth be told now, I didn't want to miss any of the picture – so I nominated one of the others as escort and stayed in my seat.

Eleven years later, I read *Anna Karenina* while on holidays at Shoreham, the holiday house of the Missionaries of the Sacred Heart on Victoria's Mornington Peninsula. When I came to the part where Anna stands in front of the train to kill herself, I felt compelled to stand up and walk around so powerfully emotional was the translation of Tolstoy's prose but also, and particularly, my vivid memories of Vivien Leigh, in black and white, standing on that railway line in the smoke and on the path of that oncoming train. That is one of the times when I did retain a visual image.

It's now time to move on to the priest/film journey and the various steps of that process.

I am going to add that, while I have given thought to suggestions that I write this story (and did write some material in 1987), I have begun this morning, 27 October 2008, with hand-written pages in a notebook on a Ukrainian Airlines flight from Kiev to London, Gatwick. It's an indication that the answer to the question, 'How did you ...?' is going to be a time journey, a places journey, psychological, theological and spiritual, an Australian story, a Catholic story, a religious life story, a priest's story, a film reviewer's and writer's story, a meld of all these elements.

If reading this story now seems like a good idea to you, I invite you to come along with me.

2. CATHOLICS 1940s STYLE

OF COURSE, you can't generalise about Catholics. Catholics in Latin America have lived quite a different tradition and outlook on religion and practice from those of us from the Irish Catholic lineage. So, this is a glance at Australian Catholics in Sydney of the 1940s. I am not sure that I am a good old-time Australian Catholic. I never experienced a Redemptorist fire and brimstone parish mission. I never went to a Christian Brothers' school!

A good friend of mine who has a flair for the cynical observation often tells me, 'Let me be serious for a moment.' And then he adds, 'And if you tell anyone, I'll deny it.'

Let me be serious for a moment. No denials. It gives me a chance to go back to wonder about the way that I was brought up religiously and morally in those days, about what was deeply ingrained and how that had to be handled in adult life with the changes of the decades. It also gives me a chance to check on what I needed to evaluate in trying to review and write on films from my religious point of view.

The setting is, as I have mentioned, Maroubra Junction, a suburb about 12 kilometres (seven miles in those days) from the centre of Sydney, on the way to Botany Bay and past Long Bay Gaol to La Perouse. It is as descript and as nondescript as any suburb around there but it has the great advantage of being close to the Pacific Ocean and the beaches, especially Maroubra Beach and Coogee, the former rather open with the touch of the wild waves on expanses of white sand, the latter rather smaller and cosier, rock and cliffbound. The houses look much the same. Dad built ours in the early 1940s, a time when the paddock opposite was open and sandy and which is now South Sydney Boys High School. Further down the street was the beginning of Pagewood where General Motors had opened a plant (and our cousin Colin had a job there). That's probably enough attempt at description. For further imagining, just think 'ordinary', think 'average middle-class' or a few rungs below.

One regret I have is that I started school in 1945. No, that's not the regret. The regret is that I don't remember anything of the dropping of the atomic bombs on Hiroshima and Nagasaki (the latter on my sixth birthday). I do remember ration coupons (collected at the RSL in Anzac Parade across the road from the top of Wise Street) but I wish I could remember how we reacted on those now dreadful days.

I was born (as your maths would just have informed you) in 1939, 8 August in fact, which is a great timesaver in filling in documents, and Philip on 3 February 1942. Ancestry was mainly Irish. There was a great-grandmother who was English. She was Elizabeth Morris who married Martin Malone in 1871. They had 17 children who all lived to adulthood (which means that she was pregnant almost continuously from 1871 to 1895). I suppose that's what they mean by sturdy stock. On my mother's side, we thought our grandfather (not a Catholic but he married one, Margaret Healy, the Irish thing again) was Scottish but we recently discovered he was born in Dunedin and came to Australia when he was 36. (Suddenly, *The Lord of the Rings*, etc, seemed much better than first thought!, but the accent still seems funny). Makes me wonder about the cinema at Summer Hill which we used to see from the train to Liverpool and beyond. We thought he owned it, 'grandfather's picture show'.

Possibly worth mentioning that Martin Malone (one of the Garden Malones of Braidwood, not one of the unrelated Coach Malones, from the Southern NSW goldfields, who later moved his gardens to Dundas, outside Sydney) is said to have had a stockwhip at the dining table for discipline and quiet. This irked my grandmother who was one of 13 Madigans from one of the 42 pubs down the Clyde Mountain from Braidwood in Araluen. Philip Madigan did not allow drunkenness, did not allow swearing, would not cash a man's cheque without his wife's consent. Mary MacKillop stayed there on a visit and her sisters lived in the pub for many months while the convent was being built. Now, that's a Catholic family tradition.

School. And this is where the Catholicism of the 1940s becomes more conscious for me. We started at the local Catholic primary school, up till then St. Aidan's, but at this time changed to Holy Family parish, Maroubra Junction. I spent three years there, Philip one. The move to boarding school in 1948 will wait till later because it will have an even stronger influence on our attitudes – and also our going to the pictures.

Let me tell you a story that might indicate something of the piety and the strictness of those days.

It is First Communion day, 27 October 1946, the feast of Christ the King (a celebration introduced into the Church about 20 years earlier in rather triumphalist mode – maybe something of a counter to Mussolini and his Fascist Italian government of the time). Dad was there but my mother was at home in bed, too ill to come.

We had been very well prepared. We boys had our white shirts and our ties, our navy blue short pants. The girls had their white frocks and veils. We had also been extremely well-rehearsed in the way we would process up the aisle, genuflect and move into the pews to preserve the order in which we would come up to the altar rails. We would receive the host on our tongues and swallow without chewing it (chewing the host was unthinkable, something dreadful, perhaps like biting Jesus, though we were told it was not that; it was a 'reverent consuming' of the host). We had our prayers, our prayer books, joined hand postures, eyes cast down, devout with the words of the hymn, 'Where my blessed Jesus may repose on my First Communion Day.'

Afterwards there was the certificate, the medal and the First Communion breakfast in the kindergarten classroom. Dad, I remember, stood at the door, giving out ice creams. It was to be a great and holy and memorable day. And it was.

Now comes the story within the story.

In those days, the Church rule about fasting before Communion was very strict, nothing to eat or drink from midnight until after receiving Communion. (It changed in the 1950s and now the fast is one hour and there is no limit on drinking water). The rule was absolute. One of the boys to make his first Communion that day, whether he understood the fasting rule, forgot or whatever, he drank some water from the school bubbler. That was the end of it for him. No First Communion that Sunday, no celebration. Instead, during the week, quietly and unobtrusively, he made his First Communion. But, of course, it was not the same for him as with our celebration. I remember (now with some embarrassment at my rigid mindset) that we thought he should have known the fast regulations and not put himself into such a position. It was his fault. We were seven at the time – and already our little adult mechanisms were at work, mine anyway.

Looking back, I wonder if I had been trained to be a little adult rather than a child in these religious matters, especially in obeying and fulfilling obligations. I don't mean the sense of guilt that is a cliché tossed up regularly to label the down side of a Catholic education. Yes, some developed guilt feelings but, for many of us, I think it was more duty feelings with a touch (or more than a touch) of scruple. Anyway, I think that this was true for me.

This is connected with the role of confession. First Confession preceded First Communion. Even though we were seven, the presumption was that we needed some serious soul-cleansing before we were worthy to receive Jesus in Communion. Examination of conscience was part of our instruction and everyone expected that seven-year-olds be taught this careful, sometimes thorough, examination and to list one's sins, to recognise them, great and small, to identify them and articulate them to oneself and then to the priest in the confessional. (Obviously plenty of room for becoming a bit scrupulous here.) Having articulated them, one was to be sorry for them, repenting and determining never to sin again – and, in our heart of hearts, presuming that one day we would never sin again. A bit perfectionist! As I remember, we were trained for precision and for confessing our guilts. We were trained to be clear and rational about our sins and our capability of committing mortal sin. And this kind of Catholic conscience, heavy at times in succeeding years, was the way we approached and assessed life.

I would like to add, without any breaking of the seal of confession, that I was at first shocked and then dismayed when I began to hear confessions in the 1960s. So many adult men had not progressed beyond what they learnt at seven. This was in Italy where the men had learnt to add *bestemmiare* to their list, 'blaspheming', or 'swearing', just part of the routine. But, then, back home well-dressed businessmen would come into the confessional, maybe after a tough board meeting, and then, in childish tone, confess that they had missed their morning or night prayers three times. So, while as children we were expected to be adults, with little further adult development available for Catholics, many adults remained rather infantile in their conscientious self-evaluation.

But, in those days, it was difficult to locate precisely where pre-rational and rational lay. The 'age of reason' was reached much earlier then! We were supposed to have reached it by seven and children, treated so often as little and growing, were in some facets of their lives, as far as religion was concerned, subject to adult expectations. Aspects of odd precocity, a greater self-consciousness, especially of wrong and being blameworthy were part of this heritage. At least, I think it was for me. It was very much a Catholic thing, enhanced by the presuppositions of the Catholic education system as it functioned at that time and the way one practised one's faith: morning and night prayers, abstinence from meat on Fridays, Sunday Mass-going, devotions and going to confession regularly. While we knew that these were highlights of our religious experience and were enhanced by the Catholic environment of home, school and parish, the Irish tradition and a pride in assertive Catholic defensiveness were the way that we lived our Catholicism: quite self-conscious, very rational.

catechism answers and clarity, often brief and brisk, were a keynote and the ever-present striving to get things right. One was supposed to be right, not wrong.

This is something of how I remember we were in the mid-1940s, though there is one idiosyncratic story. We belonged to the Natural Health Society of NSW. We had a cousin, Jim Kelleher, living up the street. He was the editor of *The Catholic Weekly*. Dad gave him a story (which proved very embarrassing when reprinted 20 or so years later when as a student I was sent to Rome and Jim Kelleher reprinted it): we didn't put flowers on Our Lady's altar; we put fruit, bananas and oranges! We were Catholics and proud of it, set apart from the rest of Australian society even though we were in it. We had religious beliefs and gave our consent to these whether we had tried to understand what they might mean or not. We had ritual practices which were sacred. We had a Church to belong to and priests and nuns to tell us what to do. Bishops did not yet loom large!

3. FILMS AND CODES

NO, I haven't forgotten about the pictures. But, I thought it best to offer a background of how we were thinking as Catholics when we went to the pictures.

Cinema began on the continent of Europe despite Thomas Edison's 1891 patents and his experiments with cameras and developing film stock. It was the Lumiere brothers from Lyons (with their symbolic name of 'light') who offered the first public screenings in Paris on 28 December 1895. At first, something of a craze for many people, cinema soon established itself as a medium of record, of instruction and religion and, what still dominates, entertainment. The Salvation Army opened its film unit in Australia in 1899. Catholic responses to cinema were mixed but generally welcoming, although Pope St Pius X in 1912 was not keen on churches being used for screenings. In 1928, in the Pays Bas (Belgium, Holland and Luxemburg), the International Catholic Organisation for Cinema (OCIC) was established (important for this story as I was the last president of OCIC before it merged with Unda, the International Catholic Organisation for Radio and Television, also founded in 1928, in November 2001).

The European approach to cinema was in the tradition of appreciation of the arts, a positive approach as a context for any criticism or negative experiences.

The U.S. tradition, maybe because of the strictly devout foundations of that country in Non-Conformist religious refugees like the Pilgrim Fathers (and Mothers) and the pervasive predestination and prosperity spirituality that derives from Calvinism, has tended to take a moralistic stance as a priority and a base for further considerations. In Australia, the moves towards respectability and federation in the 19th century, meant that there is more than a little of that U.S. approach right here. As time went on, with the Catholic influence and intervention in the U.S. concerning movies, this approach was adopted by the Catholic Church in Australia. It was not quite as simple as that and, as I later became involved in some of the changes, this topic will come up again.

If you are familiar with the work of Martin Quigley, Fr. Daniel A. Lord SJ, Will Hayes, Joseph Breen, the Hayes Office and the American Motion Picture Code, skip this section and we will meet up again on the southern highlands of NSW and boarding school in Bowral. If you are not, I hope this explains why the judgmental approach to movies and their morals took hold by the 1930s, was loosened in the 1960s, and began to lose its strict control.

One of the reasons many religious people in the US, Australia and other countries could be sure about the pictures and be calm was that the Hayes Office had been established. It 'cleaned up' the movie industry which had been labelled as permissive by the early 1930s. A Motion Picture Code was established that governed what could or could not be put into a movie to get a seal of approval. The perennials of sex and violence were actually well-known before the 1960s!

A look at the work of the Hayes Office together with the Code and some Catholic contributions to the American policing of the Code, especially by the Catholic Legion of Decency, can show us where the Church (and most of Australian society) stood in those days.

The production Code was the work of Martin Quigley, a film trade journal publisher, along with Fr. Daniel A. Lord, a Jesuit moral theologian and Will Hayes, President of the Motion Picture Producers and Distributors of America inc. In 1929, Quigley was alarmed at what he saw as a departure from accepted moral standards in many films. Most of the material came from plays designed for sophisticated city audiences. In Quigley's view, this material was not acceptable for the wider cinema audience. With the collaboration of Fr. Lord, he produced a production code which was adopted by the Hollywood Producers' Association and ratified on 31 March 1930. It was seen as a means for self-regulation for the industry. However, it was not obligatory to follow the Code until 1934. Interesting to note that Cecil B. de Mille asked Fr. Lord to celebrate daily Mass on the set of *The Ten Commandments* (1927).

Given the overall supervision by the Hayes Office during the 1930s to the 1950s, especially by Joseph Breen from 1934 to 1953, a man who knew the movies and also how they were received outside the U.S. (and whose copious notes are now available), the films of those days were not particularly controversial. If they became so, this was the result of publicity hype rather than content or treatment. It is something of a surprise nowadays to see some pre-strict application of the Code films (a benefit of Turner Classic Movies), the sophisticated and amoral tone of Ernst Lubitch's *Trouble in Paradise* (1932), with elegant thieves getting away with it, or the partial nudity in Rouben Mamoulian's *Dr. Jekyll and Mr. Hyde* (1932) or Cecil B. De Mille's *Cleopatra* (1933) and *The Sign of the Cross* (1934). Small budget features with tough prison themes, like *Ladies They Talk About* (1933) with Barbara Stanwyck have references to butch prisoners and their behaviour and madams talking about their careers, matters that would be merely hinted at in later films. Popular gangster films of the 1930s were sometimes given moralistic introductions to highlight the message that crime doesn't pay.

The Code was a conscientious attempt to apply to cinema ethical and aesthetic principles concerning the art and to regulate its effect on audiences. It embodied caution about the power of film and a felt need to protect audiences and take responsibility for what was shown on screen, placing limits on what could be viewed and how the material was presented. The movie moguls wanted their films to be successful at the box-office, so they followed the cautionary approach. This gave the administrators of the Code, Will Hays and Joseph Breen enormous power over the film-makers. Frustrated and wily writers and directors clashed with the Office but were inventive in finding ways to get round the letter of the Code. Many films that were to become classics like *The Maltese Falcon*, had dialogue re-written, sequences edited and clipped, and relationships obscured or made ambiguous for the sake of the Code. The film of Vito Russo's book and illustrated lecture, *The Celluloid Closet*, has some interesting revelations with scenes from *The Maltese Falcon*, *Rebecca* (and Mrs. Danver's sensual touch and contemplation of Rebecca's wardrobe) and, even, the stroking of javelins in *Ben Hur*.

The Motion Picture Code's general principles read:

1. No picture shall be produced which will lower the moral standard of those who see it. Hence the sympathy of the audience shall never be shown on the side of crime, wrongdoing, evil or sin.
2. Correct standards of life, subject only to the requirements of drama and entertainment shall be presented.
3. Law, natural or human, shall not be ridiculed, nor shall sympathy be created for its violation.

This Code was formulated during the Prohibition era when Al Capone and other gangsters were involved in protection rackets and the bootlegging distribution of liquor. It was released in the first year of the Depression – and the famous criminals like Dillinger or Bonnie and Clyde were about to rob banks.

A long and detailed set of 'Particular Applications' followed, including regulations on presentation of murder, crime, drug trafficking and addiction, and liquor; sex was to be discreet, presented 'in such a manner as not to stimulate the lower and base emotions'; subjects like abortion, sex hygiene, venereal disease were forbidden (in fact, during the war, many films were made about sexually transmitted diseases for the health of the enlisted, and abortion was added in 1951); vulgarity had to be guided by the dictates of good taste; examples of excluded profanity were listed, including 'damn' (which did get through with Rhett Butler at the end of *Gone with the Wind*) and 'hell'; there were detailed prescriptions on costume, dance and decency. Much violence was excluded under 'repellent subjects'. Religion was not to be ridiculed and 'ministers of religion in their characters as ministers of religion should not be used as comic characters or villains'.

It is easy to see why the 1960s presented a challenge to the Code.

The Code applied only to American studio productions but clearly set standards for industries around the world, especially if the foreign product was to be screened in the United States. Since French or Swedish sensibilities are quite different from those of the United States, many foreign language films gained a reputation for being daring or risqué.

The most powerful (but not only) religious lobby group was the Catholic National Legion of Decency:

> It seeks to obtain and maintain fundamental moral standards on the screen. It desires a screen which will not endanger the moral welfare of children and citizens and, therefore, not jeopardise the moral welfare of our country.
>
> It issues, regularly, classifications of films in terms of Christian morality. It presents these moral ratings to the public in order that the public might be informed of the moral character of films currently exhibited and, thereby, be enabled to act wisely and choose for themselves, and for those entrusted to their care, screen entertainment which will not threaten moral and spiritual welfare.

Catholic commentators in recent years have pointed out that, while this approach to cinema might have generated a moral perspective, even if rather simplistic in its judgments on what is good and what is bad, it excluded so many deeper human and moral themes that it contributed to a 'dumbing down' of American cinema at the time – something which many say has not been remedied yet!

The Legion began its work with the Catholic Alumni, women who had attended Catholic schools who were prepared to see films and contribute to classifications. This might have led to a significant contribution by lay women to the Church. However, by 1934, some bishops had issued statements against films, even threatening that viewing some films was a mortal sin. A Legion loyalty oath was developed and promoted amongst Catholics to be faithful to the Legion's advice.

Later, the Legion would take strong stances against particular films that seemed to flout the Code but by the mid-1940s, the movies were generally 'respectable' and audiences knew what to expect. The Code filtered the Catholic moral mentality and the Legion classified each film. Australian Catholic classifications, the work of Fr. Fred Chamberlin who established the Australian Catholic Film Office in the 1970s, followed the American lead from the time of the Legion as well as during and after its transformation into The National Catholic Office for Motion Pictures. Its influence can still be seen in the style of review and classifications from the United States Conference of Catholic Bishops, recently removed from the official Conference and now part of Catholic News Services. If that arouses some curiosity, then a partial list of films which received a C, Condemned rating from the 1930s to 1980, courtesy of Wikipedia, can be found in an appendix. However, I have no memory during my growing up years of talk of the Code or even of the Legion of Decency in Australia.

Vatican authorities had by this time acknowledged the work of OCIC in Europe. Pius XI, a pope who focused attention particularly on social issues while facing the reality of Mussolini and Italian Fascism, of Hitler and Nazism, issued an Encyclical Letter to the whole Church on cinema, *Vigilanti Cura (With Vigilant Care)* on 29 June 1936. While praising the newly established Legion of Decency, the letter highlighted the power of film:

> Good motion pictures are capable of exercising a profoundly moral influence upon those who see them. In addition to affording recreation, they are able to show noble ideals of life, to present truth and virtue under attractive forms, to favour understanding among nations, social classes and

races, to champion the cause of justice, and to contribute positively to the genesis of a just social order in the world.

This is a letter of papal encouragement rather than one evoking fear.

While we weren't aware of all of this American work when we simply went to the pictures, I hope that it becomes clear how the experience of the Code and its consequences fitted rather well into our Catholic world view of the 1940s.

4. SISTER MARY PHILOMENA

I WAS WONDERING why I chose Sister Philomena's name as the heading for this phase of my life, my schooling and my cinema journey.

Sister Philomena could be a pretty formidable figure, short and stocky, but, as I look back, she was extraordinarily affirming. In February 1948, Philip and I went off to boarding school, Our Lady of the Sacred Heart College (OLSH), he just turned six (so a mighty step for him) and me at (Fellini's evocative number) eight-and-a-half. I don't know how it was all arranged, but there we were on the Southern Highlands express travelling to Bowral, over a hundred kilometres south of Sydney. As the truism puts it, Bowral, the home of Don Bradman, was to be our home and our home away from home for nine years.

The sisters, from the religious congregation called The Daughters of Our Lady of the Sacred Heart, took in children who had difficult or problematic family lives. These situations were not all bad. For instance, one of the boys in my class was Geoff McCabe, son of the Australian cricketer, Stan McCabe. With the weeks taken for travel to Europe and other match destinations by boat in those days, Stan McCabe and the team had to spend a great deal of time out of the country. (One of the benefits of Geoff being at school was that his father and several of the cricketers like Lindsay Hassett, Ray Lindwall, Bill O'Reilly and Keith Miller came to visit and took us for some practice lessons. Some stood as sponsors for our Confirmation; my sponsor was selector, Chappie Dwyer though I never saw him again). Looking back, I have no memories that anyone felt looked down on or discriminated against. We were all there at school, together. So, for the record, I enjoyed my years at Our Lady of the Sacred Heart College, Bowral.

We were 150 primary school boys and we each had a number, going up further towards number one each year. (I eventually reached number two, number one being my Missionary of the Sacred Heart confrere, Peter Harvey-Jackson.)

In retrospect, the College was rather exotic in its way but at the time we thought this was all quite normal. Sister Philomena was an educationist with a penchant for success which could be rather elitist, her hope being that her successful boys would continue their secondary education with the Jesuits, at Riverview College in Sydney, which many did. That will not happen in this story. But, her influence and the kind of school she ran had a profound effect on me, and it suited me very well.

There had better be some reflections on the education in general and with some particulars before getting on to the cinema part – and the yen was certainly there because I remember that Sister Mary Consolata told us on the short walk, en masse, up from Bowral station to the College, that we had pictures every week. No wonder I was instantly captivated. To my now embarrassment, I asked her whether we would be having *Bush Christmas* and *Pinocchio* since I had missed seeing them. (We didn't and it took me many years to eventually catch up with both.) Where did this come from, by the end of 1947? I don't know, but I am still on the lookout for the films I have never seen (and God inspired Ted Turner to buy the MGM library for the TCM channel [which added the Warner Bros. collection] for those of us who feel the need for completion in our viewing).

For this section, I am going to borrow from myself, something on Sister Philomena that I wrote years ago in a more succinct writing phase, for which you will kindly make allowance:

> There were only three classrooms in the college. Each held two class groups who were educated at the same time. At most schools, the traditional listing was first class to sixth class. Not here. We had Grade B and Grade A, then Elements and Rudiments (our cousins identified these as Third and Fourth classes at their local parish school), then Grammar B and Grammar A.
>
> Though we knew no better at the time, surely it must

have done wonders for us to arrive at the end of our primary schooling achieving Grammar A.

Curriculum was a specialty. We (at least, I) delighted in quizzes, intelligence tests, re-living history, exploring geography, writing stories, putting on our own little plays (often modelled on Greenbottle and co and their hectic school in radio's *Yes, What!*), reading and reading and reading (both Captain W. E. Johns and *Biggles* and Mary Grant Bruce's Australian stories) and the pictures at least once a week. By the time we were ten, we had begun geometry over and above our arithmetic. We also started to learn Latin and French.

But it was not just busy brains. We had busy hands as well with crafts and hobbies. On Saturdays we got out our fretsaws and slabs of wood, pieces of masonite and three-ply and we meticulously cut out trays, teapot stands, place mats. And we drew on them: cats, horses, the whole zoo. And we painted. The tangy smells of oil and turps easily come back to mind, royal blue skies, emerald green grass and fairy-tale swans that defied whiteness with scarlet beaks (and those are just some of mine!).

So, busy brains, never idle hands and, of course, sport for a healthy mind in a healthy body, especially in the Bowral air and cold. I have to admit that I didn't realise Bowral was so cold until I had left it and others spoke of how freezing the place was. Sport was pretty conventional in those days: cricket and rugby union. However, there was the annual athletic carnival, with four teams in their own colour T-shirts, in reds and greens tucked into extra large Bombay bloomer-style shorts which you had always modestly changed into using your dressing-gown. And, for showers we always wore the linen trunks that we fetched from the 'togs' box at the end of the amber dormitory – our different dormitories had colour names and they were adjacent to 'lavatoriums'; it was all right putting them on when they were dry, but in that cold climate, they were usually still wet and wintry cold, edging them up slowly, again under our dressing gowns to avoid the clinging damp until the last moment. [I am adding an editorial note: we had better come back here later as it indicates that this inculcated modesty did not necessarily prepare us well for the franker era to come].

But the athletics carnival was great, like a fete, families visiting, and sprinting, high jumps, broad jumps, sack races, egg and spoon ... a sunny holiday day.

Speaking of holiday spirit, we often went for a walk, three by three along Craigieburn Road towards Berrima, wearing balaclavas (long-forgotten, except for old-fashioned bank robber disguises, woollen helmet/masks) when it was cold, one hundred and fifty boys in overcoats, with mittens to protect chilblained hands, sticky with ointment. And, on Sundays, we went to Bushtown, a large area just in from the road: trees, bush, creeks, rocks, playing and walks, and tins of scrumptious camp pie, baked beans and spaghetti. Bushtown was a straightforward luxury. (And healthier, with time more effectively spent than do many children today bent over play-stations, perfecting aggression and the killer instinct, chomping fast foods!)

I've left religion until last. Sister Philomena was no stint in religious education. Catechism was a pushover – she stimulated all our learning, religion included, by making it competitive, with gold star competitions, our capitalistic touch. We knew the lives of the saints. That conjures up another embarrassing memory. Apparently, I read well enough and had a good enough voice to be chosen to read aloud from Joan Wyndham's books like *Six O'Clock Saints*. Where you might ask, did this happen? Actually, I was in the projection room, called the bio-room, along with the two 35 mm projectors, standing at a microphone with loudspeakers in the hall. This was before the film started – pious crowd control! – and also when we (often) stopped after the first reel of a suitable film and the word went across to the elderly sisters in the nursing home that they could come to see the film and we would start again. The reading of the lives of the saints served as a devout intermission filler.

The celebrations of the Church's year were on the tips of our tongues

– you name it – 17 October, for instance, feast of St. Margaret Mary Alacoque. (For the eagle eyes reading this, it was 17 October but the 'optional memorial' was later transferred to 16 October, so it is not an error!). We were not only well-educated, we were well-pious: Mass every day, Confession every Friday, Novenas, Rosary every night after tea (the younger ones not in the pews but, with little chairs on the side aisle, pushing limbs into crevices between chapel floor planks to make whitened grooves on our knees) and processions round the classroom corridors, sometimes outside for bigger days like Corpus Christi, and up and down the classroom aisles, chanting hymns behind a banner of St. Joseph, Our Lady or the Sacred Heart or the Sacred Heart.

Back to the films and what they contributed to a cinema education.

At OLSH (we were not allowed to pronounce it Olsh), we were very lucky. No restrictions on movie-going. I have read the stories of that doyen of UK critics and prolific writer, Alexander Walker, a Northern Ireland Presbyterian who envied the Catholics in his town who were allowed to go to the pictures when he wasn't, or the story of film buff, researcher and movie-lover, Brian McFarlane, speaking of the struggles with his father (and some subterfuges as well as using his imagination) to see a film. We had at least one film a week in the hall, with 35 mm prints, and sometimes mid-week in the Elements and Rudiments classroom with 16 mm prints.

In the new hall (big screen and curtains), we had popular and more recent films, the G and PG movies from the 1940s that turn up on TCM. We saw plenty of Margaret O'Brien (*Bad Bascomb, Three Wise Fools*), Jackie 'Butch' Jenkins (*The Human Comedy, My Brother Talks to Horses*) and the two together in *Our Vines Have Tender Grapes*. We saw *The Secret Garden* (and marvelled at the door opening to the garden and moving from black and white into colour). We saw Judy Garland as *Little Nellie Kelly* (just saw it again on TCM after more than 60 years), colourful homespun stories like *Home in Indiana, Scudda Hoo Scudda Hay, The Homestretch* (where we got to know and dote on Maureen O'Hara, Jeanne Crain and June Haver.

The fact that they were Catholics also helped!). There were plenty of British films like *Scott of the Antarctic* or *Hue and Cry* and *Great Expectations* (where we jumped when Finlay Currie as Magwitch stepped out from behind the gravestone and startled Pip and us).

Like any good (that is, more highbrow) cinema at the time (we didn't go in for two films with the supporting feature), we had 'featurettes', called 'shorts' in our day. We saw many, many, many of MGM's *Passing Parades*, *Pete Smith Specialties*, James ('and so we say farewell to...') Fitzpatrick travelogues, Paramount's *Talking of Animals*, Columbia's Three Stooges. Cartoons were favourites. We seem to have had a lot of Mighty Mouse and Heckle and Jeckle from 20th Century Fox.

In the classroom we saw quite a number of silent films. There were some scary *Cat and Canary*-like thrillers. After all, it was just over 20 years since the introduction of sound. But, we also saw some classics from the 1930s like *The Sign of the Cross*, giving us the chance to have Charles Laughton's face implanted in our imaginations as Nero until *Quo Vadis* came along and Peter Ustinov, strumming and singing while Rome burned, took over.

If you have ever seen Giuseppe Tornatore's Oscar-winning *Cinema Paradiso* (1988), you will know what is coming next. Yes, despite the Motion Picture Code making most American movies respectable and decent, there was that matter of kissing and what that might imply, which, of course, it didn't to us at that stage of our development, but did put wariness and suspicions into our subconscious about love and what we later discovered was sexuality, and a reality that didn't bother us at that time on the screen, either, human nudity. On many levels, Catholic children like us in the 1940s who, we now realise, lived rather sheltered lives, were prepared for growth and maturity, but not in this area. It wasn't just the Church. It was the times, and that was where we were stuck. Did we later put a mental hand over these scenes? I know one priest who used to remark about how often he dropped his rosary beads and had to bend down to get them to avoid a risqué scene. He was just joking – I think.

An anecdote to illustrate what happened. June Allyson and Kathryn Grayson (well-known to older audiences and devotees of MGM classic musicals) should have been more than safe. Off we went on the first reel of *Two Sisters from Boston*. Kathryn Grayson had left home in Boston (I can't remember why) but finished up on a stage (saloon or vaudeville, I think, probably the former) where she had a long dress, a parasol and a bonnet and sang in her operatic way until ... she turned round and there was no back on her skirt. Perhaps it was burlesque. We did survive that scene. Then her sister, played by June Allyson, went to New York to find her and was shocked at this behaviour (as we were). But, then (and I've forgotten the reason) June had to go and take Kathryn's place. She did, turned round, no back to the skirt and, I think, she fainted ... Enough for us. It was over 40 years later that I was able to see *Two Sisters from Boston* on television and find out what happened to Kathryn and June.

One of the funny things in *Cinema Paradiso* was that, when the parish priest stopped the screening in the piazza and an offending kiss was literally excised, the projectionist spliced it on to a reel of similar cuts. Years later, the young assistant comes back and plays the reel. I wonder what our OLSH reel would have been like!

So, yes, Sister Philomena did put her hand over the lens so that we would not see kisses. We did see them if we went to the pictures during the holidays. I actually don't remember them, though I must have been, as I suggested, subconsciously alerted.

I do, finally, have to express gratitude to Sister Philomena for her breadth of vision, her affirmation of her students and providing us with a wide-ranging study background as well as a religious sensibility as we moved into our futures. Sister Mary Philomena was probably a blend of Mr. Chips and Miss Jean Brodie, but we were the better for it.

5. NANA AND AUNTY SHEILA

IF IT WAS right to name the previous section of this book, Sister Mary Philomena, it is even more right and proper to acknowledge the importance of our grandmother and her youngest daughter for their love and care in the crucial years of our childhood and adolescence.

Bessie Malone (who, as you might remember grew up in her father's hotel in Araluen, that respectable pub where the Sisters of St. Joseph could stay without undue concern) was a small strong woman who had given birth to six children, was widowed after 30 years of marriage, and who had strong and determined opinions. At the end of 1949 when Dad had moved to Melbourne and changed his life and work completely, our Uncle Phil, a Franciscan priest, picked us up from OLSH for the Christmas holidays and drove (a euphemism for his style behind the wheel) us to Woollahra, 1 Tara St, just off Ocean Street as it goes down from the gates of Centennial Park towards Edgecliff Post Office (later the underground station) and Double Bay. Our house, a solid two-storey building, was built by my grandfather in the late 1920s. It was situated on the lesser, poorer side of Ocean Street, the Paddington side, which later became more swanky and gentrified. As my grandmother wished, we lived in a Franciscan parish (St Joseph's, Edgecliff) but we were equidistant with St. Francis, Paddington, where Uncle Phil was guardian and parish priest from 1954. We were devoutly situated.

Aunty Sheila was the youngest of my grandmother's six children. She worked in the public service (and taught me early to touch type, something for which I have been most grateful, renewed at this moment as my fingers glide over my Toshiba laptop). She never married and looked after her mother until she died (in bed at home) in 1971 at the age of 88. Sadly, Aunty Sheila developed dementia in her early 70s, but kept an eye on Philip and myself (and my film reviewing) long after we were ordained.

I liked living in Woollahra. It was truly home. Nana and Aunty Sheila were kind and firm and it never occurred to me not to do what they asked and expected. We received love and care. Holidays at home from boarding school were joyful times and Nana was never short of an entertaining story from her own life. I came to Tara Street when I was 10 and left to go to the Novitiate when I was 17. Philip was there from ages seven to 17.

Dad came up to Sydney for Christmas holidays. From 1951, Philip and I flew to Melbourne for the May holidays. So, seeing and being with Dad was joyful time. He adapted after Eileen died, gave up work in advertising, radio and sport, went to Melbourne where he worked at Greenvale TB Sanatorium (later a home for the elderly) as a wardsman for 10 years or so, other jobs briefly after that but, with his discovery of lawn bowls, he became an avid player (as he was of rugby league, professionally, during the Depression, cricket and golf), an untiring apostle for bowls and greenkeeper for many years at Carrum. He was the most cheerful man I have known, plenty of affirmation and plenty of flirting, though he never married again (perhaps his mother was against this), but, as he wittily punned, he had several 'near missus'. Yes, he cracked puns, incessantly, and loved wordplay, contributing to Lawrence Money's *Boot in Mouth* column in the Melbourne *Herald* for years, sending in slips of the tongue from radio and TV sports commentators.

I would invite you, if you wanted to know more about Joe, to read a story I once wrote about him, and a tribute when he died in 1997. You will find it in the postscript to this book.

(I am beginning to feel a little guilty: what no childhood traumas!)

Two things I would like to recall that are relevant to the film journey.

The first is that there was a discipline in our going to the pictures during the holidays. I don't know who stipulated it, but we were never to go to the pictures more than twice a week – no consolation to those whose parents would not let them go at all. And we did abide by that.

At first we went with Nana and Aunty Sheila. We went to the Savoy, like all good Catholics, to see *Monsieur Vincent*. We also went there to be amazed at *Fantasia*. One of the happiest movie memories is our all going to see the Marx Brothers at the Regal at Bondi Junction, *A Night at the Opera*, where we laughed, as the ads might say, 'hysterically'. For a while, Nana would take us into town (we had both trams and buses), line up and buy the tickets – I have memory of her queuing at the St. James in Elizabeth Street for *Annie Get Your Gun* – and our going in while she shopped and collected us afterwards. I think it was when I turned eleven that it was judged that Philip and I could go into town by ourselves (good old safe days!).

We saw films like *Come to the Stable*, with Loretta Young and Celeste Holm as nuns, comedies with Bob Hope and lots of Dean Martin and Jerry Lewis (before the French pedestalised Jerry Lewis), though they don't seem so funny nowadays, and spectacles like De Mille's *Samson and Delilah*. I can still see that chunk of temple roofing hurtling straight into the stomach of one of the Philistines as Victor Mature, now a long-haired and blind Samson, brought down the Temple of Dagon on himself, on Hedy Lamarr's Delilah and all. (Who said children aren't impressionable? – but they can maturely deal with a lot of scenes like this one!)

Many of the films don't seem so great as we look at them again. But they played an important part in the development of imagination, part of the special experience of going into the theatre, and, at the Paramount's Prince Edward Theatre in Elizabeth Street, the Wurlitzer and Noreen Hennessy at the organ rising out of the pit. It was the grandeur of pre-multiplex cinemas, the darkness, the curtains, the increasingly wide screens during the 1950s, colour, glamour, stars, magical effects and the dreams and fantasies of the plot. The imagination was active and excited. Not a bad thing.

The second thing

This is the story of Tut. I think it will be the story to help you realise how kind and strong both Nana and Aunty Sheila were. (And it has a movie connection, discipline-wise.)

You are wondering who or what is Tut. Actually, she was our grand aunt, Nana's youngest sister, Lucy Madigan. A bit more explanation. She was the little darling, her father's delight. The story went that he was playing with her when she was quite small, playing the way doting fathers do with baby, tossing her up and catching her. The story doesn't have the detail of how the accident happened. She hit her head on the roof, damaged her skull, damaged her brain. She was never quite right afterwards. She became Tut and grew into a little old lady.

Before the middle of 1950, we used to accompany Nana on the 360 (Dover Heights) or the 333 (South Head Cemetery) to Central Station and then take the 460 (Campsie Station) to Ashfield, to the Good Shepherd Sisters convent, one of those immense 19th century buildings that looked perfectly suited to France and European landscapes and climates, a smaller-scale *Nun's Story* establishment. The sisters had accepted Tut as a subsidised border. She lived with the other, younger women, Magdalenes. It was a long time later that we understood who the Magdalenes, dressed like nun postulants, actually were, women, some from the streets, who were getting their lives together again. No bother for Tut. The Magdalenes and the sisters were kind to Tut, although (the Catholic thing) she could be grouchy about some of the sisters.

Our visits to Tut were on any day of the week and the visits were fortnightly.

Then in mid-1950 Aunty Sheila bought a car, a Ford Anglia, and our visits were changed to Saturdays since Aunty Sheila was at work during the week. Every holiday, every fortnight, no matter what, we visited Tut and took her out. You may be curious as to what taking her out entailed, especially as her legs were bowed and she was rather dwarfed, with a loud nasal twang to which the insensitive were often insisting 'I beg your pardon', finding her difficult to understand. She had the gift of being oblivious to the staring passers-by, the gawky curious glances or the heartless smirk. We parked near Burwood shopping centre and the goal of the trip was to wander Coles and Woolworths, she looking at odds and ends and trinkets (and we, if we had a little money, buying boiled lollies or broken biscuits). After that, a picnic in the park and then a visit to one or other of the many cousins (remember 17 Malones and 13 Madigans) who lived in those inner western suburbs, and this included afternoon tea.

During the drive Tut chattered unrestrainedly about her life over the previous two weeks. We could have been driving round the block again and again. The important thing was the talk.

Nana had cared for Tut for years but, as Nana grew older, she needed some help and the Good Shepherd sisters were real rescuers. But, Tut did have a holiday at Tara Street every year after we went back to school, sleeping on the front balcony which Philip and I shared. Tut died at the age of 61.

And what has that to do with going to the pictures? By now I might have given something of an impression that I am a planner and that is right. One of the joys of later years in preparing a day of reviewing, and fitting as much and as many as I could, was studying session times, determining what was feasible to see without wasting too much time in between screenings. That could partially account for how I have been able to see so many. It was a bit the same in those younger days, checking the theatres around us for double feature programs. Two for the price of one has always appealed to me. The Coogee Boomerang (never heard that name for another cinema either) used to have two main features for their double every week, one from the Hoyts circuit on its first week of release, the other from the Kings circuit on its second week. So, one could do the calculations and plan ahead. But, the days for the visits to Tut meant no picture-going and the sacrificing of the anticipated program.

Which meant that during our holidays we had an experience of priorities and that family, care and concern for those less well off than ourselves was of paramount importance. It's a lesson I hope I have learnt.

6. CHEVALIER COLLEGE

PHILIP and I did not go to the Jesuits or to Riverview. We didn't have the money for the fees. Was Chevalier College the next best thing? Educationally, not at all. But, for an influence on both our lives, essential.

Being 12 was a peculiar experience. After seven years of primary school education (and reaching the top with Grammar A), one suddenly found oneself at the bottom of the scholastic ladder on entering secondary school. A new learning curve, or a new learning ascent. The old patterns of study which, it never occurred to us would ever change had to give way to the new.

Chevalier College. The school was run by the Missionaries of the Sacred Heart (MSC). In Australia they had ventured into secondary education with the establishing of Downlands College in Toowoomba in 1931. Fifteen years later, Chevalier was opened five kilometres or so outside Bowral, on the way to Moss Vale. Rather enclosed British countryside scenic looks. So I was not exactly in new territory. The school was rather small. Wooden classrooms and dormitories and, at the beginning of 1952, a new hall (where significant film experiences were in store for me). We had priests and brothers on the staff, quite a lot for the small number of boarders and the 'day-bugs' who came in each day from the surrounding towns.

At Chevalier, we were offered a reasonable education, though I don't think the academic standard was particularly high. Priests might do long years of philosophy and theology training but this does not help them much in preparing to teach secondary school subjects or deal with adolescent boys. Somehow or other, we all managed.

We studied (even half an hour after morning Mass and before breakfast), went to classes, played the expected sports, cricket and rugby union (no matter how badly). We joined the cadet unit – we were too small to go to camp the first year and were told at the passing out parade to tell the presiding officer that we were 14. We said our prayers, Daily Mass became optional at times and whoever thinks that 1950s boys were more devout than today's concerning Mass has a highly romanticised memory. Religious teaching was constant, culminating in an intellectual study of apologetics (the explanation and defence of faith). We used our memories, though I don't think we understood too much. Try Sheehan's *Apologetics* and the meaning of Transubstantiation. But, that was the subject meant to get us ready to face the world, begin our jobs and enter into marriage and raise families.

Somebody asked me recently what I thought I was going to be when I grew up. Memory tells me that in the early secondary years, I didn't really think about it. Later, I may have thought I would study to be a teacher. While we had to make life decisions at 15 (if we left after doing the Intermediate Certificate at the end of third year) or by 17 (if we stayed to do the Leaving Certificate exams), that future didn't seem so urgent.

The priests and brothers showed a humane face of the Church in personalised education and guidance. Needless to say, there were harsh words, the strap, some unjust sixers (and some angry grudges against individuals which took some time to get over), but my memories of Chevalier in those days are happy. (I think I have forgiven our first year football coach who made us run around the upper football field sixteen times because we mistook the day for starting practice and then used us as buffers for his crack under-14 team, pushing against scrums, standing waiting to be tackled on rather hard cold ground and hearing him urge them to wind us – which they sometimes did. Yes, forgiven, not forgotten!)

These days it is commonplace to see the 1950s in films as a quiet time, a conventional time, the Eisenhower years in the U.S., a time when the nuclear family could be itself in middle America and in Robert Menzies' Australia (though, come to think of it, I did not, as I have suggested, have much experience at all of the nuclear family). The American films of the time, still respectable and decent, mirrored to other admiring cultures the American way, Australia included. Perhaps it was the aftermath of the Second World War, perhaps the cold war security of knowing the rightness of our way of life. Perhaps it was simply a breathing space, the lull before the 1960s. The 1950s seem much gentler than our own times. When the *Back to the Future* movies were made in the 1980s, Michael J. Fox discovered that when he time-travelled back 30 years to 1955, he found his bobby-soxer mother, his gawky father and Ronald Reagan and Barbara Stanwyk in *Cattle Queen of Montana*, screening at the local cinema – which had become the 'adult' theatre of the 1980s.

We did have our own difficulties at the time. We saw *Guilty of Treason*, with Charles Bickford starring as Cardinal Mindzenty of Hungary being tortured by the Communists. We were against the Communists and scared of them. Fr. Aussie Sheridan, who used to read us *Father Brown* stories as an incentive to do better in maths class (we did) and the final guillotine chapters of *A Tale of Two Cities* before we went to sleep, also told us tales of the Chinese Communists advancing down to Australia, taking over the country and torturing Catholics. Bamboo sticks poked under fingernails still come to mind. Red scares and yellow perils.

This next bit is somewhat embarrassing. At school in New South Wales we didn't know too much about Archbishop Mannix in Victoria, Bob Santamaria or The Movement or The Split. The Labor Party seemed quite normal to us – except for its leader, Dr. Evatt, because of the Petrov Affair and suggestions that he was really a Communist. 1954 was a momentous year. In February, as a family, we lined up outside St. Vincent's Hospital in Darlinghurst to wave to the Queen as she drove by (extra days of holiday granted for the occasion). Back at school, we went down by train to Wollongong to join the children from the south coast and the southern tablelands in the oval to wave to her again. Then we saw the films made about her tour.

But, during the Easter holidays, Mrs. Petrov, wife of an official at the Russian Embassy in Canberra who had decided to defect, was dragged by police from her plane to safety at Darwin airport. Espionage down under! We went back to school to write essays about the Petrovs. I found mine. I was caught up in the spirit of the times:

If all things are considered, it is good that this has happened here and it is hoped that the affair will bring the Australian people to their senses concerning communism.

Sir Robert Menzies (for whom and for whose party I have never voted) would have been more than satisfied with my sentiments and my rhetoric.

By good chance, I have just watched a documentary, *Trumbo*, on the screenwriter, Dalton Trumbo (best known these days as the writer of *Spartacus* and *Exodus*). While it tells his story, it is really about the Cold War paranoia that overtook so many in the West from the mid-1940s. We were afraid of the Communists, who had been our allies during World War II. (The revelations and truth about Stalin were not really revealed until the information came from his successor, Nikita Kruschev in 1956, which shocked and disillusioned many of the world's Communists). These were witch hunt years in the United States with the House Committee for Un-American Activities, the McCarthy enquiries. The movie industry was under suspicion and many of the card-carrying Communists who saw the party as a means for social reform during the 1930s and 1940s were summoned, asked to name other Communists and, when they refused, were tried and some (including Trumbo) jailed as hostile witnesses. Other patriotic stars and directors co-operated and named. Lillian Hellman has called this era 'Scoundrel Times'. Many of these film workers were blacklisted for years, losing homes, marriages breaking, their children hounded. A film like *Trumbo*, with its many quotes from the author's writings and the clips from the times as well as the later interviews are a sobering reminder of the cost of unjust loyalties. Philip Noyce's *Newsfront* is a film reminder of some of this attitude in the Australia of the 1950s. We absorbed it at the time.

When I mentioned the hall at Chevalier, I suggested that this was a place that looms large in my film memories, looms in a very happy sense.

February 1952, my first month at secondary school (when King George VI died) gave us three films that we would not have seen at OLSH Well, maybe the first, *Words and Music*, the MGM biography of Rodgers and Hart. But, with the next two we moved from the G classification (For General Exhibition) to A (For Adults). We saw a World War II thriller, *Five Graves to Cairo*, and another tough thriller with Burt Lancaster, *Rope of Sand*. Things were to be different. But, there was one blow. For economy's sake or discipline or both, the new Rector, Fr. Jack Burford, told us that there would be only three films a month. A Saturday per month with no film! Possibly, the most consistent feature of the choice of films over my five years was Greer Garson. Fr. Burford had a passion for Greer Garson, so we saw *Mrs. Miniver* (of course), *The Miniver Story*, *Blossoms in the Dust*, *Random Harvest*, *Pride and Prejudice*, *Goodbye Mr Chips* ... and *Julia Misbehaves*. But Julia and Greer will be part of a problem to be considered later.

So far, I have suggested that I had escaped traumas (except for Fr. Jack Tyler – forgiven not forgotten – and the football practices), but here is one. And the agent of the trauma was Fr. Sheridan. I suppose it was an inevitable result of Catholic attitudes of the time and the effect of the Legion of Decency kind of militancy.

We were all collectors when we were young: stamps, marbles and (oh dear!) cigarette cards were popular with us. I also had some scrapbooks of film advertisements. It had all the hits of 1952 neatly cut out from the papers and pasted up. Some of the priests used to enjoy looking through them and noting the progress. Aunty Sheila, in fact, was not so keen on it, perhaps a little worried about the views of the priest friend who used to repeat, 'Peter knows all about the pictures.' (If I ever fulfilled one prophecy, more or less, this was it!). But Fr. Sheridan did not like the scrapbook or the ads at all. Marlene Dietrich appeared that year in a western *Rancho Notorious*. Decades later she said she was still proud of her legs but, here they were, the be-all and end-all of the film it seemed, half a page of the Sydney *Sun* and *Mirror*: split skirt and exposed leg.

But, that was not the worst. An anti-marijuana film, salaciously titled *She Shoulda Said No* was also emphatically advertised. The skimpily-clad, arched backwards form of the degraded heroine, wine-glass stem in hand, I now realise meant that she had certainly said 'yes'. But, perhaps I didn't discriminate too well at that age, and there was the ad in the scrapbook. I was surreptitiously summoned after lights out to Fr. Sheridan's room. Deeply upset, he spoke to me with pain and conviction about the evils of these ads, concluding vehemently (and he was a small-statured man and I still remember his intensity), 'The devil himself drew these pictures.' He confiscated the scrapbook and burned it.

These were sobering thoughts for a 13-year-old and made for an uneasy conscience.

It has suddenly dawned on me that I should Google the film and see if the offending poster is there. It isn't but there are four others, not quite as overt as the one I described, but in the vein nonetheless, so you can see for yourself. I discovered that the actress had been arrested with Robert Mitchum at a party where pot had been smoked; she was invited to star in this film because of her celebrity – and a way for her to make amends. The film was also known as *Wild Weeds* and *The Devil's Weed*.

This is probably the moment to take up a theme from the OLSH days of modesty and, of course now, sexuality. Our lives at Chevalier were still quite sheltered. We had to learn to be a bit more robust in the locker rooms and the showers, especially at cadet camps, much more open than at school – or lining up all together, in the altogether, for the medical examination and that touch and cough routine. With Catholic principles, puberty was looked at very seriously. We had inherited the casuistry of the Jesuits of the 17th century when they opened schools and were very strict concerning thoughts, words and deeds, favouring the intrinsically evil approach to sexual matters both slight and serious. I was very lucky that my Uncle Maurice, one of the wisest and kindest of men, took me through the basic matters one day at lunchtime upstairs in the shop he owned at Erskineville. I appreciated his calm and matter-of-fact explanations.

In 1954, instead of a preached retreat (they could be deadly), Fr. Burford invited an older MSC priest, Fr. Eric Dignam, to stay at Chevalier for six weeks and to give talks in the religion class slots. Fr. Dignam related well to the boys, spoke in the classroom with ease and common sense, frankly and with no fears or phobias, about sexual issues. For him, every boy had a 'heart of gold'. He was gentleness itself in confession, lifting the weight of the world and of feeling-guilty consciences. Actually, we didn't know very much in those days. Saying 'shit' was pretty daring. A furtive cigarette was strong disobedience. There were girls at the Dominican Convent, not far away in Moss Vale, but we scarcely met them, though dancing was introduced at old boys' functions – we were expertly coached by Fr. Harold Baker whose father served as an energetic MC at the dances, where we waltzed, did the foxtrot and paraded with the Pride of Erin. There was some socialising in our last years at school and tennis games during the holidays. That was about it.

Despite the lately burnt scrapbook, I was invited by Fr. Gerry Kelly, who showed the pictures, to join him as projectionist and to help him choose the films. (Later, when I went through something of a puritanical phase and mentioned that we had seen some films which were not so good, he remarked, stroking his head as he always did, 'Now you know what I had to put up with'.) But, that was 10 years later. It's time to go up to the projection room.

7. THE PROJECTION ROOM

YOU HAD to climb up a steepish, banister-less set of wooden steps to get into the projection room. We had a 16 mm projector, places for reels and rewinding spools of film, a gadget for splicing when a film broke – and this little gadget will soon make more of an appearance than you might have been expecting.

Well, here I was at 13, happy to learn how to project and to do the other chores required in a projection room. As we watched the pictures, we let our imaginations be stirred, we relished the stories. But, we also began to understand that there was more to them than the attractive surface and that we too could become film critics. In the projection room, I discovered *Focus*. Not the focusing of the projector, but a Catholic film magazine from the UK with articles and reviews by longtime reviewer for *The Tablet*, Maryvonne Butcher (whom I just missed meeting 40 years later when she died) and longtime reviewer for *The Word*, Fr. J. A. V. Burke. Reading them avidly, I learnt about film reviews and themes that were dramatised in the films. The magazine began in 1948 and folded in 1958, but, for me, *Focus* was a light in my life. It was a great joy to learn in the 1990s that it was partly an organ for the International Catholic Cinema Organisation (OCIC) which I later headed.

Here's a distraction for which *Focus* should not necessarily be blamed! I found an exercise book with my third year essays including reviews of the British film, *The Oracle*, and John Huston's *Beat the Devil*. I might not have known what I was going to be when I grew up, but this review tells me that I would not have minded being a film reviewer. (Skip this if necessary! I had just turned 15):

> This is a review of the film which was advertised as 'John Huston's comedy successor to *The African Queen*'. I have heard of the merits of *The African Queen* and I find this an

extremely worthy successor. 'Focus', a film review, writes that the characters are of an Evelyn Waugh calibre and I definitely agree. The ridiculous situations are along the lines of *The Loved One*.

There is not much of a story at all. We find ourselves in a dirty Italian port with a bunch of crooks, their agent and his wife who have met and are friends with what seems to be an aristocratic English couple. In truth they come from London's East End.

The crooks are really amusing in themselves. Robert Morley, tall and enormous, Peter Lorre, short and fat. There are two other members, a tall, thin foreigner and a small, sinister Major Ross. Oh, I almost forgot, 'handsome' Humphrey Bogart, of course, is their agent.

We follow them through their adventures in the town and in a semi-derelict steam-ship bound for Africa where the crooks intend to possess themselves of a uranium field (illegally, of course). Their plan is halted as they have to disembark in mid-sea into a small rowing boat. They are captures by Arabs when they land but are freed with the aid of Bogart and a clever piece of satire on Rita Hayworth and Aly Khan.

The acting is superb! You would be hard to please if you did not enjoy this film, for it is as the papers say, 'a prancing comedy'.

Oh well, one has to start somewhere, somehow!

Just a word concerning programming. Sometimes I feel that I am a touch competitive. I wanted each year's program to be better than the last. With the help of *Focus* and other reviews, we did have some top-rate films. Fr. Kelly allowed me to choose films that some might have hesitated about for school screenings. We had Marlon Brando in *The Wild One* and *On the Waterfront*. (It was years later that I discovered *The Wild One* was banned in the UK at this time). We had Grace Kelly in *The Bridges at Toko-Ri* and *The Country Girl*. We had *The Caine Mutiny*. We missed out on *The Greatest Show on Earth* and *The Student Prince*, prints not returned in time for us (though we were sent Greer Garson – again – in *Scandal at Scourie* as a substitute). We showed the Alec Guinness Ealing comedies and many British war films. Looking back, perhaps we were a bit highbrow for a secondary school, but there was plenty of entertainment, even Bob Hope and Dean Martin and Jerry Lewis. We enjoyed Danny Kaye in *Knock on Wood* and, later, 'the chalice from the palace with the pellet with the poison' in *The Court Jester*. Yea, verily, yea.

Not everything was plain sailing. We went big on *Quo Vadis* and even obtained a poster from MGM to display on the notice board. We were big on notices and 'Coming Attractions'. Unfortunately for *Quo Vadis*, MGM's advertising campaign chose to highlight Patricia Laffan's Empress Poppaea rather than Deborah Kerr (another favourite of the time – we even had Marlon, Greer and Deborah in *Julius Caesar*). The poster pictured the empress reclining sensuously and (though this was not in the film itself) with her skirt split and displaying leg. Legs again! Not suitable for Chevalier Notice Board exhibition! Our solution: a green crayon matching the colour of her dress brought the material down to a more modest draping – and boys and staff were none the wiser.

Marlene Dietrich's legs and Patricia Laffan's legs were not the only legs to cause us trouble. There were those of Esther Williams (hardly surprising because she was so often in the water in her films) and, perhaps a little shockingly, those of Greer Garson herself. Greer first.

As mentioned, she appeared in *Julia Misbehaves*. Fr. Kelly thought that two scenes were unsuitable, so up in the projection room we set to work cutting and splicing. We were more effective in censorship than those who simply put their hands over the lens. At the beginning of *Julia Misbehaves*, Greer, a showgirl (if you can believe that) is besieged by creditors and escapes by taking a bath. Reginald Owen as her agent appeals to her to come out. She replies nonchalantly and in her ladylike tones (neck to toes in suds), 'I can't. I'm in the nude.' 'Well, get out of the nude', replies the exasperated agent.

The Chevalier boys and staff of 1953 never saw or heard that. We had made up for the laxity in applying the Motion Picture Code. Nor did the audience see Greer do a song and dance routine with acrobats where she sang, 'Oh save me, oh save me, my house is on fire', and was lifted down a tower on to the stage. The trouble was she was wearing a mini-kilt. We put the pieces back quite deftly and sent the print back to MGM. This seemed odd to me even at that time, so a bit more ingenuity for next time.

Next time was on the college sports day of 1954. Parents joined boys and staff for the screening of *Million Dollar Mermaid*. Esther Williams portrayed Australian-born swimmer and entertainer, Annette Kellerman. To this day, I am sure that most of the audience do not realise that the film contained a telling shot of Esther in a one-piece bathing suit in 1908. (*The One Piece Bathing Suit* was actually an alternate title for the film). She was filmed from the waist down in close-up walking along a Boston beach. This episode led to a court case about decent beach wear in those early 20th century years. I didn't want to, literally, cut the film, so Fr. Kelly agreed to a compromise: projector running, off with the projector light, at the same time, with co-ordinated fingers, on with the hall lights; 30 seconds and the scene has run, so off with the hall lights and, at the same time, on with the projector light. The film was not cut. Audience sensibilities were not offended. People may have thought we had a technical glitch in the projection room but on we went.

I just Googled *Million Dollar Mermaid* on the website of the U.S. Catholic Conference of Bishops and found its Legion of Decency classification and review. There is a comment that the one piece bathing suit raised eyebrows in Boston at the time but the classification is A1, Unobjectionable for all audiences. The review finishes, 'Sentimental but easy-to-take family fare.' Fr. Kelly had been too strict. But, that is how we were.

There are many stories from the 1950s along these lines. A different American story is that of Cardinal Spellman of New York who took exception to Jane Russell's suggestive costumes in a minor frothy musical comedy, *The French Line* (1954). He urged and persuaded people to picket cinemas in protest. He did the same in 1956 for the release of Elia Kazan's version of Tennessee Williams' *Baby Doll*. We were the Church Militant. (Googling again, I find that while the review of *The French Line* mentions sexual situations and innuendo, and was classified as Condemned, it has been re-classified as Unobjectionable for Adults!)

Part of Cardinal Spellman's motivation may have been the fact that there were stirrings of protest in Hollywood against the Code. A celebrated case was another minor comedy, *The Moon is Blue* (1954) with William Holden, Maggie McNamara and David Niven. Based on a play by F. Hugh Herbert who had been writing plays and films for years, it used words not permitted by the code, 'pregnant' and 'virgin'. Director, Otto Preminger, decided that it was time to flout the Code and make a test case.

But, something was also stirring in the Catholic Church of Australia of the 1950s. The impetus was from movements started through the inspiration of a Belgian priest, later Cardinal, Canon Joseph Cardijn, the Y.C.S. (Young Christian Students) and the Y.C.W. (Young Christian Workers). They did not develop in Sydney which had the C.Y.O (Catholic Youth Organisation) but flourished in Melbourne and other dioceses. Socially aware, vigorously active, prayerful and thoughtful, these Catholic Action movements meant that, while things seemed to be steady, there were possibilities of doing something more. This made more immediate sense in the Europe of the 1920s and 1930s with the rise of Fascism and Nazism.

In Australia, Fr. Fred Chamberlin, who had been ordained in Melbourne in 1946, became interested in OCIC, which itself was connected with the Cardijn movement, founded in 1928. Fr. Chamberlin paid his own way to OCIC international meetings at the end of the 1940s and early 1950s and later decades. He became national chaplain to the Y.C.S. A serious film buff (who had written a letter of congratulations and encouragement to *Focus* in its first year), who worked with young people for film appreciation, published two influential pamphlets, *Films and You* (1950) and, a collection of articles, *You and the Movies* (1952). With many current films referred to, these booklets were popular and stimulating. *Films and You* went through five impressions from October to December 1950. A total of 20,000 copies were printed.

In the projection room we had copies of both booklets along with *Focus*. I read them and re-read them and absorbed them. Fr. Chamberlin will play an important part in this journey later on.

Meanwhile, back in Woollahra on holidays, the same conditions were in place: going to the pictures twice a week, and the visits to Tut each fortnight.

In 1951, there was a change. Philip and I flew to Melbourne for a holiday with Dad, which we did each year bar one to 1956. There were screenings for the residents of Greenvale Sanatorium and we saw those. There was a bus direct from the Sanatorium to Flinders Street outside The Majestic, enabling us to get into the city quickly and discover the Melbourne equivalents of the Sydney cinemas. The early 1950s was a period of some action and spectacle films. Maybe *Kim, King Solomon's Mines* and *The High and the Mighty* seemed better because we were seeing them in Melbourne. It was also the era of Cinemascope with *The Robe* and, for those not biblically-oriented, *How To Marry a Millionaire*. The 3D phase was short-lived, and I saw only one with glasses, *Kiss Me Kate*. We also went to a local cinema in Puckle Street, Moonee Ponds, not dreaming that Edna Everage lived close by!

One good thing which emerged from this period was that I went to have my eyes tested and had to wear glasses. I still remember the shock when I came out from Geddes in Elizabeth Street and could read the signs on the shops opposite. I didn't know you were able to see so clearly! No wonder I couldn't catch the balls in cricket. And, for the record, the first films I saw with improved eyes were a double feature at the Coogee Boomerang: *Vera Cruz* and Neville Shute's *A Town Like Alice*.

8. A CHOICE

HAD YOU asked me at 5.30 pm on 25 June 1956 what I was going to do with my life, I wouldn't have been able to give you a firm answer. The only answer up to this time was a 'no' or 'never' to Fr. Bill Ryan who taught us Latin and Greek when he asked, daily, 'When are you going to Douglas Park?' (the small town and area outside Campbelltown where the Missionaries of the Sacred Heart had their Juniorate and Novitiate). Had you asked me at 8.30 pm on 25 June 1956 what I was going to do with my life, I would have answered (and have never changed my mind or doubted since) that I would be a Missionary of the Sacred Heart. I later learnt that I function best with intuitions, so an intuition that led to a life choice.

What happened was that at our table in the refectory, the subject came up about living in the seminary in Melbourne. Most said it would be awful. Dad had taken Philip and myself for a visit there during May 1954 to visit our cousin, Fr. Darcy Morris, and the superior of Croydon, Fr. James Power, the priest who had, the year before, said in his sing-song and repetitious way, 'Peter knows all about the pictures.' We had been introduced to Roland Kaupp, the first Chevalier old boy who had joined the MSCs.

I ventured the opinion at the table, that it wouldn't be so bad. And, whatever the spiritual, theological and vocational spin you put on it, that was that. Philip had already made up his mind to go to Douglas Park into fourth year in the Apostolic School, which he did. Our genial Dad made no objections whatever, even at the prospect of not having grandchildren. He did offer the opinion that we wouldn't have much difficulty in community life as we had spent many years already answering bells. In later years, he was interested in everything we did and always signed his letters, 'your proud Dad'.

One of the consequences of this decision was facing the fact that I would not see a film for, at least, another eight years during the period of training. (In case you are feeling some stirrings of compassion, this did not happen!). But, I must have had a vocation, willing not to see a film, giving away the library of novels I had been building up (reading a new Agatha Christie every afternoon during the Leaving Certificate exams and being a member of the *Sun-Herald* book club for some years).

Before I went to the Novitiate on 24 January 1957, one of our disciplinary rules was allowed to be broken. Different relatives wanted to say goodbye – and take me to the pictures. Not only more than twice a week but twice on the one day, *Private's Progress* in the morning and *High Society* in the evening. Three days before I went to Douglas Park, as a family we all went to the Kings Cross theatre, Dad, Nana, Aunty Sheila, Philip and myself to see a double feature program, the civil war film, *Great Day in the Morning* and the Judy Holiday comedy, *The Solid Gold Cadillac*. And, that for the time being was the end.

What was the Novitiate like? *The Nun's Story* might offer some leads. We were eight novices for the priesthood as well as a group of men training to be brothers. Not having been in the Apostolic School (I asked not to; we had an anti-view of the boys we met from the school when they came to Chevalier to play cricket), I had no idea what to expect and accepted it all as 'normal'. We were also very young, some of us turning eighteen that year and some just a year older. But, that's how it was. Our contemporaries were embarking on work training or further studies. You were expected to have made up your mind at this age in those days.

We were earnest, very earnest. One of the first things I wrote down in my notebook was 'Near enough is not good enough.' The novice master was Fr. Frank Butler who had taught us at Chevalier (which meant that I wasn't as terrified of him as some others were who had not met him). There was an atmosphere of apprehension, if not of fear, and sincere 'striving for perfection', as the spiritual books used to say. One of our mistakes (that lasted too long into my life) was to presume that perfection could actually be reached if we tried hard enough and we were the ones who were going to do it. That dangerous presumption is doomed to disappointment and disillusionment.

The routine was quite severe and unrelenting, but we took it for granted and many of us survived. Up at 5.00 am, more bracing as the mornings grew colder, then breathing exercises breath more and more visible as the weeks went on, an hour's meditation in the chapel, Mass (we were forward-looking and enjoyed the 'Dialogue Mass', reciting the Latin responses as a congregation). There was study, Latin classes, manual work in the vegetable gardens, chicken-houses, tomato jam-making. There were conferences, study of the Constitutions, prayer times and exercises, speech practice. And meals, mainly in silence except for feast days and specials, bush walks to the shrines dotted around the property and swims at Pass Creek because the schoolboys went to the Nepean River swimming hole, cold showers, except for a hot one on Saturdays, recreation together, talking, sewing-mending and peeling potatoes. Then meditation points and early to bed.

There were hysterical times. Too much seriousness and silence begets the release of uncontrollable giggles. Even the then exhortations, 'Brothers, think of the Passion' didn't really help. But a swift rebuke from the novice master and you never felt less like laughing in your whole life. There were will-bending exercises like the Chapter of Faults, where we confessed to the group any external misdemeanours, a great opportunity for the novice master to let rip on how bad we were and to humiliate us. The expected response, always given, was 'Thank you, Father.' It was the same with reading in the refectory. Reading too fast, 'Just sit down, Brother, for five minutes while we catch up.' 'Thank you, Father.' Agreeing with instructions for work, 'That's right, donkey, nod your head.' At least that was better than others having to read over the novice master's loud mutterings of how badly you read or his continuous tinkling his bell at the table.

The high point of the novitiate was the 30 Day Retreat from mid-August to mid-September, using the Spiritual Exercises of St. Ignatius. St. Ignatius was a master of spirituality and keen psychologist. Following his process of prayerfully discerning was an experience of conversion of heart and a contemplation of the pattern of Jesus' life, death and resurrection. It helped us to see our call, our coming commitment our life in the MSCs and in the Church. We may have been too young to appreciate much of this retreat, but it was a significant time of our lives.

One of the difficulties in all of this is that I could not remember what I was like before the Novitiate. The year of the novitiate and the direction of the novice master had the effect of turning me on my head, and the prospect of getting my feet back on the ground seemed nearly impossible. Fr. Butler did offer me a cheery piece of advice during the 30 Day Retreat when I was feeling down, 'Just go and dream about *On the Waterfront.*' But, he had also avowed to rid me of my 'celluloid fever.' He was not in favour of films. He saw them as worldly, potentially corrupting. He had us almost ready to vow that we would never see a film again. I need to include now what otherwise might have been a postscript. After his eleven years as novice master, Fr. Butler was appointed to Papua New Guinea and found himself screening films in a parish open-air theatre in Port Moresby. Then in 1975, chatting in Sydney, he moved off to his room but remarked with his frequent stammer, 'R-righto, just g-g-go and write you review of M-m-machine Gun Kelly.' An acknowledgement, even approval, of what I was doing? I hope so,

However, I felt even more guilty during the summer break before our profession of vows. It involves another practice, 'modesty of the eyes'. We were encouraged to keep our eyes down and to remain recollectedly undistracted. My crucial moment came in January 1958, on a bus trip to Shellharbour Beach for a picnic, one of the very few times outside the novitiate. We drove through Wollongong, and I knew where the cinemas were. To look or not to look to see what was on. The great temptation, despite our never seeing a film again. I'm afraid, as you might have guessed, that striving for perfection failed: Burt Lancaster, Tony Curtis and Gina Lollobrigida in *Trapeze*!

And, then it was coming to an end. Our novitiate was not as strict as some others. I remember we listened to records one night in June and then again on Christmas night. (Shock, horror, the next year we heard the novices actually watched a film, *The Mountain*. What was Fr. Butler up to?) We had visitors on Boxing Day, only close family. There was a rule in the novitiate that we did not speak about or mention the apostolic schoolboys. Which meant that all the other novices could talk about their brothers and sisters but I was not allowed to talk about Philip. Communication with family was by one letter a month. There was no contact with school friends which, regrettably, brought severances of friendships that time and circumstances could not mend. Then the next group of postulants arrived and it was time to make our vows. The eight students for priesthood and two brothers made their profession of poverty, chastity and obedience on a hot steamy day, 26 February 1958.

On reflection, I realise that we missed 1957. I am still surprised sometimes at seeing a film title I am not familiar with and then finding its release date was 1956, 1957 or 1958. We also missed the arrival of Elvis Presley! We did go out some evenings to see Sputnik. We went outside the grounds only to doctor or dentist or for a picnic. We did not read the paper or listen to the radio. Much of our energy actually went into devising more and more practices that would mortify and test us. These seem now to be excessively fidgety: not crossing our legs, not cutting corners on paths, not picking leaves from trees as we passed, opening and closing doors silently. But, these were the benchmark of our striving for perfection. We were determined to honour these practices for the rest of our lives and not be influenced against them, especially by any of the seminarians in Melbourne, some of whom seemed 'lax'. We thought we were spiritual but we were spiritually proud and priggish.

On the 25th anniversary of my profession, 1983, I went to review *An Officer and a Gentleman*. It was a very popular film, especially with Richard

Gere's performance as the navy novice with Louis Gossett (Oscar for Best Supporting Actor) roaring commands, imposing the strictest discipline and enforcing meticulous practices on the recruits to batter them into submission and make men of them. Even the Joe Cocker and Jennifer Warnes' Oscar-winning song 'Up Where We Belong' reminded me of our single-minded, spiritualised-for-the-cause, striving for perfection, 'Up There'. I thought that things had changed over the quarter of a century in the humanising of training and discipline. Perhaps I should have seen *An Officer and a Gentleman* on a different day, or go to see it again. But I have no desire and never have.

9. ON THE SCREEN AGAIN

AFTER WHAT Fr. Butler urged us not to do (see any films), it might seem strange to see such a heading as 'on the screen again'. But, it happened far more quickly than I could have imagined.

However, let me put an image and an anecdote to you that might suggest how we were on the day after making our vows. This is the image. The eight of us are dressed in our black clerical suits, the broadest of collars, our black hats. We are setting out for Melbourne on the *Spirit of Progress*, the night train. 27 February. It is hot. The carriage is small and self-contained, a 'dog-box', just enough for us to be sitting four on each side with no real room to manoeuvre. Looking primly dapper, we are prepared to be self-sacrificing, 'mortified' since it is Lent and this is what life is supposed to be like. There is some respite after the all night vigil sitting up ramrod straight. We stop at Albury to change trains because of the different state rail gauges. John Hanrahan's father is there to meet us (the Hanrahans live in Albury) ready to take us to Mass and to breakfast before we catch the Victorian train. That train must have been comfortable (at least in comparison) because I have no memory of it. Spencer Street (now upmarketed to Southern Cross). Br Lambert the senior student there to meet us. A car ride out to Croydon, Mt. Dandenong and the television towers on top of it coming closer until we have arrived and have been welcomed by the students.

The prospect of seven years of enclosed studies, no movies.

Not in the least!

Actually, the first months were hard going. The senior students appeared 'lax' to us and some took it on themselves to shake us up. Since that time, I have always disliked the phrase, 'I want to whisper something in your shell-like ear ...' That was the quietly sudden interruption to the five minute break before night prayers. Somebody was actually whispering in my ear, warning us to, what we might now say, 'lighten up'. I don't remember the detail, but I do remember the shock to the system because we thought we were 'practically perfect' (there's more than something very prim about Mary Poppins too!). We still did our study, did our best not to cut corners on the courtyard paths and to open and shut doors quietly. This latter was practical. There was such a large number of students in those days, nearing the 70 mark, that we juniors did not have a room to ourselves for the first two years at Croydon, six of us in a balcony dormitory-style and studying in the classroom (next year being promoted to a front parlour with only four of us, a desk each as well as a bed).

At Easter 1958 the crisis came. During 1957, what now might be seen as a breakthrough occurred, though it had a touch of scandal at the time. A relative of one of the students had brought out some 16 mm prints and a projector to screen some films for staff and students, the first time ever. The first films for 1958 were to be *Prince of Foxes* and *Love That Brute*. Many were looking forward to this. Some of us were not. Our first year group met on Good Friday in our classroom and determined that we were definitely not going to go.

I don't know to this day who told Fr. Drake, the superior of the community, but on the Saturday morning after breakfast, he got us together on the cloister outside the refectory, spoke strongly (he had a loud and attention-demanding voice), told us how hard-ground into us our ideas were – and told us we had to go to the pictures. It seemed the beginning of the end. (I was told years later that Fr. Drake said to someone, 'I told him to go to the pictures and now he sees 500 a year. What have I done?')

We went.

Actually, *Prince of Foxes* was one of the films I had chosen for screening at school, so I knew it wasn't so bad. A first seed of doubt. I have never had an opportunity for seeing *Love That Brute* again, a hope now over 50 years old.

There were three or four more movie evenings that year and some the next: *A Kid for Two Farthings, Double Indemnity, The One that Got Away* ... some already seen while at school, some new films, more adult themes. So, for the record, it was only 14 months between seeing the last film I thought I would see for eight years and that compulsory Easter night.

For me, the scholasticate (the word for 'seminary') became an exhilarating place. We had to grow up in so many ways. It was a place to regain and develop some sanity. Philosophy studies suited me and were stimulating after the year's break from school, a different type of gap year! Fr. John Savage was one of the best of teachers. Fr. Dennis Murphy, not long back from overseas study in Scripture opened up the Old Testament for us, books we knew nothing about. I thought that if I were to do something after ordination, it would be to teach some Old Testament studies (which did happen, teaching Scripture for 30 years and more). We were introduced to Liturgy (but I found that I was exited from the choir, voice deficiencies), did small courses in astronomy, biology and began to learn Italian as there were so many migrants from Italy that it would be useful to have some knowledge of the language for pastoral purposes. We also did a three year course on Church History, the taking of notes (pronounced 'noots') by Fr. Frank Brady. Part of our folklore is imitating Fr. Brady's eccentric pronunciation and his getting his words and phrases mixed up: the year ten eleventy four, Gregory the Gate standing on the threshold of the Middle Ages, and the Roman Pontiff Sope Celestine the Sird. Mischievous students asked him to repeat spellings like Guggenberger, 'G-U-juggle-g'. He had jokes written in the margins of his noots, like the one about the theologian, Origen, who wanted to be martyred but his mother hid his clothes – 'and he could hardly go out wrapped in thought'! It was the same in his ethics classes, a contract being an agreement between two parties joined by a 'juridical blonde'.

But, it was the spirit of the group and the vitality inside the place (we went out only for regular hikes and bike rides) that I found best. Four three act plays were put on each year, generally in professional style.

Though for our Christmas 1958 play, some disasters struck. The dimmer would not work and so Mary (me) and Joseph had to exit in full view, with some thinking it was already the flight into Egypt. And one of our Filipino students as one of the Magi offered the gift of 'mirth'. Other performances included *Rope*, *Arsenic and Old Lace*, an abridgment of *The Rivals* and, later, *A Man for All Seasons*. (While I had some initial moments as Lydia Languish, I could later be both Henry VIII and Thomas Cranmer in *A Man for All Seasons*).

There were several in-house magazines for essays, stories, poetry, *Stella Matutina*, and one for philosophy, *Eureka*. We had Forum every Saturday night, prepared speeches, debates, impromptus where I learnt I had a capacity for putting words together and presenting them. Television came into Australia only at the start of 1957, after some previews during the Melbourne Olympics of 1956, but no television for us. We saw the front and back of *The Age* and could listen to radio news. We did get our first look at television in mid-1959 when the ABC did a program on life at Croydon, *Out of the Monastery*, where we combined being 'normal young Australians' with being monastic-style religious. The superiors hired a set to watch the program – and afterwards we were allowed to watch *In Melbourne Tonight* with Graeme Kennedy.

But, we read. Biography, spirituality, Catholic culture (Chesterton, Christopher Dawson, Frank Sheed...). during term and novels and plays during holidays. We had a three weeks break in midwinter and six marvellous weeks away from Croydon at Shoreham on Westernport Bay, fresh air freedom (comparatively speaking) and, the first year, 500 miles of bike-riding and 100 miles of walking, all over the Mornington Peninsula, down and up (where unavoidable) Arthur's Seat, and to Sorrento back beach and Portsea. It took some time to adjust to Croydon, but second year, 1959, was one of the happiest of my life.

A new stage in my approach to films.

It was not just a Catholic thing to be wary and suspicious of the arts (despite a 2,000 year history of support and development of the arts). It is a feature of many religions (or of their sub-groups) and of Christian denominations. One remembers the zeal of some of the 16th century reformers like John Calvin or John Knox who were reputed to hold stern religious attitudes towards frivolity. The Puritans in England (think iconoclastic Oliver Cromwell) were the same. It is often said that the Puritans were opposed to bear-baiting, not because of the pain to the bear, but because of the pleasure it gave to the baiters. And, it is said, Puritans are afraid that someone, somewhere, somehow, might be enjoying themselves!

In more recent centuries, Catholics were influenced by their own kind of Puritanism which was developed in Belgium and France, Jansenism. Jansen was bishop of Ypres, influenced by his interpretation of the writings of St. Augustine. The practical side was developed by such Parisian figures as the Abbe St. Cyran and the community of Port Royal, of which Blaise Pascal was a member. In France, there was another, rather opposite, movement, focused much more personally on the inner life and feelings of Jesus, which was developed by Francis de Sales, Vincent de Paul and others, a counter to the rigidity of Jansenism.

One hallmark of earnest religion has been the work ethic. No pain, no gain. Another has been to see evil, and the devil, in entertainment. Despite our alleged hedonism (and Australians do like surf, sun, drink and gambling and those who believe otherwise are 'wowsers') there is also a puritanical streak, sometimes showing itself in stoic endurance of hardship and sometimes in self-righteous attacks on a lowering of community standards. Witness the Australian eagerness to satirise Yanks and Poms and the critiques (which imply that people should be far better than they are) that form part of the satire of Edna Everage and Les Patterson, courtesy and discourtesy of Barry Humphries.

The wowser, puritanical expectations make it difficult for film reviewers, Catholic, to think of themselves sometimes, or be seen by others, as doing something worthwhile, because they are spending time on an occupation that is peripheral, frivolous or merely entertaining!

I have amongst my books, a 1932 publication by R. G. Burnett and I. D. Martell, *The Devil's Camera, Menace of a Film-Ridden World*. (Uh-oh). The dedication reads, 'To the Ultimate Sanity of the White Races'. To skim through it, you would think it was attacking the world that was emerging from the 1960s, or was an attack on current 21st century attitudes, hardcore pornography of sex and violence, the mockery of religion. Instead, it is a commentary on the 1920s and the early 1930s, the period of the writing of the Motion Picture Code.

In 1957, we might have described the tone of the book as excessive yet have believed in many of the points it was making even if there was vehement rhetoric in its high-minded attack and aggressively racy paragraphs. A sample of the overstated case might pique interest and curiosity:

> Have you ever considered what a sex-steeped world would be like? Do away with marriage and replace it with free-love, and civilisation would collapse. Life, robbed of the restraints supplied by culture and education, would become a grotesque parody of the sordid and abandoned films that the British censor sometimes lets through, and in a few generations would slip back into the twilight of history; the civilised Empires of today, having their moral foundations knocked away, would crash into oblivion. It sounds far-fetched, fantastic perhaps, but throw your memory back twenty or thirty years. Did you ever dream in your wildest moments that sex could hold the sway it does today; that you could watch a complete stranger slowly disrobing entirely for your entertainment? Of course not; yet it has come to pass. Beware that time when you glance back in twenty or even ten years' time you are not similarly amazed at what you failed to foresee in 1932!

Even noble scaremongering often lacks credibility.

It was the Forum gatherings on Saturday evenings that helped me to think again about films and be reminded of what I was like before the Novitiate, of Fr. Chamberlin's booklets and *Focus*, of writing reviews and seeing meanings in films.

The Croydon student discussions about films focused on *Seven Brides for Seven Brothers* which had been screened there in 1957. Many of the older students had been scandalised by it. While the novitiate had worked its effect, I could not see that *Seven Brides for Seven Brothers* was in any way bad. Dad had taken us to see it during the Christmas holidays three years earlier and we had enjoyed it. The anti-film stance began to waver. At Forum, some students spoke about the films we had seen. They took rather a pious approach, reading Catholic themes into the Jewish *A Kid for Two Farthings*, and waxing lyrical about the end of the Korean War film, *Battle Hymn*, taking its romantic symbolism of two pines, one representing the hero chaplain, played by Rock Hudson, the other a Korean girl, united in eternity, even further than the sentiment of the film intended. It seemed too much. A more down-to-earth attitude started to take root again.

We were helped immeasurably by our director of students, Fr. Jim Cuskelly. He opened up spiritual and theological horizons twice a week in brief and telling conferences. He helped us to get in touch with the exciting developments of the late 1950s under the leadership of Pope Pius XII (on biblical studies, theology, a spirituality of the heart, liturgy and participation; the pope also publishing an encyclical letter on cinema in 1957 suggesting that we ought to know how moving images worked as communication). This pope, despite the questioning of his reputation concerning his wartime activity or inactivity on behalf of the Jews, and of his aristocratic and aloof personality, addressed himself in audiences, speeches and letters to the contemporary world and its development.

A special series of conferences for our first year group made all the difference. Put simply, Fr. Cuskelly explained how we had been moulded in our novitiate year, all coming off the assembly line perfectly square (as indeed we were). The next step in our formation had to be the wearing down and smoothing of the sharp-jutting corners and edges so that we would become our own rounded characters. In 1958, this was freeing, enabling us to get on with the business of living and developing (and rid ourselves of self-focused rigid judgments). Crises, such as crossing our legs or not (the novitiate had been against it), were resolved by 'Please yourself', and we started to take more responsibility for our lives and decisions. If ever I want to embarrass myself, I have only to read Jim Cuskelly's *A Heart to Know Thee* (which I did as a mainstay during my retreat before ordination). He wrote it from his experience of the students and their personal growth. It is about us. Whether we acted on it or not, we were offered the gift of common-sense in our approach to everything.

Receiving this kind of formation as I was turning 19 was a gift. Fr. Cuskelly will reappear in 1962 with an even more common-sensed practical application of the common-sense he offered us at this time.

10. WIDER HORIZONS: ANU

WE HAD gone to Croydon in 1958 fully expecting to stay there until our ordination in 1964. It was not to be. Providence had far more in store. Because Croydon was overflowing with students (those were the days!), the MSC administration built a house of studies on the Federal Highway, Canberra, just inside the northern border between the Australian Capital Territory and New South Wales (actually, next to a drive-in, which will also make some appearances in this journey). The two junior year groups from Croydon set out by bus at the end of February 1960 to open up the Canberra monastery. We had another welcome Albury stopover at the Hanrahans.

We certainly had to take responsibility in Canberra. Our group had become the senior group. The monastery was not finished when we moved in. Planks to walk up to the entrance. And there was no sewage system until July. It was no joke lining up at the sheds out at the back fence on frosty, then freezing, Canberra mornings (or having an emergency during the night and having to run downstairs from the front wing where our rooms were into the dark and cold). And then there was the detail of students commissioned to tip the contents over the back fence on to an open paddock. The grounds were full of thistles. A library had to be set up (my job). After packing the Croydon books destined for Canberra (mainly philosophy), we found that the tea chests could not be carried up to the library because the metal on the bottom would cut the floor tiles. The job took years to finish since the design of the library for 10,000 books was based on a shelving height that could hold only the smallest paperbacks.

But, we were in Canberra, another world, a small city in those days, around 54,000 people. Lake Burley Griffin was still being excavated, not being filled with water for another three years. You could walk cross-country from our place to Mt. Ainslie with no properties or fences to stop you. The cemetery, soon to be in a suburb, was a long way from Civic Centre. The picnic spot was way out at Cotter Dam and the Molonglo River. At the back of the monastery, we could climb over the fence and go directly to the top of Mount Majura. And, on a personal level, Philip had completed his novitiate and made his vows in February and he and his group had arrived in Canberra to begin their studies.

For three of us, there was another surprise, even more challenging. The MSC superiors believed in education, so we were to begin an arts course while doing our seminary subjects at the Monastery. In 1960 we were enrolled at the Canberra University College of Melbourne University, following the Melbourne University curricula. But, revolution was in the air. Well, not quite. Negotiations were under way that year. At the beginning of 1961, we became the School of General Studies of the Australian National University, with our own curricula, designed by our own lecturers. We were very lucky in those days. While lectures were given and office meetings held in the old wooden huts in Childers Street, a new and modern building was opened in 1961. Our lecturers in English I (and we were only 20 students) included A. D. Hope, Hope Hewitt and Bob Brissenden, and the same for English II (about 13 students). Professor K. C. Masterman taught us Latin (six in Latin I and down to four in Latin II). Manning Clark was the professor of history with Geoffrey Fairbairn lecturing in History I (The Rise of Christendom, 27 students) with Manning Clark.

The Australian National University experience proved to be another great stimulus and, significantly, an unexpected opportunity to be out of the enclosed world of the monastery and out in the streets, in the lecture rooms with ordinary people. In those days, the Catholic Church promoted tertiary education for religious and clergy and there were lots of us, all in clerical suits and nuns in older style religious habits on campus, rather out of proportion to the number of ordinary students there.

At Chevalier, we had studied Latin and Greek, so Latin I seemed an obvious choice. If we live any purgatory here on earth, doing Latin proses and translating unseens week by week has to be it. We improved our classical background and read the principal classical authors. Lectures during my four years studies in Rome were in Latin. Later, at Daramalan College in Canberra, I taught Latin to fifth and sixth formers for a year and a half, so I feel I have done my duty to Latin.

English literature, not to the fore at Chevalier, was much more to my taste and gave a solid literary background for the later work in film. We didn't fail our first year, John Franzmann, John Hanrahan and myself. In fact, we did very well.

At the end of 1960, after three years in what were called temporary vows, we were to prepare to make our final vows, our lifelong commitment of poverty, chastity and obedience as Missionaries of the Sacred Heart. That was on 26 February 1961. Lifelong commitment.

The three of us were asked to stay on for a full-time year at ANU and were joined by another of our group, Kevin Bowden, who had been teaching the year before at Monivae College. And some from the group behind us also began their studies. Ten of us now at ANU.

Full-time, a marvellous year, 1961. We did Latin II (no comment – or, rather, a reminder of the previous comments on proses and unseens). English II meant reading and reading (with no television distractions at the monastery). This was a more coherent course than that imposed by Melbourne University. This year, Shakespeare, Elizabethan and Metaphysical poets, Jacobean drama and, something of a shock to sensibilities and sensitivities and the broadening of these, a special course in Restoration Comedy (which the novitiate did not quite prepare us for). But, with the intelligent guidance of A. D. Hope (who might have felt at home himself in the 17th century), we learnt more (and better) than we had expected.

I am very much indebted to Manning Clark not just for opening up

Australian history and the desire to major in it, which I did, but for his sardonically insightful perspectives on history and the history of the Church. In History I, The Rise of Christendom, he took us through the origins of Hinduism, Buddhism, Christianity and Islam. He had a particular focus on the reformation period. His quiet, provocative humour was funny, even when you were on the wrong end of it. With such small groups, 27 of us in this course, he knew everyone. He relished the potential embarrassment. Arriving late for the first history lecture, I was told, as I searched for a seat, that the course could begin with the date of the birth of Christ or, if preferred, the death of Cleopatra. He kept insisting that I not be embarrassed. No good protesting that I wasn't, as, red-faced, I finally got to a desk. We came to expect and enjoy the gibes and learnt to be comfortable as Catholics in this 'secular' environment. Manning Clark was not biased for or against any denomination. Explaining 19th century Russia, he used large books of paintings, walking up and down the front desk, with nuns and us in our regalia, showing us vividly coloured images of beer-swilling or vodka-toting clerics. 'Look, drunken priests'. Then, suddenly, most apologetically, 'Orthodox priests, drunk, not yours.' Only momentary relief when, with that tremor in his voice, 'Of course, yours were like that too.' Aced! Later, explaining Tolstoy's testing of all religions, he quoted James Joyce's *Portrait of the Artist as a Young Man* in support. When asked if he had tried Protestantism, Stephen Daedalus replied, 'I've lost my faith, not my self-respect' – and this with a bow to the Presbyterian minister in the front desk. He also bowed to two of us, in clerical dress, at the back of the room when he quoted Macauley on Anglicanism being between austere Calvinism and 'Rome, with its crowd of pantomimic gestures!' Then he said that he liked this so he would read it again. Another bow.

I would like to pay tribute to Tom Inglis Moore for his course on Australian literature. There were only half a dozen of us but, each week, as we sat around the table in his office, we explored and read voraciously the poetry and the novels of 19th and 20th century Australia. It was a marvellous opportunity, Professor Inglis Moore's personal friendships with writers, his knowledge of and enthusiasm for the literature (at this time still under-appreciated and under-taught in our schools and universities) was an inspiration. Patrick White was our special topic in 1961. Since A. D. Hope had slated *The Tree of Man* in a review some years earlier, *Voss* was our focus for White. During the year, White published *Riders in the Chariot* which we immediately studied. One likes to think one makes personal and independent judgments when one is young, but I still admire *Voss* and have never re-read *The Tree of Man* despite its favourable re-appraisal.

These were very literary years for me. Very little television and scarcely any films. During the Christmas holidays at the end of 1960, we went to down to Bowral, to Chevalier College (no comparison with the memories of Shoreham). I was grateful to Fr. Bryan Strangman for choosing some films for us, Peter Sellers hilarious in *The Mouse that Roared*, the inevitable *Heaven Knows, Mr Allison*, but also Hitchcock's *Vertigo* and, a favourite from school days, *The Man Who Knew Too Much*.

The main cinema event of 1961 was attending a screening of *The Nun's Story*. The poor manager of the Star cinema in Queanbeyan must still be puzzled as to why his specially invited audience of nuns and brothers behaved the way they did. We laughed. We particularly laughed at the penance sequences in the gloomy Belgian convent, with Audrey Hepburn kneeling and kissing the feet of the sisters under the refectory tables. Of course, it was the release of tension, the reaction to seeing up there on the big screen images of what we had all experienced and were finding it a relief to be away from. Going to the cinema for the first time in over four years, and we laughed at what seems now to be one of the best films dramatising the old styles of convent life. More serious and threatening was the sequence where the superior told Sister Luke to fail her exams for humility's sake. We were never told to do that. Rather, Fr. McDougall, the provincial superior, told us it would be a tragedy if we failed. We didn't. We had become quite competitive.

You may remember with some sympathy my failure with 'modesty of the eyes' at the end of the novitiate, looking at the signs outside the Wollongong theatre advertising *Trapeze*. In Canberra, we were told not to look across at the drive-in. But, it was difficult (a superhuman demand) not to glance at the screen and notice shorts like *Autumn in Vermont* and the credits roll for Laurence Olivier and Marilyn Monroe in *The Prince and the Showgirl*. On warm nights, the air carried the sound more vividly. I spent much of the night before final vows listening to Bing Crosby, Mitzi Gaynor and Donald O'Connor singing in *Anything Goes*. One delayed compensation was that I had thought on seeing the leaves in *Autumn in Vermont* that it would be wonderful to actually go there. Mid-October, 1989, mission accomplished, even after almost 30 years.

The windows on to the drive-in were useful later in 1969. Fr. Joe Chown, the superior at that time, was always in a hurry. He had ducked in to see the James Bond actioner, *On Her Majesty's Secret Service*. When George Lazenby married Diana Rigg, he ducked out during this happy ending to beat all the other cars out the gates. He was momentarily aghast when we told him that was not the end. Fortunately, he was able to watch the last five minutes, and the unhappy ending, by looking out the window.

After the wonderful year of full-time university studies, it was back to Croydon to continue with our theology. It was a very quiet place after Canberra, fewer students but the same routines. 1962.

The main thing that happened, cinematically and morally speaking, was *Pillow Talk*. *Pillow Talk*?

The situation. There was some tension between our superiors in Canberra and Melbourne and between those students who had studied only at Croydon and those returning from Canberra and the university. Several of the Croydon group were still in the anti-*Seven Brides for Seven Brothers* phase, very suspicious of the secularism of literature studies. One had written to me in Canberra the year before, particularly upset and scandalised that we were reading the erotic poetry of A. D. Hope, especially his *Imperial Adam*. He assured me that his values were diametrically opposed to mine. Others asserted that their manual work was their recreation. We had debates on the matter, in private and during Forum and, I think, we agreed to differ.

Whether it was the literature-secularism discussions or the two years of focusing on literature, I must have been in a supercilious and return-to-priggish frame of mind and arts criticism. The doctor who had earlier brought out the 16 mm films for the students was, fortunately, still doing it. After Easter, he brought a double, *Hey, Let's Twist* with Chubby Checker (we looked down our noses at that one) and the Doris Day-Rock Hudson comedy, *Pillow Talk*. Along with most of the others, I walked out. What could I have been thinking? Seeing *Pillow Talk* (in its entirety) on television 25 years later – it took that long to catch up – I could sense the moment I had left. Despite my journey towards open-mindedness, I had been caught on 'suggestive sex-talk'.

Once again, it was Fr. Cuskelly who helped us. Fr. Murphy, our Scripture lecturer, went round the class first to get our responses to the lively and shaking twist film. A clear majority was against it. He pointed out our 'superior' attitude towards this innocuous, current dance trends musical. Fr. Cuskelly took the Dogmatic Theology class to ask our views on *Pillow Talk*: smutty, off-colour, etc.

Most important paragraph now coming up!

He then made a point that has been a significant reminder all these more than 50 years and one which has guided me in reviewing and which I like to pass on in articles and in teaching. He told us about Francois Rabelais in 16th century France, his warm and satirical humour which was considered bawdy (and we had studied Shakespeare – let alone Restoration Comedy – the previous year). Rabelais thought that everything human, no exception (even sexuality), could be the subject of humour. We were not being human if we could not accept that. I have forgotten how Fr. Cuskelly put it exactly, but the possibility of every topic being the butt of jokes was something of a revelation. We had succumbed to the temptation of being puritanical, prudish, wowsers. Later, American Jesuit, Michael Moynihan, made the same point, that if there is something we cannot laugh at, we have made an idol of it and it needs to be knocked off its pedestal.

I wish I could say that I put this insight into practice at once. Later that year, I was in a screening of *Strangers When We Meet* and I walked out of Kim Novak's trance-like soliloquy about a sexual encounter. But it did not take 25 years to make good on this one 'in its entirety'.

Six years later, after Fr. Cuskelly had been elected superior general of the Missionaries of the Sacred Heart, a group of us were with him at a theology conference in Sydney. We had a night off and went to the local Manly cinema to see *Where Eagles Dare*. I had been reviewing for almost two years by this time, so thought I should express some gratitude for the Rabelaisian insight. It had been one of the most important moments for me – and then Fr. Cuskelly confessed that he couldn't even remember the incident or saying what he did. Well, I have continued to remember, especially as films over the decades are more Rabelaisian than we ever imagined they could be!

The other significant experience at this time in developing an appreciation of films and meanings was discovering American Jesuit William Lynch's *The Image Industries*, a small book that I was to re-read over the next five years. I had encountered Lynch's writings at Canberra when I was given his book on literature and its religious dimensions for my 21st birthday, *Christ and Apollo*. It was exciting to find that Lynch knew films and could open up their themes. *The Image Industries* took me further steps on from the schooldays study of Fr. Chambelin's *Films and You* and *You and the Movies* and reading *Focus*.

Looking at *The Image Industries* again, I note that the hold of the Motion Picture Code was lessening in the late 1950s. Simone Signoret's 1959 Oscar-winning performance in *Room at the Top* was a case in point. In the struggle with television, the movie studios developed their technology with more refined camera and projection work, stereophonic sound and widescreen processes. Films became not only wider but longer, bigger and brighter (and sometimes more thematically meatier, thoughtful and provocative). Best Picture Oscars remind us of this: *The Bridge on the River Kwai, Gigi* and *Ben Hur* from 1957-59; *West Side Story, Lawrence of Arabia, Tom Jones, My Fair Lady, The Sound of Music* from 1961 to 1965. For those who noticed the gap, the 1960 winner was the black and white drama, *The Apartment*, which beat *Spartacus* and *Exodus*!

At this time, then, something of a reversal of Martin Quigley's 1929 experience occurred. The Code had been introduced because theatre drama had been more sophisticated than film which commanded the average audience. Now that television was fulfilling that popular niche, cinema could go back (or forward and further) in treating themes more seriously and more frankly. William Lynch looked at this new American image industry and made comparisons with the British, European and Japanese industries which had never been subject to the code. The book's dust-cover indicates what Lynch was about.

> The author of this book disregards the more superficial aspects of television, and goes to the heart of the matter. The imaginative life of a nation plays a vital part in its health or sickness: what sort of effect upon the imaginations of a people by this mass medium – the image industry?
>
> Christian comment on this subject all too frequently restricts itself to Jeremiad denunciations, and dismal attempts to categorise entertainment according to the inches of shoulder displayed and the number of rude words per minute. *The Image Industries*, while sharply critical of the flood of infantile fantasy which threatens to belittle the mental status of the viewer, is not hamstrung by such negative sterility. Its concern for the development of a visual imagination maturely created and thus spiritually healthy; and for the whole defence of human dignity which this implies.

With reference to topical films of the time like *Twelve Angry Men, Rashomon, The Brothers Karamazov, The Blob, Bonjour Tristesse* and *South Pacific*, Lynch explores themes of fantasy and reality, freedom and fixation, imagination and human dignity. The book might not cause many ripples now, but for me, five years after the novitiate, it was sacred writing.

There was a possibility that this journey story might now settle down to three-and-a-half more quiet, reclusive, study years in Melbourne before ordination. But, as said before, it was not to be.

11. HIGH SEAS, STUDIES – AND THE VATICAN COUNCIL SHAKES THE CHURCH

WHATEVER we might have been like in 1962, the Second Vatican Council had the potential for shaking up Catholics – perhaps an understatement. It seemed odd, riding in from a holiday bike ride at Shoreham during January 1959 to hear students sitting on the verandah talking about an Ecumenical Council. Those were church meetings we learnt about in Church History classes. But, that is what the elderly, genial 'stopgap' pope, John XXIII, had called, a gathering of all the bishops of the world, to begin in October 1962. That meant almost four years of preparation. We had studied Councils that focused on teaching and theological questions. This Council was meant to be pastoral. It was meant to dialogue with the contemporary world, a world that was definitely changing, whether we realised it or not, as we entered the 1960s. Some staunch traditionalists complain about how the Council damaged the Church. On the other hand, faced with such change and desire for freedoms, we might wonder how small and isolated the Church might have become had there been no Council.

My re-entry into Croydon was about to come to a swift end with a question from the provincial superior, Fr. Leo McDougall, whether I would like to study in Rome. Since, in those years, only ordained priests went to Rome for specialised studies, I thought that the province must be doing quite some forward planning since I would not be ordained for another three years. Naturally, I said this was a pleasing idea. It was 22 July and suddenly he said, 'If you are to go, you will have to be gone by the end of August!' What do you think, what do you say? Since he told me the decision had not been finalised, I was to keep this to myself – so, plenty of thinking, nothing to say. Unexpectedly, six days later, the Provincial Council had a meeting and agreed that Bill Lyons, who was studying in Canberra, and I should go. As a confrere who was work-oriented and blunt cheerfully said to me after the announcement, 'They never send the obvious ones, do they?'.

The short time for getting things ready meant hurry for passports (the gaunt, short back and sides, clerical photo – a contrast to the longer haired and bearded photo of 15 years later, but I would never have dreamed then that I would ever look like that). A visa for Djarkarta, the first foreign port of call during the voyage, vaccinations, traveller's cheques (I hadn't been managing any money at all for almost six years). It meant two weeks' holiday in Sydney with Dad, Nana and Aunty Sheila with a visit to Philip in Canberra on the way back to Melbourne, and farewells for four years. I still don't know why, but the Croydon superior, Fr. Eddie Kelly, explicitly forbade me to go to the pictures (still *The Devil's Camera?*), so I missed out on a free ticket to the St. James Theatre to see *The Parent Trap (*and that took another 30 years to see). In a moment of less rigidity, I realised that television had not been forbidden, so we did watch *Mrs. Miniver* (and Greer Garson was more than safe) at another aunt's home.

Bill Lyons and I set sail from Port Melbourne on the *SS Neptunia* on the evening of 2 September 1962. I was not long 23 and Bill would celebrate his 23rd birthday on 5 September (when we were seasick). While we had been to the university, life had still been fairly enclosed and now it suddenly opened up in ways that I could not have anticipated. Fr. Cuskelly, always plain and common-sensed, reminded us that wine is drunk at meals in Italy (and we had never drunk alcohol) so we might as well get used to it on board. Claret and champagne were surprisingly bitter that first night. But one can get used to most things.

There we were, going to the other side of the world on a voyage that took 33 days.

Despite strong will, getting up the first morning (and it wasn't at all rough), I got dressed and suddenly felt that sinking, focused, bitter feeling in the stomach. While I did survive a day in Adelaide, visiting our parishes and going up into the Adelaide hills, the three, beautifully sunny days across the Great Australian Bight, meant bemoaning sea-sickness, as the ship rolled from side to side at the same time as plunging forward and rising as it sailed ahead, a kind of corkscrew movement that seemed to presage a month's misery. When we got to Perth, I was amazed how the kneelers in St. Mary's Cathedral wobbled and swayed. Of course, after that initiation, all was well and, no matter what the ship's movements, all continued well for the rest of the voyage.

I can add that the ports were wonderful, though some of the experiences were more than a little hairy, as we used to say. In that Soekarno era in Indonesia (three years before *The Year of Living Dangerously*), we had to wait on board until mid-day before being allowed off. But, Fr. Bedaux was there to meet us and, glancing at the police with actual guns, something we had never seen, off we went to look at Djarkarta with Fr. Sol. Crowds, heat, open drains, new sports arena, taste of rice and Asian food, pot-hole roads. We were definitely out of Australia. Then Fr. Sol had to bribe the soldiers at the wharf so that we could get back on the *Neptunia*.

Singapore was not like it is today. There were litter and open drains back then and no legal penalties. But, the shopping for bargains fever was already alive and well. I had better mention our stop in India (instead of the usual Colombo). We went to Cochin in Kerala, right into the harbour and the city but were not allowed to land since there was a cholera epidemic. For almost 17 years I could say that I had been to India and never set foot on it. Actually, the next stop was the difficult one, though we naively went through a potential riot. This was Aden, then a British protectorate, an opportunity to experience something of the Middle East. I should add that besides Bill and myself, there were three Christian Brothers and a Jesuit all going to Rome. And, there were three Australian bishops, several from Indonesia and India and some priests and nuns all off to Rome, so quite a clerical and religious gathering. We six Australians had heard the warning about not going into the old city, but didn't quite know where new finished and old started. We got a taxi away from the wharf and did end up in the old city, and learnt for the first time the business (not the art) of haggling and bargaining. After wandering around like tourists trying to be unobtrusive, we decided to economise and take the bus back, quite cheap in fact. Except that school girls kept running up and down the aisles, eyeing us off and demanding of us, 'Nasser good!'. Our memories of Colonel Nasser were from the Suez crisis six years earlier, but we had no difficulty in assenting, 'Nasser good'. It was only when we got back to the boat that we were told that it was the schoolgirls who had incited the riots in Aden a couple of days before. It's all Yemen now, and security might be much worse.

While this is becoming a mini-travelogue, I still want to add the wonderful day in Cairo, getting into a launch to take us into Suez for a bus ride, through the desert, to the city, the Nile and, of course, a camel ride to the Sphinx and the pyramids. I still feel in awe of the pyramids. We were allowed to go up part of the way and into the Great Pyramid. Then it was a night trip to Port Said, via a meal in Ishmailia (goat someone said) where a man in the toilet area wanted to sell Brother Rod Doyle some dirty postcards. Rod was a model of courtesy, simply, 'No, thank you.' (I had thought this scenario just a traveller's comedy routine, but there it was in surreal life). Since I have mentioned Cairo, I had better give equal time to Messina and a bus trip down the east coast of Sicily to Taormina and its amazing amphitheatre (coming up a bit later in a different context).

The trip was very long, and often tedious, but the ports made all the difference.

Quick plane trips eventually superseded boat travel, except for cruises, during the 1960s. Our boat, the *Neptunia* was small and on its last trip from Australia to Europe. It was to be pensioned off for a South American run. On this voyage it was a one class boat and we had the freedom to move around anywhere. It belonged to the Flotta Lauro line so had a chaplain, a friendly-enough Maltese dynamo of a priest who celebrated a speedy Mass. One of the Australian bishops was Eris O'Brien, archbishop of Canberra-Goulburn, a popular head of the church whom we knew from Canberra days. He was a noted Australian historian, a learnt man, much more at home in the university world of thirty years earlier, speaking about the poet Christopher Brennan as if it were the day before. It was the present he had difficulty with: what deck he was on; how to get to deck drill, how to get back to his cabin, ordering bacon and eggs for breakfast while he relived the past. On being served, he remembered he didn't like eggs. We were sitting with him. 'Do you boys like eggs?' 'Yes, Your Grace.' Then, with a skilfully furtive glance to check whether the steward was watching or not, he divided the poached eggs and flicked us one each, leaving himself with a sliver of over-crisp bacon a centimetre wide. We enjoyed listening to Archbishop O'Brien.

Also on board were Bishop Edward Doody of Armidale and Bishop Thomas Fox of Broken Hill. First time sitting with bishops. Bishop Doody was very refined, wondering why people seemed diffident in approaching bishops for conversation. He suggested they were shy. 'Shy? Shite', said Bishop Fox. I forget why, probably due to the shock of the episcopal expletive.

Another passenger on board was Mrs. Dora Bartels of Melbourne. She and her husband, Carl, were on their way to Rome for the canonisation of Peter Julian Eymard, founder of the Blessed Sacrament Fathers, who staff St. Francis' Church in Melbourne. In the latter part of the 1940s, Mrs. Bartels had been suffering from severe angina pectoris and was given no hope for recovery. In July-August, 1949, a worldwide novena of prayer had been organised for Peter Julian's feast day, 3 August, everyone praying for a cure. As Mrs. Bartels told it, the day came and almost went. Carl went to work. The children went to school. All were more than a little disappointed. In the afternoon, Mrs. Bartels got out of bed to do a little cooking – and never went back. The process for the investigation of the miracle took years, complicated by the fact that in the mid-1950s, Mrs. Bartels was written up sensationally in a tabloid – and the process was re-opened. She thought that she was one of the few people in Australia who had been officially declared sane.

She was getting over the Bight sea-sickness and we met sitting on the staircase before Mass, trying to keep steady. But, she was fit and agile. For instance, she was able to clamber up and down the amphitheatre in Taormina while Carl, who had an artificial leg because of a World War I injury, had to sit, rest and wait for us. At the time of the canonisation ceremony, December 1962, the Vatican had overbooked seating space and some seat-grabbing friars had to be ousted from the Bartels' reserved places. We couldn't even get in. The drape in St. Peter's Basilica showed a pious, pink-nightied, slim Mrs. Bartels (a less than accurate portrait) with eyes uplifted to heaven. When she saw it, she sighed and, paparazzi-like a reporter immediately appeared to ask her if she liked it. One doesn't usually meet a miracle woman, or such a genial and unassuming one. When I got home, I used to visit her. She did not die until the 1970s.

Yes, we did have films on board. One night they were in Italian, the next night in English. And they were crowded, especially with the Indonesian and Indian Catholic contingent. We saw Bob Hope in *Alias Jesse James*, the thriller, *Edge of Eternity*. *The Apartment* was in Italiano, too difficult to pick up the dialogue. There was also an opportunity to see my first serious and frank drama, the kind of film William Lynch wrote about in *The Image Industries*. It was Robert Preston and Dorothy McGuire in William Inge's *The Dark at the Top of the Stairs*, an enjoyable and challenging experience. The main memory is of seeing *Strangers When We Meet* (which, I mentioned, I walked out of not having yet assimilated the Cuskelly advice about film topics and treatments). There was Kim Novak recounting her sexual fantasy. There was the crowd of Indonesian and Indian bishops and clergy sitting there with rapt attention. Understanding every word?

We were met in Naples because one of the bishops from Indonesia on board was an MSC – and this meant a side trip to Pompeii and a fine meal on the train where we learnt the meaning of *primo piatto* and *secondo piatto* and that the *primo piatto* of pasta was not the main course.

We arrived in Rome on 5 October and began to settle into an international scholasticate with Italian as the common language. That took a while – until, one night, sitting in front of the television news, I realised that I was understanding it. (One of the strange consequences of this language lag was that I was completely unaware of the crisis of the missiles of October, not watching the television; of course, we were completely focused on the Council these same days).

The first time I saw St. Peter's was the morning the Council opened, 11 October 1962.

During the years of preparation for the Council, John XXIII had set up the Secretariat for Christian Unity, established contacts with the heads of churches, such as the Archbishop of Canterbury, and started to travel around Italy. The day our passports were stamped, 'Italia', was 4 October in Messina, the feast of St. Francis of Assisi. That day the Pope travelled by train to Assisi. This was the day that Marxist poet, novelist and film-maker, Pier Paolo Pasolini was caught in his hotel room in Assisi because of the crowds gathered for the Pope. He read the Gideon Bible and decided to make what became *The Gospel According to St. Matthew* and dedicated the film to John XXIII.

An experience I will always be grateful for is that of being in Rome during the whole period of the Council. On the day it opened, we left the house in wet weather. Then it fined up. If you see *The Shoes of the Fisherman*, notice that in Pope Kiril's (Anthony Quinn) coronation scene, the piazza is wet. They used footage of the crowds present at the opening of the Council – we were on the left facing the basilica. It was a memorable spectacle as the thousands of bishops, robed and mitred, preceded John XXIII on his Sedia Gestatoria up the steps to the Basilica. The doors were shut and then the Pope gave his prophetic address about opening the windows and letting in the fresh winds of the Spirit.

Rome is not necessarily the best place to live if you are devoted to the Catholic Church. The human face of Rome is too often like a Fellini grotesque (his ecclesiastical fashion show in his *Roma* is obviously caricature, but...). During the Council we would hear of the in-fighting, the factions, the intrigues, devious methods for making points, of temperamental cardinals and bishops, reporting of theologians, and one would encounter the unimpressive functionaries whose be-all and end-all is ecclesiastical bureaucracy. We read Morris West's books with relish, appreciated the dilemmas for Monsignor Blaise Meredith, the Devil's Advocate, and tried to work out who was who in real life from *The Shoes of the Fisherman*.

We were able to attend all the public ceremonies of the Council. In fact, pictures of St. Peter's without the seats for the 2000 bishops still look somewhat odd to me. Archbishop Virgil Copas MSC of Port Moresby was among the bishops staying at our student house. I had the opportunity to do various jobs for him, especially translation work. He obtained several tickets for me to be present at actual sessions of the Council, one in 1964, the other in 1965 when there was a vote on the extraordinary *Declaration on Religious Freedom*. Gazing down the length of St. Peter's from the Papal Altar, looking at the bishops at work, witnessing formal interventions as well as casual conversations and the to-and-fro traffic for morning tea, watching Episcopal stretching of legs and trips to the toilets, I could see the human Church which trusted in the Spirit of God. That Church seemed profound, lumbering, exasperating. Suddenly a voice behind me, 'What are you doing here?' more like 'Vot are you doink here?'. I offered a hasty explanation to the MSC Superior General, Fr. van Keerckhoven, that I was in the right place and not a trespasser.

One small job of translating into Latin was for Dutch Bishop Koop MSC from Brazil. In a note concerning married clergy, urging this, he had left out the figure six from his statistics. I added in the Latin for six, 'sex'. It is not everyone who has added sex to a submission to Vatican II.

We experienced the death of Pope John XXIII and the extraordinary three days in June 1963 when thousands and thousands filed past his body lying in state. The hyperbole about the funeral of Pope John Paul II came from journalists who had no idea of the immensity of the ceremonies and crowds for John XXIII.

We went over to St. Peter's for the first ballot of the conclave and saw black smoke. The next day, we tried again. Then, as we got off a tram, 'E bianco' (it's white) from a Spanish confrere who went running up the Via della Conciliazione. We stood at the front of the barriers for the announcement but everyone was sure that it would be Cardinal Montini and he would call himself Pope Paul VI. It was something of an anticlimax when it was and he did.

The day that Paul VI was crowned (outside St. Peter's), I was standing next to a father with his little daughter. He hoisted her on to his shoulders for a better view. Then, over the PA system came a solemn voice, in Latin, 'Sic transit gloria mundi' (So passes the glory of the world). The little girl asked her father, *'Cos' ha detto, padre?'* (What did they say?). He replied, *'Entra nella gloria del mondo'* (Enter into the glory of the world). I suppose that is what it really looked like. But, soon after, Paul VI got rid of the papal tiara.

For four northern autumns, the Council made its way through discussions on liturgy, on the Church, on Scripture, on the Church in the modern world ... Discussions on the vernacular in the liturgy in November 1962 and celebrating first Mass in April 1965 in English.

And, on 8 December 1965, Paul VI brought the closing session out of the basilica and the Council ended with St. Peter's doors open, the bishops outside and thousands of the people of God in the piazza to witness the end of the achievement and the final launching of updating and renewal.

A diplomatic complication meant that President John F. Kennedy could not attend the coronation. Vice President Lyndon Johnson was the official U.S. representative. However, Kennedy had been in Milan and arrived in Rome the day after. He laid a wreath at the Victor Emmanuel Monument. Whatever the back problems he suffered, as we learnt later, he jogged up those stairs with an agile spring, quite an impressive glimpse of a live president. It was under five months later that we were celebrating an evening of music for the feast of St. Cecilia, 22 November, when someone interrupted with the news of the death of President Kennedy. It was only the next morning at lectures at the Gregorian when the impact for Americans dawned on us. The students from the American College stayed away, apprehensive about what might happen, uncertain of the consequences of the assassination. We underestimated American responses and fears at the time.

Rome is a city of contradictions. We lived down the road from the Forum and the ruins of the palaces on the Palatine Hill and the Circo Massimo. Walking to the Gregorian University every day, we passed the arches of Constantine and Titus, Trajan's column, just near Piazza Venezia and the Victor Emmanuel monument. Churches galore. Centuries of art and history. Culture so different from what we were used to in Australia but which had begun migrating there at the end of World War II. Assisi was peaceful and beautiful, just the place to spend some days after ordination. We had holidays twice at Castelletto Ticino on Lago Maggiore at the foot of the Alps, with bus trips all around the north, to Milan, Verona, to Monte Rosa, into Switzerland and Lausanne and Interlaken. Our trip to Bergamo meant a visit to the home of John XXIII just after he died. His niece, Suor Angela, a Daughter of Our Lady of the Sacred Heart, suggested we go when he was expected to be there on holidays. However, we met his brothers, old farming men who greeted us when we arrived, 'Would you like to see the cows?' We would – and then 'Would you like a cup of wine?', then a glass of the roughest red wine you ever tasted.

The history of the Papal States resulted in a situation where piety and devotion are mixed, to say the least, with some anticlerical hostility.

High Seas, Studies – and the Vatican Council Shakes the Church

Mass attendances in Rome were not large, although the parishes on the outskirts of Rome where he helped out after being ordained were more vigorous than those at the inner city shrines. However, an experience at Easter 1966 stays in the memory as bringing home these Italian church realities.

Cardinal Lercaro of Bologna used to invite the student priests in Rome to come his archdiocese to help with the Holy Week ceremonies. Bologna was a Communist stronghold. I realise now that 1966 was just over 20 years since the end of the war but that seemed a lot longer in those days. The experience (shades of Morris West and *The Devil's Advocate*) became vivid with three days at Pioppe di Salvaro in the Adda valley, 50 kilometres west of Bologna. The parish priest didn't have a car, only a motorbike, so a quick tour of Bologna, hanging on for dear life, then out to the village in the mountains. Pioppe had only a few hundred inhabitants with three Mass centres. The welcome from some families was warm, 'Padre, you speak Italian so well ...' On Good Friday evening we held the Stations of the Cross through the streets. The 12th station, recalling Jesus' death, was at the town reservoir where the occupying Germans had shot 70 hostages. This was not my culture, but I was absorbed in theirs. The next afternoon, it was confessions several kilometres back down the mountainside toward Bologna. In this village, there were only two hundred people most of whom worked at the one factory there. The parish priest told me as I finished to look at the various people outside the church, a woman whose husband was killed by the partisans and the man who had killed him, now a factory supervisor, who stood there checking who went to confession and who did not. Easter Sunday Mass was for a small group at the third church, high on top of a nearby mountain – which meant another fling on the back of the motorbike.

But we were in Italy to build up an international MSC community and to study theology. Community was the hardest task. We were disappointed at first that the Italian we had learnt was not strong enough for conversation. We found in the house an English-speaking group who studied at the Jesuit university, the Gregorian, and a French-speaking group who studied at the Dominican university, the Angelicum. It was not always easy settling in and adapting. After a year and a half, Bill Lyons found it too difficult and returned to Australia. There was always a small group of Australians plus Brother George Lockhead, the cook at the General House who welcomed us monthly and fed us up with sandwiches and cakes since the food where we lived was, euphemistically, 'basic'. Our Dutch cook reminded us of the privations during the war. For a while in 1964, we regularly had old boiled potatoes, tasteless boiled leeks and large chunks of horsemeat and watered down wine. The pasta days were a treat. We managed because there were so many other things going on. A letter to the Superior General elicited only the response that we needed some mortification in our lives!

Theology in Rome was fascinating but the traditional methods of teaching and learning were in their dying days. There were lectures and exams (almost all oral), lectures to four hundred to five hundred students, no personal supervision. Assessment was by speaking in Latin to Latin formulations of doctrine. However, there was a mini-thesis to be done and some exciting electives. We had the opportunity to sit at the feet, so to speak, of distinguished international Jesuit theologians like Rene Latourelle, Bernard Lonergan, Frederick Crowe, Zoltan Alzeghy and Josef Fuchs. These methods were not for the faint-hearted, nor were they effective adult learning – but you made of it what you could, and we read and read and read.

12. DIPLOMA: CORSO DI FILMOLOGIA

IN THOSE years, Rome offered more film experiences than I would have had in Australia.

We saw films on television, often introduced with commentary by expert Gian Luigi Rondo and guests like Ingrid Bergman. Our timetable may have been old-style and we lived the vow of poverty a bit more tellingly than at home (walk everywhere, no buses or trams, coins a rare enough sight, our long, black religious habits, quaint from an Australian point of view – but permission to ride bikes did come eventually, after we were ordained deacons!). There could be problems. Our unpredictable Australian superior (who had succeeded a kindly Frenchman) would not let us watch Laurence Olivier in *The Entertainer* (*'troppo sporco'* – too dirty) nor *Wedding Breakfast* (*'troppo femminile'* – too feminine). But we still did see many films. The dubbing of foreign films into Italian was expert. Seeing a film later in English, you had the same experience as seeing it in Italian. However, with *West Side Story*, they gave Russ Tamblyn a deep dubbed speaking voice while the songs remained in English, leaving Tamblyn to suddenly range into a squeakier higher pitch. The songs in *The Sound of Music* (minus 'A Problem llike Maria' and 'Climb Ev'ry Mountain' since it was thought Italian audiences would not come at nuns singing like this) were also dubbed. It was the same for *Mary Poppins*.

Try this to the melody and rhythms of 'A spoonful of sugar makes the medicine go down': *'Con un po di zucchero, la pillola va giù*!' Fits perfectly! An easy guess is the translation for 'Supercalifragilisticexpialidocious'.

But, there was a difficulty. Church law forbade local clergy from going to public cinemas, on pain of excommunication (it was said). Rather drastic. However, there were screenings for clergy in Rome. The best-attended of these took place at the Oratorio San Pietro (next door to the then Holy Office, previously Inquisition, more latterly Congregation for the Doctrine of the Faith). The first time I went, I was rushed on to a tram by some eager Spanish confreres, not knowing where I was actually heading, running fast along the street (in habit, of course), was jostled (a Roman ecclesiastical pastime, although the nuns were better, and rougher, at it than the men) and finally got in to see *Ben Hur*. I was pinned against a wall, about 10 metres from the screen, at a 30 degree angle and so packed in that I could not have slid down to the floor even if I had wanted to. Over three hours later ... At least I knew I could stand *Ben Hur*!

We had the opportunity to see the current blockbusters as well. Otto Preminger (of defying the Code with *The Moon is Blue* fame) was awarded a papal medal during the Council for his film, *The Cardinal*. There were special screenings for the Bishops. Some weeks later, at a more intense screening of *Judgment at Nuremburg*, the projector broke down. The hisses and boos from the future ministers of the Church outdid any Saturday arvo kids' audience. One angry man, moved by the scene and remembering the Ku Klux Klan trying to burn Tom Tryon's Cardinal, yelled at us, '*Non siamo nella Giorgia*' (We aren't in Georgia). But I don't think the point was taken.

An extraordinary memory is seeing *The Sound of Music* (minus the songs already mentioned). I have never experienced such rapport between film and audience as when a thousand clerics all fell instantly in love with Julie Andrews. The emotion was palpable. I mentioned this to a group of women in the parish of Coogee three years later. They seemed singularly unimpressed, then declared, 'Julie Andrews? ... aahh, Christopher Plummer!'

At this point, for amusement and to highlight cultural differences and emphases, we used to collect Italian titles for foreign, especially American, films. *Sessualita (Sexuality)* capitalised on the young Jane Fonda in the ads, but we found out it was *The Chapman Report*. Lana Turner and Dean Martin were in *Come Ingannare il Mio Marito (How to Deceive My Husband)* which was really a comedy about Lana hiding her gambling addiction, called *Who's Got the Action?*. The best of all was *Tutti Insieme Appassionatamente (All Together Passionately)*. And that was, in fact, *The Sound of Music*.

More importantly, there were opportunities for film study. Catholic groups were screening *Lawrence of Arabia* for discussion. At times, there was an ultra-seriousness that drove one away. Scarcely had the curtain closed on Ingmar Bergman's *Through a Glass Darkly* than the priest-director of the Cine Forum was on stage asking what we thought of it. Somebody immediately offered a pious interpretation. I had to go out for air and time. I learnt then never to discuss a film formally before an audience has had time to stay with the film or to chat informally about it for a breather. The worst Cine Forum was at Propaganda College (where Australian diocesan seminarians lived) as part of a course on film appreciation. The film was *Becket*. Before the film started, we were told that some scenes had been deleted as they were 'below human dignity'. Watching *Becket* later in the year (next to the Holy Office, in fact) and deciding to time the offending scenes, I found that the first 45 minutes had been cut, the complete segment of Becket's life before his being ordained as bishop. This was 1965 and the question rose: Who censors? On what bases?

It was in Rome that I had the first opportunity to do some film study and get a small diploma certificate. Spurred on by *The Image Industries*, I enrolled in 'Corso Elementare di Filmologia' conducted by Jesuit Enrico Baragli on behalf of the Studio Romano della Communicazione Sociali.

The first document discussed at Vatican II, October 1962, had been the Decree on Social Communications, a symbolic start (or an easy option to begin with). Fr. Baragli was one of the writers of this document. Everyone now agrees that it is not a particularly startling document but it was a big start and social communications became one of the 'signs of the times' with the Church not being outside media or on the margins, but actually involved.

For us the course was excellent, an encouragement for our own appreciation in film-watching and offering ideas for teaching courses ourselves. We considered technical aspects of film. We looked at films as art, as commercial, as offering moral issues. We saw Mario Monicelli's *I Soliti Ignoti* (translated as *Big Deal on Madonna Street*) and Juan-Luis Bardem's *Calle Mayor (Main Street)*, both favourites in my memory. We actually went into some real cinemas for these screenings. When we were seated, Fr. Baragli asked us where the best place for watching the film actually was. We found we were about 10 rows too far back. We needed to be a third of the way down the cinema, centre, because of the geometry between the screen size and an equilateral triangle for our eye focus. Perhaps it's the church syndrome and we feel safer and less obtrusive at the back. Unfortunately, even today ticket sellers at our multiplexes assume that audiences want to sit right away from the screen.

This relationship between eye and screen was brought home to me while sitting with a film study group in Canberra watching Audrey Hepburn being terrorised by Alan Arkin in *Wait Until Dark*. When I saw it in the cinema, in the correct spot, everybody jumped and screamed – and continued to do so while blind Audrey crawled across her dark kitchen, gripped by Arkin, to close the refrigerator door and so turn off the light, to save herself by literally putting him in the dark. But, in the hall, down the back, nobody jumped. Nobody screamed. That terror was going on up there on the distant screen. We were observers rather than participators. I wonder when I read reviews, or hear people saying they didn't like the film much, where they were sitting and whether they had merely observed the film at a distance and did not have the experience of being involved in it. (Later confirmed during my life as a reviewer and comparing notes with those who distanced themselves at the back.)

The course, the opportunities to see films, reading and theology were coming together. As usual, we had an in-house magazine for student writing, *Voces Romanae*. I see that in 1965, I was venturing the suggestion of a theology or spirituality of films. The article was both aggressive and defensive. Memory tells me that many people at the time did not think this was such a good idea – 'why not a spirituality of fish? ...'

I was lucky to be able to try out some writing on films and moral stances as well as the perennial tensions between education and entertainment.

Some of our Irish students were friendly with a man who was starting up a Catholic magazine-paper in Dublin. He was on the lookout for articles so I wrote on 'Facing up to Films' and 'Entertainment vs Education'. I don't know whether the paper ever got going but the articles were not printed. However, after a two year wait, they were published in the Australian review, *Twentieth Century*, and then formed the first two chapters in the book, *The Film*.

But, the stimulus for this kind of thinking was the Council discussion on the Church in the Modern World and the pastoral document, 'Constitution', which emerged, *Gaudium et Spes* (known as *The Joys and Hopes* ...). It took the world seriously, expressed a theology of creation as something good and encouraged dialogue with science, technology, culture, the arts – as well as considering the serious social questions of personal dignity, the family, peace and nuclear war. Promulgated in 1965, this was exactly a century since Pope Pius IX had issued his *Syllabus of Errors*, a document containing papal hostility towards the emerging 'isms' of the 19th century. In nos 53-62 of *Gaudium et Spes*, there is a lengthy consideration of 'The Proper Development of Culture'. It states:

> thus each nation develops the ability to express Christ's message in its own way. At the same time, a living exchange is fostered between the Church and the diverse cultures of people.
>
> To promote such an exchange, the Church requires special help, particularly in our day, when things are changing very rapidly and ways of thinking are exceedingly various. She must rely on those who live in the world, are versed

in different institutions and specialties, and grasp their innermost significance in the eyes of both believers and unbelievers. (no. 44)

Great times, stimulating times. (Though in 2013, a conservative Australian commentator remarked that she thought the Holy Spirit was out to lunch when the bishops began to talk about *Gaudium et Spes* – and/or that the bishops had had too much lunch). Paul VI, in his first encyclical letter, *Ecclesiam Suam (His Church)*, had advocated dialogue within the Church and between the Church and the modern world.

In 1965, we had to choose a seminar for our degree, a Licentiate in Sacred Theology, and prepare a topic for a mini-thesis. At the Gregorian, Fr. Karel Truhlar, a Jesuit from Yugoslavia, was offering Theology of Recreation – and it seemed just the right topic to gather together all that I had been doing (theology, not just recreation!). Truhlar encouraged us to pursue the lines of theology of creation and *terrestria* (earthly things, earthly realities, perhaps better translated, 'down-to-earth things'). He encouraged reading and discussion and being venturesome in our writing. My final topic was a study of French writer, Henri Bremond, and his book *Priere et Poesie (Prayer and Poetry)*.

This mini-thesis looked at the human capacity for knowing, loving and appreciating the beautiful. Following the lead of Joseph Marechal, a Jesuit who taught in Leuven, I was attracted to a philosophy of humanity that saw that in all our finite experiences, there was an openness to something more. There is a human capacity for more. While we cannot demand an infinite fulfilment of our longings, we are open to receive the infinite. This means that in our day-to-day experiences as in our most profound experiences, there is an implicit desire for the infinite. In knowing finite truth, we are open to more, to infinite truth. In willing finite good, we are open to more, to infinite good. In appreciating finite beauty, we are open to more, to infinite beauty. God's revealing infinite truth, goodness and beauty, we sometimes call 'grace'.

As regards the arts, and cinema, this means that as we listen to poetry or music, contemplate a picture or a sculpture, read a novel, attend a play, watch a film, to the extent that we are responding to truth, goodness and beauty, we are open to the infinite. This is the language of philosophy. It can be the language of religion. It gave me some formation for the experiential insights into the search for and exploration of human values written about by William Lynch.

13. ORDAINED, THEN ...

I WAS ordained a priest on 3 April 1965. We were the first group, seven of us, to be ordained in the chapel of our international MSC house of studies. We began to think big when we were given the all clear from the authorities in Rome to ask any bishop to ordain us. It was not, in fact, all clear. A Spanish confrere and I approached Cardinal Josef Beran, recently released from Czechoslovakia by the Communists, Archbishop of Prague, a witness to a persecuted Church in the manner of Cardinal Mindzenty of Hungary. Cardinal Beran was gracious and agreed to perform the ceremony. However, the Vicariate of Rome was politically wary and concerned about detente with the Soviet Union. They feared that Cardinal Beran might use the opportunity to speak out against the Communist authorities and hinder Vatican negotiations for greater Church freedom in his country (only three years or more before the Soviet tanks rolled into Prague against Dubcek).

The Vicariate tried to do the right thing. They sent Archbishop Pericle Felici. Pericle Felici, a large, robust, conservative prelate, was the General Secretary of the Second Vatican Council. He presided over the organisation, made matters run smoothly and spoke to the bishops in session in a slowly-paced, over-emphatic Latin that they would have little excuse not to understand. But, the efficient running of the Council was an enormous achievement. He was later made a cardinal and presided over the commission for the Church's reform of its law, the new Code of Canon Law. Good photographs were taken at the ceremony. I have one of the ritual kiss of peace. Embraced by this large and influential archbishop, I am held by staunch tradition and the emerging of a renewed Church. At least the photo offers a symbol of orthodoxy.

We were seven ordained that day. Seven of our 1957 novitiate group were also ordained in 1964-1965. We knew these were times of change.

I don't know that at that time we thought that anyone would decide to leave the priesthood, probably not. The departures, more and more extensive would begin three years later and escalate over the succeeding decades. In fact, from the Roman group, two left and two joined the diocesan clergy. Three of our Australian group left.

On special occasions, especially anniversaries, someone asks, 'If you had your time over, would you do it again?'. Reflecting on my life, I would answer, 'No.' I have few regrets, in fact, and I meant the commitments I made and that has been my life. I need to offer some explanation. In the 1950s, it was taken for granted that a boy who sat for his final examinations at school and then joined a religious order would become a priest. And that's what we did. That's what I did. However, the debates after Vatican II have made us realise more forcefully that belonging to a religious community is important in itself. The founder of the Missionaries of the Sacred Heart, Jules Chevalier, 19th century Frenchman, had a vision for a de-Christianised or post-Christian France, of rediscovering the warmth and compassion of God's love, especially in the human and humane heart of Jesus Christ. This vision spurred him on with 19th century and romantic zeal to send the men and women of his religious foundations literally to the ends of the earth with missionary enthusiasm. He spoke of a new heart for a new world. This is the vision I have wanted and enjoyed living. In fact, most of my life has not had a great deal of specifically priestly ministry. So, if I had my time over again, knowing what I know now, I would be a Missionary of the Sacred Heart without being ordained – and avoiding being part of the clerical and clericalised world which, in more recent times and with scandals, is not an easy place to be.

It was almost time to return to Australia and get to work. Hopes to write a doctoral thesis on the theology of Graham Greene's writings turned out to be merely dreams. My Australian superior had sent a report home on me suggesting to our Provincial Council that I was mixing with the wrong types in our international scholasticate. Some of them were top theologians and canon lawyers, some to become assistants to the Superior General or Provincials. Water under the bridge now.

Pope Paul VI brought Vatican II to a close on 8 December 1965. The doors of St. Peter's basilica had closed on the day of the opening of the Council. Then Pope John XXIII spoke of opening the Church's windows. The final ceremony of the Council was, significantly, outside, on the steps up to the basilica, open for anyone who wanted to be there. In symbolic gesture, the Pope received representatives of all branches of work and learning, highlighting the dialogue between the Church and the modern world. The principal document from the Council was the *Constitution on the Church (Lumen Gentium, Light of the Peoples)*. The title is a reference to the book of Isaiah and the figure of the ideal servant (the pattern for Jesus in the Gospels) who acted gently, not imperiously, and who was prepared to lay down life for the sake of others. Already the formal (and formalised) externals of the Church were being adapted to the contemporary styles of a pluralist world rather than being the externals of a powerful Christendom. It was with jaunty stride (and speeding on our bikes through the Roman traffic) that we went to final lectures and exams at the Greg in clerical black suits rather than in the ankle-length Roman soutanes.

One last thing. A benefit of overseas travel was the opportunity to do summer schools in England. The British Council is a wonderful institution. We English-speakers were frequent visitors to its Rome headquarters. We borrowed extensively from the literature library. We attended seminars and lectures. We went to screenings of films like Olivier's *Henry V* and *Hamlet*. The Institute also offered scholarships to spend six weeks of study at summer schools in England. I was fortunate in being awarded scholarships in 1965 and in 1966.

Summer 1965 (very wet and ruinous for shoes) I was at Stratford-on-Avon, a six weeks course on Shakespeare. Lectures, seminars, discussions with actors like Eric Porter who was playing both Shylock in *The Merchant of Venice* and Barabbas, Marlowe's *Jew of Malta* (Barabbas, said Porter, was an extravert while Shylock an introvert with an in-grown soul), trips to Birmingham, Oxford, Coventry with its new marvellous cathedral, Tintern Abbey, and the season at the Memorial Theatre with Paul Scofield as *Timon of Athens*, and the soon-to-be-heard-of Glenda Jackson, Judi Dench, Janet Suzman, David Warner, Ian Richardson and Ian Holm. It was only five shillings for standing room to see each play again. I encountered John Bell and Anna Volska (Anna was selling guides to the Shakespeare Exhibition and asked whether I was Australian, no loss of accent after three years away) who were studying in Stratford and was able to baptise their daughter, playwright Hilary Bell, in 1966.

John Bell's Shakespeare Company has had a powerful impact on theatre in Australia. I am indebted to him for his bringing me into rehearsals for *Hamlet* for a day at the end of the course, watching the processes with David Warner as Hamlet and Glenda Jackson as Ophelia, her metallic speaking voice breaking into a very sweet singing voice.

Hilary Smith and her husband, Michael (a parole officer), ran The White House, a bed and breakfast just opposite the Church. A Jesuit, Fr. Hubert Delaney and I were advised to stay there but early in the course, we were invited to be part of the family, the first 'ordinary' family I had stayed in, ever. The Smiths offered wonderful warmth and friendship. Later John Bell and Anna moved into The White House. Hilary, their daughter, is named after Hilary Smith.

At the end of the course, before going to London to stay with cousins, see the city, go to plays and travel up to Scotland as far as Inverness and back, I wanted to visit Worcester and Gloucester but the tour was cancelled. Why? The coach director said it was Friday, 13 August and there were not enough takers. But, there was an afternoon trip in a smaller bus which took us to the Cotswolds, to Stow-on-the-Wold and Bourton-on-the-Water. The latter has one of the best witchcraft museums in England. So, that is where we spent the afternoon of Friday 13 August 1965.

The next year was at Exeter College, Oxford, boarding at the

Catholic chaplaincy where the chaplain was the fine British priest, Michael Hollings. The course was England, 1870-1966, politics, literature and music. Again, fascinating material from Dickens to Iris Murdoch, Gilbert and Sullivan to John Cage and the Beatles. 'Eleanor Rigby' and 'Nowhere Man', instant classics, for study. The D'Oyley Carte Company was performing almost all their repertoire at Oxford that summer, which made me realise the plays were rather silly but the music and lyrics made them shine.

Then, a visit to Ireland for the first time. Rain the first few days, then fine. From 1966 to 2009, I visited Ireland six times, a total of 25 days and, after that initial rain, the weather has always been fine! (The day in 2009 at the cliffs of Mourne – and a chance to be in Clare where the ancestors came from – was so placid we wanted a bit of wind and waves! More like *Ryan's Daughter.*)

Rules in religious orders were still a bit tight. Our provincial superior (no mean traveller himself) told us not to gad about Europe or gallivant. He told us to travel directly from point A to point B. But, it is marvellous what one can see in a direct trip from Rome to London, getting on and off trains, Pisa, Florence, Innsbruck, Munich, Heidelberg, Cologne, Aachen, Liege, Leuven, Brussels! He didn't specify how long it took to go from point A to point B!

One other thing. What were cinemas like in the rest of the world? Pricey and plush for *My Fair Lady* in London's West End. Seeing *The Tokyo Olympiad* near the Moulin Rouge was a tourist visit. *How to Steal a Million*, plus the Rockettes, at Radio City Music Hall was part of flying home through the U.S. (because I thought I would never be in that part of the world again, obviously not gifted with prophecy!). Travel arrangements had changed in four years, so home by plane. There was a plane strike in Europe that summer of 1966. When I finally got to Shannon to fly to the US, it was a Friday afternoon... and, the travel company in Rome had neglected the visa for the US. Too risky to fly there without a visa. One could be stranded – and fined $1000. So, reluctantly, I changed the ticket back through Asia, thinking guiltily so that's what happens when you go over the superior's head because he said no to the U.S. and the Provincial said yes. I won't prolong the sad story, but I decided to spend a weekend in London at my cousins, see a play, see London for the last time. And, next morning the strike ended. Change of plans, stay till Monday, get a visa and out to Heathrow. When is the next flight? Boarding now, off to the US, New York, Los Angeles. What had happened about God's will and the superior?

Getting on the Qantas flight in August 1966 (and tiredly trying to pay attention to Henry Fonda and Joanne Woodward in *Big Hand for the Little Lady* on the monitor lined alongside the cabin luggage racks) meant that study was over. Life, be in it.

14. ECCLESIASTICAL PEEPING TOMS

AUSTRALIA in the mid-1960s was involved in the worldwide turmoil of questioning, re-thinking and loosening the hold of the past. Because of distance from the northern hemisphere, communication times and our own pace of doing things, we might have been behind the changes going on in Europe and the United States – but we always catch up in our own way and in our own time. For someone who had been living in the cloistered atmosphere of the seminary and then four years away, a newer Australia of 1966 became the status quo.

Harold Holt had succeeded Robert Menzies, after 16 years, as Prime Minister and there were serious consequences for his genial cry, 'All the way with LBJ!' This meant even to the war in Vietnam and conscription. President Johnson visited Canberra in October 1966, staying at the Ainslie Rex Hotel but entering via a back door to avoid our small crowd milling in Northbourne Avenue in protest. Within a few years there would be draft dodgers, court cases, young men and women, sometimes just out of school (boys I taught in 1967 in Vietnam the next year), and the large demonstrations in the major cities against the war, the moratoriums.

We began to hear more about drugs, notice that some of the high schoolers seemed to be on them, realise that big drug organisations were operating in our part of the world. Inner city areas, university campuses experienced unrest, excitement, a drop-out counter-culture and causes for protest. We heard about the hippies in San Francisco and flower power and the word 'psychedelic' was a sign of the times.

The Second Vatican Council had concluded on 8 December 1965 and Paul VI had gone to New York to address the United Nations (which became a background to the plot of *Rosemary's Baby*). Observances and regulations that we Catholics had taken for granted were now open for discussion. Eager changers hurried ahead; others stood their ground and tried to be immovable. Most people went with the changes in a spirit of renewal and updating. There was a fair amount of iconoclasm, the knocking down of images whether they were statues or the garb worn by clergy and religious. The Mass was in English, sacramental rituals were being re-written, different kinds of catechisms and religious textbooks were being published, greater lay participation in worship, study and church administration was acknowledged. In retrospect, this renewal seems to have moved rapidly in many areas despite the impatient demands and disappointments, complaints about moving too slowly at the time.

Many enterprises slowed down in the 1970s and 1980s – and since. Some people lost their enthusiasm and gave up, others stayed with it, even when they experienced some severe backlash, and tried to keep moving with renewal.

Who would have, or could have, imagined this kind of 1960s ten years earlier?

Before looking at what was happening with movies and the 1960s – and quite a deal of change was happening – I would like to situate myself and my ministry in the second half of 1966.

I was asked to fill in for a term at Daramalan College, Dickson, in Canberra's northern suburbs. The Missionaries of the Sacred Heart had opened this Catholic boys' school in 1962, a year notable in Australian Catholic history for the strike that took place in nearby Goulburn, when students from the Christian Brothers College and the Mercy Sisters College took a fortnight off and went to the public schools to enrol. This action led to the government eventually granting state aid to Catholic schools.

1962 also saw the beginning of implementing the Wyndham scheme in New South Wales and the Australian Capital Territory, a change from five years secondary schooling (which we had undergone) to six. A broader curriculum had been developed. Daramalan was building up its numbers and its classes year by year with the scheme so that the top class remained the top class for the six years. The school was a day school, something of a new venture for the MSCs who conducted boarding schools, like Chevalier College, with some day students.

Almost every MSC who was ordained from 1963 to 1968 spent some time at Daramalan. In 1967, five of our novitiate group were on the staff. I think we did our best, but few of us had any kind of teacher training let alone a professional qualification. There was a good spirit in the school, a spirit of building something new, although something of a 'them and us' with the rest of the Australian MSC province. At this time, families were moving from Sydney and Melbourne as more and more public servants went to work in the capital. Suburbs were in constant expansion. There was a feeling of a young city with people establishing roots, settling in. Again, it suited the times.

Looking back, I see that returning from Rome after so many years and being parachuted into the school and into classrooms seems more than a bit bizarre. However, in September 1966, I began teaching 34 periods a week, a range of subjects form First Form Social Studies, Second Form English, Third Form Australian History to Fifth Form Latin. There were joys, exasperations, mistakes (a little strapping once to Stephen Howarth in desperation – and hope he has forgiven and forgotten – but soon to be abandoned as a means of discipline – remembering those times when we got the strap at Chevalier) and energy given to earning one's living in the classroom. As during school days at Chevalier, the MSCs were generally friendly, although there are always the funny stories. John Northey (we later learnt that he had cancer and was dead by 1970) was a huge presence. James Bond in *Thunderball* had been released and the kids called Northe, 'Thunderguts'. You could hear him roar, 'You will obey me', from nearby buildings. His method of objecting to an adjacent class's noise quotient was to get his class to count from one to 10 getting louder and louder (and sending back the boy who came to request quiet on behalf of his teacher with a six).

In 1967, with the Wyndham scheme complete, we had to get ourselves better organised as a school. There were two primary classes as well as the full secondary school. More by necessity than by planning, we set up structures of discipline master, study directors and form masters. This was ordinary organisation for education, but for many of us (in our late 20s or early 30s), this was new. And we had to learn on the way. After working at Daramalan, staying through 1967 before going to the seminary as was originally planned, I believe in learning by experience, although some of the actual experiences I would gladly have foregone, especially supervision at bus stops, Under 13 C cricket coaching (and defeats) on Saturday mornings. But working with the boys and young men, helping them with career decisions (I had landed Sixth Form Master and Director of Senior Studies despite minimal age and experience) and listening to parents was, of course, most valuable.

In case you were wondering where the films have gone, let me take one released in 1985, set in a New York Bronx High School, 1965-1966, as a way of illustrating something of what we experienced at Daramalan. The film was called *Heaven Help Us* (how apt!) but was given the title, *Catholic Boys*, for its Australian release. Some Catholic reviewers took the film to task for exaggerating the severity and authoritarianism of the teachers, the behaviour of the students and their non- or anti-religious attitudes. Reading these reviews, I was very surprised. I could match any incident in *Heaven Help Us* with what happened at Daramalan. Seeing events and characters compressed into a hundred minutes running time certainly spotlights problems, but still mirrors reality. I found the film a tonic reminder of those days, the good and the bad.

I enjoyed the classes, Fifth and Sixth Form English Literature, less so Latin. Religion classes were very hard going at that time, and making subject matter credible, interesting and relevant, often defeated us. The fact that Religious Education was a subject that was of no use for a Higher School Certificate assessment did not help student attention or participation at all.

We corrected essays. We supervised. In *Heaven Help Us* there is a school dance supervised by the priests and nuns. I think the film did overdo the 'no touching' comments from the eagle-eyed staff and the homily about temptations. But, there we were, in our clerical collars, smiling, keeping an eye on everyone, noting who went out of the hall, alert to smoking and worse, living with the din of the music. But the dancing style of the times meant that the boys and girls did not actually touch. They were too busy twisting in their own space for that. The dances and the friendships, the advice, kept us down to earth. And, of course, we had to learn verbal caution, remembering that the kids would pick up every meaning, double or treble. Headmaster, Fr. Jack McCowage (who years later still referred to us in these early teaching days as 'wet behind the ears') did not help matters when, at the end of an Assembly, he announced, 'Would the masters and mistresses now carry on as usual.'

We must have had the energy because several of us completed our BA degree at the Australian National University, taking up where we had left off five years earlier to return to Melbourne for seminary studies. Back to English Literature and Professor A. D. Hope. Back to History – this time Australian History which was beginning to seem more interesting and relevant and on the school curriculum. Back to Manning Clark with the same controversial comments or his dramatising of history and his imagining of William Charles Wentworth's conversation on deck sailing into Sydney Harbour 10 years after the crossing of the Blue Mountains, the style that was to make his *History of Australia* unique. But, it was not easy keeping alert, or even awake, during this part-time study.

And now back to the question of how films were faring in Australia and in the Church.

The film to focus on for this period is Mike Nichols' version of Edward Albee's *Who's Afraid of Virginia Woolf (*1966). Elizabeth Taylor and Sandy Dennis were to win Oscars for their performances. Richard Burton and George Segal did not (Burton losing to Paul Scofield as *A Man for All Seasons*). Stories are told of Warner Bros. nervousness, whether they should release the film or not since it was frank in its content and treatment. The play had won a Pulitzer Prize but it had been withdrawn because of the crudity. The Motion Picture Code? The Legion of Decency? As it turned out, all was well. But it is the background of the nervousness which is important.

The films of the late 1950s and early 1960s were long and sometimes spectacular blockbusters. However, the influence of playwrights like Tennessee Williams (even though versions of his *Cat on a Hot Tin Roof* and *Sweet Bird of Youth* were 'sanitised' for the screen), William Inge and Edward Albee in the U.S., the 'kitchen sink' playwrights and novelists from England, like John Osborne, Shelagh Delaney, Alan Sillitoe and John Braine, and the increasing distribution and popularity of films from continental Europe and Japan, meant a much more serious, more adult approach to film subjects.

Some directors and producers defied the Motion Picture Code and films that were considered to be sleazy in tone were made in Hollywood. The spotlight fell on one, Billy Wilder's 1964 comedy, *Kiss Me, Stupid* with Kim Novak, Dean Martin and Ray Walston. Objections were made by the Legion of Decency about the offhand and satirical, treatment of marital infidelity. Billy Wilder recalled the cast and crew and re-shot more acceptable material. In 1966, Otto Preminger, who had defied the Code with *The Moon is Blue* in the 1950s, released his film of the South at the end of World War II, *Hurry Sundown*, without the seal of approval, because of a saxophone scene with Jane Fonda and the suggestions of phallic symbols (never heard of them before but now something we were learning about, introduced by somebody's reporting of 23 such symbols in Blake Edwards' *The Pink Panther* in 1963).

But there was disagreement within the membership of the Legion of Decency. A number of Catholic critics, particularly Moira Walsh who reviewed in the Jesuit Journal *America*, felt that the principles behind the Legion needed re-consideration and that the atmosphere of renewal within the Church needed to be applied to the approach to films. A controversial case occurred in 1965 with Sidney Lumet's moving film, *The Pawnbroker*, when an actress bared her breasts in a brief sequence. How should the film be judged? How should it be classified? The Legion gave it a 'C', Condemned, rating. The ensuing discussions led to a re-writing of the classifications and a change of name for the Agency. (Controversies about *The Pawnbroker* were not just a Catholic thing. Released at the Gala Theatre in Sydney, it received media coverage and advertisements suggesting that this was either a censorship breakthrough or the end of the world.)

The change of name from Legion of Decency, with its evocation of a militant group crusading for a cleaner and proper way of life, to National Catholic Office for Motion Pictures, a matter-of-fact name for a Church agency interested in film, meant a change in watching and assessing films as well. The Office continued to view films and classify them but offered an advisory classification rather than something which binds conscience, although it could give the impression that it was conscience-binding. The Office has tried to review appreciatively rather than suspiciously and has a better working relationship with the industry. (Since 2005 and a controversy concerning *Brokeback Mountain*, making its classification stricter, morally offensive, as well as the withdrawing of the review of *The Golden Compass* in 2007, there has been a more cautious approach from the Bishops Conference and a stepping back in the way reservations are singled out and expressed. Then the Bishops Conference cut off the Office and reviews were taken up by the Catholic News Service.)

This new situation became clear in 1966 with a screening of *Who's Afraid of Virginia Woolf*, arranged for the Catholic Office representatives, the Warner Bros. executives fearing the worst, perhaps even to shelving the film. They seem to have been greatly relieved when the film was classified with the newly introduced A-IV category, 'Morally unobjectionable for adults, but with reservations' because of subject and strong treatment of themes. This classification emphasised the 'morally unobjectionable' with the necessary reservation to be seen in the light of the overall classification. In practice, many readers saw the word 'reservations' rather than the 'morally unobjectionable'.

Who's Afraid of Virginia Woolf was screening in Sydney when I arrived home in 1966. As expected, there was controversy in Australia. The advertisements included a statement attributed to the Australian Censorship Department to the effect that the film was so strong that it would never be screened on television.

(For the record, it was first screened on television in 1972).

The reviewer in Sydney's *Catholic Weekly* had given it a thoughtfully favourable critique. Letters critical of the review and alarmed about threats to community standards were also published in the *Weekly*. To my surprise, Aunty Sheila urged me to go and see it. I did and, like many others, was impressed. The prolific English critic and film-buyer for ITV Television, Leslie Halliwell, remarks in his entry for the film in *The Filmgoer's Companion*:

> But its chief interest for historians will be that it further extended the bounds of what is permissible on public screens, its unbridled treatment of matters sexual being decorated by 'blue' jokes and expletives.

This is not historically accurate but it is perhaps symbolically accurate. *Virginia Woolf* was one of the major films, like *The Pawnbroker* or *Alfie*, which treated serious themes in serious and intelligent ways. All these films received Academy Award nominations. Oscars in those days were not usually given for way-out films.

'The times, they are a-changing.' I remember that I wore a clerical suit to see *Virginia Woolf* and found myself reported to the Provincial Superior for seeing such a film looking like a priest. I went to see *Alfie* wearing ordinary clothes and found myself reported for not wearing, clericals. We were busy about many things in those days. And John Northey coined the label for us, Ecclesiastical Peeping Toms!

The question of censorship and moral principles was also being discussed in the Australian Church. Father Fred Chamberlin had by this stage become a significant figure in regard to films. He wrote for the Melbourne Catholic paper, *The Advocate*. He served on OCIC juries at various international film festivals. He expressed concern about standards in films in a pamphlet, *Children and Adult Films*, in 1964. Its sub-title was 'A case for restrictive legislation' and it had a foreword by the retiring Chief Film Censor, C. J. Campbell. It raised the problem of Australian censorship which, at the time, had no classification that had legal binding to prevent children from seeing any film. This meant too great an availability of adult films for children and consequent cutting of these films for adult viewing, where children could be present.

Already, there was an increase in exploitative films available, accompanied by lurid advertising which, as usual, meant that the film did not live up to it. However, there was public concern. Parents are usually alarmed and moral action movements get into gear. This was the period of television controversy with the satiric *The Mavis Bramston Show* and auxiliary bishop of Sydney, Thomas Muldoon's public threat to sell his Ampol shares to make his point to the sponsor.

Father Chamberlin was following the Legion of Decency classifications for the Catholic Church. He now proceeded to adapt them to those of the National Catholic Office for Motion Pictures, introducing the A IV classification, Morally Unobjectionable for Adults, with Reservations. Almost immediately the classification was read wrongly as 'Morally Objectionable' and readers interpreted the reason for the reservation as the cause of the film's really being objectionable. Father Chamberlin regularly reprinted his explanation of the advisory nature of the categories (rather than their being imperatives). He also used an 'Advised Against' category. The 'To Be Avoided' category was dropped during the 1970s. Needless to say, the Catholic joke in Melbourne was to look up the Advised Against and To Be Avoided films to discover what to go and see.

Within a few years there would by public discussion on the whole issue of censorship and changes to the Commonwealth classifications which have remained, with some additions, for over 40 years. That will be the next step in this journey.

One arena where I was able to become more involved actively with film issues was film reviewing in the MSC magazine, *Annals*, later *Annals Australia*. The magazine was established in 1889 as *The Annals of Our Lady of the Sacred Heart*. It became a very popular publication and taken in many Catholic homes. It carried devotional articles on the Sacred Heart and on Mary, on missionary activity in the Northern Territory and Papua New Guinea and throughout the Pacific. It catered for adults, children and for Catholic schools. In an authentic touch, Fred Schepisi had the boys in 1953, sitting outside the Superior's office, in *The Devil's Playground*, reading the *Annals*.

In 1966, the assistant editor, Paul Stenhouse, took over as editor and used his training in layout and photography to give the magazine a more contemporary content and look. With the lack of fresh catechetical material for use in schools, he and Frank Fletcher devised a catechetical supplement which was introduced in the February 1967 issue. For the next 10 years, the *Supplements* earned a solid reputation for quality of content and design and the wide ranges of illustrations, quotations from different points of view and questions for relevant topics. Some parents and teachers were initially reluctant to look at issues of drugs, capital punishment and abortion which featured as early as 1967 and 1968. Until the proliferation of American material during the 1970s and growing local production (and the coming of the photo copier), *Annals* was popular and widely used in schools.

I was glad to be part of the *Annals Supplement* preparation team, a group of brothers and nuns from a variety of congregations and schools who contributed material, discussed content and layout and gave a religious authority to the work. Later there was involvement of the MSC students researching quotable material. Later there would be a Catechists Guide, a number of which Paul Stenhouse asked me to write (sometimes in the car on a Sunday morning parked in parish grounds between Wandin and Mt. Evelyn Masses).

It is interesting to look at the *Supplements* with the hindsight of experience and to understand the ways we were thinking at the time. Our *Supplement* on Censorship was early in the piece, the sixth, in July 1967. We provided points on pro-censorship and anti-censorship and texts from authors as diverse and Pope John XXIII and T. S. Eliot to D. H. Lawrence and papers and magazines like *Time Magazine*, *L'Osservatore Romano* and Sydney's *Daily Telegraph*. I was able to write an article to accompany the *Supplement*. I see a sentence in bold type: 'This means that we are our own most important censors' and the observation that 'what was shocking for one generation is often not even disturbing (is sometimes laughable) for the next. We can see this for ourselves with some of the "daring" films of 25 years ago'. I don't remember what I was referring to, probably Howard Hughes' *The Outlaw*, which boasted a sensational(ist) poster of Jane Russell, which I had seen on television in 1966. I just looked up the Internet Movie Database which notes the controversy:

> Although the film was finished and copyrighted in February 1941, it was not shown theatrically for another 2 years, mostly because of censorship problems which required cuts and revisions. By May 1941, the PCA agreed to approve the film, but Howard Hughes found that many state censor boards wanted a lot more cuts that he was not willing to make, so he shelved the film until 5 February 1943, when it was finally shown theatrically in San Francisco in the 115-minute version that we essentially see today. It caused quite a sensation, especially since Jane Russell and Jack Beutel performed a 20-minute scene that was cut from the film after each showing. More hassles about its possible release in New York caused Hughes to shelve the picture once again.

When re-released in San Francisco on 23 April 1946, the theater owner was arrested for showing a film 'offensive to decency.' The MPAA maintained that Howard Hughes switched prints and did not show the version that was approved. Hughes resigned from the MPAA and filed a $1,000,000 lawsuit demanding triple damages. He lost the suit and all the appeals. Despite the legal battles and many bans, United Artists continued to roadshow the film in 1946 and 1947 and it set records almost everywhere it was shown. Originally banned in New York, it was finally shown on 11 September 1947 when the ban was lifted.

The argument was that censorship is often imposed by authority rather than by ability to discern what is really good and what is really bad. My article ended, a bit exhortatively, with conviction, 'Censorship is always a means. The end to be achieved is the Christian development of every person in the community and of the community itself.' Oh, to be 27 again! And this is not the last word on the topic for this journey.

We were enthusiastic in those days, eager to reach out and help, to become involved in religious education and the media, wanting to face up to issues and help people to face them rather than avoid them. Our sphere of influence was limited.

During 1967, Paul Stenhouse did some photo-stories in *Annals* on two films with religious backgrounds that were screening in Australia, Pasolini's *The Gospel According to St. Matthew* and *A Man for All Seasons*. It seemed like a good idea to introduce film reviews in *Annals*, highlighting films that were current and of interest to our readers, Paul wrote the first one himself, 'The Glory that was *Camelot* (almost)'. That was almost the end of the reviews as soon as they started. Paul had gone along to the preview and had not liked the film much, despite its splendid sound and look. Warner Bros. publicity was not impressed. After this not exactly auspicious start, what to do next?

During the Liturgical Congress in Melbourne in January 1968, we saw a few films on the side. One was *To Sir With Love*, Sidney Poitier as teacher, E. R Braithwaite, in a difficult London school. It had not opened in Sydney, so that was the one to go with. At the Sydney preview, everyone was given an apple in a plastic bag as they went in. Sometimes advertising gimmicks are part of the show. *To Sir with Love* was my first review. The second was *Far From the Madding Crowd*.

'Those at school will like it. Most teachers, while yearning for such success, will nevertheless get a big lift from seeing it' – the end of the first review, *To Sir With Love*. It is now thousands of reviews later.

15. 1968 AND ALL THAT

1968 BEGAN a new phase for me, over and above the film reviewing, with my appointment from Daramalan College out to the monastery on the Federal Highway where I had spent 1960-61 studying. I was to teach Old Testament and some Theology, both of which were congenial. I was also to teach Philosophy, much harder for me, let alone the students, one of whom told me that he counted all the nails in my office floorboard during his pauses in the oral exam. I was also to work in the formation of the students as persons, as members of the congregation and on their road towards ordination. This too was congenial, although I was soon to realise that my training was not specifically for this and that hunches and goodwill went quite a part of the way. This was called experience. And experience helped you go a lot more of the way. I was to do this work at Canberra and back at Croydon for the next 16 years. But working with students in a seminary in 1968 was quite different from the same work in the decades before that. It was the end of the 1960s.

One of the advantages in being born in the final or early years of a decade is that you can look at your life in the patterns that the commentators on society and history use. Your life corresponds to those decades. It helps to interpret what has happened to you and how you have changed. Of course, this is quite arbitrary, this focusing on the 1960s or the 1970s instead of the period, say, 1964-74. But that is what we tend to do. And it suits me and my life decades.

When you are younger, you are not thinking of the meaning of the decades of your life. It is a bit awesome to reach double-figures. Nowadays, you have become technically adult at 18 but the celebratory 21st birthday party is yet to come. But, reaching 30 ...

The closing years of the 1960s were, as I recall, full of energy and life. How much of my perception was due to being in my late twenties and approaching 30, I am not too sure. Perhaps a great deal. Some memoirs of the 1960s evoke a period of confusion, excessive experimentation with values and lifestyles, loss of identity and moral decline. The 1960s are spoken of by many as a regrettable mistake. Not for me. But, I think, we were spurred on by the challenges. Life was not as predictable as we had assumed 10 years earlier. We were involved in throwing off the narrowing, cramping formalism of the past, in concern about present crises and eager to shape and re-shape the future. Even in a religious congregation and in a small seminary in Australia, this was possible.

1968 was a key year. The French look back to the turmoil in Paris of that year, the university protests, riots at the Sorbonne. In the minds of some French writers and film-makers, it seems to be the watershed and the emergence of a new period in French history. In the Soviet Bloc, 1968 saw the end of the more liberal regime of Premier Dubček in Czechoslovakia and the Russian tanks drove into Prague. (And for readers who like visual research, there are many films about 1968: Paris and *The Dreamers, Born in 1968*; Prague and *The Unbearable Lightness of Being*; many films on Vietnam like *Full Metal Jacket, Platoon* and, if you would like quite a contrast to this serious fare, I can recommend Nadia Tass's tongue-in-cheek version of the first Australian siege in the summer of 1968, Wally Mellish and his girlfriend, Beryl, and the baby, Lesley, along with the flatfooted police and officials in *Mr. Reliable*.)

In the Middle East, the maps of Israel and Jordan had changed with the 1967 six-day war and the boost to Israeli self-consciousness and the antagonism of the Arab world. 1968 saw Richard Nixon's successful presidential campaign and the escalation of the American presence in Vietnam and the conflict of viewpoints on the waging and winning of that war. John Wayne's enthusiastic, even jingoistic pro-US presence in Vietnam movie, *The Green Berets*, was released in 1968. Another film, released in 1975, that invited its audience to look back to 1968 and re-assess what U.S. society was like and its expectations of the Nixon administration was Hal Ashby's *Shampoo* with Warren Beatty, Goldie Hawn, Julie Christie, a blackly sardonic look at the permissiveness and wheeler-dealing of the time in the light of Watergate and Nixon's resignation.

In Australia, there was (more comparatively quiet) university unrest, antiwar protest and people puzzled by the shifts of values reported on television from the U.S. and Europe and, increasingly, from Asia. John Duigan's *The Trespassers* (1976) dramatised that period in inner Melbourne suburbs. He took up the same theme, but with a Sydney setting, in *Winter of Our Dreams* (1981). John Duigan was a co-writer and director of the 1987 mini-series *Vietnam* which effectively dramatised the late 1960s again, scored high ratings, and was watched by a large number of Australians.

Nobody knew it then (though many hoped) but it was the final stage of Liberal-Country Party coalition of conservative government that had begun under Sir Robert Menzies in 1949 and was to end on 2 December 1972, with the beginning of the Whitlam years, with the slogan, 'It's Time'

And the Catholic Church?

In Australia, the changes proposed by the Second Vatican Council were beginning to be implemented. Many thought changes were being hastily enforced. Others groaned over delays. Looking back, I am amazed at how quickly many of the changes were accepted. It was always difficult to bring about changes or 'renewal', given the range of attitudes and levels of understanding of their faith amongst the people in the pews as well as in the clergy. Bishops were certainly not of one mind. Catholics in the Archdiocese of Melbourne were encouraged to fresh perspectives on the celebration of the liturgy or the teaching of doctrine which were forbidden along the Calder Highway in the Diocese of Sandhurst, centred on Bendigo.

There was confusion, but there was also a re-discovery of hope and a shift of emphasis from children and primary and secondary education in the Catholic system to adult education and responsibility and more participation in church life and administration by the laity. After all, key ideas in the principal document from Vatican II were on the universal call of all men and women to the fullness of Christian life. There was also a separate document on the laity, urging a church in which the priesthood of all members was highlighted to give a different perspective on the priesthood of the ordained bishops and priests.

The intervening decades have seen many books written on the Catholic Church in this period. Ecclesiastical horror stories of repressive education systems have not been wanting. Collections of funny and not-so-funny incidents have been published. Those who lament a lost Church have condemned this period. In the mid-1980s Michael Gilchrist, of the Catholic Institute of Education in Ballarat, advertised in the Catholic papers for and then edited stories of 'excesses' at this time – strange celebrations of the Mass, members of religious orders becoming more 'worldly' and about-to-leave priests. His book *Rome or the Bush* (1986) is one of savage sadness (not without invective!) about the changes in the Catholic Church. It was followed by *New Church or True Church* (1987) in the same vein, where my courses at the National Pastoral Institute merited attack on one page and praise on the next.

An event that he highlighted and one which was significant for the Church at large was the issuing of the Encyclical Letter by Pope Paul VI, *Humanae Vitae (Of Human Life)* in July 1968 on the vexed questions of human life, sexuality and contraception. An expectation had been built up over four years for this statement from the Vatican. During the Council, the contemporary and urgent questions of sexual morality had been discussed in the preparation of the document on the Church in the Modern World (*Gaudium et Spes*). However, Paul VI reserved the question of artificial contraception for his own consideration and set up a committee to investigate the issues as carefully as possible. This raised doubts of conscience for many Catholics. No matter how often the traditional teaching against artificial contraception was reiterated, the fact that there was a Papal Commission studying it seemed to say there were doubts about the prohibitions. The years went by with many Catholics, especially in the United States, taking stronger and more vocal stances about the issue. It was the same in Australia. By the end of 1967, it was rumoured that 1968 was to be the year of the Vatican statement. There were also rumours that a majority of the Papal Commission was in favour of 'lifting the ban'. The questions were discussed in seminary courses on moral issues, in adult education groups that were now emerging, in the press. I think many of us thought that the statement would be Paul VI's adoption of the so-called majority viewpoint.

It was not. I have particularly vivid memories of the night the encyclical was issued. Daramalan was sponsoring a series of lectures on current theology issues for parents. We had had the evening on Scripture. That last Monday night in July, I was to speak on the Church. We heard the news at 7 o'clock and, if there is anything to make one check what one is going to say on the Church's teaching authority, it is the issuing of a significant encyclical on a controversial topic. We had a fair crowd that night and more than the usual number of questions, but I don't remember any of them. Dealing with the encyclical and its impact was enough for that day. By the way, the next talk was to have been on conscience. It was never held.

There was enthusiasm for the encyclical by those who expressed respect for tradition and expected and wanted papal documents to express and re-affirm that tradition. In the ensuing controversies in the newspapers, Catholic journals and forums, this group highlighted the question of authority and papal infallibility. While the accepted literary mode of the Pope's encyclical was of 'ordinary teaching', a number of writers declared that it was 'almost infallible'.

Others, disappointed by the contents and tone of the document, emphasised that theology has always said that this kind of document deserved great 'respect' but, since it was not infallible teaching, it did not demand total 'assent'; the issue still needed to be carefully analysed and studied.

Humanae Vitae had a profound impact on the Church in Australia. Many Catholics expressed disillusionment and stopped practising their faith. Others bypassed the encyclical. Others, both clergy and laity, acknowledged it with respect and, conscientiously, continued to study the issues and their theoretical and pastoral implications.

The Australian Bishops almost at once issued a very brief statement of loyalty. Hierarchies from other countries took longer to consider the encyclical and produced more comprehensive statements in their interpretation. These documents ranged from the 'almost infallible' stance to the 'continue to study' stance. Paul VI's letter, quite a long one, did have, in fact, a pastoral and compassionate tone for couples struggling with circumstances and conscience, encouraging their continued participation in the Sacraments of Reconciliation and Eucharist. It was discovered, by comparing versions in English Catholic papers, that the lines stating this were omitted from the translations first printed in the press in Australia.

While I hope these last paragraphs give some indication of how things were at the time, *Humanae Vitae* touched the MSCs in Canberra, with a (sometimes literal) vengeance. For those readers interested in the Church-Cinema interaction, you will have to go on hold for the time being, since this was a significant Catholic happening for us.

Two priests, concerned about the impact of the encyclical on people with whom they worked and had talked over these issues, decided on the Thursday night, 1 August, to write a letter to the *Canberra Times* offering a broader, pastoral interpretation of the encyclical. A first draft was circulated next morning amongst the MSCs at Daramalan and at the seminary. In the afternoon, a second draft was signed by five priests (one later rang the *Canberra Times* to withdraw his name as he reflected on the growing serious impact of the publishing of the letter). On Friday afternoon, the letter was hurried, without the respective superiors seeing it, into the *Canberra Times* office for printing on Saturday, 4 August.

I did not sign the letter. It seemed to me too quickly written and needed further definition if it was to be helpful. In hindsight, it would have been better for someone who disagreed with the letter's content to have read it and commented. But there was an atmosphere of urgency that week. Letters from confused, upset and staunch Catholics had appeared in the papers. Some priests were interviewed round Australia. Moral Theologian, Passionist Nicholas Crotty, who had anticipated a different encyclical wrote some articles for *The Australian* since so many who knew him – and he had given the 1968 retreat for many MSCs – were wondering about his response; he took the broad interpretation. Fr. Walter Black MSC, who had suggested that the encyclical would take this broader view, wrote articles affirming loyalty to the Pope. It was that kind of atmosphere.

In the letter went. The editor sensationalised it by inserting a front-page blurb about four priests who were contradicting the Pope. It was nothing like riots in the streets of Paris; but it was dramatic enough for Canberra.

Early Saturday morning, Max Douglas, our Superior at the seminary, decided to ring Fr. John McMahon, the Provincial Superior, to let him know what had happened. There was no need. The Archbishop had already rung him. The following week was unforgettable. No Church crisis has ever been the same for me. And I learnt comparatively early in life that one can survive ecclesiastical crises.

Archbishop Thomas Vincent Cahill of Canberra Goulburn took a very dim view of the letter and immediately issued a statement to radio and television which was to be read at all Masses in the diocese that weekend. It denounced the MSC letter and declared that the only doctrine to be put forward in the diocese was what 'the Pope and I teach'. At one Mass, a parent of boys at Daramalan, who was employed at the Diocesan offices, stood up after the reading of the Archbishop's statement and loudly declared, 'I believe in contraception', genuflected and walked out. (He was a Dutchman.)

The Archbishop certainly let the Provincial and the Superiors know what he thought of the MSCs. Not good. However, he was persuaded by his Chancellor not to penalise the four priests by suspending them from priestly ministry but only to ask they not to preach or hear confessions for the time being. But, unfortunately, the archbishop did not interview the writers personally for five days – and then found out that what they were saying was, in substance, no different from what hierarchies from other countries were saying. He even spoke admiringly of their zeal as priests. However, it was too late in the week for that.

In the meantime, reporters were ringing, wandering through the monastery seeking whom they might interview: segments for TV programs like *This Day Tonight* were set up but did not come off; to avoid reporters at the airport, John McMahon travelled back to Canberra from Sydney by train to Goulburn and then by car. I seem to have spent a lot of time during that week driving the Provincial to meetings and trying to argue the legitimacy of the stance for theological reasons. Fr. McMahon started to refer to 'our opinions'. The days before the interviews with the priests were spent in looking up theology books to find language that could be agreed on. John Hanrahan, the originator of the letter, was sick in bed and was visited at the monastery by Archbishop Cahill. They agreed on some Latin terminology – and all was almost well when the Archbishop noticed a Hans Kung volume on a pile of books by the bed. And then the Archbishop did not stay for the afternoon tea spread that had been prepared for him!

The hubbub died down within a fortnight. But the *Humanae Vitae* episodes linger in the memories. Michael Gilchrist, for instance, referred frequently to them in *Rome or the Bush*, even using the epithet, '*Humanae Vitae* dissenter', to refer derogatorily to Michael Fallon who subsequently contributed a great deal to theological and scriptural awareness in his speaking and writing over many years. The rest of 1968 was somewhat difficult, people reporting some of the priests to the Archbishop for any statements they disapproved of, tensions because of varying stances in the Church in Australia on the issue of contraception – and the Archbishop's desire that none of the four priests remain in his diocese. They were moved.

16. FORMATION/SEMINARY WORK

THIS PART of the story will not focus on film work so much. If the prospect of reading about formation work in seminaries in the late 1960s and early 1970s does not rouse much curiosity, then I would advise skipping this section. One of the main reasons it is here is that, of course, it was an important part of my life. But it is also the background to the beginning of my film reviewing as well as of the considerable changes that were to begin this time in Australia with an investigation into and consultation about cinema censorship – which will be taken up in the next section.

I spent four years, 1968-1971 at the monastery in Canberra working in formation, working with young adults who had been through a novitiate year like, yet unlike, what we had gone through just over a decade earlier. The students were moving towards making their 'final vows', a perpetual profession of poverty, chastity and obedience in commitment to God and the Missionaries of the Sacred Heart. It was important for me personally because it became a time of reflection on my own life with the benefit of personalised and psychological language that was not available in the late 1950s and early 1960s, though the conferences and writings of Jim Cuskelly at Croydon prepared us well for this. To that extent, it was confirming of the life that I felt I had been called to.

Not everybody experienced those years in that way. For many, it was a time of re-assessment, a time of realising that the initial commitment was not as well-grounded as was first thought. When one looks back at the formation styles of those years, it is easier to see why there should have been such a re-assessment. In a society that relies on traditions and external forms, it is easy to remain where one is. Even if it is painful or there seems to be no way out, one is supported by the structures, the rituals, the group who are doing the same thing regularly. There is a strength in routine and many living by the same routine. Thus men and women were able to stay together in marriage. Many men and women were able to remain as priests and/or members of religious orders.

The former formation program was geared to these structures and support. The candidate, often as young as 12 years old, went into a junior or 'minor' seminary for trainees for the order. The Missionaries of the Sacred Heart called their junior seminary at Douglas Park an 'Apostolic School'. (Since I went to Chevalier College to school and went directly to the Novitiate, this was something I never experienced). The school was fairly isolated, generally in the country, had students of only the same sex, allowed visitors, social contacts and holidays at home but not too frequently. The pattern of living and timetable was that of a boarding school but also an adaptation of the program and timetable of the religious order. Most of the boys who went to the Apostolic School did not stay. It was a time for deciding about priesthood and vocation.

There is a helpful film to look at for background to this kind of formation, Fred Schepisi's autobiographical story of his time in the juniorate of the Marist Brothers in Mount Macedon, Victoria, *The Devil's Playground* (1976). I noted that Schepisi's central character, Tom, was 14 in 1953 (as was Schepisi himself), so I could identify in time with him. Many of the routines were exact enough and, when they were heightened with dramatic and poetic licence, the points made were true enough. Schepisi highlighted the enclosed group of boys and of staff, the strict supervision by the Brothers, kitchen chores, the annual retreat (with Thomas Kenneally as the Franciscan friar attempting a sermon mixture of Joyce's *Portrait of the Artist as a Young Man* and the traditional Redemptorist hellfire imagery) and the soft drinks and cakes party afterwards.

The film also showed the loneliness of young boys away from home and family, the dangers of exaggerated piety, mortification and boys, already belonging to a religious order, in the throes of puberty, bewildered and ignorant and yet preached at threateningly.

I had to see the film twice, once to see what was there and deal with that and then to appreciate and enjoy it. As a confrere remarked after seeing it, 'Just as well they didn't make a film of our days at Douglas Park!' I should add that, for the sake of the drama and his contemporary audience, Schepisi used a 1970s frankness in language and knowingness, especially within the Brothers' community that was not actual then. One can understand the self-consciousness in the attacks on *The Devil's Playground* and the claims that it was unrealistic. But as a drama about a Catholic group in the early 1950s, it was full of insights.

The Formation program of those years meant that the initial focus was on personal commitment and an intense and strict religious experience to steer a person to that commitment. It was only after the vows (in a men's religious order) that the candidate moved on to community living and studies. The 'lay brothers' (the term used for brothers, the men in the order who did not choose ordination, which ran the danger of reinforcing a two class membership of an order) had two-and-a-half years of training before first vows and usually went straight into the apostolate, the order's work force.

Some newly professed found that they could make a commitment to God but that community life was too difficult. Some stuck it out heroically, believing in their call. Many were exhorted to continue in this heroism and did. Others left. One of the difficulties in living this type of community life, as I realise now, for extroverted personalities, is that study and prayer (individual activities by and large) were priorities; there was a great deal of silence; there was little outlet for ministry activities; the life was congenial for the introverted student type.

After ordination (or after the Novitiate years, for brothers), the priest began his ministry. Even though in his mid-20s, he was inexperienced in communication with people (even sermons had been given to lecturers and fellow students), often lacked social know-how and ease and often found the early years of priesthood very difficult in terms of adjustment, work demands, social and emotional demands and, we would say now, finding his identity as a person, as a man, as a priest. But the structures were supportive and not so many left the religious and priestly life.

Fred Schepisi had tackled this subject before he made *The Devil's Playground* in a 1973 feature, *Libido*, a collection of four short films on the theme of human passion. Schepisi's segment was written by Thomas Kenneally, entitled *The Priest*. It starred Arthur Dignam as the priest and Robyn Nevin as a nun. The priest was in 'vocational crisis', experiencing difficulties with some Catholic teachings, self-identity, and his affectivity, wanting the nun to leave her convent and marry him. Reviewers at the time focused on the priest, his psychological stress, bizarre behaviour and hallucinogenic medical treatment. But Kenneally, of course, had also written the dialogue for the nun, who chose a more restrained and orderly procedure for leaving her order. The theme of tortured clergy of all denominations recurred in Australian films of the 1970s, especially Jack Thompson in *The Chant of Jimmie Blacksmith*, Charles Tingwell in *Peterson*, Frederick Parslow in *The Last Wave*.

Speaking of films on this period, there is an interesting American telemovie that is worth looking at. It is based on a book called *The Nun*, but the producers called the film *Shattered Vows*. Valerie Bertinelli is the star; Patricia Neal appears as the Novice Mistress. The title is inaccurate. The nun does not shatter her vows but leaves appropriately at the end of a long period of questions and discernment. However, it does remind us of what it was like for an enthusiastic young religious to go through the tight formation process, be frustrated, especially by severe clergy suspicious of nuns changing their traditional roles in the mid-1960s and discover theological and scriptural study and new forms of ministry. The unfortunate title sounds like a novel by Andrew Greeley – who did, in fact, offer some arresting best-seller images of the Church at this period.

The process, traditional but not psychologically helpful, was: commitment, community, ministry. What we had to do in the 1960s and 1970s in formation work was to reassess this, experiment with ways of training and, as they were tested, incorporate them into new programs and reverse the order: ministry, community, commitment. The 1960s actually encouraged this in every walk of life and the Church was now explicitly asking that this be done. The religious orders were asked to re-write their charters, their 'Constitutions' in the light of Vatican II's renewal.

Adaptation was being asked for:

> The manner of living, praying, and working should be suitably adapted to the physical and psychological condition of today's religious and also, to the extent required by the nature of each community, to the needs of the apostolate, the requirements of a given culture, the social and economic circumstances anywhere, but especially in missionary territories (*Decree*, No. 3).

While religious orders had been adapting to changing circumstances in the past (as they moved into foreign countries, saw the need for re-organising study programs and began to train members at universities and colleges), it was now not merely a matter of necessary alterations. It was to be overall adaptation of the style of religious life. Not that this had not been done in the Church before: in the 13th century, the mendicant movement of such orders as the Franciscans and the Dominicans meant that the monastery was no longer the pattern for all congregations; in the 16th century, the Jesuits let go many of the community traditions that had remained (like the Divine Office of the Church sung in choir) as they moved into a much more active ministry.

This was our charter, particularly from 1960. At Canberra, we had the advantage of a broadening experience for the students, attending courses at the Australian National University. From 1967, we were able to send every student, whether he had matriculated or not, to study two units: Philosophy I and History 1, The Rise of Christendom. Some then went on to complete their Arts degree. The repercussions of this arrangement were that the students' study horizons broadened, they were using a range of terminologies, not merely confined to ecclesiastical jargon, exposed to philosophical systems different from those of the Church and alternate interpretations of key characters and events in the Church's history. They were also attending lectures with a cross-section of Australian students, men and women, Catholics and not. In 1969, a time of student protest and organisational disarray, the Students' Representative Council of the university asked one of our students, Bob Irwin, to stand for presidency of the Council; he was elected and successfully led and unified the Council.

At home, it was not so easy. One of the controversies of 1968 was whether the students should be allowed to smoke and to drink. Obviously, the traditional rules were against this. It was not easy to resolve in favour. (This was not a discussion for or against smoking for health reasons – that was to come soon after.)

A focus of change was the Provincial Chapter of August 1968 (two weeks after the *Humanae Vitae* crisis – and held in Canberra). The task of the congregation in those years was to discuss a new draft of the Constitutions for re-writing and final approval. It was both tedious and exhilarating to participate in these discussions. I had been asked to be part of a working group for two weeks in June to go through all the written submissions for the Chapter and to create some kind of order and agenda, an opportunity to be in touch with the mind and the feelings of the Province. But the significant thing which, I think, we underestimated at the time, was that young men at the beginning of their religious life were sitting down with the middle-aged and with the older men, to discuss core issues of the vows of chastity, poverty and obedience as well as argue about freedom and more flexible timetables. It was quite a change in methods for coming to decisions and for government. Exhilarating for the young who could be quite impetuous, wearing for the older men who could easily become angry and contemptuous.

Over the next few years we experimented with ways of developing the potential of the young men and integrating them into the MSCs. We were only a small staff and were learning as we went. I think we were moving well with the times even though we made mistakes and confreres were sometimes less than sympathetic (understatement!). We were to hear more and more of 'Why don't they ...?' This took its toll. Many of the students did not stay. Perhaps they came too quickly to their decisions about leaving. With an increasing number of priests and brothers making decisions to leave, even after many years of commitment and ministry, it was surprising, sometimes shocking, often saddening as friends of many years went different ways, sometimes keeping in touch, many preferring not to, giving themselves a chance to establish a new life.

In the meantime, Canberra was a stimulating place to live – and plenty to do. Supplying for weekend Masses at Bungendore or Captain's Flat and as far as Bega, Dalgety and Jindabyne (and a visit to the top of Mt. Kosciusko on Christmas day after the Masses). There was a growing number of lay discussion groups, meeting to reflect on the documents of the Vatican Council, providing stimulation and a challenge to translate Church formulas into everyday English. There were ecumenical deanery meetings and a haven at St. Mark's Library, an Anglican centre with fine book resources but also a centre for visiting local and overseas visitors and short courses.

This was also a period of retreats for religious orders and a variety of groups. These retreats could be for six to eight days or for a few days for school classes. I rashly volunteered at the end of 1967 to go to Cronulla for a retreat for De La Salle Brothers who had asked for a priest to sit in on their discussions and say Masses. It turned out to be more than this. The starting day is easy to remember as I was standing on Redfern station when I heard on a passenger's transistor that prime minister, Harold Holt, had disappeared at Portsea. I wished I could disappear when I arrived as an older, crusty-looking Brother looked at (through?) me and said, 'So, you're the retreat-giver.' Brother Xavier's bark was worse than his bite, although he told me when I spoke of the heritage of founders, that St. John Baptist De La Salle, their founder, had battled with parish priests and that this what he handed on to them. When he went back home to Orange, he increased his subscriptions to *Annals* to 50!

Actually, in those years, retreats took me to different cities. There was a slogan, 'Have retreat, will travel.' I went to Taree, Dubbo, Rutherglen, Melbourne, Broken Hill and an exchange with the Redemptorists where I gave the retreat to their seminarians in Ballarat (aged 28, which the MSCs noted was the opposite of the Redemptorist sent to give the retreat to them, 82!) The sisters allowed for an experiment, using a film screening as part of the retreat, a stimulus for discussion and prayer.

I do remember the Superior asking me in October 1969 if I would give three retreats to Marist Brothers during the Christmas holidays. I said yes and then asked where. 'Auckland.' Just as well I said yes! Six weeks in New Zealand. The groups were large, 150 in Auckland and 90 in Masterton. The Brothers ensured that I saw as much of the country as possible, from Rotorua to Lake Taupo, Wellington, Christchurch and four days around the south island with three geography teachers, to Mount Cook, Franz Josef Glacier, a beer at 10.00 am at a hotel in Hokitika and a sunny journey through the Haast Pass. And a stay at a motel for the first time in my life.

In Hamilton, some of the Brothers asked how I reviewed films so off we went to the local theatre to analyse the film on show. It was George Lazenby in *On Her Majesty's Secret Service*. A very serious discussion of James Bond followed though, in retrospect and with comparisons, it is the least effective of the Bond movies.

Last thing for this period! It was back quickly from New Zealand because that same superior in Canberra felt that the Formation team should contribute to the Education Ministry which seemed understaffed. I was the contribution.

It meant going from the monastery back to Daramalan during 1970 for 20 classes a week as well as doing the normal teaching and directing at the monastery. As it turned out, it was not a normal year. There was another Provincial Chapter with documents, committees, meetings. The editor of *Annals*, Paul Stenhouse, got the mumps and I had to go to Sydney to help the August issue through. The novice master had a car accident and was ill from July, so I acquired his 16 students for directing. But, then, we were full of energy.

The return to school was a healthy reminder of how teenagers ticked. The school was much better organised (and much larger) than three years earlier. There were more buildings, including a separate area for senior school (and, should they smoke or not?). I enjoyed (mostly) the opportunity to teach fifth form English (novels, at three – different – levels), sixth form English (drama, at three – different levels). And there was also religion – an almost impossible task in those days. Adaptation was at its height and students, instead of being quietly uninterested, puzzled or bored, were now vocally uninterested, puzzled or bored. I consoled myself with comparisons with English classes. I'm sure that if there had been no assessment with its consequences for their lives and work, the students would have been just as rowdy and minimally interested in English as they were in Religion.

I think the greatest success I had with fifth form English at level 3 was a discussion about the box-office takings for *Easy Rider*. We found out the number of seats in the Gala cinema in Sydney, estimated the average audience size at each session, how much per ticket ... and did our sums. It did interest them that this popular film had such a following and gained so much profit. But, further talk about themes was disappointing. Tom Laughlin's first *Billy Jack* film, *The Born Losers*, an exploitation film, was also screening at the time. Motor cycles was the common denominator. The class couldn't see any difference between the two films, actually preferring *The Born Losers* because the story line was better and clearer. Of course, the narrative appeal is strong for most audiences. It made me realise that this group, not keen on reading the novels on the syllabus, still liked to read so we had some English classes where they could bring along any book they liked. And they did, a lot of pop material, but they were reading. And they were happy to show it to me – though I found it a bit difficult scanning page 16 and page 37 of *The Virgin Soldiers* to try to determine exactly the part that these 16 and 17 year older found 'really hot'.

But it was a valuable experience, though hard work, to be back in the classroom. And there were other surprises. After a fourth form religion class where I had invited our MSC student (and now aboriginal elder), Pat Dodson, they were enthusiastic. 'Is the boong brother coming back?'. Canberra, 1970!

17. A CHANGING FILM LANDSCAPE

CANBERRA, formation, school, university in the small but growing national capital was the context in which I began the film reviews for the *Annals*. It shaped the initial choice of films for consideration before we moved to reviewing all releases. It helped shape the style which was basically a personal response to the film, an attempt at appreciation rather than a negative critique or condemnation, the hope that the tone of writing, the choice of words and phrasing would help readers to estimate how the film worked for the reviewer and whether the reader would like to see the film or not. I've always relied on the government classifications to indicate suitability rather than the classifications of the American Church reviews.

During 1968 I reviewed only 12 films. Later we were to review the same number or more per month. I started with *To Sir with Love* and *Far From the Madding Crowd* and then one of the films which still remains me one of the greatest for me, Stanley Kubrick's *2001: A Space Odyssey*. *2001* was only moderately successful when it opened in April 1968. Those who saw it then had the experience of being enveloped in the Sydney Plaza's Cinerama screen, the way Kubrick intended it to be seen. The prologue with the apes and evolution gave way to the waltz rhythms of *The Blue Danube* and 2001 space travel – and then the long mission beyond Jupiter, the clash with computer HAL and the hurtling psychedelic journey of Everyman to Everytime and the hope of human rebirth. Six months later there were spacecraft circling the moon. July 1969 saw humans on the moon's surface. But, *2001* is still the cinema-poem of human and technological progress and its meaning. I'm not sure that that is what we thought as we emerged, dazed, from the preview into George Street.

But the film for review and controversy in 1968 was *The Graduate*. The preview was one of those industry-functions where the drinks beforehand bring out well-oiled sniggers at the sex-jokes but can hinder the appreciation of the film's worth. It was the first test of how to write an appreciative review of a mature and worthwhile film for a magazine read at schools and in homes. So, the film was written up as 'first-rate', but 'not one which I would recommend indiscriminately'. A recommendation: 'The theme and the presentation – it is sexually explicit in the frank rather than the titillating manner – are of adult interest. But I would also recommend it to thoughtful senior high school students who sometimes tend to share the cynicism and the idealism of *The Graduate*.' And then the smart crack which might make amusing reading but which can be so destructive of a film. One got away with it here, 'The real feeling for Mrs. Robinson, whom nobody except Jesus could love'.

The review of *The Graduate* brought in the first letter of criticism of my reviews though there was only the one. It made me aware of the need for a reviewer to communicate with the readership and not just write for oneself (or fellow reviewers, which is quite a temptation). I think this is still the basic approach I take. At least, I hope so. A concerned mother wrote to the editor of the *Annals*. Her feelings were typical of the times (and, of course, are still echoed today):

> As a Catholic parent, and one who tries to supervise what type of pictures my family views both on television and at the theatre. I am at a loss to understand why a film entitled *The Graduate* was recommended by your magazine as being suitable for sub-senior and senior students.
>
> Allowing myself to be swayed by your views on this picture without really finding out what possible enjoyment or should I say benefit, would be derived from this movie, I allowed my 15-year-old son to go along with a couple of his sub-senior friends to see this program.
>
> I have since found out for myself what they viewed and I cannot tell you how very angry I feel about this.

I feel this type of picture generally would have the worst effect on either a boy or a girl of this age group.

Please answer this letter as I feel very let down with your magazine over this very important matter. As far as I am concerned, what a person views is there in the mind for always.

Letters like this need the personal answer. When I think back, I was 28 at the time of writing the review and, perhaps, more confident than I should have been, although I was encouraged to persevere in perspectives on films like this by the review of *The Graduate* in the Melbourne Catholic paper, *The Advocate*, where psychologist reviewer, Ronald Conway, noted that the film 'had a lot of valuable truth and blackly humorous comment'; 'The film implicitly states proper values.' He recommended it for the filmgoer who could make the necessary reservations (15 September 1968). Perhaps I was overestimating the abilities of school students but I also think many parents were underestimating the abilities of their children in discerning between good and bad.

The reviews have also brought on some amusing stories. In January 1969, a preview of *Rosemary's Baby*. The columnist on the back page of *The Australian*, 'Martin Collins', took a dim view of a film about devil-worship. As always, the talk fanned curiosity. Paul Stenhouse and I went to the preview in Sydney, clerically attired, and found it powerful: 'for an adult audience, it is an absorbing, if unsettling, experience'. Next day, the Sydney *Sun* reported on the preview. Apparently no-one followed the Martin Collins' lead, the news item simply including a piece of non-news, 'Two priests were seen to leave the theatre without comment.' Nobody asked us.

I had better mention that I received an unanticipated boost from John Northey, now in Sydney and, with his cancer, not long to live. Paul Stenhouse rang me in Canberra to say that he was going to take John to the press preview of *The Killing of Sister George*, the British comedy-drama with lesbian themes. I urged him not to. But, I had misheard! He had already taken him but had to leave the film early as he did not expect it to run so long. John decided to stay and see the film through. He found it a good film. I asked him should *Annals* review it. '*Annals* should review all controversial films'. It was the period of *If...* and *Midnight Cowboy*. No longer an 'ecclesiastical Peeping Tom', I had an unofficial imprimatur to go on reviewing whatever came up. And, of course, a lot of 'whatever' did come up – and continues to do so. (Three years later, one of the students joining the pre-Novitiate in Melbourne looked at me with a shocked and/or pained expression when he realised I was to be his director. The Marist Brothers in Newcastle had forbidden him and his classmates to read the *Annals* reviews.)

1970 offered a controversial film of a different kind, the political thriller Z, directed by Costa-Gavras and winner of the Oscar for the Best Foreign Film of 1969. (Costa-Gavras was later to direct *State of Siege*, set in Chile, as was his *Missing*). Paul Stenhouse and I decided to co-write an article for the June 1970 *Annals* looking at the film and the Right-wing, Left-wing dichotomies (with the exclusive language of the times). We began:

> Demonstrations in our streets, the Moratorium, Police and non-violence, May 1970. Condemnation, and rebuttals; Communist, Right-wing; U.S., Liberation. Australia, although distant from the intensity of the world scene, is stirring in its placid semi-apathy. What of our presence in Vietnam, conscription, napalm, guerrillas, torture and massacres and corpses floating down the Mekong River?
>
> Many consciences are at work and people are awakening to find themselves either on the Right or the Left, with a brand attached ('Made in Russia' or 'Made in the U.S.A.'). There is a great need for Australians today to focus on this alertness ...

A Changing Film Landscape

Far from the sensuality and individual search for meaning so popular in today's films, this absorbing experience is social and political – testing one's own presuppositions, attitudes and beliefs now.

We drew on the writings of Erich Fromm's *Man May Prevail* to look at the film and link its considerations of the paranoiac mentality to look at the character assassination and political exploitation of the Communist bogey in Australia and Western countries:

> This often goes hand in hand with a fanaticism that is always self-righteous, where principles override all else. This attitude seems to result from a failure to realise that principles are abstract, while people are real. It is only through people that we really understand principles. Z shows the Right as composed of principled men, whose principles compel them to trample over other men's lives and rights in the interest of politics and Society as they see them. While we do get involved militarily and politically as a result of our principles, there is a constant need to reexamine these principles which have led to our involvement. It is not a question of compromising principles but of really understanding them in the first place.
>
> Another feature of the extreme Right in their attacks on political and social opposition is the way they project the defects they refuse to face in themselves onto their opponents.

And so we concluded:

> Man's social history is the interaction of Left-wing and Right. The western world claims it is Right. Z is an indictment of an extreme which claims stability, Christianity and God for its support. It seems also to assert that Christianity has been

inextricably linked with a rigid orthodoxy which easily resorts to violence to impose itself. *Z* is an excellent film, a moving and timely alert to our own social attitudes.

So, it was not just how much screen nudity and frank language that preoccupied us that year!

One focus of controversy for Catholics and censorship arose in 1969-1970 and it concerned nuns and the changing perception of nuns. For instance, senior secondary teachers wanted to see films like *The Graduate* that their students were enthusing about. Should they go to a cinema in their religious habits, even as they were being modified and modernised at this time? What would people think? What would Catholics, especially parents, say?

One solution was to provide opportunities for sisters to attend special screenings together, screenings only for sisters. Father Chamberlin showed some good films, some controversial films like *Here We Go Round the Mulberry Bush* and *Midnight Cowboy* in Melbourne. Dr. Muller undertook screenings in Sydney, especially at the Ritz in Randwick (the Brigidine Sisters owned the lease). These were good as far as they went. At least they provided an opportunity. Sometimes TV personality Bill Collins came to introduce them – enthusiastically. When in Sydney from Canberra, I went and found myself sometimes disappointed when the audience did not know how to handle the film, how to respond to serious material (sometimes there was self-conscious laughter) because of inexperience in film-watching. There were some discussion periods afterwards, a good opportunity for clarifying responses and discovering how film conventions worked.

A case in point was *Midnight Cowboy* where a group of Good Samaritan novice nuns could talk about the images, where Jon Voight's hustler, Joe Buck, changed from his moccasin cowboy outfit into ordinary sports clothes and they knew that he had changed personally and made a life-changing decision. They appreciated the moral point. Older sisters, trained in reading, missed this because of their reliance on words and the need for explicit statements about moral points. Of course, this was true of so many older audiences (and still is for many highly intelligent academics who are word-bound). But, it was a very good move at the time and appreciated by the sisters.

Another way I found helpful in this regard was to use films in spirituality seminars at the time, and during retreats for down-to-earth reflection on themes. I have special gratitude to the Mercy, Dominican and Presentation sisters where we experimented with this use of films. Films for seminars included *Rachel, Rachel* and *The Fox*. Retreat films included *The L-Shaped Room* and *Love with the Proper Stranger* and, even with a group of MSC's, *The Subject was Roses*.

In seminars we watched the film in the evening, leaving participants to talk about the film informally. We then considered some theory on film appreciation the next day, and screened the film again 24 hours later. I suppose it was a bit risky for all of us at the time, but it seemed worth it.

There were some funny moments. At a Mercy seminar in May 1969, the only film screening in the theatre there was *2001: A Space Odyssey*. Not a wise programming choice for the miners of Broken Hill, and there were only a few others watching it with us. But, the teachers in Junior Secondary classes were keen to take the opportunity to catch up on some of the films the Senior Secondary teachers had been allowed to see. Fortunately on the last evening of the seminar, *Poor Cow*, a social-realist film by Ken Loach, opened at the drive-in. Off we went, three car loads of us. Of all things, it rained (sprinkled, really) in Broken Hill that evening and, with the wipers going through the session, the battery went flat in the most ancient car. The theatre attendants came over to jump start the engine and made casual conversation about the show. The supporting film was a thriller with Stewart Granger and Susan Hampshire called *The Trygon Factor* and featured international jewel smugglers disguised as nuns in an English country estate. The helper assumed that this was the film we came to see. No, *Poor Cow*. Said he, a bit concerned, 'That was a bit rough, wasn't it?' Exclaimed the high school principal, 'But that's what we came for!'

Word of the screenings in Sydney and Melbourne got about and created a heated correspondence in the Catholic papers, generally condemnatory of the sisters. The Major Superiors of Women's Congregations in Sydney were concerned, especially at the poor image many Catholics had of nuns and their maturity. Their esteem and respect tended to put the nuns on a pedestal and treat them as unreal or ethereal beings. Monsignor John Leonard, a regular columnist in the *Catholic Weekly*, wrote some heavily censorious columns against the films and the sisters. Letter-writers indicated that sisters should not be exposed to this kind of material, unwittingly typing them as immature and incapable of dealing with reality. Meetings were held in Sydney with Dr. Tom Connolly of St. Patrick's College, Manly. I was invited to join a group to prepare a statement about films and the principles behind watching and appreciating the modern material.

These remarks about reviewing are also offered as context for a significant debate in Australia in those years and one which was to change legislation and affect community standards. This was the Censorship debate of 1970-71 leading to the introduction of new censorship classifications for films (which, with one new classification, the MA, in 1991, are still used in Australia).

18. DON CHIPP AND THE CENSORSHIP DEBATE

ONE CANNOT write anything substantial about film in Australia without considering the parliamentary debate on film censorship.

To set the scene for this debate. I have already referred to Fr. Chamberlin's pamphlet and his case for more restrictive legislation. The situation in Australia was that the censorship system was the freest for children. There was nothing to stop them seeing any film publicly screened. To protect the children, films geared towards adult audiences had to be cut. This meant that censorship for adults was very tight. With the number of franker films, not only from continental Europe or from Japan, but also from the United States where film-makers had been clashing with administrators of the Motion Picture Code and a new ratings body had been set up in 1968, the Motion Picture Association of America (MPAA), with the task of classifying films (not a government body), there was an increasing amount of nudity, a growing use of blunt and cruder language and more 'realistic' violence, even brutality. (Memory tells me that the first time I heard the word 'shit' in a film was in Antonioni's *Zabriskie Point* (1968); the word 'fuck' was not allowed in Australia until the new classifications came into use on 1 January 1972 and was a principal reason for the Restricted classification for *Klute*.)

By 1970, the Liberal Minister for Customs and Excise, the minister responsible for censorship in the federal Government, Don Chipp, initiated a parliamentary debate on this topic. He point out that it was the first debate on the issue for over 30 years, since 1938. In his statement to the Parliament on censorship, June 1970, Mr. Chipp indicated some principles in a philosophy of censorship. The basic principle was that of freedom.

Freedom was not to be understood in the lame and untenable,

individualistic sense of 'do what you like and blow everyone else', but freedom as a positive value of human living. Freedom can be seen as that fundamental human capacity of acting for the best: seeing and judging what is the best course of action, finding the appropriate, selfless motivation and acting accordingly, without coercion from outside or compulsion from within. This is the ideal, responsible freedom to be aimed at. Education itself could be said to be a process for developing this capacity for responsible freedom. This freedom is a basic right of every man and woman, a fundamental value. The aim of society should be to guarantee and promote this freedom and, if it is challenged, to defend and protect it.

Mr. Chipp highlighted the concept of censorship as a 'necessary evil'. This leads to the principle of accountability from the censors to the people. A further principle was the criterion of community standards. Mr. Chipp was more concerned here about asking for advice rather than stating anything definitive. And, the amount of censorship should be as little as possible, within the limits set by community standards, he emphasised that parents, have the prime responsibility in censorship; 'the community simply cannot sit back and expect the Government to protect it'.

This summary highlights the importance of individuals and families to exercise appropriate censorship. This is not an alien idea. Whenever we see something that we do not like, we automatically shut our eyes, look away. This is an appropriate self-censorship. This appropriate censorship can be exercised at any time. The focus is on individual and family responsibility. Mr. Chipp also highlighted the reality of a pluralist society and, therefore, the nature of compromise to reach a working solution.

Not everybody agreed on the principle of censorship as a 'necessary evil'. Some commentators stated that it was a 'necessary good'.

The 'necessary good' proponents saw censorship as a value in itself. They seemed to base themselves on an understanding of human nature as intrinsically evil, evil of its very nature and, therefore, prone to go out of control, a prey to evil. Human beings need censorship to be their better selves.

Theological polemics at the time of the 16th century Reformation had the Reformers emphasising corrupt human nature while Catholic teaching argued that we are redeemable. There is a strong pro-censorship stance in some of the strongly traditional reformed churches. However, it is surprising that so many Catholic groups are strongly in favour of censorship as a 'necessary good'. It may be the pessimistic influence of Jansenist spirituality that so highlights our sinfulness and the pain of Jesus Christ's passion and death, that the struggle against temptation and evil is so firmly in focus. But mainstream Catholic tradition and theology would be in favour of censorship as a necessary evil rather than as a necessary good (elaborated at some length in a Pastoral Letter of 1992 by Cardinal Roger Mahoney of Los Angeles.

The contrast in opinions is clear when the inevitable question is raised as to who is to do the censorship and are the censors more virtuous and less corruptible than others. And who gives the right to the censors to have this power over others? If censorship is a necessary good, this question seems unanswerable. UK campaigner, Mrs. Mary Whitehouse, was very conscious of this. In a radio interview on her campaign against videos that exploited violence, especially sexual violence, the so-called 'video nasties', she stated that, although she was against them and knew how bad they were, she had never viewed one and never would. If she saw one and she was not corrupted, she could be challenged on her basic stance.

Censors working for censorship as a necessary evil know that they are not better than others but have been empowered to administer community standards which, of course, are not fixed standards. The censors are accountable to government and to the public. Indication of reasons for censorship decision should be available. The consequence of this is the possibility of appeals against particular judgments and continued discussion until decisions (perhaps compromise) have to be made. This procedure holds in Australia.

The distinction between subject and treatment becomes more important. If censorship is a necessary good, then a list of proscribed themes can be issued (as with the U.S. Motion Picture Code) and the censors need only ask 'what' the film is about. If it is about adultery, violence, then there can be objections. But, again as in traditional Catholic moral theology, intention and circumstances have an influence on the morality of an action so 'how' the subject is treated becomes the all-important question. For Australian society since 1970, 'community standards' (including good and humane taste) has remained the most tangible of the 'how' criteria for censorship of films.

Thus legislation uses three words: obscene, pornographic, indecent. For instance, illustrations appearing in medical text books might be obscene; the same illustrations in a magazine at a newsagent's might well be pornographic, the intention being to titillate a sensual response in the person looking at the illustration. Indecent, however, is somewhat harder to pin down. It seems to be a general word covering both obscene and pornographic. Because there are changes in sensibility and taste, things which are not decent (fitting or becoming) in one age are decent in another. Contemporary swimming gear, decent on the beach, might be indecent on a salesgirl (well, maybe not now) at a supermarket and might have been called indecent on the beach decades ago. Just as with violence, the context gives the tone to what is presented and how it is presented.

If you have persevered in reading these comments on censorship issues, you will have a better idea of how I have responded to films. In retrospect, I am very glad that I experienced this debate in the early years of my work in MSC formation and in reviewing and writing on film. Looking back, I am amazed at the difference between the approaches of the 1940s and those of the late 1960s. And I am glad that I was part of the Church's involvement in this dialogue on censorship. But you might be in the frame of mind to read an anecdote or two about Don Chipp's process, some of the efforts made by himself and his staff in consulting the public and people involved in the film industry and commentators on film.

The most famous incident was the 'Blue Movie' evening at the National Library in Canberra, 13 April 1970. Needless to say, it was a full house with parliamentarians, film personalities, well-known to lesser-known reviewers. In fact, it was at this event that I first actually met Fr. Chamberlin. The program listed the material we were to see, short **excerpts** cut from films coming into the country in the late 1960s. Up till that time I had never seen so many rapes and kicks to the groin in one showing (far fewer, in fact, than those in Tarantino's *Grindhouse* and *Inglourious Basterds*, let alone the *Kill Bill* movies). Of course, the cuts were out of context and could seem better or worse than they were in actual context. Explanations concerning the films, their tone and the length and time of the cuts were given. A sample: *PJ* (a thriller with George Peppard):

> Two separate cuts are shown here. In the first, the star George Peppard fights for survival against a bar of homosexuals. In the first sequence he impales an attacker's hand on the bar with the spike of a belt buckle. In the next he breaks a bottle and uses the jagged neck as a weapon. In the final sequence, a man is dragged along by an electric train and crushed against an underground tube wall.

Looking at the program, I see the titles include Fellini's *Satyricon* (a two-minute cut), Ingmar Bergman's *The Virgin Spring* and *Persona*, Antonioni's *Zabriskie Point* and *Two Women* for which Sophia Loren received her Oscar (25 seconds from a rape sequence). There was also a sex encounter scene between Coral Browne and Susannah York (about three minutes long) from *The Killing of Sister George* – which made me wonder whether John Northey would still have said that *Annals* should review all controversial films. Other films included popular features like

Rough Night in Jericho, *Heaven With A Gun*, *The Adventurers* to soft-core pornography like *Fanny Hill* and *Sinderella and the Golden Bra*. The piece de resistance turned out to be a highly resistible soft-core feature, *The Babysitter*, already cut by the distributors and running for 65 minutes. After a brief synopsis, our program declared:

> The film is presented exactly as imported except that at five points during the film areas of censorship concern have been marked with red-crayoned level-crossing type warning crosses. Of the five marked sequences, three have been categorised as questionable on the grounds of overt sexual indecency. The two others are scenes of violence.

The exercise was an interesting one, especially in trying to match the cut material with the version screening for public audiences. For instance, *Zabriskie Point* was in release at that time. The exercise also got people talking and writing with the result that in 1970-71, there was a great deal of public discussion about the principles of censorship and methods for film classification.

The Department of Customs and Excise got in touch with individuals to discuss the issues. The officer I was invited to meet in Parliament House was a former seminarian who had a Doctorate in Philosophy from Louvain (no small qualification and expertise). He listened attentively and gave me the satisfaction of speaking and being heard. The other thing the Department did was to invite reviewers to sit with members of the Board during a censorship screening, to observe the Board in action and to compare notes. The theatrette was in the basement of the Imperial Arcade in Sydney, a secluded spot. I arrived for my turn and sat in with four members of the Board to watch an English-Danish co-production *One of Those Things* with Judy Geeson. It wasn't much of a film. However, there was an amount of nudity and some drug-taking sequences. The members were busy with pen and paper noting the scenes and checking watches to get accurately the position within the film and how long the sequences under review ran. At the end I thought I should be a bit strict and that the film would receive an 'M' certificate ('For Mature Audiences').

Postscript: The film was given a restricted certificate (18 and over), but when it was released, it went into one of those small sex-cinemas for a short season. And its title was changed for Australian release to *The Wanton*.

By the end of 1971, the new classifications were ready and became law. Skip this next paragraph if it offers too much detail on the new classifications! The most general classification, 'For General Exhibition', stayed as it was. What used to be 'A' (Not Suitable for Children) became 'NRC' (Not Recommended for Children). The meaning of the classification was 'Not Suitable for Children Under 12' but many parents thought that it meant any children – up to 18 years of age. In the mid-'80s, this classification was changed to 'PGR' (Parental Guidance Recommended), an American title already used in Australia for television. The 'SOA' (Suitable Only for Adults) became 'M' (For Mature Audiences – for those 15 and over). The important classification was the 'R – Restricted' certificate, a new classification to be legally imposed. Patrons and theatre management were to be held responsible. The classification restricted screenings of such films to those over 18.

The minimum limit was initially six years of age for most states. But, after some experience, the minimum age was lowered to two. Having sat in a darkened theatre with about half a dozen reviewers to see some exploitive sex and violence in *The Sins of Dorian Gray*, I was conscious of a three- or four-year-old child sitting with us and wondering what impressions were being received – the fact that what was seen and heard were impressions rather than a coherent story has both good and bad aspects.

The night at the National Library showed how themes and treatments had been changing. *Midnight Cowboy*, Oscar-winner for 1969, was cut for release but *Women In Love*, Ken Russell's version of D. H. Lawrence's novel, had frank love scenes and a talked-about fire-lit nude wrestling scene between Oliver Reed and Alan Bates which was not cut. A good film, it meant that I had to do more thinking for reviewing all the films for schools and family readers:

> The film also explores the nature of erotic love, the paradoxes of its completeness and incompleteness, and the place of erotic love and of mutual friendship as the solutions to the meaning of life. Everyone knows that Lawrence is direct and that the film is also direct. The film is an honest groping for answers, although the necessity and taste of the love scenes and the wrestling scene can be argued. It is clearly not a film for adolescents, and its themes are so specialised as not to be of general interest. Apart from satisfying some curiosity, it was probably dull and hard to follow for many who went to see it.

And then came Russell's flamboyant fantasy-portrait of Tchaikovsky, *The Music Lovers,* which shocked many who thought it was in the vein of The *Sound of Music* (just as some thought *Midnight Cowboy* was a western and *Goodbye, Columbus* a period drama about the explorer). At the preview, the Publicity Manager of United Artists went round to each grouping there to assure them that they would enjoy the film. Tchaikovsky was well represented: music, ballet, drama, religion, homosexual community. What were we to see? I enjoyed Ken Russell's flamboyant posturing and over-the-top symbolism. My review was sent back by a reader: 'Many clever devices are used', with 'devices' crossed out and changed to 'devils'. But on a lighter note, there were tears at ordinary screenings of *Love Story* – except that the loud sniffling meant that some self-conscious patrons in the audience got louder giggles.

Theatres were closing down in the city and in the suburbs. It was a bit depressing going to see interesting films in the cavernous emptiness of the old picture palaces like the Sydney State, Regent and Capitol. The

Capitol in Haymarket was a bit different. Interestingly, the long ban on horror films was lifted in the late 1960s and the Capitol became the haven for Hammer Studios' horrors, Dracula and Frankenstein stories with Christopher Lee and Peter Cushing as well as Roger Corman's stories from Edgar Allen Poe with Vincent Price. It was a time of catch-up and developing a fascination for this genre. But they used a particularly strong disinfectant at the Capitol – which will always be associated with horror films. The most vivid memory of words, images and odours was the end of Corman's *Tales of Terror*, an enjoyable Poe anthology. The final Poe quotation referred to the dissolving of the 'living dead' hero (Vincent Price): 'All that was left of Mr. Valdemar was an oozing liquid putrescence'!

One of the liveliest experiences was sitting in the lounge at a Boxing Day matinee of *The Return of Count Yorga* (a vampire). The Capitol was full. I was sitting next to a young man and his girlfriend. I thought they were more absorbed with each other, but when Count Yorga flew down a corridor at us, she screamed and, from then on, she screamed and screamed. And a good matinee was had by all. (Not all the films shown there were horror stories, but it was a bit hard for three of us (out of an audience of five) in a 3000-capacity theatre to laugh at Phyllis Diller in *Did You Hear The One About The Travelling Saleslady?*, trying to hitch a ride on a carriage by raising her long-length skirt, showing a bestockinged ankle – and the horse rearing and bolting!

One last thing at the end of this section, but not film-focused. During 1968-69, I was able to follow up study at the Australian National University with an MA Qualifying work. The specialisation was in Australian history, which required an essay of 15,000 words. I decided to look at origins. After all, Braidwood was not too far from Canberra. The title was 'The Catholic Church on a Goldfields Parish; Braidwood, Araluen, 1852 to 1869'. It was enjoyable but painstaking work, delving into archives in Braidwood, St. Mary's Cathedral, Sydney, as well as libraries, especially the Mitchell and National Libraries. It was often difficult to find material and to put it together. Some theses had been written in the 1960s on significant Catholic Church figures but, up to this point, there was not the interest in history, archive preservation and family trees that was soon to come. The 1970s, thankfully, saw a boom in Australian historical research and writing as well as a move to keep material in archives rather than throw it out. And, of course, this was accompanied by the renaissance in Australian film-making that began in 1972.

Just a word or two about the thesis. Father Edward O'Brien, the first parish priest of Braidwood, was a good records-keeper. They were preserved in the St. Bede's presbytery in Braidwood. But they are missing from his subsequent appointments in Adaminaby and at St. Benedict's Broadway in Sydney. Incidentally, Father O'Brien turned out to be an extraordinary man. Sent out to Sydney from Ireland, he was appointed to be the first parish priest of the Southern Goldfields. He had wanted to go to India but the authorities thought his health could not take it. He was a man of vision, very active in moving around the parish, ecumenically concerned and interested in getting his parishioners to read and to discuss topical issues. At the age of 70, he retired and became a Jesuit! He made his novitiate and worked in the North Sydney parish until his death in 1900. Not your typical Irish clergy.

Reading about the mid-19th century, one is surprised at the vigour of the churches. The Irish piety was strong and Archbishop Polding had dreams of an English Benedictine spirituality centred in Sydney. Not everything was peaceful, of course. The Australian press's response to *The Syllabus of Errors*, a serious document issued by Pope Pius IX in 1865, condemnatory of the intellectual and social movements of the century, is far more vitriolic than press response to, say, *Humanae Vitae*. This research was to become more important as the interest in discovering an Australian theology and a distinctive Australian spirituality began to become significant.

19. *THE FILM*, A CHEVALIER BOOK

TIME to write something about films and the Church, some kind of synthesis of where I stood after all, getting to thirty! And, John Northey had called me an 'ecclesiastical Peeping Tom'. So, during 1969, writing *The Film* (not a highly imaginative title) and the mills of publishing grind slowly so that it did not appear until the middle of 1971. Paul Stenhouse produced it. It was called a Chevalier Book, acknowledging the founder of the Missionaries of the Sacred Heart, Jules Chevalier. This led to the establishing of a publishing organisation, Chevalier Press.

Paul wrote a blurb for the back cover which, I think, summed up well the hoped behind the writing:

> The film is an outstanding modern means of communication. Many of us, underestimating its potential, either ignore it, or regard it as minimal. Nevertheless, the film is here to stay. The artistic and industrial sides of the movie business are developing daily, but what about our understanding?
>
> 'The Film' is an attempt to assist parents, educators, and those interested in the social impact of movies to develop in themselves and the young people whom they educate, reasonable Christian attitudes towards this most important medium.

That was more than 40 years ago. And it still sounds right! In retrospect, I think I have believed in promoting reasonable Christian attitudes. Some of the material from the articles I wrote in Rome for the Irish paper that never was proved a useful way into the book, *Facing up to Films* and *Can entertainment educate us?*

That meant looking at moral presuppositions, first highlighting the approach that considered the principles of duty and obligation. Obligations are clear. Moral imperatives govern behaviour. It is easy to classify and categorise sins. Thus, only the subject matter needs to be considered and judgments about suitability and unsuitability of the film can be made. This approach leads to declaring that censorship is a necessary good. This puts the matter more starkly than might be necessary but a writer to the *Catholic Weekly* wrote a letter at the time protesting the favourable review of *Oliver* because the film presented children stealing.

A longer-held moral stance would be more Christ-centred, use Gospel formulations for moral behavior and take account not only of the behavior but of the intention and circumstances in estimating moral worth. The rediscovery of this moral approach, fostered by the Second Vatican Council, has also meant a healthier dialogue with those who do not share Christian beliefs, fruitful in a pluralist society.

The seemingly off-hand contrast between entertainment and education meant a consideration not of how they differed but of how they complemented each other. Satisfying entertainment (not mere time-passing) and mature education which helps us to be our better selves are two aspects of personal response to what is put before us. There need not be any dichotomy between them.

In trying to find a way to show how film storytelling draws this better response from us, I was able to resort to some ideas of St. Thomas Aquinas, whom we had read for philosophy and theology. Films appeal to our basic human drives: to be, to live; to love; to be in society. There is also the religious drive to transcend ourselves and reach out to the infinite – and St. Thomas says, 'which we call God'.

But, that is easy to say. The 'how' the stories are told raises the problems. Hence a chapter called, rather cleverly I thought in those days, *Privacy in Public*. One of the issues to emerge was that fear was at the core of many reactions: fear of sexuality, fear of violence, fear of the unknown. But, probably, the strongest was the very fear of fear. If anticipation is said to be better than realisation, anticipatory fear can be worse than being immersed in the dangerous situation. We know that we can often rise to the occasion and heroic action can be our response rather than any fear. Not always, but more frequently than not. I still think that fear of fear governs our caution concerning films that receive controversial media attention. We do not have to like horror films, for instance, but we might cope more effectively than we might think. There were also the questions of censorship, community standards, criteria for judging the appropriateness of nudity as well as the key distinction between 'what' is presented and 'how' it is presented, there being no limit to what is presented (as the sinfulness displayed in the scriptures reminds us); the limits, the standards and taste come with the 'how' of the treatment.

One of the key ideas that appealed to me was to see films as parables, using parable in a general sense of a story that has a moral point to make, explicitly or implicitly. Christians are familiar with the parables of Jesus. However, he had the advantage of spiritual insight and teaching that artists and writers do not have. His parables, like that of the Prodigal Son or that of the Good Samaritan, are what we might call 'answer-parables', whereas our films offer 'question-parables'. Perhaps some creative artists presume some divinity in thinking that their creations are answer-parables.

If films are question-parables, it means that the questions can be demanding, surprising, shocking and that the directions in which the search for values goes can lead to byways and dead-ends. If searchers knew exactly where to go, there would be no search, no mistakes, no ugliness. The search is often painful, dirty. And that is what the films show. Christians, Catholics, often wish that books, plays and films would avoid this ugliness and just be 'nice'.

In October 2010, the reviewer for the U.S. Bishops Conference ended a treatment of a light comedy, *Life As We Know It* (classified 'Limited' because of issues, not 'Offensive') in this vein: '... (aspects of the plot) lead to the crossing of several moral boundaries. Add to this scenes illustrating Eric's heedless lifestyle – the subject of some of the script's more questionable one-liners – and the presence, among the central pair's eccentric collection of new-found neighbors, of two homosexual partners whose bond is treated as equivalent to those of their married friends, and 'Life As We Know It' ends up falling far short of life as it should be.

The Film expressed ideas developed during the 1960s. It was over twenty years later that I listened to discussion by international theologians (especially German-speaking theologians) who chose to use the phrase 'De Profundis' ('Out of the Depths') films to describe the films of search, the question-parables. Much more on that when we get to 1993!

The implication of this question-parable approach is that the films often portray a search for values and that this search can be called 'religious'. Which raised the question whether many explicitly religious films are really religious, especially the sex, sand and sandals epics – which Philip Adams referred to, in an ABC radio discussion with me, as the Cecil-b-de-millstone around the neck of the Church! The rest of the book pursued the ways films can search for God: the presentation of positive values and the presentation of values set within the normal, seamy, mixed-up context of daily living. There is satire, the laughter at the world the satirist is dissatisfied with and wants to be more perfect. There is the grim search for God and there is the hopeful, human-resilient search.

We added an appendix to *The Film, Teenagers and Moviegoing*. Best to do some research on what teenagers were actually seeing.

The 'sex content' attracted the Form 4 boys (aged 16 on average). One would have thought from their comments that *Bedazzled* was all about Raquel Welch as one of the Seven Deadly Sins, no prize for guessing which one. She was Lilian Lust, 'the Babe with the Bust'. In fact, her appearance lasted little more than five minutes. But, by and large, the boys and girls were all budding censors. These films were considered suitable for them to see, but definitely not for their younger brothers and sisters. As one fifteen year old said of *Bedazzled* and films like it, '... I don't think anyone younger could get the full meaning out of them. They'd probably go for the sex'.

Yet, they could also refer to the censors as 'narrow little minds'. 'Censors are perverted'. 'Australian censors are prudes'. Where did all this come from? Parents, teachers, the media ...? I presume similar results would emerge from surveys done today.

Fred Chamberlin had acted as the official Church censor of *The Film*. The book was critical of a number of his classifications in *The Advocate*, but he read the manuscript impartially and commented with consideration.

There were several reviews in the secular media. One I liked was from ABC commentator, Suzanne Hayes:

> Another virtue of Father Malone as a moralist is his seeing each film as a whole, his awareness of how some films use material disgusting to him to make a point which is morally agreeable to him ...
>
> He has succeeded in writing an intelligent, perceptive book about the moral impact of films and on what makes them appeal to the public, but the moral attitude which deliberately permeates every page may prevent some readers from gathering the many valuable insights.

Oh dear! And that is what Brian Jeffrey thought in *The Canberra Times*:

> ... in *The Film*, he has chosen to hang what amounts to little more than a long sermon on a few recent films, in an attempt to clarify the points he wishes to make ... the book is a series of homilies ...

Dear, oh dear, oh dear!

Just one more.

Glancing at James Murray's column in *The Australian* one morning, a sentence caught my eye:

> Obviously going to the theatre is not on his list of Lenten denials ...

Who was it? A quick glance – me! Murray editorialised as the end of his sympathetic review,

> But whether it is evidence of a desperate swan-song from the dying church, or of a new dynamic in religious self-criticism, some of the books now appearing are about 'the real thing', and have to be taken seriously.

In fact, this was the case in the United States. More articles, books, film study guides were appearing there and had been brought to Australia. William Kuhns wrote of *Environmental Man*. Ron Holloway and Henry Herx in Chicago were writing, lecturing, organising screenings and discussions. Following their cue, I began in 1969 writing discussion sheets on most of the films I saw. This continues to the present and, despite the thousands done (and now finding a permanent home on a website), I am still thousands behind. Ron Holloway was to go to Europe and promote this film culture until his death in 2009. Henry Herx became the reviewer for the U.S. Bishops Conference until 1999, both men contributing to religious film awareness for decades. At a conference in 1993, John R. May, also a writer on films and religious culture gave a paper where he named and examined the Catholic work and publications from this period and into the 1980s – and I am pleased to be seen in that company.

So, what to do? Write another book.

Films and Values was written in 1970 but did not see publishing light until 1978, time enough to add an appendix on the trends of the 1970s which had become quite marked by then, including war lunacy, the occult, disasters, animal menace, science fiction, vigilante thrillers, terrorism, nostalgia, spoofs, as well as the newly re-established Australian film industry. Were you involved in a trivial pursuit competition, you might have looked at those categories listed and pick some examples, like *M*A*S*H*, *The Exorcist*, *The Poseidon Adventure*, *Jaws*, *Close Encounters*, *Death Wish*, *Black Sunday*, *Picnic at Hanging Rock*, *Blazing Saddles*.

The gist of the new book was the search for values, taking 10 specifically for exploration.

The themes were Environment (*Point Blank*), Communication (*The Heart is a Lonely Hunter*), Loneliness (*Midnight Cowboy*), Marriage (*3 into 2 Wont' Go*), Love (*Goodbye, Columbus*), Freedom (*Easy Rider*), War (*M*A*S*H*), History (*The Damned*), Change (*Z*) and Vision (*2001: A Space Odyssey*). Not a bad collection on the whole, most of them still well-known and respected.

What I would like to do is to include some quotations from the book (not mine, those from reputable authors) which had a strong influence on me. The context was the so-called Death of God. The word to describe the change the world experienced in the 1960s was Alvin Toffler's *Future Shock*. By the middle of the 1960s, *Time Magazine*, always trying to keep its finger on the pulse, was able to print a cover story, 'Is God Dead?' (8 April 1966). (If you watch *Rosemary's Baby* again, you will remember that the devil impregnated her during the 1965 visit of Paul VI to the United Nations in New York – seen on the TV sets during the film. During her pregnancy, in 1966, Rosemary visits the gynecologist and picks up a magazine to read. Polanski has her looking at 'Is God Dead?' Topical for the time, and topical for the film's themes.)

Theologians in the UK and the US, like Bishop John Robinson with *Honest to God* and Paul Tillich on God as the ground of our being, were writing of the demise of the traditional understandings and some suggested a moratorium on the use of the word, God. It is interesting to remember that the Catholic Church at this period began to use the Hebrew title 'Yahweh' in its liturgical readings of Jewish Scripture texts. God-values also received substantial criticism at this time of change and protest.

However, three years later, *Time Magazine* (27 December 1969) saw God's resurrection. The Jesus movement, prayer movements, and charismatic renewal had emerged. 1970 saw theatre productions of *Jesus Christ, Superstar*, followed by *Godspell* (with both being filmed for release in 1973). If God had died – or had been perceived as dying – values still seemed to be flourishing. Values do not die.

Here are the quotations.

> When, therefore, a society has crystallised a conception of God which is false, the professed atheist may be more religious than the theist. (Professor J. MacMurray. The quotations from Professor MacMurray come courtesy of Fr. Bernard Bassett SJ in his book, *The Noonday Devil*.)

Which reminded me of the verses by W. B. Yeats in *The Second Coming*:

> Things fall apart; the centre cannot hold'
>
> Mere anarchy is loosed upon the world.
>
> The blood-dimmed tide is loosed, and everywhere
>
> The ceremony of innocence is drowned;
>
> The best lack all conviction while the worst
>
> Are full of passionate intensity.

This seemed to be true of 1970.

In terms of Christianity, this was expressed by Spanish Jesuit theologian, Juan Alfaro, one of our lecturers at the Gregorian University.

> Christian faith demands that it be put into operation in the circumstances of daily existence; it is one of the radical decisions which is always asking for new concrete decisions. The temptation to rest in a decision once taken is a permanent menace to the faith. Our experience of the faithful bears witness that we can make the faith vain in an existence of superficial, immediate interests and conventional conformism, renouncing the tension of new decision: this is the hidden sin, no less grave for being hidden, of infidelity to our faith. To the extent that the believer refuses to be committed to new decisions of faith, he ceases to be a

believer; to the extent that the faith ceases to influence his concrete choices which make up his existence, it ceases to be faith and becomes belief without faith, faith without faith.

Is this what happens to so many kneeling in the pews who go through motions and whose lives bear little resemblance to what they have professed in church? Even faithful believers still need to assess whether they are becoming 'formalist' in their religion, whether they are becoming pharisaical.

A last quotation which helped me understand better the commands of love of God and love of neighbour:

Professor MacMurray posed a paradox that is unpalatable for the theist and which an atheist might be quite reluctant to subscribe to. In fact, it sounds scandalous. But, St. Francis de Sales, for instance, had a gentle wisdom that took into account the realities of the human situation which are themselves paradoxical. He says that of all the human emotions, love of God comes last. The Pharisee might be surprised to hear this; the atheist would not – and neither would the sincere theist. Theologically, love of God comes first and love of neighbour second; psychologically (and this is how all human beings must live), love of neighbor is stronger, and more immediate, than love of God. Psychologically, we search for and find God in our neighbour and in our world. The Pharisee tends to forget this and exalts the love of God which he finds in his own feelings; the atheist, searching for (and not finding) values in this world, is as likely to find God.

Maybe best to finish this section with a word about family. Come to think of it, the Malones were an ordinary family. On my mother's side, the Rogers, we were not so close except for my mother's next sister, Olive, who lived at Kensington not far from the Monastery. She was a very kind, very simple, even naïve, woman whose marriage had been dissolved by the courts but – and I think most unjustly – she was unable to receive an annulment. She was very kind to Philip and myself, outings, gifts and great joy in just being with her. Her older brother and her youngest sister had children but lost contact. Speaking of Olive, Aunty Ol, I should add that eventually she married in her sixties and looked after her husband who tended to treat her like a servant and forbade her to go out. We could call in to see her but she could not even attend Philip's Silver Jubilee of Priesthood in 1991 even though it was being held close by at the Benedictine Abbey at Jamberoo. The saddest part of all is that it was only months later that one of Olive's friends let us know that she had died.

In the meantime, for the Malone's it was visits to Nana and Aunty Sheila in Sydney, to Dad in Melbourne, his annual pilgrimage north to see us all (travelling at 40 mph and sometimes less!).

The most significant event for us in these years was a death. Nana, certainly a diminutive but very strong matriarch died, on 21 May 1971 at the age of 88. A woman of generosity and convictions, she was deeply religious, a member of the Third Order of St. Francis (as was Aunty Sheila), a patient listener, especially on the phone, to a lot of relatives with their problems.

When she became ill in early May, the close family gathered. Her oldest son, Phil, was a Franciscan, Fr. Maurice. Dad came from Melbourne. Her other son, (the actual) Maurice, lived in Sydney – we had seven cousins there. Of the three daughters, one, Lucy, Sister Marie Therese, was a Benedictine at Pennant Hills. Mary, Sister Mary Philip (too many Philips and Maurices!) was a Presentation sister. By a pleasing coincidence, Cardinal Gilroy of Sydney had lifted the enclosure rule for the Benedictines and Carmelites at the time of the visit of Paul VI to Sydney. This meant that Aunty Lucy could come to stay at the family home she had never seen and go to the papal events with her mother and sisters. She did.

As with so many old people, once the family gathered, Nana rallied. Two weeks after we left, she quietly died in her bed at home, Mary and Sheila with her, a peaceful death. For the funeral Mass, St. Joseph's, Edgecliff, was full. Surprising for a moment only, that a small elderly woman, who scarcely travelled beyond Sydney, should have touched so many lives.

20. CHANGES, MORE THAN ANTICIPATED

BY YOUR thirties, you are expected to have settled down, studies and training over, life commitments made, job security ensured. At least, that is how it seemed to be in the 1970s. One's thirties ought to be a consolidating decade rather than branching out or reaching out for something different. For someone in a religious order and ordained as a priest, this might have been expected as well. Seminary studies complete, other studies as well. Commitment made for life. Appointments in ministry decided, though they could change suddenly and unexpectedly and simply be announced and obedience would take care of the rest.

At the end of 1971, when all seemed to be in place, at least for the time being, I received one of those sudden and unexpected announcements. It seemed that I had become part of the old brigade and had to move. It was all rather complicated in MSC formation in those days. First of all, our superior in Canberra, Joe Chown, decided that he should leave the priesthood. However, he was conscious of the criticisms of the province about Canberra monastery – not enough discipline, with the university a bit too worldly, not enough time and training for prayer – so he decided that a clean-out was in order. Frank Fletcher was to come to Canberra and get things right. Denis Feeney, not long ordained but director of the pre-novitiate students, should come to Canberra from Melbourne. And all would be well. I had better add hastily that it wasn't and that within two years we would close the seminary in Canberra and move everyone to Croydon.

But the announcement was that I should go to Melbourne to give the incoming staff a chance to start a fresh approach. A bit alarming at the age of 32 to find that you had done your dash.

But, providence again, provided a new beginning and, as I write this, except for a year in Sydney in 1998, Melbourne has been my address ever since. Even while overseas, Melbourne was my address for the British government (always entering on the six monthly visa stamp) and for the Australian government (who allowed me to travel, even permitting support after my reaching pension age). It is strange that when Dad was turning 39 he changed his life and moved to Melbourne – and lived longer there than he did in Sydney. Here was I now coming to Melbourne – for now more than four decades. And, Philip was transferred to Melbourne in 1999 and is keeping up what now seems a family tradition.

I should say at the outset that my thirties provided quite a range of challenges and branching out. This was on a personal level, an MSC formation level, an academic level – and more opportunity to interact with cinema in Melbourne than if I had stayed in Canberra.

1972 was probably the strangest year I have experienced (and my students reminded me as my birthday came round that 33 was the perfect age to be crucified!). Well, perhaps, 1972 wasn't quite as hard as that.

We began with the first of the formation conferences that were to become an annual event, a meeting of all those involved in MSC formation work from Vocation Recruiter to Novice Master and various directors. The meeting in Sydney at Kensington was for six days, very demanding, hard going. But it was the personal interaction and soul-searching that took their toll. While there were workshop themes, the model for our interactions was the T-group, Sensitivity groups popular at the time. Hard going for those not used to this kind of self-examination and disclosure. Lots of anxiety and often some tears. We needed an outside facilitator to help us to come to grips with our personal stances, our hidden agenda and interpersonal tensions. At least we were prepared to put ourselves through these processes, no matter how harrowing some of the moments were and how uncertain we felt. The input sessions were a relief!

Five men who participated in this conference were later to leave the MSCs. American commentators had noted in those years the pressures on men and women working in formation and how a substantial percentage of them left their congregations. But, if we were going to ask our students to go through psychological testing and counselling, we had to do this ourselves. I remember listening to a confrere assuring all of us that something we were criticising in him was not true at all. But, it clearly was. A resolution – that if a group criticised anything in me like this, I had to believe them, even if I didn't think it was true!

At least this tough week led to our following many of the workshops in our formation work. We resolved to meet regularly, all of the formation personnel (Vocations recruiter, pre-novitiate director, Novice Master, director of the professed students, director of the 'late vocations') to review the progress of the students. One of the facilitators at the week was a Melbourne psychologist, Margaret McHardy. Later in the year, she introduced us to Transactional Analysis, a system for analysing and assessing the way we interact with each other. We realised that much of formation in the past consisted of a process which could be characterised as Critical Parent – Adapted Child, rather than Adult-Adult interactions.

One of the members of our TA group became a close friend, Mary Scarfe. Mary has been a marriage counselor for many years. She was one of the first female lecturers to be employed by the Yarra Theological Union, something rather extraordinary in the 1970s but, thankfully, something we now take for granted. Mary has been a wonderful friend and support all these years. She was a great resource for the students at Croydon, listening, probing, enabling them to discover some of the problems that worried them. She was always gently firm – one of the students (now a Queensland High Court Justice) came home after a session with 'Madame Lash'! In her retirement, she now lives just up the street and round the corner from us.

This is what was happening in the 1970s. Psychology was opening up and practitioners were applying so much of the theory to formation practice. Quite exhilarating, stimulating as well as challenging. In retrospect, I know that I learnt a lot in these years, especially when Frank

Fletcher, who had been called in to change Canberra in 1972, moved with all the students to Croydon in 1974. Frank was one of those 'prophetic' types who could see how things could change and the directions in which they were going. Not everyone could see these perspectives from Frank's point of view and were wary or sceptical – compounded by the fact that Frank was not born practical and was not expert at boiling water or other pragmatic basics. I found that Frank was a man of great insights who introduced us to the writings and approaches of C. G. Jung.

We had also introduced psychological testing for our students. The tests seem quite basic now, but at least it was part of the approach for students to understand themselves and for directors to find ways of developing character along with spiritual formation. The Minnesota Multiphasic Personality Inventory MMPI was one of the tools used by American Marianist, Dan Winters, who conducted our testing for a number of years. He warned us that one of the students would never suffer a heart attack or develop an ulcer – but he couldn't guarantee that this man would not cause heart attacks in others or give them ulcers. Dan Winters wasn't wrong!

This focus on human development and the interest in practical psychology was also valuable for thinking about film. I remember the book about Freud and film by Harvey Greenberg, *The Movies on My Mind*. From the 1980s on, as we shall see, we drew on the insights of Jung and his psychological types for film reflections.

In writing this, I am hoping that you will see how the seminary approach was changing from the older styles to a style that respected the student as a person with a goal of individual and spiritual maturity. We are reminded now that we emphasised the individual (as did Western society in the 1960s to the 1980s – and beyond) rather than society, community and the common good. But, it was a necessary pendulum swing from the approach where the individual was swallowed by society.

Religious congregations were coming to grips with a rapidly changing world, societies with new needs and demands as well as life altering within the congregations themselves with planned and unplanned decisions. They were re-writing their Constitutions which, in the early decades of the 20th century, had been streamlined to fit the new Code of Canon Law, sometimes drained of the inspiring words and ideas of the founders. Provincial and General Chapters were held to urge re-discovery of the 'charism' of the founders. For the Missionaries of the Sacred Heart, the quest was to find again the inspiration of Jules Chevalier in the France of the 1850s compelling him to establish his congregation. Did 20th century situations resemble those of 19th century de-Christianised France and to the world at large, especially in countries far from Europe where Christianity had not been preached? Could the language of Vatican II express for modern listeners the same kind of spirit? And the traditional focus on the person of Jesus Christ, especially through the sentiments of his heart, 'devotion to the Sacred Heart', was it still relevant as a motivating force? Was there a contemporary spirituality that made sense to Christians and would be credible to non-Christians as well?

Given the tightness of structures and administration in the Church and the crises during the 19th and 20th centuries when a modernising movement arose, it was to be expected that not everyone would welcome change, especially when it did not seem like change but more like the wiping out of the past and of venerable traditions. There is always the temptation of 'what was good enough in the past ...'. But, this was practice, prayer and observances that were not just good enough in the past. They also had an important sanction from central Roman authority and were recognised by Catholics everywhere.

But, timetables in religious congregations were re-structured in the late 1960s and early 1970s, an acknowledgement that electric light had shifted working hours back into the night and the traditional times of rest (dusk to dawn) could never be maintained, except in an enclosed cloister, and that what was called the 'Greater Silence' from the end of night prayer to the end of the morning prayer was not practicable. Monastic hours could not be kept by active religious. It was acknowledged that the variety of works in different communities was a more realistic guide to timetabling than generalised regulations. Needless to say, timetable changes first occurred through individual necessities and decisions rather than through corporate assessment. (It would have made a great difference in 1966 when we had to leave *The Avengers* and Patrick Macnee and, of course and especially, Diana Rigg, which began at 8.00, to go to night prayer at 8.30!)

It was a time of looking at the vows of poverty, chastity and obedience and exploring their relevant meaning as well as their depth of commitment to God and to the congregation.

Lively discussions ensued, articles in popular periodicals like the *American Review for Religious*, *Sisters Today* and *The Australian*, *Sursum Corda* abounded. Many congregations began their own magazines for these issues. We had *Encounter*, started by Frank Fletcher in 1964, an in-house magazine for the discussion of pastoral, educational and spiritual problems (later changed to 'spiritual initiatives') which many of us contributed to. And it still continues.

There was a focus on chastity: a commitment to celibate life after the pattern of Jesus and offering an availability of the total person for mission and service. I remember (embarrassing moment again) that in the late 1950s, we filled in personality test forms for Jim Cuskelly. For the alternative, 'emotional or unemotional', I raced to answer, 'unemotional'. There was something strange, uncontrolled, weak about 'emotional' — I definitely did not want to be like that. We had an image of severe Catholic stoicism. And, there was that tradition of *numquam duo* (never just two together) and warnings against the dangers of 'particular friendships', which many of us did not understand in those sheltered years. The rediscovery of affectivity, brought home vividly and clearly to us by talks from Walter Black which were healthy and liberating, meant less rigid personalities and a warmth of love and friendship and a maturing of the celibate commitment. He spoke of 'general sexuality' which acknowledged gender and sexual realities for all, celibate or not.

This focus on affectivity meant that many priests and religious began to realise that they had not appreciated their affective needs and drives and repressed them more than they had consecrated them. Many went through soul-searching and decided to leave their congregations and marry. Statistically, in the Australian Missionaries of the Sacred Heart, over 100 priests left from 1968 on, perhaps as many brothers and certainly more students than that who opted not to continue to vows or to ordination.

There were many who were angered by the pace of change, the impersonality of so much Church interaction, the long, legal processes (and seemingly intrusive questions and invasions of privacy) for dispensations from orders or vows, that they left without them. It was difficult for them, painful for those who remained in the congregations and often felt cut off after years of friendship and shared work, puzzling and dismaying for people who could not understand the decisions or the climate that led to the decisions.

Others wrestled with the now surfaced issues of sexual orientation. In 1998, after one of our confreres indulged in some pernicious letter-writing and judgmental opinions which were not justified, the Provincial Chapter of that year debated these issues and expressed a policy on equality and acceptance of all members of the congregations, no matter what their sexual orientation, who were committed in celibacy to the congregation.

With poverty, it was different. Poverty, again following the pattern of the Gospel, is a commitment to service, of availability of time and resources, rather than a pursuit of wealth, career and reputation. On the one hand, there was some eagerness to be rid of congregation assets or, at least, the large institutional buildings which had stern memories in their stones. And much of this did happen. This was something like Morris West's dream at the end of *The Shoes of the Fisherman* where Pope Kiril wants to sell off the Vatican treasures to pay for wheat for the starving Chinese. (But, should such valuables simply finish up at the Texas ranch of some wealthy American philanthropist?) On the other hand, with the increasing professionalism required of the traditional works of education and nursing, for instance, the rises in the standards of living in the Western world and the aspirations of emerging nations, congregations and individuals were expected to have more and more things. This is a creative tension for a group and a challenge to individuals who have to gauge how much and how little they need for the ministry that they are called to. Opinions still range from the desire for professional excellence to what some satirically referred to as 'a romantic preoccupation with dirt'!

Official Church documents and the re-written Constitutions of many religious congregations take up the phrase that had its origins in Latin America and the experience of large-scale social injustice and 'structural sinfulness', 'a preferential option for the poor' (dramatised in a film like *Romero*, the last years and the death of Oscar Romero in 1980 for his stances on these issues against the oppressive powers that were in El Salvador). This was a challenge for congregations and individuals to review their priorities and lifestyles and meant an enormous shift in activities, a lessening of involvement in big institutions and, where there is still this kind of institution, a shared ministry and administration with the laity – from schools, to hospitals, to parishes, to youth work (though in many places there is still a firm, even hard, clerical hold).

The image of obedience was not unlike that of Audrey Hepburn as Sister Luke in *The Nun's Story*, a kind of blind obedience that did what was said in the name of God, the assumption that the word of a religious superior was the will of God. Renewal meant and awareness of obedience as an 'adult' activity and style, again like that of Jesus himself, rather that the response of a bossed-about child. It appears now that much of what was commanded in the name of obedience was the personal whim of an individual who had a position of authority. (Still with a film example, one that is really worth seeing on this issue is *The Father George Clements Story*, the African American priest who defied Cardinal Cody of

Chicago in adopting children, later commended by John Paul II; Louis Gossett is Father Clements and a lively Carroll O'Connor as the Cardinal and listening to many of his lines which illustrate this whim kind of command).

Now qualities and processes of discernment are required. Words and phrases like co-responsibility, principle of subsidiarity, accountability, appear in the descriptions of obedience (not a guarantee, of course, that everybody understand this or puts it all into practice). As members of religious orders undertook more personal development, more professional expertise, adult education and 'ongoing formation' became key elements of religious life.

The prayer movements, from Charismatic Renewal to Centering Prayer, were of great benefit. Not everybody prays best in the same way, at the same time and in the same place. Freedom to pray as one found best had meant more prayer than less.

Community living has benefited by the humanising changes and religious congregations have learnt a great deal from the shift to small groups in particular areas, bonded together in prayer, work and mutual support. This was seen in the movement of 'Basic Christian Communities' in Latin America, Africa and the Philippines. Although this was never the theory, unity, in practice, had often meant a group of individuals living in the same house, held together by conformities. The new atmosphere of give and take, the human bonds, the shared spirituality had helped to renew the older style communities.

So, this is the kind of reflection we were involved in in the 1970s. Of course, there was the continual tension of degrees of change, maintenance of works already undertaken, prophetic vision and new directions. There were also the personalities, agreements and clashes, inevitable in any group.

An anecdote might make the point.

During 1972-73, we had what was called a 'Board of Inquiry', though someone in a moment of exasperation wondered whether we were really 'bored of inquiry'. I was nominated a secretary, a very interesting experience: how were our finances? Should we close a school – yes, but not the one I work in. Our Formation program? By the end of a long week in 1972, we had almost grown into the chairs we were sitting on. The next session, mercifully, was only for a weekend in 1973. We were involved in discussions on prayer and work, rules and MSC spirit. Some of the Board, interested in new ways of praying and more personalised prayer, wanted the Board to give time to some actual praying for discernment. Another group, many older, several of whom had denounced the trendy young religious who didn't say any set prayers, wanted the Board to get on with discussion, time was limited, and, besides, we had said a short prayer at the beginning of the session and that was enough. It seems trivial in retrospect, but that morning it highlighted the dichotomy between those who saw everything in black and white terms (with past practice good and present practice wanting) and those who sensed new and fruitful directions. The vote went against praying – but some interacting over morning tea enabled us to go back and practice what we preached. We took time to pray together.

The Provincial Chapter of 1974 was preceded by a process of getting in touch with the charism of Jules Chevalier by taking time to remember and talk about what it was like to be a Missionary of the Sacred Heart, what was central to that experience and where we had received that tradition, the experiences of the pioneer priests and brothers in Australia. A document, produced at the end of the process, listed what each one saw as key to what was coming to be called a 'Spirituality of the Heart': a perception of Jesus Christ as a personable man of tenderness and warmth, compassionate and self-sacrificing who was worth following.

All of this, besides being significant for me as a person in a religious congregation, was background to my work in Croydon for 12 years.

The changes in our formation system reflected what was happening in Australian society and in the renewing religious congregations.

In the late 1960s, we were trying to move ahead, trying to make our programs suitable for the times. On the other hand, we were still holding on to many of the practices of the past which would, in fact, soon go. The structure of formation and training in a hierarchical manner was still the accepted way: a faculty with its own ethos and status, a student group with its particular status, quite differentiated from the faculty with separate common rooms, 'top' dining table and the use of titles. The brothers' situation reflected the past. They did the serving and their table was near the scullery, the 'bottom' table.

By 1970, this did not seem an appropriate way for training. With the shared enterprise of re-writing Constitutions and talk about equality of members, something had to happen. There was a greater familiarity and less formality between staff and students, sharing of common rooms, for instance, for television, the use of Christian names and a more friendly and relaxed atmosphere in the seminary. The acceptance of candidates for training prior to a novitiate meant that they were not committed to vows or the full life style of the vowed members of the community. They needed a less pressurised, more personalised regime. We increased the length of this pre-novitiate period to two years and then to three, with the third year an experience of living and working in one of the ministry communities.

By 1972, the phrase 'formation by association' was more frequently used. It was a statement of principle that helped shape what we would do at Croydon during the 1970s.

Not everybody agreed with the principle. Not everybody was with the way that it was applied. Some staff members fought it strongly, meeting after meeting. To a plea that we be allowed to experiment, even to make a mistake, one man said no. As I found out later with something that I could not agree with, it is easier to say no to a situation, even to the experiment of making a mistake. But, if I remember the parable of the Prodigal Son, for instance, the point is made that God permits us to make mistakes and, no matter how bad the experiment, all is not lost.

The repercussion of this principle included a re-organisation of the house and the staff accepting the fact that they would lose some of their past privacy and that they would have to live and work closely with those in the formation program.

When I arrived at Croydon, there was a group of thirteen beginning their training to be priests or brothers. This meant regular interviews and direction sessions, some counselling. It meant group conferences, study supervision. It meant gradual introduction to the MSC way of life and spirituality. We had our moments, our crises, our goodbyes. But that is ordinary enough.

I began to learn far more about how Australian young men ticked in 1972 than I had in the previous four years. I learnt the possibilities of trust and friendship, the need for sensitive observation of how they were rather than how they ought to be. I realised more and more that the sheltered family life of the past was a thing of the past and that family hurts lodged deeply and were not easy to speak about. Angers, envies, laziness, fears. And, so many of these candidates were boys, just out of school (where they were sometimes forbidden to read the *Annals* film reviews!). They were at teenage stages of growth, of Erickson's crises of identity and of conflicts between isolation and intimacy. How could needs be met in a seminary life? There were the ordinary problems of sexual growth, compounded by the confusions of the emergence of awareness of homosexuality leading to homophobia. There were also the problems of the 'excellent' Catholic family and the high level of expectations imposed wittingly or unwittingly on the good son who thought that he was being called to priesthood.

I suppose we had some training for this kind of work but so much had to be learnt as we went. Praise to experience! But it also meant that we had to collaborate as formation team and try to avoid too many mistakes. If I had this time over again, I would certainly not accept candidates into a seminary training program before they were 20 (at least) and only if they had a variety of experiences and were psychologically mature. But that is what all the documents said then. There was also the pressure, 'what about 'giving him a go?'.

An important change in formation concerned the training of students for the priesthood and of students who would not be ordained but rather be brothers. 19th century traditions tended to make a class distinction between priests and brothers in religious orders, the brothers being second-class citizens, often doing, menial work, in comparison with the priests. Much of the formation was separate. In the late 1960s, we experimented with a training school for brothers at Douglas Park and then opted for formation together. Many a meeting was held on these issues with much concern expressed by some older brothers. Before the 1974 Provincial Chapter, I had to go out to Tullamarine Airport to meet a brother on the Council to talk over preparation of documents as he flew down from Sydney and then flew back. He remembers our working lunch at the airport as our James Bond day. Since those years, there has been a stronger emphasis on the equality of priests and brothers as members of the congregation.

The Novitiate group was also at Croydon in 1972, nineteen of them, young and older, some with one year of training, others with two, but all from that period of confusion. Most did not stay the year, most others left afterwards. Some had breakdowns; others, try as they might, could not fit into the lifestyle. The year was punctuated with Novitiate crises. There was, as well, a smaller group of men who had made their vows some years before and were moving towards ordination, towards a priesthood that seemed less certain than when they started and in an atmosphere of conflict about formation by association that tended to put them down as MSCs. There were similar problems at Canberra which led to a student conference at the end of the year, a torrid but ultimately fruitful meeting that enabled the students to air their longings, grievances, but to do something constructive. Elected student representatives came to all future formation conferences. The year was a learning experience for which one is grateful but which one would not like to repeat.

1973 was just as complex but a bit easier. Harvey Edmiston, who had had the unenviable job of getting the Pre-Novitiate system going and after two years was appointed Novice Master, was sent to the United States for studies in mid 1973. I was asked to take on the Novice Master's job for six months along with working with the Pre-Novitiate group. Fortunately, most of the key events of the Novitiate had taken place before Harvey left.

However, in Canberra, the arrangements at the Australian National University whereby all our students attended History I and Philosophy I would come to an end. Meetings. And more meetings. The decision was made to close the Canberra monastery after 14 years of life and everyone moved to Croydon.

In terms of our Pre-Novitiate program, the first year was at Croydon, followed by second year at Canberra. Not only was I to inherit a combined First and Second Year group in 1974, but also the Third Year. With Harvey Edmiston still in .America, there was no Novitiate. It was a big group, but I knew them all and it was a consolidating experience, working with those I had directed in 1972 and seeing how they had. changed and grown. We decided that the third year of Pre-Novitiate was a good idea and brought in something new: an Experience Year, a year of working in an MSC apostolate, before the Novitiate Year. The Novitiate year would have more meaning since the novice would have a better awareness of community living and the work, its demands and his ability to cope. The group also scattered round Australia, a chance to be away from each other for a year. We used to meet together at Douglas Park after the first term (they went at first mainly to schools, later to parishes) and then I visited them at work later in the year. There were some weeks of assessment and reunion each December. I thought it an excellent idea. Not everybody did and the working communities' did not always know how to handle the student. But that is part of life. This program lasted until 1983, so 1975 onwards saw, at last, a Pre-Novitiate program that seemed to meet the needs of the individual's training and was approved of (at least officially) by the Province.

Probably the most interesting experience year was had by a group of three in 1976. They had all joined at 17, straight from school. The idea was that they should have a work experience and fend and manage for themselves. They did and did well. The house they found was in Riley Street, Surry Hills, which often got mentions in newspaper write-ups of corruption and police scandals in New South Wales. It was an attempt to help individuals grow. Again, there was not unanimous approval, but I remember a lot of MSCs would call in there for a meal and for support.

I remember these years happily despite the uncertainties, the hard work and the inevitable misunderstandings, criticisms and lack of support from so many of the Province. Maybe it was just what I needed: a great number of warm friendships, trust, the shared reward of personal breakthroughs, the opportunity to be a father and father-figure. I am grateful to my own father for providing a genial model. Harvey Edmiston and Frank Fletcher showed how MSC formation could work and were the greatest support although, I am glad to say, we did not agree on everything. But I learnt a great deal from the wisdom of each, Harvey for his dedication and Frank for his vision and (although it alarmed the students he directed at times) his tenacity for what his vision told him was right. It almost always was.

21. AN ACADEMIC WORLD

THERE was another changing area in the Catholic Church as well as in other churches in the 1970s, that of theological education. I was fortunate enough to be fully involved in the re-shaping of courses and the development of curricula, an experience that kept us in touch with movements within the Church and, with the ecumenical structure of the Melbourne College of Divinity, with all the churches. This alone was a reason to be in Melbourne in the 1970s.

Without going too far back in history, it can be noted that seminaries, institutions for the training of students for the priesthood, were a product of 16th century thinking. The experience of the Black Death in Europe in the 14th century and the consequent hasty ordination of men without education or personal training to be administrators of the sacraments for the sick and dying led to an ignorant clergy, often a scandalous clergy. Martin Luther, for one, reacted vigorously against clerical abuses. They were one of the cogent reasons for a reformation. To counter this ignorance and scandal, the Council of Trent (1545-1563) decreed that seminaries should be established, text books written and printed (thanks to Guttenberg and the printing presses), and a program of at least two years' philosophy and four years' theology be undertaken and strictly examined before ordination. The Roman-centred Church wanted better standards of education for priests and, later, uniformity in theological language and understanding. The newly established Jesuits undertook the running of many seminaries.

In Australia, the practice during the 19th century was to import clergy from Ireland or England. The Australian-born were not considered suitable enough to be promoted to orders – some ecclesiastical colonialism. At the end of the century, Cardinal Moran of Sydney reversed this procedure and built that imposing seminary for local candidates, St. Patrick's College, Manly, later a venue for teaching cuisine (and, perhaps best-known for its chapel where Nicole Kidman married Keith Urban!). The capital cities established their own seminaries in the following decades, as did the religious orders. The staffs were qualified, frequently doing their further studies at Roman universities, text-books were continually being written, the courses clear and the treatment orthodox. The first Australian-born Missionary of the Sacred Heart, Archibald Shaw, was ordained in 1899, ahead of the lifting of the embargo on locals for diocesan priesthood.

Seminaries were closed shops, self-sufficient. Each seminary, each order had its experts, its Faculty. There was little exchange of lecturers. Seminarians of religious congregations met each other rarely – and then it was often curiosity value, riding by bike to Box Hill to see what the Franciscan students were like.

During the 1950s, there was encouragement from Rome for seminaries to look again at their curricula and move towards some creative developments. After all, the new information on biblical literature, languages and archaeological sites meant an overhaul of scripture courses. Pope Pius XII issued a document in 1956 that asked seminaries to use developments in education to assist in planning and re-writing courses.

We prided ourselves on our self-sufficiency. At a meeting in Canberra in 1969 to discuss the theological resources in the city, a Dominican pointed out that they had all their resources within their four walls. But, by 1969, most congregations did not, in fact, have all their resources within their four walls. For one thing, the Second Vatican Council had asked for higher standards of theological education and had initiated so many developments in thinking and action, such a range of official documents, new presentations of Church law and a host of subjects relevant to the modern world that needed to be studied that no seminary could maintain a complete and adequate staff.

When the Jesuits left their Sydney seminary at Pymble in 1968 and moved to some terraced houses in Melbourne, in Parkville, near

Melbourne University and near the colleges which comprised the Melbourne College of Divinity and joined them, Cardinal Knox took an initiative for the diocesan seminary to become part of the college and the religious order seminaries to join as well. The orders had been feeling the need to share resources and by the end of the 1960s, the different experts in particular areas were going from order to order giving their lectures, the Passionists in Templestowe, Franciscans in Box Hill, Carmelites in Donvale, Missionaries of the Sacred Heart in Croydon. This brought some freshness into courses in these years. Since the houses were in the eastern suburbs of Melbourne, they joined what was known as the Upper Yarra Consortium.

The Melbourne College of Divinity is an interesting institution in itself. It was constituted by an Act of the Victorian Parliament in 1910 and represented the Anglican, Baptist, Presbyterian, Methodist and Congregationalist Churches and by co-option, the Churches of Christ. There were quite some developments in the 1970s. The Jesuits had joined with the Anglicans and the other churches to form the UFT (United Faculty of Theology). Later, Methodists, Presbyterians, Congregationalists (with the exception of the 'Continuing Presbyterians') formed the Uniting Church in Australia and become a significant church presence in the country.

Amendments to the Act in 1972 enabled the inclusion of representatives of Catholics and the Churches of Christ in the College. Also, in 1972, amendments to the Act enabled the College to introduce a degree over and above the Bachelor of Divinity they had been offering. The new degree was a primary degree in Theology, the B. Theol. (Bachelor of Theology). It was a degree to be taught by 'associated teaching institutions'. The degree was introduced in 1974, a significant move in ecumenical co-operation in the teaching of theology with a qualification recognised by other universities. And, over the decades it has led to further degrees and diplomas as well as a range of Masters and Doctoral programs.

However, the question of the early 1970s was the kind of affiliation Catholics should have with the College and how the associated teaching institutions should be constituted. The first question was whether the religious orders would accept Cardinal Knox's invitation to join with the seminary. At first, yes. Then, as religious orders are sometimes wont to do, no. They would form their own teaching institute. While some of the orders whose houses of studies were close to the diocesan seminary did, in fact, become part of what is still Catholic Theological College (CTC), those in the Upper Yarra Consortium decided that it sounded better to be called the Yarra Theological Union (YTU). In fact, with the Redemptorist students and staff leaving Ballarat for Melbourne at the beginning of 1972, the Consortium was getting larger but was still an arrangement which one might call a clerical 'gentlemen's agreement'.

You might like to skip this but it does reflect reality and how exasperated some in the College, let alone mystified outsiders, responded to the acronyms: the MCD made up of UFT, CTC, YTU, with the latter incorporating OFM, MSC, CP, OCarm, CSsR. The SJs were in UFT while the OMI and SDB were in CTC. Those latter initials are for the different religious congregations (which could be Googled for further enlightenment or bafflement). But, back to the real task. What were we actually doing?

One of the interesting initiatives of the Consortium was to have the courses for the first year students of Franciscans, Passionists and Missionaries of the Sacred Heart (before their novitiate) together. Since I was coming from Canberra to be pre-novitiate director of students, this meant that I was involved at once, discussing if and how it would work. One cautionary thought was that the students would lose their order's identity. Let me tell you from experience that this was never the case, despite three students in the early years moving to other congregations. Rather, identity was reinforced, often in a jingoistic, better-than-thou, attitude! – which needed tempering. This first year course was to include an introduction to theology, to the Old Testament, to the New

Testament, Communications, and we travelled from campus to campus (comparing the relative merits of what was for morning tea, (to our embarrassment, we provided leftover cold toast at Croydon). Students working together (rather than simply meeting for football matches or to hear an overseas lecturer, as had developed during the 1960s) was now something substantial.

And this quickly developed. At the end of June, 1972, classes were called off for three days and students, lecturers, formation personnel and some congregation leaders met to discuss the future of seminary collaboration. Discussions were heady. Butcher paper points and diagrams were imaginative. What followed is one of those minor miracles: we made the big step, to forego our independence and establish a theological union, to be one of the associate institutes.

We decided that St. Pachal's Box Hill, the Franciscan campus would be the centre of the Union. It had the advantage of being closer to the city although accessible to eastern, north-eastern and southern suburbs. The name of the institute was far harder to come by, something telling but also something modest. Despite difficulties that many interstaters expressed, especially those from Sydney who thought that the Yarra River was so brown it must be flowing upside down, Yarra Theological Union was agreed on – and became a significant name for what is still a significant associate institute. A first president of the YTU easily emerged, Humphrey O'Leary, a Redemptorist, and a surprising blend of Canon Lawyer and charismatic enthusiast. He led us effectively through the process in June 1972 and, with infinite zest and patience, led us through meeting after meeting, exercising a skill in diplomacy and attention to painstaking detail. (Yes, I certainly did vote for him!)

Then began some years of hard and constant work but fascinating, not necessarily for the reader and so will be described more briefly than not. As staff, we were required to go to departmental meetings, faculty meetings, business meetings to look at traditional courses and see how they might be presented in the context of a theological degree. We also tried team-teaching, we experimented in lectures, seminars, tutorials, workshops and ventured away from blackboards to overhead projectors, to pre-power point audio visuals (slides, music and so on) and film.

Ministry was a buzz word at the time. Part of the exhilaration was moving away from the drily abstract treatment of so many theological and moral issues. If only we had known those 1936 words of Pope Pius XI about story and film being more effective in teaching than abstract reasoning!

We did not want to be too academic in an ivory tower sense (though many of our lecturers did stay more comfortably there). We wanted to meet pastoral needs and for relevance to guide our contents and treatment. Different types of assessment were tried, written and oral.

The bonds between the staff from the different congregations were important with so much time and energy spent in those meetings and discussions. In the late 1960s, besides the interchange of lecturers, we met at annual Theology Conferences, a chance to compare notes, hear speakers, debate. Now we met often and developed friendships and collaboration between the orders.

It was the same in teaching students from the different orders which has led to friendships and collaboration in ministry ever since. The concerns of the formation personnel were also considered and so regular meetings were set up for what Tony Kelly, from the academics' point of view, used to refer to as the 'Formation Lobby', who were a support group, learning from the ways of doing things which meant dropping some of our own ways and adopting others.

This is a moment to acknowledge the enormous contribution of Tony to YTU, president for many years, lecturer and author (and more lately on the Papal Theological Committee). Not that this did not prevent us from mimicking Tony's orotund Redemptorist resonance, his articulate and recondite vocabulary and his preference of double negatives over simple positives. I had better acknowledge that I have used one of his phrases for decades now when I meet some people whom I uncharitably think of as self-opinionated – he remarked of a German missionary from India who was lecturing at YTU. 'Ah, these veteran German missionaries, they are not plagued by self-doubt!

By 1974, YTU was ready to participate fully in the teaching of the Bachelor of Theology degree.

But by 1974, one of the main consequences of all these changes being in place was the arrival of lay students. Seminarians would not (and should not) study isolated from the rest of the Church. In February 1974, YTU opened its classes to lay students and a large number of sisters and teaching brothers. In fact, within a year or two, laity and religious would outnumber (and frequently out-achieve) the seminarians in each course. One of the features of YTU in its early days, and quite a feature of UFT, was the number of talented lay women who obtained their degree (often in long part-time work), went on to doctoral studies and became a more substantial presence in the Church. On television and in the parishes of the past, it may have been 'Father Knows Best', but the developments in wider theological education means that this may not necessarily be so.

YTU was important for me personally because, apart from the daily and demanding formation work (and a review or two or three ...), this is where I taught and earned my living. The latter is, perhaps, an overstatement, lecturers receiving a modest stipend as an acknowledgement of their work. In the end, the lecturers at the time were substantially supported in financial matters by the religious orders themselves.

During the Canberra years, I 'taught' (I think) some philosophy but my main areas were Theology of Faith and Revelation and a thematic study of the Old Testament. With an eye on notes from Roman courses, I devised a theology course that looked both 'academic' and 'modern' but gradually modified it to relate more to the experience of faith, of a personalised perspective on a revealing God (rather than on truths revealed and doctrines). But, the Old Testament was my favourite, remembering the enthusiasm that Dennis Murphy engendered in us at Croydon in the late 1950s as we were introduced into a work of imagination, poetry, prophecy and 2000 years of religious experience that was also the heritage and spirituality of Jesus Christ. It was a challenge to try to elicit from class groups something of this zest for what had been generally closed pages of the Bible for Catholics, to try to help them be more at home in the Old Testament world.

At YTU, I was able to move into the Old Testament area, for the first year students (but also later teaching a course on the Prophets and, particularly, a course on a New Testament Jesus in the light of the Old for all students). The main course was a one-term overview for first year whose aim was this 'at homeness' which would give students courage to go on to more detailed courses of exegesis and interpretation. Some years, the courses, especially for lay students, were held twice. It is a pleasure to look back and realise that I was able to effect the introduction to the Old Testament for several hundred people.

One of the features of the YTU first year course was the introduction to theology called 'The Mystery of Christ' as devised and taught by John Flynn, a highly imaginative confrere and theologian who drew on a great range of literature and believed that theology is grounded on and built on religious experience, 'autobiographical faith'. When John went to Sydney in 1975, I gladly inherited the course and taught it with my own variations for nine years until the end of 1983 when the numbers joining religious orders were dwindling (and the number departing during the first year increasing). It was time to bring it to a close.

The Mystery of Christ was a great but enjoyable challenge. It was a helpful course for a pre-novitiate director to teach. It put me in contact for years with the students and formators of the different orders, and those of several women's congregations as pre-novitiate sisters joined the first year program as early as 1973.

I like to think we were pioneering some creative ways of doing theology in The Mystery of Christ. The attitude behind it, at least for me, was what Henri Nouwen called, in his book *Creative Ministry*, 'redemptive education'. Redemptive education, according to Nouwen, was to be evocative, respecting potentials with students making them available to each other. Instead of 'Yes, but ...', 'Tell me more'. Knowledge is not meant to be a property to be defended; comparisons are not relevant. The process is to be bilateral (education by association) rather than unilateral (the competent instructing the incompetent). It should be actualising rather than alienating.

We interacted, discussed, workshopped, watched films, play-read *The One Day of the Year*, Alan Seymour's provocative 1963 play on Australian attitudes towards Anzac Day, invited guests, analysed letters to editors, wrote essays, did role-plays and made collages. I was a bit put out (putting it politely) when the former provincial of the Dominicans on hearing about the collage on Ministry in the Church, the assignment for the term's assessment, asked whether they were doing 'theological kindergarten'. But, anyone can toss off an essay, especially in the short time of a written exam. The time taken to research and select material for the collage, finger it with scissors, get the paper and paste and decide on positioning pieces with meaning, and later explain it to the class, was well worth the jibe.

Our first term aim was to look at ourselves as critical Australians, Catholics, adults. During second term we looked sympathetically at religion, world religions, atheism and the credibility of Christianity and the person of Jesus. This involved some historical delving as well as looking at literature, art and Christ-figures. Third term took us to ourselves again, stories and storytelling and, finally, to our autobiographical faith. In the late 1970s.

We did have some moments in the films I chose to help us introduce theology and the mystery of Christ. *The Devils* (yes, I did use Ken Russell's controversial look at an aberrant Church each year) raised eyebrows but led to lively and helpful discussion. We stayed with Ken Russell with *Tommy*, quite a favourite for symbols, music, song and Christ-figures.

The growth of the Melbourne College of Divinity was not the only adult education development in Melbourne during the 1970s.

One of the institutions established for religious women in 1970 was Assumption Institute, designed for about 50 women to spend a year working on personal agenda as well as attend a series of courses on key areas of scripture and theology. From 1972, some workshops on film appreciation were included in the program. These I really enjoyed and found that the sisters on the course were far more open to fresh perspectives on films than some of the more brain-focused courses at other centres. I could take big risks in showing controversial films to these sisters who were willing to respond emotionally and thoughtfully to films which explored the darker side of the human condition than they were used to. I particularly remember screening *The Sailor Who Fell from Grace with the Sea* in 1977, a film that received an Advised Against rating but which had a great deal to show about relationships. One of the best discussions on a film that I recall. As numbers declined in religious orders, there was less need for Assumption Institute and it closed in 1990. There had been a priest director at one stage but those who managed the institute were sisters. But, for the closing Mass, given the situation on priests, they wanted to invite the past director but he was out of the country. The lot fell to me. As we began our celebration it occurred to me to mention that if anyone wanted to know what 200 to 1 looked like, here it was.

The other important institute in Melbourne was the National Pastoral Institute (NPI), established by the Australian Episcopal Commission which offered a one year Diploma in Religious Education. It opened in 1973. Again, as with Assumption, students came from all over Australia, Papua New Guinea, New Zealand and beyond. A major focus of NPI was on methods of adult learning, student participation in and responsibility for curriculum and programs with a vision for a changing Church in a changing Australian society.

Later, further needs of students brought in a Diploma of Ministry, possibilities for part-time study, ministry supervision programs, a youth ministry training course and Diplomas in Education for Justice and in Social Communications.

It was an accident, my becoming involved in NPI. Gerald O'Collins SJ was engaged to teach a course on Theology and Revelation. Just before the opening of the first course, he was transferred to the Gregorian University in Rome. I had worked on Catechetical material in the 1960s with a group that included Rosemary Crumlin, a Sister of Mercy from Parramatta. (A major project was called *Come Alive*, an interesting and colourful text for secondary study, which incurred some Episcopal displeasure and disapproval, and a condemnatory booklet which wags nicknamed *Drop Dead*.) Rosemary was a driving force behind NPI and asked me could I come to teach the course on theology. This enabled me to be exposed to a learning style that was less academic-achievement oriented than the YTU.

Offering short courses in such places meant meeting a wide range of people (though not remembering names with faces) and the establishing of bonds throughout the country. These wider horizons also provided a balance to the more intense working within the walls of MSC formation.

I have not written the last on NPI because, while I continued part time for the next 10 years, I did spend five years full time there until its closure at the end of 1988. So, there will be more about NPI and Rosemary and others.

Still speaking of theology in the 1970s, another field of interest was the MSC periodical *Compass Theology Review*. It was the brainchild of Dennis Murphy who had taught us Old Testament in the 1950s. As he moved amongst groups eager to learn more about current issues in theology, he was struck by the reporting of theological questions and controversies by the media, both newspapers and periodicals like *Time Magazine*. This was especially true of articles discussing Vatican II where journalists wrote simplistically and often with an eye to sensation – not that this has changed in the decades following but now everyone can blog and the discussions often become more simplistic or heated or bigoted. But, we can leave on-line theology until later. *Compass* was intended as a more popular magazine which would provide information and balanced update on theology and controversies.

While *Compass* was successful and has survived, the original goals were not attainable, especially in a country with such a small population as Australia. Dennis Murphy realised that those who know theology do not necessarily have journalistic skills while those with such skills can rush for copy rather than explore. He was after a 'creative continuity' in theology, in touch with solid tradition but with an insightful and visionary openness to the contemporary world. He added that we have to avoid something which became more prevalent in succeeding decades and is still with us, 'theological terrorism'.

It was not easy to get a new theology review into production. MSC superiors were wary and did not put up the money. When the first issue, June 1967, was prohibited by the Superior Generals of several women's orders, they might have felt they had a point. The 'hot' topic that caused concern at that time was Original Sin. John Oostermeier of Spectrum Publications took the business and financial risks and the five issues for 1967 were published within five months. Dennis Murphy edited *Compass* for only one year. An illness meant that in 1968 Peter Hoy became the second editor. *Compass's* reputation (for and against, mainly for) flourished and attracted a wide range of Australian writers.

Towards the end of 1971, Peter Hoy was not able to manage producing the magazine and Dennis Murphy asked me if I would take it on. Moving to Melbourne made it more possible for me so I accepted and edited it until the end of 1998 (over a 100 issues it pleases me to note!). We negotiated with John Oostermeier and in 1973, Paul Stenhouse and Chevalier Press undertook the full publishing responsibility. In 1976, it became a quarterly (which it still is). It was smaller in size than the original issues and kept a modest circulation. With the coming of the periodical *Pacifica* and its academic content and style (now the periodical of the MCD), *Compass* affirmed its choice of being a review of what we called 'Topical Theology'.

I would like to think that *Compass* has been sometimes visionary, sometimes adventurous, always interesting. It aimed to be read as well as admired! Special features have included Theology and Story before it became more trendy (as well as when it did). Urgent issues like Women in the Church, Urban Theology, Marriage and Divorce, Lay Ministries, Women's Spirituality, Men's Spirituality. It even housed some of the Hagar the Horrible cartoons to illustrate the Myers-Briggs Type Indicator. In 1996, an issue (with contents on the back) also became a book to celebrate the centenary of cinema with representatives of churches and faiths in Australia, *From Back Pews to Front Stalls*.

However, one of the key issues that has become prominent is the consideration of Australian Theology, mirroring what happened in Australia, especially in the years before the bicentennial of white settlement in 1988. We started with a Tony Kelly paper, 'Towards an Australian Theology' in 1972 and kept progressing year by year (helped by seminars at YTU and NPI), realising that the experience of God in Australia was distinctive because of the geography (the great advantage of so much desert plus Uluru at the heart of the continent to chime with biblical imagery), history (of the millennia of aboriginal presence sustaining the land as well as the centuries of the latecomers since 1788) and the environment (just think of descriptions of the coastline from north Queensland down the east coast, across to the west, up to the Kimberley's and back through the Northern Territory to Queensland). I think *Compass* made a significant contribution in those years to local theology which has increased and multiplied. Some fruits of this thinking and writing were gathered together in two collections I edited, *Discovering an Australian Theology* (for the bicentenary) and *Developing an Australian Theology* (for the Jubilee year of 2000).

Theology was a tradition of wisdom, mysticism, prayer and preaching before it became a science, an ordered body of academic knowledge in the Middle Ages. While this latter way of doing theology became the norm for seminary studies, 'sure knowledge', the wisdom tradition must continue. With the focus on church and ministry, theology and its language addressed to particular 'publics' must also be ministry-centred. *Compass* still attempts to provide a theology review containing theology as wisdom, as science and as ministry.

22. MEANWHILE, FILMS AND THE 1970s

FIRST, the effect of the introduction of the new classifications for Australian society. An interesting case in point was a British film version of James Joyce's *Ulysses* with Milo O'Shea and Barbara Jefford. Produced in the mid-1960s, the film was refused registration in Australia because of its use of the frank language and the role of sexuality in Joyce's poetic narrative of a day in the life of Dubliner, Leopold Bloom. There was a minor sensation in 1967 when the film was allowed to be screened in New Zealand. Many Australian show business personalities and media commentators crossed the Tasman and reported to the deprived Australian public about this daring film. What made it more sensational was that the New Zealand authorities would allow the film to be screened only to segregated audiences, sessions for women only, sessions for men only. By 1972, there was a calmer approach to controversial films and *Ulysses*, which was really an art-house film of limited appeal because of its fidelity to Joyce's complex and verbally strong novel, had a modest run in Australian city cinemas. Advertising and PR hype relied on the validity of anticipation being better than realisation.

However, there was an immediate crisis, artistic and political, causing censorship officials to be worried at the beginning of 1972. It was Ken Russell's *The Devils*. Russell is often referred to by critics as cinema's 'enfant terrible'. A photo of him on a cross with a crown of thorns appeared on John Baxter's biography, *An Appalling Talent*. Russell was frequently arresting, sometimes shocking. His 1960s television portraits of Elgar, Delius, Isadora Duncan and others were unconventional, juxtaposing biographical plot, music and accompanying images (on the principle of free-flowing imaginative association). This often offended viewers, especially purists; others found his flamboyant extravagance exciting. He was soon to turn to cinema portraits of Tchaikowsky (*The

Music Lovers), Mahler, Liszt (Lisztomania), Valentino, Byron and Shelley (Gothic) and give them this treatment.

And so, *The Devils*. The plot, derived from Aldous Huxley's novel and John Whiting's play, concerns a convent of Ursuline sisters in Loudun in France and their Jesuit confessor in the time of Louis XIII and Cardinal Richelieu. The women in the convent, many unwilling to be there, a religious vocation being foisted on them by family and society, were prey to aberration and madness. Church histories and studies in 17th century spirituality indicate that this was the case as were the bizarre events in Loudun. Their fanaticism was used by Richelieu to set up treason trials, order executions and annex Loudun. Russell was fired by the story and shows religious mania, sexual repression let loose and a decaying society holding on to the formalities of religion while abusing it. The plot, the visuals and some episodes of the demented superior, Mother Joan of the Angels (Vanessa Redgrave) fantasising about Father Grandier (Oliver Reed) with herself as an erotic Mary Magdalene at the foot of the cross with Grandier as Jesus coming down from the cross and embracing her, caused, needless to say, some protests. Was the film blasphemous?

Mr. Chipp's department consulted. The point was made that the representation of blasphemy was not blasphemy itself even though it might be considered offensive. The Democratic Labor Party (which was the political party that separated from the Australian Labor Party in the anti-Communist spirit of 1955, The Split) had reservations about the new classifications and *The Devils* found it all too much for them. As it was, the film went out with a boxed warning on every advertisement stating that, although events portrayed were historically accurate, some people would find the treatment too strong. It was a way of keeping the classifications and addressing public opinion and community standards. I reviewed the film at the Australia Twin Cinemas in Melbourne. A young man escorted his girlfriend up the steps afterwards and paused and declared loudly and disgustedly for all to hear, 'Fuckin' awful show.' What language was the Restricted Certificate protecting us from?

Actually, the issue that made most impact on the Australian public in 1972 was screen violence. It was not just an Australian thing. The early 1970s produced a number of well-made, significant films, which depicted and explored violence.

The Oscar-winner for Best film of 1971 was *The French Connection*, for 1972 *The Godfather*, both recipients of a Restricted certificate. *The Godfather* was an excellent portrayal of the Mafia and their codes of honour, their network of crime and power, with Marlon Brando's convincing Don Corleone and the even more frightening portrayal of corruption of Al Pacino's Michael Corleone. And audience shudders at the horse's head in the bed. The orchestrated violence, especially of assassinations intercut with the baptismal ceremony (and the irony of both godfathers), brought a bloody but effective film to a close.

Top box-office films (and Oscar nominees as well) included Stanley Kubrick's *A Clockwork Orange*, Sam Peckinpah's *Straw Dogs* (and a release of his previously cut *The Wild Bunch*), John Boorman's *Deliverance*, Don Siegel's *Dirty Harry*. Quite a year with those titles. All are now considered classics of their kind. These films, along with Charles Bronson in *Death Wish* (1974) raised the crisis of law and order, the ability and inability of the law and law enforcers to administer justice and, if it could not, did groups or individuals have the right to take the law into their own hands. This is still one of the important screen questions and contemporary moral issues. Head might say 'no', but heart and emotions say 'yes'.

Orchestrated violence was seen in *Straw Dogs*, *Deliverance* and, especially (and literally orchestrated) in *A Clockwork Orange*, Kubrick's expert version of Anthony Burgess's grim futuristic parable about society, environment of violence, prison and the false optimism of aversion therapy and human freedom. Sam Peckinpah had used this in *The Wild Bunch* (1969), with its slow-motion of flesh torn and blood spurting. Here was stylised violence. The portrayals of violence in a violent world still cause dilemmas, especially after *Reservoir Dogs* (1991) and *Pulp Fiction* ushered in a new genre of mordantly funny depictions of violence.

Should films mirror society? Does screen violence desensitise audiences? Or are many audiences not yet sensitised so that it is not a matter of desensitising?

At the time of the release of *A Clockwork Orange*, a court case in Victoria indicated that a boy attacked his parents after seeing the film. But, the boy was disturbed and might have been set off by the *Roadrunner* instead. And, of course, there are the millions who did not leave the cinema and act violently after seeing *A Clockwork Orange*. As with any controversial area, it is the richness and variety of life that most people experience that puts exposure to a disturbing area into perspective. Those who are fixated on one area can be unpredictably triggered.

Of course, the R-Certificate meant that many more visually explicit sex films were released commercially. And, many of them (quality or not) were money-spinners. However, most tended to be of the soft-core sex films relying on abundant nudity, breathlessly contrived seductive sequences and simulated sex acts. The kind of pornography on DVD release and on websites nowadays was not allowed into Australia officially. But, at this time, Australians were curious – naturally.

Drive-ins caused some concern. Managements began to screen the sex films and the exposure was over-exposed to those living nearby – and to unaware citizens driving along suburban roads. Coming from Dandenong along Stud Road, one came over a hill at Rowville to be suddenly confronted by giant square metres of flesh. Often a road hazard.

But, after 12 months, many adults realised that, if you had seen one you'd seen many, many others. Within years, the mainstream audience had seen enough. In fact, for many, the repetition, the contrivances and the predictability were boring.

There are some funny stories associated with the advent of the sex films. Sometimes they were screened at more prominent, reputable cinemas. I remember going in 1973 or 1974, as reviewers were doing at the time to check on a sampling of these films and a proper cinema was a better place to go. The film in question was Clinic X-clusive, at the highly respectable Forum cinema in Flinders Street. (Later, it became a centre for Evangelical services and Neil Jillett from *The Age* newspaper referring to its closing down as a cinema saying that it had 'gone to God'). It was raining and I was actually wearing a raincoat (never again!) Usually, the older ladies in the Greater Union business office rang through and the tickets would be ready at the box-office. This time (early in the morning), the manager was taking the tickets at the door, answered the phone and across the foyer I heard, 'Father Malone'. 'Yes.' 'This way, please.' A hasty, self-conscious conversation followed:

'I see only a selection of this kind of film.'

'Oh, we don't usually show this kind of thing.'

Perhaps I should have heeded the title of the supporting film, Come Away, Peter.

There is always an initial curiosity and I was a little suspicious of critics who claimed that the sex movies had become boring. But, when I realised that for 20 minutes or so I had not been paying attention to *Love Games in Florence* but had been planning exam questions, I knew they were right.

The formation and theological involvement of the early- and mid-1970s had a strong influence on my approach to film. The experience in education and personal development highlighted the need for a similar approach to film. This was happening, slowly and spasmodically, in Australia in university courses and what became Colleges of Advanced Education and, alter, received university status. Schools were slower to take up media awareness courses and education in appreciation. So too were the seminaries. Perhaps some of the films and their reputations alarmed parents and teachers. Advertising, radio and television promotion certainly do. This often meant a reluctance in taking cinema seriously. It is easier to pass it off as just entertainment or be upset about its threatening of accepted values and standards.

Before considering the moves within the Catholic Church to establish some programs of media education, it is worth looking at the kinds of films released in the 1970s and the trends.

We changed the format and layout of the *Annals* reviews at this time. After four years of comments of mixed length with several stills, we were influenced by the pages in the popular magazine, Movie News. Each issue had a page with a blurb about forthcoming movies accompanied by a still. We introduced two or more pages of reviews each month, each review just over 100 words in a wide panel, a still in the centre. It highlighted the visuals well but meant that some films could have done with more comment, others with less. However, we kept to this format for the next 10 years.

Being in Melbourne was a definite advantage for extensive coverage in film reviewing. Instead of catching something in Canberra or fitting in sessions during visits to Sydney, I was able to see films as soon as they arrived on Melbourne screens. Many of the cinemas operating at the time have disappeared: Chelsea, Odeon, Esquire, two Metros (despite creaky leases of life as Palace and Mayfair), Bercy, Bryson, Swanston ... The famous State on the corner of Flinders and Russell Streets had become two cinemas, Forum and Rapallo. They were taken over by the Melbourne Revival Movement in 1986, 'Gone to God', as critic, Neil Jillett, remarked. Of course, the 1970s saw new cinema complexes being built for Hoyts, Greater Union and for Village.

One of Melbourne's strengths at that time was its variety of suburban cinemas that offered 'art house' films. While the Camberwell Rivoli, the Longford, Trak (the latter long since gone) and others experienced good and bad times, they continued to present quality films. Old halls at, say, Croydon and Murrumbeena used to show popular as well as rarely screened films. The Richmond Valhalla, Carlton Movie-house, Melbourne University's Union Theatre offered specialised, double bills, With the coming of video, each has had to re-think policy but, by and large, they survived into the 1980s. Another feature of those days was the drive-in, handy if you wanted to review something locally except that in, the early 1970s the fog used to close in at Croydon or Wantirna and you would he issued with Fog Passes to get you in to finish the program another night.

Another feature of Melbourne film-going that I enjoyed was meeting the people, almost always women, who worked at the box-office, selling, tickets, giving people program information on the phone, giving advice about the suitability of the films, checking student cards and preventing (sometimes with a surprising and uncharacteristic vehemence) under 18-year-olds from getting into an R-film like the unwily 15-year-olds who bowled up to see Sylvester Stallone's *Cobra* (Rated R) and asked for a half-price ticket for children! For many years, I enjoyed chatting, with these friendly women, always obliging, often interested to check out opinions and often (in the early days of the R-certificate films) eager to protect me from some of the films on show. You got a feel of how the business was going, how successful films were or not, who was the audience for particular movies (like bikies slashing seats at martial arts shows or the teenage girls sighing over Rob Lowe or Tom Cruise), how management was managing or not. There were some characters too.

Norma had highly-lacquered artificial hair that surprised you with its size and shape, used more make-up and mascara than necessary, a spinster of impossible to determine age who lived with her sister, looking after their mother, but she was also one of the most kindly persons you could meet, one of the world's best affirmers. Everybody was good. Her moment of glory, proudly recounted, was presenting a bouquet to Vivien Leigh on the occasion of the screening of *Gone with the Wind* for the centenary of the Civil War.

Bill was a pensioner with the oldest of clothes (said to be supplied by St. Vincent de Paul shops), a beanie, a scruffy beard and bad eyes, who had sat in the front row since I had begun to review in Melbourne. In the 1970s he used to snore mightily. I sometimes think I should see Clint Eastwood's *Breezy* again and listen to the dialogue. The usherette woke him several times! And with only a half-dozen in a smaller theatre, one was aware of Bill's snoring. He was always there in the front row and usually on the day the film opens. Shuffling in and out, chatting to the staff, seeing films like Places in the Heart that he really liked, six or seven times. As Norma said, 'He is a character!'

A benefit of living in Melbourne at that time was that some overseas celebrities visited Australia to promote their films. By the 1980s they were being rushed from studio to studio, busy with radio and television interviews. In those less hurried days, *Annals* was able to do some interviews. Topol was in Sydney to promote *Fiddler on the Roof*. Although running late, he spent some time with us, a genial man but much younger than his make-up as Tevye would lead an audience to believe. He stayed talking to Paul Stenhouse and came downstairs to a conference with representatives of Sydney's Jewish community arm-in-arm with the clerically-dressed Father Stenhouse. Interfaith show-biz.

I had the opportunity to speak with Richard Attenborough when *Young Winston* was released. An articulate man, he had a great deal to say about his films and the British industry. He made a point when I asked, with a bit of snobbery, I realise now, concerning 'the movies', about the relationship between films as art and films as commercial commodities: would I preach in an empty church? No matter how eloquent the sermon, if it reaches only a small congregation, it has only a narrow effect. Yes.

Cicely Tyson promoted *Sounder*. Again, an articulate actress with views about the ways in which racial issues were being portrayed and the status of black actors and actresses. She expressed disgust at the wave of tough crime-busting or private-eye thrillers. *Shaft* would probably have been the most popular of these. She felt that there was a need for the more basic humanity of films like *Sounder* to be seen and appreciated. Acknowledging the success of Sidney Poitier, she, like many critics, felt that *Guess Who's Coming to Dinner* had good intentions but Sidney Poitier as a United Nations doctor stacked the odds too much in his favour.

Charles Jarrott and his star, Joseph Bottoms, (young and particularly deferential to the director) came to promote *The Dove*, part of which was filmed in the Northern Territory with John Meillon.

An opportunity to discuss his plays and films came with Robert Bolt's visit for his *Lady Caroline Lamb*, the film that he had written and directed for his wife, Sarah Miles. He had also written *Ryan's Daughter* for her. While objecting to the word 'moralist' and its overtones, he agreed that confronting life and the way it is, or should be, lived inevitably draws one into the areas of values and morals. Inevitably he found himself a moralist. He said *Lady Caroline Lamb* was 'a regretful attack on the Romantic notion of doing one's own thing.' He stated that 'the Romantic impulse to follow emotions through, to live heartily in the moment has a vitality and verve about it that are valuable. This doing one's own thing, the modern catch-cry as well as the old, can, however, manifest itself in poses, theatrical impulses and gestures. It can and does appear overwhelmingly attractive.' Doing the proper thing, however, which ultimately Bolt guardedly endorses, can appear staid, unimaginative and lifeless:

> And with the hypocrites of society, one has the further problem that in private they do their own thing, but publicly give evidence of extreme propriety. They are believers in the 'virtue' of discretion, which somehow allows them the best and worst of both worlds. The elegant aristocrats of *Lady Caroline Lamb* were experts at this and condemned Caroline, not for the excesses, but because she was excessive and restrained in public. She could not be discreet.

1973 was a year that raised again questions about 'movies and morality'. After a year of the R-certificate, it was time to do some assessing of the effect of these films on us. Controversies were still possible. The main controversial film of 1973 was *Last Tango in Paris*. It came with a fanfare of praise and some loud condemnations. It had some respectability as it received some Oscar nominations including Marlon Brando for Best Actor. The local publicists played on this. Usually reviewers received a double pass for previews. This time the pass was solely for the reviewer and had to be confirmed. What we saw was a powerful film of despair. It was blunt and frank in its language, dramatised some desperately gross sexual behaviour. But it was a well-made film, mirroring contemporary experience not for every audience, of course, but one which I found I could praise: 'A telling and detached film communicating the frustrations of ageing and the non-sense of life ... Bleak and sombre outlook, though allowing that several graphic sexual sequences and constant sequences would be unacceptable to many audiences.' The review was also published in *The Catholic Weekly*. I received no letters of complaint.

Some of the thinking that appeared useful in *The Film* went into a series of articles for *Annals* in mid-1973 on 'Movies and Morality', on ways of establishing standards by focusing on patterns of human development, on censorship and fear and the fear of fear, on the ways we respond to stories.

I innocently thought that Paul Stenhouse was furthering his presentation of material on this topic when he invited me to write an editorial for him for the August 1973 issue. It was only after I had written it and he had printed it above his own name that he told me that there had been complaints from a priest in North Queensland about the *Annals* reviews and that the matter had gone on the agenda of a meeting of the Queensland Bishops. The articles and the editorial put forward the *Annals* viewpoint. This proved acceptable. The latter paragraphs still seem valid:

> One of the difficulties about appearing in print is that words assume an authority they don't properly possess. Father Malone, and others whose reviews appear in *Annals*, are merely a few reviewers among many. Their reviews are not meant to be the only ones read. It must always be remembered that a viewer's (and, of course, a reviewer's) assessment of the moral, aesthetic or dramatic quality of a production depends on the person's background and degree of maturity. It cannot always be assumed that a reviewer has adequately assessed the impact a film will have on people

of differing ages and backgrounds; account must be taken of the personal and subjective nature of even the best reviews. If people appreciate *Annals* reviews (whether they always agree with them or not) they will generally trust then: as reliable and can check their judgment with the ideas of local reviewers in the daily and Catholic press. To expect more from such reviews is to have extravagant expectations, Moreover, reviews even in Catholic papers do not absolve parents, teachers or viewers generally from the necessity of observing the censor's classifications and catching up on at least a sampling of the movies themselves in order to form an overall and personally sound judgment.

However, the controversial film of 1974 was *The Exorcist*. An eerie, curious atmosphere about the preview and then (a gimmick) someone ran screaming down, the aisle of the East End Cinema and out a side exit. Somebody remarked that Catholics could accept the plot of *The Exorcist*. William Peter Blatty said that his story had a basis in actual events. The film had Jesuit advisers and actors. Non-religious people would think of it as a Dracula horror-equivalent. What about those who grew up as Catholics and had left the Church? Could Satan suddenly inhabit a human being? The film, despite the ugliness, the devil's crass language and green-slime special effects, was very popular. Caustic New York critic, Pauline Kael, said that it was the greatest pro-Catholic poster since *The Bells of St. Mary's*.

Our *Annals* contribution to film awareness in 1974-75 was Bill Collins. Already a television host and always an enthusiast, he wrote study guides to particular films. At a home screening for Paul Stenhouse and myself, he showed us Robert Taylor in *Quentin Durward* and, during blank footage for commercial inserts in the Channel 7 print, did indeed rouse us to look forward to speeches by Robert Morley and some swordplay on a large bell.

Seeing all the films for review was made possible by the film companies, the management of the cinemas. Up to 1972 I had to rely on preview tickets and paying. At the beginning of 1973 the companies made available tickets and passes. And not only a personal ticket but a double pass. This was of great benefit to confreres and friends and, I hope, of benefit to the companies by word of mouth about many of the films. There was a large number of seminarians at Croydon and I was able to invite them to screenings. It was, in passing, an interesting way to get to know students better. Some preferred particular types of films. There was a group who would be in on westerns, martial arts shows and action thrillers. A couple vied for the horror films. Some were fastidious, picking and choosing carefully. Others, sometimes surprisingly, had a wide range in taste and were able to appreciate quite different films. One advantage, I found, in the R-certificate films was in advising some students, especially those with more sheltered background, to go and see the Swedish sex documentary, *The Language of Love*. A strongly humanist film, based on some hedonistic principles, it was nevertheless a useful film to catch up on sexual information and education.

23. IN MELBOURNE

WITH TEACHING timetables and formation work, it was not usually possible to go to previews. I preferred to see the films with an ordinary audience. It gives a more realistic impression. The danger with the small preview, which the main media reviewers generally attend, is that you have the opportunity to make comments, scoff aloud at what you don't like, make the smart quip. It is also more difficult to be teary-eyed in a close group! When reviewers says a horror film is not as scary as it might be, they probably saw it in such a group. One reviewer remarked of Stephen King's *Children of the Corn* that it had few scares. But the audience screamed at the session I attended. Comedies go better with a real audience rather than sitting rather silently with introverted reviewers who like Mona Lisa, are laughing on the inside!

Practising Christians tend to be more quickly alarmed at such extensions and often fear the worst. We often then go on to speak and judge as if evil not only shouldn't happen, but should be bypassed or ignored if it does. And then we are suddenly confronted by it and may be unable to cope, running away from it helplessly or succumbing to it because we had never before acknowledged its attractions. Art has always helped audiences to face the myriad facets of human strength and weakness, of human heroism and depravity. If God saves us from our sins, he knows human evil and can forgive it and redeem it.

1977 was, of course, the year of *Star Wars*. 1976's *Rocky* (in the year of the U.S. Bicentenary) and *Star Wars*, with their optimism and touching the age-old legends of journeys and quests, chivalries and battles between good and evil, re-shaped the popular movie-consciousness that had, from the late 1960s to the mid 1970s, focused on the anti-heroes, those overwhelmed by society, the graduates and those trapped in the cuckoo's nest. With its sequels and many derivatives on the large screens and television. *Star Wars* was to dominate the world's imagination for many decades. *Superman the Movie* came in 1979. But, interestingly, it was 1978 and 1979 when major films about the Vietnam war reached the screens, *The Deer Hunter*, *Coming Home* and, one of the greatest of films (personal opinion!), *Apocalypse Now*.

Another advantage of living in Melbourne was being able to attend the annual International Film Festival. As with the festivals in other cities, especially the large Sydney festival, that in Melbourne is an event for the city. In fact, the Melbourne Film Festival which started at Olinda in the Dandenong Ranges east of the city in 1952 is the fifth-longest running festival in the world. During the 1950s and 1960s, it grew, moving to the very large and elaborate Palais Theatre at St. Kilda where it remained until 1981, and has since moved to several venues around the city. The annual June pilgrimage to St. Kilda offered a wide variety of films from many countries, some narratives, some experimental. They were supported, by a big number of short films, many of which were excellent.

It is in this context of film culture and consciousness of the 1970s that I write about aspects of media education in the Church which seemed to be one of the promising developments of the time and in which I wanted to become involved. It was time to work towards some courses, especially in the context of the Bachelor of Theology degree. But it was a slow process. The YTU introduced a 'Films and Values' course as part of the degree program in 1974. The opportunity came when the Sisters of Mercy in Victoria asked for a three-day workshop at Easter 1973 for film appreciation for teachers in Melbourne. The only way I could say yes was to have the first-year YTU group with me. And so it was. Three enjoyable days in shaping the elements for a Films and Values course, with a visit to the Carlton Movie House to watch Ingmar Bergman's *Wild Strawberries* which was on the school syllabus. I was able to draw on a course in Media in general that I had been invited to conduct during 1972 to teacher-trainees at Christ College.

One incident with the Christ College students was a learning experience. We decided to go to a film screening in the city as an exercise in criticism. Hitchcock's latest film, *Frenzy*, was screening. What better than a Hitchcock film? Actually, many things! *Frenzy* is about a rapist-strangler and the trainees, all women, found the film hard going and experienced the ugliness and the threatening situations of the victims. I then made the same mistake with a group of novice-nuns watching Robert Mitchum menace Gregory Peck and his wife and daughter in *Cape Fear*. One could not even stay and watch the film and ran out. The importance of sensibilities and sensitivities was brought home to me again, especially the experience of watching the film with a specialised group. On the lighter side was a screening of *Scrooge* to some 14-year-olds at Ringwood and the planned discussion afterwards. They worked through the complete schema for reacting to *Scrooge* in fully 15 minutes. Other seminars helped shape the course: senior boys at Ringwood talked about the films they enjoyed but which they were certain their parents would dislike and/or approve of, nor even see. A Religious Education co-ordinator decided to test this and arranged a screening of *Billy Jack*, one of the films the students quoted, at the local library. Seventy students and parents turned up. During the consequent discussion, it was the parents who spoke up with interesting angles on the film rather than the students.

Schools were trying different ways of working with film. Film was also something of an excuse for helping Star of the Sea College, Gardenvale, girls meet and socialise with Assumption College, Kilmore, boys. Screenings at Kilmore, meal, discussion. Good and worthwhile discussion, better socialising. Again a sign of those times. At Wangaratta, things were different: twilight Religious Education sessions (from about 4.00 pm to 8 pm), senior boys and girls working together with staff each fortnight. Again, film was a useful theme. I enjoyed going and always brought some of the pre-novitiate students with me to share the experience.

Not every session went smoothly, especially talks on censorship. An ironic question came from the Victorian Senator Hannan after watching *I'll Never Forget What's'isname* with a group of Christian students, 'Shouldn't it have been entitled I'll Never Forget What's'ername? One girl, not knowing who this adult was, vigorously (and skilfully) took to him to give him a lecture on understanding film along the lines of 'Surely you, surely you can't'.

A different experience was a seminar at the Brisbane seminary at Banyo at the end of 1972. After working on our moral approaches to film, we watched James Bridges' interesting film about surrogate motherhood with Barbara Hershey, *The Babymaker*. The next day was spent discussing and studying moral issues with the possibility at the end of the day of viewing the film again to check whether the seminar had changed our perspective at all. But the Christian Brothers on the course all ducked out to the drive-in to avoid seeing *The Babymaker* again except for one who did not get away quickly enough and was 'trapped' by the rest of the participants. It is not always easy facing up to films.

The NPI students tended to be readers and not so fond of film, rather uphill seminars at times with literary presuppositions being imposed on film (to its detriment) and film considered solely for enjoyment. 'So this is the third time you've seen *Nashville*, this says more about you ... 'I had better luck with a screening of *Lipstick*. *Lipstick* featured model Margaux Hemingway with her sister Mariel, Chris Sarandon as a teacher who rapes the two women and Anne Bancroft as a lawyer. When the film was screened at the Melbourne Capitol Cinema in 1976, audiences applauded fiercely when the heroine shot her assailant (who had been freed by the courts, re-employed by the Catholic school he worked in and had raped again). *The Age* critic Colin Bennett expressed concern at the time at the applause for this kind of vigilante behaviour. Fr. Chamberlin included the film in his Advised Against category in *The Advocate*. While *Lipstick*-behaviour might be condemned by the head, it gets a great deal of emotional support from the heart. I screened it at NPI to a group who were about to start a course on Moral Theology, Moral Principles and Behaviour. A bit wary because of the violence, I went down to a buffet meal with the students after the screening and was accosted by an elderly Irish sister. 'That ending, Father, it was terrible'. I prepared for a criticism of self-proclaimed vengeance. 'It was too easy for him, too quick. The bullet should have gone through him slowly, searing and burning his flesh ...'. So, the difference between head and heart response is striking. What has each to say to the other?

Some of the best workshops were with the sisters doing their Renewal Year at Assumption Institute. Perhaps it is the personal investment, but the response was always interesting and vigorous. After some preparation on looking at films, I have tried out a screening as if the group were working for the Censorship Board. Without having seen the film before or without having heard anything about it, how would they classify it for Australian release? On one occasion, the group watched *Lepke*, a gangster thriller with Tony Curtis. Their verdict, an M certificate. In fact, it had been given a Restricted certificate for its violence (in *The Godfather* vein). However, the group argued and made an excellent case for the film to be reclassified. Many of them drew on their experience of teaching teenagers and judged they would be able to appreciate the film for its strengths, weaknesses, its themes and violence. The same group responded excellently to the frankly explicit, *The Sailor Who Fell From Grace With The Sea* with Sarah Miles and Kris Kristofferson, making sound judgments about themes of intimacy and sexuality. This was quite a change from the sisters' screenings at the end of the 1960s.

At the time, a group of Anglicans was publishing a series of booklets for use in 'General Studies' at final year level for secondary schools in New South Wales and Western Australia. I was happy to write up the course as their booklet on film which came out in 1974 with the misleading title *The Writing on the Hall*.

Another vehicle for film study was the discussion sheet. The influence was American William Kuhn who had published a book in the late 1960s containing 38 films for discussion (introduction and suggested questions). It seemed a good idea. After using *Saturday Night and Sunday Morning* in a workshop in 1969, I began to do discussion sheets on most films (something of an obsession still, but with a website to give them a home) and something never finished. Paul Stenhouse published two series of these sheets (200 in each) in 1973 and 1975, mainly for school and group use. This is the moment to express appreciation to Phyl Coffey who began listening to my tapes of these sheets, transcribing them and offering all kinds of spelling and grammatical suggestions to make them clearer. The thing is that she began doing this in March 1976 and has been listening to my voice (no purgatory for Phyl after this decades-long marathon) and typing ever since. As you can see, 'thank you' seems inadequate for so much work and devotion.

In 1985 Melbourne's Catholics for Peace published another 70 on nuclear issues, *Nuclear Films* with an overview of the treatment of nuclear issues in films and added appendices by Joanna Macey on how to deal with terrifying films. The range, of popular films with nuclear themes is larger than we might immediately think. Already in the mid 1940s, some thrillers like *Cloak and Dagger* took up the issues. MGM produced *The Beginning or the End*, an early account of the development of the atomic bomb), and *Above and Beyond* on Paul Tibbett, the pilot of the Enola Gay which dropped the bomb on Hiroshima. In the 1950s there were many small-budget features, science-fiction or horror, like *The 27th Day*, which served as warning parables. The '60s offered direr warnings like *Failsafe* and *Seven Days in May*, satirical messages in *Doctor Strangelove or How I Learned to Stop Worrying and Love the Bomb* and the *Planet of the Apes* series. The late 1970s and early 1980s offered disaster films like *The China Syndrome* (1979) and those of ultimate destruction, the American *The Day After* and Australia's *One Night Stand*. Nuclear Films was launched, appropriately enough, on 6 August 1985, the 40th anniversary of the dropping of the atomic bomb on Hiroshima.

One other avenue of media education opened up in Melbourne and has offered experience and background for developing courses, the media itself, radio and television.

The Catholic Communications Office for the Archdiocese of Melbourne was an enterprising office, even when severely limited by financial support, personnel and even, at times, moral support. It flourished under the direction of Peter Thomas but was ultimately closed by Archbishop Pell in 1997. Their program *Sunday Magazine* had screened on Melbourne's Channel 7 on Sunday mornings since the earliest days of television in Australia. Channel 7 provided studio facilities and crew and the viewing time as its statutory time given for religious broadcasting. In 1988, Channel 7 offered a new programming, four 45 minute documentaries to be screened in prime time, Channel 7 offering production facilities and a director, a policy which continued until the closure of the Office. Channel 10 began filming *Mass for You at Home* in the 1970s. It continues 40 years later. Over the years, I was invited to discuss films, the Film Festival and to review. In the old days of technology we had to rely on using film stills and talk. Then came film clips.

The first time I was asked to be on a television panel was in Canberra 1970 when director Michael Wadleigh was promoting Woodstock. It was quite an event. Not the program, but the phone calls checking permission with Archbishop Cahill to go on the air. He said yes. In Melbourne it was easier being under the auspices of the Archdiocese being interviewed about *The Exorcist*.

One television experience might be worth a mention, first of all because it almost didn't happen. It was the time of the release of Zeffirelli's *Jesus of Nazareth* in theatres in 1978. I was invited to join Father Jim McLaren of 2UW and the Sydney Catholic Communications Office in presenting a program on the film, reviewing it and, best of all, interviewing Robert Powell. Unfortunately, he came during the TV crew's lunch-hour. They had them in those days and all work stopped! The Village Roadshow representative was getting anxious and wanted to call the interview off. I noticed Robert Powell gave a quiet signal that he should stay five minutes once work started again. He did. A gracious gesture that saved the program. The benefit was spending three quarters of an hour talking to him until the crew were ready.

Powell explained that *Jesus of Nazareth* had involved three years of his life: preparation, filming, promotion. He said that he had begun to interpret Zeffirelli's hope to show a humane Jesus by making him very human, portraying him almost as just one of the apostles. This did not work at all on film and so he went back to Zeffirelli's conception of Jesus, both divine and human. Zeffirelli used the art models of the centuries to visualise the Gospels. Jesus tends to become something of an icon, which helps the balance between his humanity and his being one with the Father. Powell also described the way he acted some of the sequences: over the months he built up a growing portrait: at first, at the baptism, somewhat remote, then warmer and, finally, to the Passion. I had found the recounting of the parable of the Prodigal Son a high spot. Zeffirelli, like the Gospel-writers themselves, transposed episodes and joined others. Here the parable is at Matthew's banquet with Peter outside listening and ultimately reconciled to Matthew. Powell did not learn the parable by heart. Rather, he wanted to tell the story as a story, from the heart, within this situation and content. With his fine diction, the sequence worked beautifully.

Powell found himself moved in portraying the Last Supper. As he conceived it, Jesus had had very busy days in preaching, healing, cleansing the temple, confronting the authorities. He was fatigued. He also knew that in order to achieve the meaning of his mission, he had to die. Judas, his friend, was the means to that death. In order to convey that tiredness and the need to be in communion with his father, Powell decided to play these scenes with his eyes closed. Jesus was to be fully conscious of what was happening, but he was to be in prayer to his father. Hence the impact of the Supper sequences. When the famous actors and actresses came for their scenes, Zeffirelli warned Powell that it might be intimidating. What actually happened was a greater benefit for his performance. Since, he said, so much cinema acting is reacting, the quality of a performance draws out quality response. Powell singled out Anne Bancroft as Mary Magdalene and explained that a lesser actress would not have brought such a profound response from Jesus. Powell said he was not a believer. He thought this was better for his performance, conscious as he was, that so many audiences had high expectations of what Jesus ought to be like on the screen. All in all, most audiences and critics agreed that he is possibly (even probably) the most successful portrayer of Jesus on the screen. And that is quite an achievement for anyone.

The Melbourne Catholic Communications Office thought that the three-minute weekly review would be suitable for the long-running program *The Catholic Hour*, on Sunday nights on 3AW. This started in mid-May 1973 with *Godspell*. The style changed over the years as the program developed: pre-recorded reviews, interviews, discussions about the film festivals, movie themes analysed over some weeks, live interviews, phone interviews. For a wider and more ecumenical appeal the program's title was changed to *Crossways* and the magazine format used from the early 1980s. This brief weekly film review covered a great many films over the years.

A friend pointed out an article by Anthony McAdam in the Melbourne *Herald* in September 1982, 'Nothing But The Truth?', which was a criticism of Costa-Gavras' film about Chile and political prisoners in 1973, *Missing*. After stating that almost all Australian reviewers 'have fallen all over the place in their haste to affirm their belief in the unquestioned integrity of the director and his work' and that Costa-Gavras' film is not based on documented incidents and fact as claimed, he added:

> One critic, a priest on 3AWs Sunday evening *Catholic Hour*, informed us that truth is a many-splendoured thing and that even if the film was not true in its particulars it was, nevertheless, give or take a few liberties, probably pretty close to The Truth. No doubt this was an example of how 'liberation theology' can liberate film criticism.

Had I actually said that 'truth is a many-splendoured thing', I should not have been allowed on *The Catholic Hour*! We sent a text of what I actually said to Mr McAdam, who himself often complained in print about being misquoted, but we received no reply. I think the point being made was a useful one, important for the poetic or dramatic licence that novels, plays and films take with historical events and characters:

> The difficulty in assessing this kind of film is that some audiences understanding 'true' to mean accurate in factual detail, while others understand it to mean that the issues raised and points made are valid, even if there is dramatic re-arranging and stylising of detail. (This is the kind of thinking, for instance, for biblical studies where the message is important and detail is designed to enhance this message). This means potential for endless controversy. Response to Costa-Gavras and his films has ranged from enthusiastic applause for a courageous man who has brought the abuses of political repressive regimes to the world's cinema audiences, to denunciation of him as an opportunist an unreliable ratbag.

Crossways on Sunday evenings ended in June 1987 and went to a journey-personal story -type hour on Friday night. However, a new device was used to continue the film reviews, a series of 30-second capsule comment used as radio spots during the week on 3AM programs.

When, in the 1980s, the Films and Values course was expanded to Church and Media, the experience at television and radio studios was invaluable. The hardest program, however, was an ABC discussion in 1975 with Phillip Adams. Perseverance and facts and figures were necessary as he tossed off his usual lines about the Cecil B. de Millestone around the neck of the Church and seeing *The Exorcist* at a cinema in Ireland where he was the only one in the audience barracking for the Devil! Perseverance and facts.

One of the most important results of this involvement with radio and television interviews is the realisation that one should say yes to requests on all areas of expertise. Be confident and courteous and answer the question asked and the interviewer then respects you and the interview becomes a conversation.

24. THE US, A BRIEF ENCOUNTER

WE ARE at 30 September, 1978. Pope Paul VI had died on 6 August after 15 years of leadership in turbulently changing times. His pleasant successor, Pope John Paul I, is only two days dead.

On 1 October 1978, I flew to Sydney from Melbourne to start a brief sabbatical. During 1978, there had been discussions about changing personnel at our two seminaries, Croydon and the Late Vocations Seminary at Kensington in Sydney. I was asked to go to teach at this latter, St. Paul's Seminary for older men training for the priesthood. It was a national seminary for all Australia. However, 24 hours later, Dennis Murphy, now the Provincial Superior, rang to say that it was too difficult to find a replacement for me in Melbourne. Would I stay? Yes, happily. He then suggested I plan some time away. The best period seemed to be the final weeks of classes for the year and the summer months. I would be back in mid-February to begin again. It was an unexpected sabbatical, most welcome – although I missed six weeks of classes, the only time I had missed any since beginning teaching in 1966 (perhaps a workaholic boast, tempered by someone's comment, 'more fool you'!).

As regards family story at this stage, there is little to say. The Malones by now seemed to be a conventional Australian family. There were some weddings and births with the cousins, some illnesses and deaths. There was an annulment as well as a divorce (the first that I was aware of in the family) and a re-marriage, which caused something of a shock at the time. But, overall, little startling. Dad continued to take care of the bowling green at Carrum and evangelising on behalf of lawn bowls as well as listening attentively, as I have mentioned earlier, to radio and television sports presenters and commentators and sending their verbal faux pas to Lawrence Money for his Boot in Mouth column in the Melbourne *Herald*. Philip finished eleven years teaching at Daramalan as well as studying, specialising in education and in Indonesian. He went to teach at St. John's College in Darwin. Aunty Sheila bought a unit not far from the family home. Not particularly startling.

Once on the plane from Sydney to San Francisco, I realised that once you make a move, it is easy enough to be detached and come to know that you are not indispensable. The Pope said that 'distance lends enchantment to the view', but distance enables you to see more objectively and assess what you have been doing. Whatever the limitations of personnel and situations, the seminary program we ran was effective for the time. If we erred, which we did, it was on the side of personalised training rather than on the imposition of regulations. We were trying to work with young men to help them make decisions that were adult and responsible. We wanted to counteract pressures and expectations. This means patience, staying with a man's growing, even when challenging him. It means being aware of stages of development, conflicts and crises of young adulthood as well as stages of faith development. Clearly, this is riskier than setting up requirements and standards of behaviour that many older members of religious orders wanted. Many were more comfortable with uniformity (and by conformity).

One of the major developments of the time was a 'discernment' process before students made their perpetual vows and before ordination to diaconate and priesthood. It meant honest prayer. It meant a weighing, before God, of reasons, motives for and against the step to be taken. With a director, the students would move towards a decision that they could stand by. Clearly, we do the best we can at the time and clearer discernment later means that we might change our decision. Many did. Or we can reaffirm the earlier discerned decision. Many do.

In the mid-1970s, we sent out our younger students on an experience year. Others, moving towards the end of their training years also went out 'into the field' for further experience, to parishes and schools and some to work in Japan. After ordination to diaconate, the deacons also went out for some months. There was talk at the time of Supervised Field

Education and of seminarians becoming involved in Clinical Pastoral Education programs, generally hospital-based. When I arrived in San Francisco, I found that American seminarians were required to take part in these programs which were not clerically supervised. Often religious sisters co-ordinated them and there were local lay support teams. If it was a goer in the U.S., then it would soon be part of Australian training, for better, for worse. This was certainly for the better. By the beginning of the 1980s, most seminaries had their students involved in field education. Clinical Pastoral Education programs went from strength to strength during the 1980s, in hospitals, in parishes, involving the whole range of students, men and women. Most churches supported these programs, which means ecumenical interaction as well.

As 1 look back, I think we were on the right track, but the constant watch of the Province and the criticism meant that we were often on the defensive about what we were doing. But we stayed with it. Frank Fletcher did my work while I was away. I was to return the compliment the following year when he went to complete his Doctorate in Toronto.

At this time, with the help of psychologist, Dorcas Mann, we discovered that for many the goal was to take vows or be ordained without thinking about the living of the vows for life or for being a priest – a bit like Muriel in *Muriel's Wedding* wanting to get married, to walk down that aisle, wearing the wedding dress and grinning to all and sundry that her marriage mission was being accomplished, rather than think about living a married life. We also were helped to become aware that good Catholic parents who were not putting any pressure on their sons to be priests nevertheless had a strong influence: what does a good Catholic boy do to please his parents? Become a priest. While we took the students through different stages of development, conflicts and crises of young adulthood as well as stages of faith development, many students opted not to continue. Which didn't go down well with many in the province and we were blamed.

So, 1 October. Get up in Melbourne, fly to Sydney, meeting about

Annals, take off for the U.S. at 3.00 pm. On the recommendation of friends, I was going to Berkeley for one term, a 'quarter' as they say. In the short time to get ready to go, I was not able to finalise a place to stay or an exact program of courses to follow. But, it seemed important to take the risk and try to manage when I arrived. Since that was a Sunday afternoon, I may have been more than a little presumptuous. But, as I was to discover during the coming months, Providence was more than kind. I was enrolled at the Franciscan School of Theological Studies, so there I went that afternoon of arrival. Fortunately, Kenan Osborne OFM, the director, was working in his office and suggested that I stay at the Franciscan provincial house in nearby Oakland until I found an apartment. I was pleased to have a conversation piece that my uncle was a Franciscan (to die three years later) and that we lived in a Franciscan parish in Sydney. I felt more at home when the Provincial, a genial man who became Minister General of the Franciscans, John Vaughn, had not only heard of the Missionaries of the Sacred Heart (we are not very numerous in the United States and mostly are in the East or Mid-West) but he had offered hospitality to fellow Australian MSC, Andy Howley, who had stayed on Franciscan Indian missions in New Mexico and Arizona during a Churchill Fellowship visit.

The courses were easy to arrange since I was staying only for the Fall Quarter. Time-tabling soon sorted out what was possible and what was not: a course in Christology, the theological study of Jesus, with Kenan Osborne, which was one of the most stimulating courses I have ever done; a study of the New Testament book of Revelation which I had never managed in detail; a course in spirituality of authors like Francis de Sales and, finally, a doctoral seminar I sat in on focusing on apocalyptic themes in American literature. It covered such authors as Kurt Vonegut, William Faulkner, John Barth and Flannery O'Connor, a novel a week. Attendance at lectures was not burdensome. There was plenty of time to read. There was no television in the apartment I lived in, so two months of distraction-free living there.

Berkeley is across the bay from San Francisco (under the bay in BART, the Bay Area Rapid Transit system). Berkeley is closer to Oakland. The University of California campus was well-known in the 1960s and early 1970s for its student unrest and protests. By 1978, it seemed quite sedate, many students moving around the large university area on skateboards. Jane Fonda spoke soon after I arrived, but it was in connection with social issues and voting and to introduce screenings of her films. It was hard to imagine how there had been uproar there 10 years earlier.

Up the hill from the university, in the quietly leafy suburban streets were the centres of the Graduate Theological Union. It was as if all the associate teaching institutions of the Melbourne College of Divinity were not scattered around Melbourne but in the one area with students and lecturers of all denominations (and of all religious orders) sharing courses and facilities.

I sat in on some of the sessions of the Introduction to Old Testament course for comparison's sake. The class size was similar to or a little smaller from what I had at YTU. The recommended textbook was the same as the one I used. The lecturer began with a quiz, which I did ... it all seemed familiar. It was obvious that the seminarians here were restless with dull lecturers just as they were at home. Sometimes, distance can lend over-estimation to the view (over-estimation of the U.S., that is). There was nothing to cringe about in what we had done in our work for the MCD.

However, one of the best things about Berkeley was the Sunday liturgy. Planned by the students under the direction of Jake Empereur SJ at the Jesuit-run Institute of Spirituality and Worship, it was alive, imaginative, involved the whole congregation and certainly showed how liturgy was not just individuals praying together but individuals becoming part of a group worshipping. Visuals, mime, creative combinations of Old and New Testament readings were exciting. The choir was led by two of the famous St. Louis Jesuit hymn-writers (whose hymns are still sung with enthusiasm), Dan Schutte and Roc O'Connor. A bit of the celebrity touch. Oakland Cathedral was also famous for its sound system and its involvement of a large Cathedral congregation – especially for the ordination to the diaconate of Schutte and O'Connor which I attended. While I didn't do a course in Liturgy, the Berkeley experience was something special to bring home.

Providence was best seen in my finding an apartment. Not knowing the lie of the land, I was expecting it to be difficult. But, as early as Tuesday morning, someone heard that I was looking, told me of an empty apartment nearby. A student from India had not turned up. Phone calls on Tuesday, looking it over on Wednesday, moving in on Thursday. It was, in fact, a block across the street from the main lecture rooms, a minute and a half from door to door! The rent was $5.00 a day, bedroom, bathroom, lounge room, kitchen – and furnished. It belonged to the Episcopalian seminary and the manager lent me crockery and cutlery. The only things I had to buy turned out to be blanket and sheets and coat-hangers (which I can still see if I turn round from this computer; cherished souvenirs of the first time I had lived by myself and fended for myself!). This meant two quiet months, doing things for myself, a chance for study and rest. Who could ask for anything more!

October-November 1978 were extraordinary months in the life of San Francisco.

Of course, it is a beautiful city. There is the bay, the bridges, the cable cars, and the hills with movie memories of *Bullitt*, *What's Up Doc* and *Foul Play*, which was showing at the time. There is the Episcopalian Grace Cathedral with surprising stained-glass windows of Pope John XXIII, Catholic Benedictine liturgist, Prosper Gueranger, and Jesuit Theologian, Karl Rahner. There is Fisherman's Wharf and the tour of Alcatraz. From Alcatraz, the city does not look too far away, but there is a lot of water and dangerous currents to cross. Memories of Al Capone and Burt Lancaster as the *Birdman of Alcatraz*. In late 1978, Don Siegel was filming *Escape from Alcatraz* with Clint Eastwood. Paramount had spent some millions giving the prison a face-lift and, as we toured, we saw several of the cells restored and made up for filming. South of the city is Daly City with its 'little boxes made of ticky-tack'. North is Marin County with the Muir Woods and the giant sequoias James Stewart and Kim Novak meditated on in Vertigo. And, Marin County was where George Lucas was working on his *Star Wars* series.

While there is a bit of nostalgia in writing this, I add that I re-visited briefly in 1989 but in 2010 I walked for a day around Berkeley (little change in the Graduate Theological Union area, still quiet and leafy) and around San Francisco with a trip on the Bay, to revel in memories.

However, there is a grim side to the American psycho as we well know, a violence that manifested itself in the expansion of the frontiers west and also seems to be inherent in American gangsterism and, later, the race riots and tensions in the big cities. October-November 1978 were the months of Middle East peace settlements presided over by President Jimmy Carter at Camp David. But, during the two months that I was there, San Francisco violence made world headlines. There was campaigning during October and voting in early November on civil issues in the state of California, including a proposition, 13, heavily discriminating against homosexuals in public positions, like teaching. There were vigorous, to say the least, campaigns on both sides. The Archbishop of San Francisco published material sympathetic to individual rights. The restrictive motion was lost.

In early November, the San Francisco supervisor, Dan White, shot and killed the mayor, George Moscone and the activist supervisor, Harvey Milk. This kind of violence was screenplay material, not what I was used to as reality. It produced a stunned emotional stop, disbelief followed by a shaky uncertainty. This became actual screenplay material with an Oscar-winning documentary by Rob Epstein in 1985, *The Life and Times of Harvey Milk*, then a television movie with Peter Coyote as Harvey Milk and Tim Daly as Dan White, *Execution of Justice* (1999) and, more recently and with greater oomph, *Milk* with Josh Brolin as White and an Oscar-winning performance by Sean Penn as Harvey Milk. Seeing

Milk brought back strong memories but it also fills in a great deal of background.

Then, as is shown at the end of *Milk*, 10 days later, there was worse. This was the Jonestown mass suicide. So many of the people at Jonestown and led to death by Jim Jones were originally from San Francisco. The senator who was shot there, Leo Ryan, was also from San Francisco. During those days, radio news and newspapers brought more and more detail of mass deaths that could scarcely be believed. You could not help picking up the strong emotions of the city, the bewilderment and the grief.

How to bring this journey to a lighter note from these more than sombre realities? The Pope.

On the morning of Monday, 16 October, I came back from some shopping down at the University co-op on Shattuck to find a friendly note on my door, the election of a Polish Pope. The note finished with the re-assurance that 'this is not a Polish joke'! Then we had over 26 years to test whether that was true or not. But, John Paul II will make some appearances later.

Being in San Francisco had quite some effect also on the cinema journey.

Already on the plane, I noticed that the print of *Capricorn One* had been cut, a sequence where astronaut, James Brolin, surviving in the desert eating some snake flesh and a pleasing scene tracking towards Brenda Vaccaro as a mother telling her child a fairy story. Cuts, to what purpose? With cinema at will, with huge choice for international travel these days, the censors do not have to get to work. But, in the 1990s, the birth of the calf scene in *City Slickers* was completely cut. And some mild expletives in *The Beverly Hillbillies* received frequent enough bleeps. What was considered unsuitable for the sensibilities of air passengers in the 20th century might make an interesting cultural study.

But, San Francisco was a place to catch up on films. The size of the

U.S. population meant a lot of cinemas and a large number of potential patrons. Besides the first release cinemas – and first release films have a huge media build-up – there were many cinemas, often older, seen-better-days buildings which showed double, even triple feature revivals of old and recent films. Many of them were in the Market Street area, drab in parts, where it would seem poorer and homeless people could pay the dollar or so to get into a warm and comfortable seat. The variety of films was large, some not yet available in Australia (including some of the revival run films). Prices were reasonable, especially the bargain matinees. It was a chance to see Elizabeth Taylor and Richard Burton in *Hammersmith Is Out* or Anthony Perkins in *Pretty Poison*.

I was able to keep up the *Annals* reviews as if I were still at home.

Of course, that was then, this is now. Most of the cinemas are gone. You see the equivalent films now in multiplexes, on cable and satellite channels, and they can (often should not) be downloaded.

Around the university in Berkeley, there were cinemas for students. This was where I saw Pasolini's *Salo*, wrote up my discussion material and was puzzled as to why it had been banned in Australia – but that issue comes up again when the ban was lifted in 1993, and then re-imposed some years later, and then the ban lifted again, still with controversy, in 2009.

Near the University of California campus was the Pacific Film Archive with regular programs. Three Dick Powell thrillers, Susan Hayward and Marlene Dietrich seasons. Cinema culture is strong in America, especially along the west coast.

I did have one strange experience. I decided to go by bus one evening to see John Carpenter's *Halloween*, which had just opened to much acclaim (but without the realisation that we were going to be treated to multiple murder horror movies plus *Friday 13th* and *Nightmare on Elm Street* sequels for years). It was screening in an Oakland cinema with *The Medusa Touch*, starring Richard Burton and Lee Remick. In Telegraph Street, a man got in the bus and sat next to me. The exchange of greetings meant that he recognised the accent was different. Despite all my manoeuvres and diplomacy and a growing apprehension about his story – living with his father, receiving charity handouts, little education, unemployed, wouldn't his father wonder where he was – he wanted to accompany me to where I was going. I was off to Halloween, escapees from mental institutions and knife slayings. He came, ate popcorn, watched the movies, stood at the deserted late-night bus stop with me, and finally got out quietly at his own bus stop in Berkeley. Perhaps I was too wary and suspicious. I know Halloween is far-fetched. But, it has just that edge of actuality in my memory.

I was able to share these experiences with the other Australians, priests and nuns, who were in Berkeley for that quarter, fourteen of us. That was important for my next cinema adventures.

One feature of looking at films in the United States which I did not anticipate but which presented itself was the pornography industry (seems mild now in retrospect). It soon became clear, looking at the newspaper advertisements, that the sex cinemas we had in Australia were not quite the same as those in the US. Should or should I not compare notes? It seemed a sensible enough idea in theory that I should if I were to say or write something worthwhile on the issues. But, in practice? I requested one of those nun-friends studying in Berkeley that, were I arrested or had a heart attack in one of those cinemas, she would let everyone know that I was on the apostolate!

With the 1970s discussions in Australia about the Restricted Certificate, we were dealing with soft-core, simulated or heavily cut, pornography. No matter how erotic or suggestive, the sequences were not hard-core, the real thing, so to speak. At first, there is the natural prurient, apprehensive curiosity. Then there is the disbelief that this material is being actually filmed and that I am sitting there watching it. Then there is the realisation of the absolute crassness and contrivance of what is being presented and that the criticisms of hedonism, exploitation, violence and degradation of women is right. And of men. Then there is the tedium of repetition, the artificiality of the plots, if there are any. Sometimes, there is the touch of send-up or jokiness but, by and large, the sampling I saw was, at least, ultra-earnest about sex. So much for our concern and campaigns about soft-core material when there was hard-core.

In Australia, the debates about what was to be allowed in were to come in the 1980s. And, in the meantime, the films became more sophisticated and used continually improving technology.

With the advent of video in the 1980s, the soft-core material seemed too slight for sex cinemas and so found its way to the new, at the time, video-shop shelves where adults could rent cassettes and parents and educators were rightly concerned about youngsters seeing it and how this would affect attitudes towards sexuality, especially some of the brutal material where women are raped and bashed. Bodies administering censorship had to exercise their skills on 'censorship as a necessary evil' to protect adult freedoms and to protect impressionable young people. It is easy to see how individuals and groups offended by this material become zealous for 'censorship as a necessary good'. The 'sex cinemas' then advertised hard-core material. For some time in the 1980s it was available (though not to be displayed) in video shops. But public opinion and pressure led to bans on this X-rated material. However, it remained available in the Northern Territory and the Australian Capital Territory (and, therefore, by mail). The spread of AIDS in the 1980s changed some of the behaviour in the hard core films. It became more cautious in its permissiveness, especially with the use of condoms. Campaigns against such material are often inevitably alarmist. This in no way condones the films, but it puts the alarm into proportion. As always, effort put into preventative education is far more effective in the long run.

In San Francisco, there were two kinds of pornography: heterosexual and homosexual. In the Mitchell Brothers cinema, one Wednesday evening in Berkeley, I counted only 15 people. You paid and went in. In the cinema screening homosexual films on Nob Hill, the procedure was more complex. It operated as a club and you had to sign in and receive a membership card. It was a Saturday evening, fairly crowded and, I then realised, a pick-up centre. I misread the information on the card as I went in (after resisting the temptation to write Dennis Murphy or Frank Fletcher instead of my own name) thinking that the management was offering to help patrons if they were bothered or hassled. Re-reading it afterwards, I found it said:

> We believe in an atmosphere of freedom for individuals. If you are harassed or restricted by any unwelcome police agents or entrappers please notify the management and we will provide legal representation for you at our expense.

I am glad that I went to see these films at the time. It gave me a more realistic picture of what was available when the video debate did come up and a realisation of what is available at a click or two on the internet.

To move to something a bit more edifying, though something which is not afraid of looking at the shadow side of human beings, the insights of Carl Jung on psychological type.

During the 1970s, especially with the influence of Frank Fletcher, we became more and more interested in what we read and heard about Jung. We started to remember our dreams and rely on Jung's indications of how we might interpret them (that every aspect of our dreams are facets of ourselves). We pored over Man and His Symbols and began to dip into Memories, Dreams and Reflections. I was fortunate in San Francisco in finding the C. G. Jung Institute and participate in several weekend seminars. John Sandford, who wrote interestingly on Jung and Christianity, books like *The Kingdom Within*, spoke at the Unitarian Church on his recent book, *Healing and Wholeness*, the first week I was there. The two seminars at the Institute were 'Satan and Psyche' on the imagery of evil and the possibilities of redemption (offered by a genial facilitator who claimed that he was one of the only 15 per cent of extraverted psychologists in the US) and 'Issues of Life, Love, Death in

Fairy Tales'. The material was, of course, fascinating and, though feeling rather amateur in knowledge of psychologies and mythologies, I was surprised how much Church history could contribute to the discussions, for instance, the story of Catherine of Siena, the young 14th century mystic, who was sent by the Florentines to urge the Pope to return from Avignon to Rome in 1378. She succeeded – not the expected role of a woman in a patriarchal society. Along with Joan of Arc, she made an impression as an Anima figure for the Jungians.

The linking of images and fairy tales with film plots was also fruitful for more understanding of how films work on our psyches. After all it was the year after the release of *Star Wars*. Joseph Campbell visited San Francisco and I was able to attend a day where he spoke on Jung and Mythology, the hero with a thousand faces, on the meanings of tarot cards, showed slides and spoke without a note.

The Boys from Brazil was in release at the time with Gregory Peck as concentration camp Dr. Josef Mengele being pursued by Nazi Hunter, Laurence Olivier. In this Ira Levin plot, Mengele was cloning Hitlers (the boys from Brazil), trying to play a Satanic creating god. Mengele was fearless and ruthless, except for hounds. The film's climax has him struggling, terrified of large, black, snarling dogs, a symbol of an arrogant man being savagely destroyed by his 'shadow'.

In an odd experience of synchronicity, I was asleep after a late night at the end of the 'Psyche and Satan' seminar, in a visitor's room in the basement of the De La Salle Brothers' community house. I suddenly woke about 3.00 am. I felt a weight on me. I looked. And looked. Staring at me, sitting on me was a black cat. I turned on the bedlamp. It was gone ... It had actually jumped on to the floor and scurried out by a high open window skylight. I was glad, after the odd surprise, that I was not as superstitious as the situation momentarily demanded.

The particular aspect of Jung's psychology that appealed to me was the personality indicator developed in the U.S., a practical application of Jungian theory, by Katharine Briggs and her daughter, Isabel Myers.

I was introduced to the Myers-Briggs theory and practice in Berkeley. The authors had spent many years improving their indicator (never a psychological 'test') and its questions and assessed the many results they acquired before publishing. It relates to Jung's understanding of the way that human beings function: their preferred way of perceiving reality, either by the five sense and by detail (sensing) or by hunches and noting possibilities, by a sixth sense, (intuitive); their preferred ways of coming to decisions, either by objective, logical processes (thinking) or by more subjective, values-oriented processes (feeling). It also determines whether one prefers to be energised by the world outside (extraversion) or the inner world (introversion) and whether one prefers decision-making or data-gathering.

What was attractive about the Myers-Briggs Type Indicator (MBTI) and its sixteen possible profiles is that it is not assessing the rights and wrongs of personality type. In fact, Isabel Myers titled her 1980 book after St. Paul's comment, *Gifts Differing*. It is also challenging, indicating ways in which we can move towards a more integrated, 'individuated', personality. Noel Davis introduced me to the MBTI, to the discovery that I identified with being an introverted intuitive who preferred making feeling decisions, INFJ (which became some of my favourite letters). Noel also introduced me to the Enneagram at the same time but I found that, on returning to Australia, the Myers-Briggs insights appealed the most and were most helpful in working with MSC students, offering them a helpful means of assessing their particular strengths and worth.

For more than 30 years, the MBTI has been essential and has taken me in several directions – in terms of prayer and spirituality, in working with groups and conflict resolution and, especially, though it did not occur to me at the time, in ways of appreciating films, screenplays and performance.

This will need a lot more consideration so I had better leave it until we get into the 1980s and 1990s and beyond.

25. THE WAY HOME

CAPITALISING on those round the world air tickets, I found that the journey home took a little longer time.

After classes finished, Mel Cotter and I went on a 7-day bus trip. An Ameripass cost $9.00 that year and you could travel as far as you liked for the week. Though we went through Nevada, amazed at Carson City being such a small capital, staying at Reno and Las Vegas, we merely did a quick tour of the casinos and their glitz. In fact, it was a good dose of reality staying with the Salvatorian priests in Reno. They ran a boarding school not unlike those we were used to. In Las Vegas, we stayed with the Franciscans who were part of the Diocesan Justice Committee for the diocese of Reno. Before we went on a quick late-night tour, we went to a local parish, mainly black parishioners, for an Advent Scripture Service in which one of the Franciscan students role-played John the Baptist and members of the congregation asked him 'What then must we do?' (Luke 3:10) after listening to his preaching of repentance. The examples very down to earth, many of them concerned with Las Vegas housing and rents and problems of family members working in the casinos. The Justice Committee certainly did not like the casinos and their lifestyle and talked about the number of dead buried in the desert. A different perspective to Las Vegas – a city which looks more pedestrian with the lights turned off and in broad daylight.

A few film memories. We went to the Grand Canyon and saw its magnificent vistas covered in snow. Afterwards in nearby Flagstaff, I remembered that this was where Glendon Swarthout's group of misfit boys travelled to free the buffalo in Bless the Beasts and Children.

If you line up for Greyhound buses, first come, first served. Gentlemen always, we stood back from the head of the queue in Flagstaff to let a group of New Zealand tourists travel together to Los

Angeles. There would be another bus soon. Soon was an hour and a half. But goodness is its own reward and we were put on a bus that was to go to Los Angeles via Phoenix. By the time we got to Phoenix, we had come down from snow to desert and the extraordinary Arizona mesas. But in early 1978 Clint Eastwood's *The Gauntlet* had been released. He had to bring a witness from Las Vegas to Phoenix by bus. However, he was being set up by the authorities. When he realised this, he let the passengers out and got together iron sheets and other metal to fortify the bus. He certainly needed it as State police and troopers fired arsenals of ammunition into the bus as he drove it determinedly through the streets of Phoenix right to City Hall. And here we were exactly in his bus-steps!

We missed Universal Studios in Hollywood: they were on winter timetables, but we used up all our tickets on rides at Disneyland which is worth going to once. Winter had the advantage as the queues were smaller. But, in Los Angeles, never in San Francisco, even walking the streets late, was I apprehensive about violence. No sooner were we out of the bus, than a taxi driver grabbed our bags and threw them into his boot to save taking black passengers who argued vehemently and loudly against him. And we were trapped in the situation with our bags locked up in the boot. Walking down some of the Skid Row-type streets, even at 6 p.m., was scary. And then to find that the Franciscan Brother who answered the door where we were staying had been bashed brutally on the front doorstep less than an hour before we arrived. Later another Franciscan, this time in New York was upset at the bad name American cities have for violence and said they were safe as long as you kept in the light and walked confidently. I found this true in New York City. I think I terrified a man in front of me one night around midnight. He could hear my footsteps and seemed nervous until I overtook him. There were plenty of taxi-drivers on the streets – but one of them might have been Robert de Niro's Travis Bickle and ask 'are you looking at me!'

The United States is a land of reality and fantasy. Non-Americans seem to know so much about it because of the images that we have grown up with. It is difficult not to be caught up in the images rather than in the reality.

The United States is also a generally friendly place. The 'Have a good day' and 'Take care' greetings and smiles are appreciated but, when they are the same two months later, you realise that it is part of the style, not necessarily a heartfelt thing.

Berkeley was welcoming and so were the many communities in which I stayed, one of the benefits of a universal Church and of religious orders all over the world. The De La Salle Brothers were particularly generous in their hospitality, especially in New Orleans where you took a limousine from the airport rather than a bus. The driver was friendly indeed, Bill Hanes. I was his only passenger except for a flight attendant who needed, if I didn't mind, a lift home. Of course not. We sped off in the opposite direction from the city into the Bayous. The attendant was grateful for the lift and brought us out a can of Coke each when we got her home. Back towards the city. Guarded and anonymous answers to Bill's enthusiastic chatter and questions until he got out of me not only that I was going to the Boulevard St. Charles, but to the Christian Brothers' School. Naturally, he has gone to school there. I had wanted to ring to make sure my letter requesting a room had arrived and that it was all right to come. Instead, Bill would have nothing less than limousine to the door, his ringing the doorbell and announcing 'Father Malone from Australia'. The Brothers were great hosts. My letter arrived the next day!

I don't know if New Orleans is a small place but I was momentarily disconcerted two days later when, wandering around the city, I heard my name called. It was Bill again. No matter how sinister New Orleans looks in Tightrope, No Mercy and, especially, Angel Heart, voodoo and all, to me it is a friendly place.

Appreciating, the range of nationalities in the United States is another challenge and, especially, Spanish as a second language. Staying at the diocesan seminary in Denver, the city of the *The Unsinkable Molly Brown*, let alone the westerns, I found myself there for the feast of Our Lady of

Guadelupe, mariachi players at Mass and all. As far north as Denver, the buses had notices in both English and Spanish.

Mass was celebrated in both languages, the meal was Mexican and a group of Mariachi musicians played and sang. Christmas was at Youngstown, Ohio, a steel city that looked very much like the settings of *The Deer Hunter*. I was told that the first shopping mall was built there, so I celebrated by seeing *Superman: the Movie*! Actually, Christmas Eve was by myself in Buffalo. Bus travel from Youngstown to Cleveland to Buffalo to see Niagara Falls, which ice and icicles down the side. The bus back to Cleveland did not leave till 5.00 am I found a church, asked the parish priest whether it was alright for me to celebrate Mass. After some hesitation, he agreed. The hot Australian summer never seemed so far away as at Midnight Mass in the snow in Buffalo. (A week later I was able to see *A Chorus Line* and enjoy the cynical remark of one of the characters: 'Suicide is redundant in Buffalo'.) It was only after arriving in England on New Year's Day 1979 and going to the Mass at Westminster Cathedral and hearing the precise but rotund English vowels that I realised, how much I had become used to being in the United States in such a short time.

The other highlight of the sabbatical was a visit to Israel. Since I had been teaching the Old Testament for over 10 years, it seemed a reasonable thing to do when in the vicinity. I was fortunate to be able to travel with Paul Stenhouse who had been completed a doctorate in Semitic Languages and Literature and was acting as secretary to Jim Cuskelly, Superior General, at the time. Paul Stenhouse knew the Middle East well. We were able to visit Athens and Istanbul on the way. From Athens we made the Greek mythology tourist trip (Thebes and Delphi) and the New Testament trip to Corinth (with Mycenae and historical centres as well) . Ancient History studies and Greek made a comeback . However, it was a new awareness to stand on the ruins of old Corinth, inland. It seemed a very small area for an ancient city. And then there was the surprise of the mountain rising sharply at the back, the legendary mountain where Sisyphus rolled the stone up the slope and it continued to fall down again, and again. Athens also seemed to be crowded with Americans, all employees, allegedly, of the Bell Telephone Company who had just been ousted from Iran on the eve of the Revolution of 1979.

We were to have much more contact with St. Paul territory than we expected. The Sabena flight from Brussels, was snowed in so we decided to go by bus from Athens to Istanbul. While we were delayed and so missed the opportunity to visit Ismir and the sight of Ephesus, I had a small experience of hostilities that stays in the memory. We travelled all night and through Salonika, finding ourselves at the Greek-Turkish border, about 9 o'clock in the morning. The Greek bus does not go through to Istanbul nor the Turkish bus to Athens. Passengers change buses at the border. There were only 10 of us and the border guards kept us there three hours. They played baseball on the deserted road. They emptied the belongings of the Greeks going into Turkey out on to the bitumen. They left the visitors' cases. There we were in the middle of Macedonia, seemingly nowhere and unable to do a thing, stranded at the whim of the Greek soldiers. When they finally let us get into the Turkish bus, the Turkish soldiers, guns and all, seemed far friendlier. However, at Istanbul airport, we had local security check, Israel's own El Al Airlines check, a final check when we were in the plane. At the Greek border, we could think of St. Paul writing to the Philippians. At the Istanbul airport, I became conscious that it was only two months since I had seen Midnight Express. With respect to the Turks, I should say that we went on a ferry up the Bosphorus one afternoon. Passengers could buy drinks of tea or coffee served in quite delicate glass cups on glass saucers. When you finished, you left the cups for stewards to collect. My thoughts went to Manly ferries and wondering whether some Sydney passengers would have left fragile glass or taken the opportunity to have a literally smashing time.

It certainly was an experience to visit Israel, to be aware of the recent history as well as of the past, to think of 1948, to think of 1967 arid realise that the De La Salle College on the wall where we stayed was almost in No Man's Land. One heard stories of aggressive Israelis as well as of prejudice. One heard stories of Palestinians arrested and disappearing in the night. Bombs went off while we were there. On a visit to Galilee we were stopped at 10 road blocks – and I was blamed. Having economised on haircuts while away and since hair and beards were longer in those days, they thought that if anyone looked like a terrorist, it was me! At the Lebanese border, we had to stop 50 metres away and just look over, unable to go across. Sitting by the Sea of Galilee on a warm winter's afternoon, we listened to the Gospel reading of Jesus cooking for the apostles as they came in from fishing. The sea was smooth and hazy. The trawler out on the lake was silhouetted how the sea and the boats might have looked like this 2000 years ago. Then the Israeli observer jets screamed overhead and it was 1979 again.

Old Jerusalem is evocative of memories and one prays at the shrines. Christians believe incarnation was here and have reverenced and fought over the sites for centuries. The Franciscans, custodians of the shrines in the Holy Land, do excellent work keeping churches and sites open and in good order for pilgrims and tourists. There are stalls, donkeys and merchandise in the narrow streets of the old city. Walking round the wall, we found an Armenian church door opening suddenly and people pouring out, almost on top of us: a funeral (like Naim?). But, of course, there are also the clergy, clinking and clunking their bags, collecting money at Golgotha and Jacob's Well and the armed soldiers wandering the streets.

We did the usual things but memories of the scratchy bits of grass on stony Shepherd's Field gave new images to Bethlehem and nice crib statues. The colours and dryness of the Judaean mountains and desert are magnificent, right down to Jericho, past Qumran to Masada and the Dead Sea. We were taken out on extraordinarily rough and stony roads to Mas Saba and to a Greek Orthodox monastery for recalcitrant monks, perched in the desert: over ravines going down to the Dead Sea. The coast was different, suburban Jaffa and Tel Aviv (we were there on the Sabbath and it was closed) to the ruins at Caesarea, up past Haifa and

Mt. Carmel to the Crusader memories at Acco. Even in 1979, it was too dangerous to go from Nablos and Jacob's Well out to the site of the old capital of Samaria. I wondered what was Mary doing travelling from Nazareth to Ain-Karim in those days!

A cinematic sidelight of the visits to these countries was to notice cinemas and what was on. A day in Geneva had great variety: a visit to the Calvin Memories in the morning, a trip of 50 kilometres back into France to Annecy to visit the St. Francis de Sales memories, then back in Geneva at McDonalds, with its plaque proclaiming that, this was the first European McDonalds, opened in 1976 and then to *Jaws II* in English with French and German subtitles. That was winter. Summer 2009 offered an opportunity to re-visit the same places in reverse order. The bright sunshine now in Annecy (and discovering that the crowd in the bus were off to Annecy because that day it was a stage in the Tour de France), the evening, cooler, darkening memories of Calvinist austerity.

I'd been to theatres in England in the 1960s, but in the 1970s you were searched before going into a morning session of *The 39 Steps*. The searching was even more telling in Israel. We went to see that very enjoyable Goldie Hawn-Chevy Chase comedy, Foul Play, in Jerusalem (which had no lack of Hollywood films screening). The cinema was closed after each session. Bomb detectors were used throughout the auditorium. When all was clear, the doors were unlocked and the searched patrons went in. There was no trouble in Rome, although it was a strange feeling to attend an ordinary session in a cinema, something I had not done during the four years of study there. The dubbing was still excellent, except for Walter Matthau's more articulate and smooth Italian voice in *House Calls*. In Athens, we appropriately saw *Escape to Athena* but also saw *Avalanche* and a martial arts epic in what must have been Athens' answer to the Sydney Capitol with food smells and cigarettes mingling with the disinfectant. Istanbul had no ads for western films as far as I could see which meant that landing at Lod airport and Tel Aviv seemed like arriving back in the United States

However, I have never seen so many advertisements for films as in Bombay. They were everywhere, especially on railway stations. India produces hundreds of features for local consumption each year and they seemed to be very popular (understatement). An Indian Christian Brother tried to get us some tickets to see an Indian musical Shalimar (with Rex Harrison also in the cast) so that we would have a local experience, but the advertisement we read in the paper, '8th House-Filled Week', proved to be too true. I am not sure how exhibition works in India, but the papers were reviewing the 1974 Sidney Poitier-Michael Caine adventure, *The Wilby Conspiracy* and the biggest hoarding I saw was in Pakistan, in Lahore, for Grace Kelly and Ray Milland in Hitchcock's *Dial M For Murder*, made 26 years earlier. The film reviews were also taking dim views of sex scenes and permissiveness which may have accounted for many English-speaking films of the time not being released.

A short visit to India was a sobering experience. Just to see so many people in the one place is astounding enough for an Australian, but the rows and rows of iron shanty sheds and the beggars means that we are very comfortable at home even when we think we are not. And this was Bombay, not Calcutta. Also, the cricket was on and I've never seen so many people with transistors to their ears going about their business. The schoolboys at the Christian Brothers' College seemed to think I was an Australian cricketer.

The other aspect of India and of Malaysia and Singapore or any Asian country is the religious atmosphere of Hinduism, Buddhism and Islam. Christianity is seen in a different perspective when it is a minority religion compared with the other world religions. Christians always run the risk of sinful presumption and need the exposure to other ways of religious experience, other myths and rituals, other religious temples and art. Australians acknowledge a 'fair go' but have an inbuilt automatic intolerance .

And back at Tullamarine on 16 February 1979 and life resumed as normal.

26. NEW JOBS

RELIGIOUS orders seemed steadier at the end of the decade than many observers might have thought in 1970. Our Irish MSC confrere, Diarmuid O'Murchu, has written on religious orders and their crises and has used the phrase 'the dynamics of demise'. This phrase was particularly apt for the 1980s. It may not have been a demise unto death, but religious orders have had to face the fact that they are no longer the large and flourishing organisations which played key roles in particular apostolates in the Church. Salesian Frank Moloney looked to the scriptural titles, disciples and prophets, as a way of describing smaller groups of men and women inspired by the Gospel charism of the founder of their congregation.

Candidates hoping to be priests or brothers joined us during the 1980s. However, most of them did not stay very long. Some were inspired by the MSC vision but found it was not for them. Others were looking for a refuge and religious congregations cannot be refuges. Of the 26 who joined us from 1981-84, only three remain. Brothers and priests continued to make their decisions to leave, some who had been ordained for a long time. Patrick Dodson, the first aboriginal ordained, also decided to leave the priesthood and the MSCs. An excellent and articulate student, he became a strong spokesman for the Northern Territory Central Land Council and a respected elder. Do religious orders have sufficient regard for the individuals who join them, for their heritage, needs, aspirations? Experience seems to indicate that congregations have set up norms and traditions too inflexibly and that individuals have been unable to stay. Or is this the nature of s religious order in the Church? Surely not.

There was a change of administration and leadership for us in 1980 with veteran missionary from Papua-New Guinea and Japan (over 30 years), Frank Quirk becoming Provincial. There was a reconsideration of Formation and decisions made for a tightening and a toughening of the Formation program, the elimination of the Experience Year and a greater trust in older methods of seclusion, prayerfulness and discipline in the Novitiate year. Personnel were to be changed. Older men were put in positions of leadership and training. Our era was over!

By the mid-1980s a decision was made to close Croydon as the MSC seminary and move the student group to Sydney A block of units was bought at Drummoyne, a western suburb along the Parramatta River, and redesigned as the seminary, called Navarre House after a celebrated 19th century French MSC Bishop who pioneered work in Papua New Guinea. The Missionaries of the Sacred Heart withdrew from the YTU of which they had been original members and went to the Theological Union at Hunter's Hill, part of the recently established Sydney College of Divinity. Comment was made that this was an act of 'nimble morality'. The concentration of MSCs in Sydney was seen as an advantage for morale. (This was the mistake I thought the Province should not have made but had to develop an attitude of allowing a mistake).

Back in 1979-80, however, we were still battling on. It was a busy and interesting time with the usual excitement and crises that you are amazed you lived through. One day in November 1979, we had to send an older priest to hospital with severe kidney trouble, another was quite unwell, phone calls to make arrangements, classes, students with worries and an afternoon game of squash for exercise and enjoyment. Whether I was too slow or misjudged, my opponent's racquet came smashing down on my glasses and the glass went straight into my left eye. Perhaps the Malones have a stoic tradition, but it seemed the right thing to take charge, keep my eyes shut to prevent further damage from the glass, be led up to the house and arrange for someone to take me to the Maroondah Hospital. Providence again. It was a Tuesday, the day Dr. Stasiuk, the visiting eye specialist came to Maroondah. Within two hours the glass was out and stitches in for 10 weeks and an eye patch for the duration. One of the realistically daunting thoughts that came as I walked up from the squash court was that I could lose the eye. In fact the glass went deep but did not cut anything essential. The unworthy thought was that the previous night I had reviewed some films. Surely God would not let *Kiss Meets the Phantom of the Park* be the last film I saw with two eyes! It wasn't, but it might have been. And plastic lenses since! (There were then two months of literally one-eyed reviews and a celebration of Midnight Mass wearing dark glasses.)

Occasionally problems arose with films reviewed and the suitability of comment or recommendation. One that led to some correspondence at the time was John Landis's *An American Werewolf in London*. A student at a leading Catholic secondary school wrote to complain that he went to see it because of my review but found that 'the blasphemy and bad language and sex scenes made me sick'. (He mentioned that his mother was typing his letter; sounded like her comments more than his.) Another reader sent the *Catholic Weekly* review which concluded: 'This sick film is popular which makes one wonder what jaded young audiences need now for their laughs/thrills.' The film had an 'M' Certificate For Mature Audiences (15 and over). I thought it a clever but very pessimistic film that works on more levels than the spoof horror of its surface. In Auckland in 1987, I was taken with a statement in the foyer of the Odeon in Queen Street. It was painted on a large poster-size hoarding and the ticket-seller said that it had been there for years. It reads:

> A plea for the art of a motion picture. We do not fear censorship for we have no wish to offend with improprieties or obscenities, but we do demand, as a right, the liberty to show the dark side of wrong that we may illuminate the light side of virtue the same liberty that is conceded to the art of the written word that art to which we owe the Bible and the words of Shakespeare.

At the end of 1981 the style of the *Annals* reviews changed. For the next three years we had a page with about 10 films listed, a 20-word thumbnail review with the censor's rating and a face in various stages of grimace to grin indicating a rating system. The bald-headed gentleman of the faces bore no resemblance to the reviewer! An aside: I don't approve of rating systems and stars; it is quite arbitrary and offers readers a lazy shortcut in selecting what to see without really finding out something worthwhile about the film; the language and word-choices of the review should be what makes an impact. In 1984 we reverted to the original style of long or short reviews according to the interest in the films. The only relief was that the face ratings were replaced by individuals or groups on seats ratings in 1986.

A sign of the growing interest in films and thematic and religious insights was an invitation to go to Canberra to speak to a Christian forum of Australian National University students and staff at St. Mark's Library on Australian cultural themes. The topics were Images of Religion in Australian Films and The Theological Implications of *Gallipoli*, its use of the dying and rising themes for an interpretation of Australian history and for myth-making. I was trying to link Theology and Story with our Australian film stories.

In case you are not interested in (or weary of) stories of polarisation in the Catholic Church, what follows is one of these – minor, perhaps, in the greater scheme of things, but one of mine.

By this stage, Paul Stenhouse had come back from Rome, acting as secretary to the Superior General and completing his doctorate on Samaritan Literature and had resumed editorship of the *Annals*. While he was away, Geoff Baumgartner was editor, working from Melbourne with the help of his wife, Carmel. I had the MSC liaison role. By 1977 when Geoff took over, there was a great deal of catechetical material coming into Australia from overseas as well as that produced locally. Photocopiers had begun to increase and multiply. The *Supplement*, as designed by Paul, had had a life of 10 years. It was time to change. 1977 was a transition year. We contracted a different author for each month to prepare material on a theme related to the religious education guidelines of different dioceses and to write a feature article to accompany the *Supplement*. During 1977 a particular catechetical need was noticed: background for Scripture courses. So, in 1978-79, we produced 18

Supplements covering the Old Testament and the New, written by several authors, including Rabbi John Levi, well-illustrated and with bibliography and suggested activities. It met the need, was a great success and gave *Annals* some motivational impetus. What to do when we finished the Scripture course? The next area of need seemed to be that of morality. Great idea – but it ended in disaster.

We outlined and advertised a two year plan for 1980-81. I will spoil the ending by saying that we were able to produce only three of the Morality *Supplements* before the Provincial, Dennis Murphy, decided to stop them. We were alerted because some letters from Monsignor Kevin Toomey of Melbourne had been sent on from Bishops expressing concern about the proposed *Supplements* and the hope that they would take note of the recent Vatican *Declaration on Sexual Ethics*. We were busy with *Annals* at Croydon (and I had the use of one eye) but the preparation of the material was, admittedly, hurried, although we had some experience in preparing the catechetical material. Although he made a careful decision not to continue as a Missionary of the Sacred Heart and was to teach at a Christian Brothers school in Sydney, David Hodges undertook the co-ordination of the material. MSC still appeared after his name on the *Supplements*. For some backing we asked Dr. John Hill, then Chaplain of St. John's College at the University of Sydney, counsellor Father Dan Winters SM and moral theologian Brian Johnston CSsR to check the material before it went to the printers. They were listed on the front page as 'Consulting Committee'. The first issue asked out general question, 'What is the basis of Christian Morality?' The focus was on commitment, commitment in relationships. The first topic was commitment to self. There was material on conscience much of it through story and case study and reliance on educators who taught development through moral stages.

Some teachers found it useful and proceeded to use the material. But some individuals under the banner of 'Concerned about Religious Education' wrote letters complaining to the Provincial. So did some

Missionaries of the Sacred Heart. The material was criticised as being subjective, not adhering to the teaching authority of the Church. But it also seems to have touched nerves because so much of the criticism was not so much academic as emotional and denunciatory. These readers were not merely disagreeing, they were offended. And they felt offended on behalf of the Church. Some schools cancelled subscriptions on the advice of their chaplains. The second issue came out on friendship and commitment but the damage seems. Monsignor Toomey was a great friend of Fr. Harry Jordan who supplied him with information and the matter went to the Papal Nuncio in Canberra who noted to the Superior General and Provincial when they visited him that '*Annals* has fallen from its pedestal'.

What to do, persevere or terminate? Dennis Murphy had a meeting with Geoff Baumgartner and myself at Croydon, looking at the next issue which was on loneliness and the feeling of rejection and included a section on masturbation. We decided to hold the sending out of this April *Annals*. It must have been one of the few times that the *Annals* had been sent out early. Subscribers, in fact, already had it. So, there are copies out there for assessment. I wish someone would write a religious education essay or thesis on catechetics in this era so that I could see some more objective evaluation of the material and of what happened.

Dennis Murphy made the difficult decision to stop the *Supplements* and the whole Moral program at once. I have to say that I found this very difficult. We had a large number of subscribers and people who wanted to use the material. Dennis saw the situation as a fresh beginning for the *Annals*. Difficult phone calls had to be made. It is very hard to be an intermediary in these cases, trying to explain both sides. The May issue had a long letter from the Provincial to subscribers taking the responsibility for the decision to end the *Supplements*: 'I have asked the editors of *Annals* to end the series of Catechetical *Supplements*. This is my own initiative and I take full responsibility for it. I am grateful for the efforts the editors have put into what is an extremely difficult and delicate task. I appreciate also their generous co-operation in the final decision.

When last year I encouraged them to take on this series, I underestimated the technical difficulties and unfair conditions under which contributors, consultors and editors would work in order to meet deadlines. There has not been time for sufficient revision and correction. I feel that this pressure of work has been largely responsible for a regrettable unevenness of material, inadequate coverage of important doctrinal matters and even some errors. None of this has done justice to our readers or to the good standard of most of the articles. I apologise for that.'

Re-reading the letter now, it seems a model of politeness, acknowledgement of good done and an exercise of leadership responsibility.

There was reference to this, not always accurately and rather unjustly in Michael Gilchrist's *Rome or the Bush*, published in 1986 prior to the visit of John Paul II to Australia, a traditionalist critique of the shortcomings of the Australian Church. It appeared at the same time as Paul Collin's look at the Church from the opposite point of view, *Mixed Blessings*. The two became media celebrity sparring partners! Gilchrist states: 'There was to be a special focus on sexual matters with such enticing topics as 'Discovery of Myself, Masturbation', 'Commitment to the Same Sex: Homosexuality', 'Contraception', 'Abortion', 'Divorce and Remarriage' and 'Prostitution'.'

This lifting is out of context – and needs that distinction between what is presented and how it is presented. Gilchrist capitalises the words 'Discovery of Myself: Masturbation' and isolates them whereas they were a part of a larger description of a theme. This overall theme was 'Loneliness and the feeling of rejection'. 'Contraception' comes under a heading, 'Reproduction' and a sub-heading 'Conception'. 'Abortion' is one heading of three, the other two, 'Being a Parent' and 'Child-care'. 'Prostitution.' is under the heading of 'The Erosion of Commitment.' The tone of some of those who wrote in 1980 can be gauged from

Michael Gilchrist's quotation from a letter by Monsignor Toomey to the Secretary of the Australian Episcopal Conference: 'The main writers of this trash are seminarians, some very young ones, and it's an insult to a pastoral priest to have these puppets putting up case histories that, in my opinion, could never, or scarcely ever, be verified in real life. It's a lie! Because I love the church, I plead put an end to this rubbish before it puts an end to us.' *Rome or the Bush* then says that the MSC seminarian responsible for the 'Discovery of Myself: Masturbation' feature left the seminary soon after the intervention of Father Murphy ... 'This is not true. Gilchrist then takes a quotation from Ruth Carter Stapleton, which had been set with headings and discussion questions and cites it as if it were written by the 'young seminarians'.

The 1980s saw some polarising of the Catholic Church in Australia and some vigorous, few-holds-barred polemics on the part of allegedly orthodox groupings of Catholics. Dennis Murphy said in his letter: 'I am not against free debate, but I am for a high level of debate in which there is an adequate understanding of the issues involved, and also of the background of the views expressed, which at times is more important than the views themselves.'

Whatever the shortcomings of the *Supplements* (and these were acknowledged), the tone of the attacks did not indicate high level of debate or understanding. Dennis Murphy also said in the same letter: 'An improved presentation or this subject in *Annals* could have worked towards a more peaceful consensus, because practical areas of agreement are quite marked. As it is, I fear its presentation, plus some unguarded language, will foster divisiveness and unpleasantness. I hope my fears about this are exaggerated.' Unfortunately, we had to close the Melbourne office of the *Annals* in 1981 for economic reasons and Paul Stenhouse took over again from, Geoff Baumgartner, turning the magazine into *Annals Australia: a Journal of Catholic Culture*. It reached its centenary of publication in 1989.

There were two areas of development during this period. The first was in Media Education, the other in more personal education, prayer and Spiritual Direction.

The Films and Values course at YTU and the seminars at places like Assumption Institute and the National Pastoral Institute continued into the 1980s, small numbers doing the courses but increasing. They were soon to receive a boost.

During 1981, the Victorian Council of Churches set up a Media Committee with representatives from most of the churches in Victoria. Peter Thomas, who worked at this time for the Australian Christian Television Association, chaired the meetings and invited me to join the committee. The range of topics discussed was as wide as the media, particular interest being taken in the treatment of religious issues by the newspapers and in the new technologies, especially satellites and the possible introduction of Cable TV into Australia. An important meeting was that at *The Age* building with the associate editors of Melbourne's three principle newspapers, *The Age*, *The Sun News-Pictorial* and *The Herald*. The newspapermen shattered any illusions we may have had about public interest in some of the issues the churches thought important. We were advised to consider how our stories interested the population at large, what angles would catch public attention. Parish pump stories, nice events and people, overseas guests, even celebrities, needed some kind of public focus before they could be considered newsworthy. One of the spin-offs of this visit was the Victorian Council of Churches commissioning one of our MSC seminarians, Bill Rimmer to examine *The Age* and *The Sun* for three months and catalogue the items that related to religion: reports, stories, articles and features, editorials, letters (with Australian content as well as overseas). His work was so thorough and clearly-ordered that Rimmer was asked to continue looking at each paper for another six months. His final report was published in booklet form by the Council. It illustrated that religion and the churches received more attention than had been anticipated and more fairly than expected. This was especially true of *The Age* which tended to focus on news and issues.

The Sun preferred news and personal stories. By contrast, the Melbourne Herald had little religious reporting or stories.

Another question was taken up by the Victorian Council of Churches Committee, that of media education in the Melbourne theological colleges. A survey of handbooks was done. One institute had a Preaching-Communications course. YTU had Films and Values. The main word on the report was the three-letter word, Nil. It seemed the right moment to expand the YTU courses to cover basic aspects of social communication and press, radio, television as well as cinema.

It would be a pleasure to write that Peter Thomas and I planned the course, submitted it to YTU and the Bachelor of Theology Board of the Melbourne College of Divinity and that they approved it. It was not so simple. YTU presented the course outline and requirements but Media, while taken for granted as part of our everyday lives, was not taken for granted as an area that merited religious reflection and critical theological attention. The Board at first insisted that students study almost a year's courses in Systematic Theology and Scripture as pre-requisites for Church and Media. There was no such requirement for students beginning Pastoral Counselling or even such a crucial area as Moral Theology. After representation and correspondence, the pre-requisites were withdrawn and the course accredited. We were able to set up a program where students could take the course over a year or even longer, do general introduction to media and specialise in one or two areas and be assessed by written and practical work.

The course still looks good on paper but it attracted only a modest number of students through the years. Lip service and praise are given to its inclusion in a Theology degree course. But, perhaps, we all prefer to listen and watch rather than critically appreciate.

It seems a great pity when people become anxious about the effects of television or video and want to make snap judgments and prohibitions or ask for quick recommendations rather than spend time and energy on preventative education. However, Church and Media received a new lease of life later at the National Pastoral Institute where we were able to set up a diploma.

Not sure whether that sounded like preaching or a whinge or both!

The other area of development was that of spirituality. Traditional patterns of prayer received great jolts in the aftermath of Vatican II. The changing from Latin as the language of the Liturgy was the most notable. Congregations who had remained generally silent were now invited to participate, to listen to their own language for scripture and prayers, speak out in prayer, to sing, to move, a great deal of energy that went into popular devotions and private prayers was now to be channeled into the Eucharist and the Sacraments. The 'God is dead' movement of the mid-1960s reflected much of the pain that Christians were experiencing as traditional values were questioned, ridiculed, got rid of. Instead of an 'other-world' or 'after-life' focus, we were to look at the world in which we lived, discern the signs of the times and see God in our world. Our spirituality was to be horizontal (unity of human beings) rather than vertical (between God and us). But in the late 1960s the tendency was to be a Christian workaholic.

A reaction soon set in, a realisation that peace, quiet and contemplation, even in the middle of busyness and struggle, was needed for the human spirit. The 1970s saw the spread of Jesus movements, prayer groups using shared prayer, the lively charismatic renewal. Individuals became interested in their spiritual journeys, their inner lives, their autobiographical faith. Links between traditional Christian ways of praying and Eastern techniques were found and practised. The personally directed retreat was taken up, especially by members of religious orders. Programs of personal and group renewal were set up. Large empty buildings belonging to religious orders were no longer ecclesiastical white elephants, but became prayer and retreat centres. Secondary students were more accepting of retreats and camps. There had been quite a change from 1965 to 1975.

This movement continued and led to a rediscovery of the variety of spiritualities in the Church's tradition and the need for training of spiritual guides with an ability to help people discern rather than impose directions. The developments in counselling and therapy were meeting the spiritualities.

Some of these elements came together for us in 1981-82 when the President of the Yarra Theological Union, Redemptorist Tony Kelly, proposed that YTU take advantage of the great variety of Catholic traditions represented by the different religious orders in Melbourne and establish a centre for the study of spiritualities. He asked Brian Gallagher to conduct a feasibility study. At a Faculty meeting in July 1982, the Centre was voted down and lapsed until Frank Quirk took it up and decided impetuously that, if YTU would not sponsor it, the MSCs would. YTU would be connected by the accreditation of some material done at the Centre, spiritual direction courses and seminars which would be the core of a Diploma in Spirituality Studies. The day was saved. It was to be a new beginning for the MSCs and, as it turned out, for Brian and myself.

Brian Gallagher had done Clinical Pastoral Education work and training in spiritual direction in Boston in the mid-1970s. He was able to set up a program in Sydney in 1979 for a group of spiritual directors to learn by reflection, interaction, practice and supervision, more about religious experience, prayer and discernment so that they could be better and more effective spiritual guides. They would also have accreditation rather than be simply putting up their shingle (as some individuals were doing at the time) and proclaiming themselves spiritual directors. Brian called the course 'Siloam' from John's Gospel story at the pool of Siloam where the man born blind went and washed at Jesus' bidding and then could see.

When Brian became Superior and Director of Students at Croydon in 1980, Siloam moved with him. It seemed a good idea, because of the work with the seminarians, for me to do the course that year. It was very demanding. It is not always easy to give of yourself, but that was what was required. If you are to direct others, you must be willing to go through the same processes yourself. We listened and learnt, interacted, spoke honestly, felt bruised and hurt at times and tried to be perceptive about ourselves, our capacity for listening attentively to others and our wisdom in offering advice. I used the *Annals Supplement* crisis for reflection. Actually, looking at how Siloam has developed and continues, our part-time course seems elementary in retrospect.

27. NEW HOUSE AND …

NEW HOUSE! Had I been asked in, say, 1970 where I thought I would be living in 1984, I would have answered that I would be living in an MSC house, in an MSC community. That proved true, of course, but not in the way that I would have ever imagined.

By 1983, I was finishing work in formation at Croydon. The Mystery of Christ course was winding down at YTU. It was time for change. Already the establishment of the Heart of Life Centre and the backing of the Province indicated a new direction. The new centre opened in February 1983 on the ground floor of a former boys' orphanage at Surrey Hills, not far from Box Hill, owned by the Sisters of St. Joseph who used much of the building for student-nuns' accommodation. Brian Gallagher set up the rooms available to us to offer a welcoming atmosphere and avoid the impression of a large, somewhat unwieldy and dark building (which it was). But we had seminar space, lounge, reading room, offices, kitchen and the use of the community chapel. It did look institutional as you entered but we tried to avoid an institutionalised atmosphere.

The 1983 Siloam group formed the core of activity there. But a growing number of people came for personal guidance in prayer. We began seminars with groups of 15 or more on topics related to spiritual experience and growth with an emphasis on experience and reflection rather than the study of spirituality: The Experience of Conversion, The Human Experience of God, The Person of Jesus, Discipleship. Many religious sisters came in the first year. There were a number of lay people who, we hoped, would find the Centre of particular help. We began workshops on local spirituality, that is, a spirituality with an Australian flavour, and entitled them 'Discovering an Australian Spirituality'. Since Brian Gallagher had investigated the feasibility of the Centre, he was in the best position to manage it. He set it going with a particularly personalised 'heart' style.

It seemed a sensible idea to live nearer to the Centre if possible, rather than commute every day from Croydon. Croydon is about 20 kilometres from Surrey Hills. What about the possibility of a small group living in a suburban house in the Surrey Hills area? Living by themselves and managing by themselves? Doing the shopping, cooking, cleaning themselves? The idea sounded attractive in theory, a different way of living MSC community, living near but away from the work and not relying on housekeepers. Obviously, many members of religious congregations live in small groups and fend for themselves but the Missionaries of the Sacred Heart have tended to live in larger communities and have a combination of brothers and priests.

We received the all-clear. To find a house. Providence seemed manifestly on our side, not only in our finding the orphanage suitable for the Centre but in being offered a house for rent by the Dominican Sisters. It is who you know. Siena College in East Camberwell owned some old houses in Hocknell Street at the back of the school. They were ultimately intended for demolition to make more room for the very limited play areas. A. small community of sisters had been living in one of the houses but were moving out to other houses. Would we be interested? Yes.

The sisters were more than generous, leaving a lot of basics in the house, beds, crockery and cutlery, refrigerator. Not being an expert in house-setting-up nor having a flair for eyeing bargains at St. Vincent de Paul stores and second-hand shops, I learnt a lot in early 1984 accompanying Brian on expeditions that led to the simple, inexpensive and effective furnishing of the house. We moved in at the end of January and began three years of living in a small suburban street until the house was listed for demolition. Providence still being on our side, we were able to move quickly round the corner to another house we could rent from the College. Then providence lapsed. Though the sisters said we could stay until whenever, whenever was up by the end of the year. Temporary living for eight months came to a happy ending when the Province bought a house in Kew (some more furnishing expeditions) and we have lived there ever since. The reason for Kew is that in 1986, the Heart of Life Centre moved to the old home of the Family Care Sisters in Canterbury where we remained for seventeen years. After some years at Wantirna, Heart of Life found a comfortable home in the rather new house vacated by the Discalced Carmelites in the grounds of the Franciscan property in Box Hill, the site of YTU.

We had had a number of visitors to share our company (or who wondered where we had disappeared to) over the first three years, the catch being that visitors had to sleep on a sofa on the floor outside my room, one of those extras tacked onto the back of the house. The new house had a visitor's room and we could welcome more people and we still had the sofa for an extra.

Needless to say, it was a great change for me, living in a small house with our own timetable and pace and supporting ourselves, but I felt the need to say it. I had barely cooked before this, but having to do it, I found that what seemed exotic mysteries turning up tantalisingly on plates could be achieved by a middle-aged amateur. I was very careful at first about how long to steam each kind of vegetable but intuition is often impatient with accuracy (sometimes rightly)! And basic meals do not always require recipe precision. I'm glad to say the repertoire keeps expanding, not least with jams and pickles (fig, lemon and plum trees in the garden). Jams are easy to make, I discovered, but since most people do not make them, they inspire a certain awe and over-estimation of cooking abilities.

The signs of the times for active, rather than contemplative, orders in the Church seem to indicate something of this kind of more basic, simplified living. In many countries this has always been the case and solidarity with the poor has taken it for granted. But it has not been the case in middle-class Australia. It has been a sensible move for us and an appreciation of the pressures on households to keep going on daily routines of budgeting, cooking, cleaning. Supermarket specials are a way of life. But I still belong to the Abracadabra School of Wishful Thinking about instant house-cleaning. One of the benefits of living in the house, apart from the visitors, is in getting to know not merely how others function but how they tick.

Obviously, not everyone is geared towards this kind of close living. After Michael Morwood, who was the other member of our initial trio, went to Boston to study, one of our Indonesian MSCs joined us to do the Siloam Course in 1986, Tarcis Wigneosomarto. It was well worthwhile for us (and I hope for him) to have a man from such a different culture sharing our kind of life – and to sensitise us to other ways of diet. After a month Tarcis told us he was hungry for rice. Later visits to Asia made me realise I could be hungry for bread. In the latter part of the year, Makino, our first ordained Japanese MSC priest also came to live with us for three months, to experience Australian life and to do some studies. We had become an international centre.

I remember that at the end of the 1960s when there was a lot of talk in religious orders about moving out of big institutions and institutional buildings in order to live a more simple life and give a different kind of witness to people in the living of religious vows, that some wanted to move into smaller houses and groups. During the '70s, members of women's congregations did this far more readily than the men. The effect has been to give me a different view of how religious groups might continue when their numbers are in such decline.

But one of the reasons we were able to make the move to Canterbury was that the Centre was to become economically self-sufficient so that we could pay our rent and our bills. And I was offered a job that also the helped pay bills. It was at the National Pastoral Institute (NPI) where I had been teaching some Theology, Scripture and Media courses since it opened in 1973. During 1983, the director, Rosemary Crumlin, whom I had known in *Annals Supplement* days of the late 1960s and who had been at NPI since its opening, was looking for a priest to come on to the staff full-time. She asked me, amongst others, if I knew someone who fitted the job description. After some days, it occurred to me that, with the work I had been doing in seminaries and teaching and being used to working in a team, I fitted the description well enough. It was thinkable that I move to NPI. Was it possible? During the two or three months that it took to negotiate the change, it sometimes seemed not. One of the biggest questions was that of MSCs working 'outside' the traditional institutions. Someone expressed the apprehension that I would be 'lost to the Province'. By September, the decision was made that I go to work at NPI, while still doing some courses at YTU and continuing to do workshops at the Heart of Life Centre. I don't know whether Frank Quirk felt bad about getting us old brigade out of formation, but the thought he ought to do something good for me, 'the right thing for the wrong reason' as T. S. Eliot wrote in *Murder in the Cathedral*.

So, by February 1984, I had a new job and lived in a different kind of community. As I think back, it was a very easy transition to a fresh mid-life beginning while being able to capitalise on the past.

One of the most significant features of Australian society in the 1970s and '80s was the boom in adult education. Courses proliferated. The number of women returning to studies increased. Men and women changed jobs and went for retraining. There was ongoing retraining, in-service work, an ever-increasing number of talks, workshops, seminars. Retired and ageing people found new interests and took on activity and hobby programs. Tertiary education used to refer to universities. Now it assumed an enormous variety. It was exactly the same in the churches. The development of the theological colleges in most of the capitals and the large lay enrolment highlighted this. The predominant number of lay teachers on Catholic school staffs was another example. Australian dioceses in 1987 introduced a program of faith discussion-sharing, 'Renew', that was aimed at the widest parish population. So much of the future of the Church had to be in the field of adult education.

Working full-time at the NPI put me in touch with this even more effectively than the work at YTU. The students at NPI come from all over Australia and some from overseas. They were not working towards a theology degree. Many already had such degrees or went on to pursue them after their year at NPI. At first, the work at NPI focused on religious education, not just primary or secondary school religious education, but religious education in its broadest understanding. However, it is true to say that during the 1970s, the majority of students at NPI worked in classrooms.

By the end of the 1970s, with the growing awareness of the role of lay people in ministry, including parishes, NPI established, a new Diploma for Pastoral Associates with particular emphasis on ministry in hospitals and parishes. After all, the charter of NPI from the Australian Bishops Conference was for the Institute to respond to pastoral needs, as its title declared. This brought a new group of students with different backgrounds as well as many teachers who felt that they had given as much as they could to Catholic education and needed to move to other fields and required training.

In discussing my possible contribution to NPI, it emerged that social communications needed to be presented as a substantial part of the course. What emerged was a Diploma in Social Communications which included study of intra-personal communication, where students could focus on personal developmental work, inter-personal communication, where students could focus on personal developmental work, like skills in interaction, counselling, and in social communications, small media and mass media. The work that Peter Thomas and I had done now found a new home and support.

We had been able to develop some 'Meeting the Media' days for groups to understand press kits, radio and television interview techniques. Significant and satisfying for us (and touristically pleasant) was a request to work with a group of Catholics involved in religious broadcasting in the Cook Islands. Sister Elizabeth Russell studied at NPI, in 1986 and arranged for us to go to Rarotonga. The 25 on the course were more than enthusiastic and produced programs using interviews, voice-overs, dramatisations, music that they had not so far been able to do. They continued to meet and plan and critique their programs. Since the seminar started at 4.00 pm each day (officially, but realistically in Pacific Time we were lucky to get going by 4.30), we had the opportunity to see the beauty of volcanic mountains as well as lagoon and reef where this most welcoming of people live.

A feature of NPI was the invitation to a number of international visitors sponsored by the Institute. They have religious education experts like Herman Lombaerts from Louvain, Belgium, Virgil Elizondo from Mexico, Maria Harris from the United States. American youth Ministry expert, Michael Warren, has visited twice. In the International Year of Peace, Jesuit activist Daniel Berrigan came for 10 days and conducted two scriptural retreat weekends. Despite some active protest from Melbourne's 'concerned Catholic' groups, Dan Berrigan made a memorable impression on all who met him. He was consistent, a man of conviction and courage and humorous plainness. Even Derryn Hinch and Terry Lane came out from their studios to the foyers to meet him before taking him in for interviews. I think he had a strong influence on us. (I like to think I had some influence on him. He went to see and *Crocodile Dundee*, which he enjoyed, and later wrote that he had taken a dying Jesuit confrere in New York to see it to give him an outing and a laugh!)

The distinctive quality of NPI was its belief in processes of adult learning. The staff believed in a distinctive style of education that respected the giftedness and wisdom of its adult students. The learning climate was important, one in which adults knew that they are respected, accepted and supported. This meant a student-staff interaction where staff contribute their expertise but were also learners. Adult learning meant students taking responsibility for their programs, contracting appropriate time-commitment, course-involvement and the pursuing of personal goals. These could include self-initiated and self-directed learning. Paolo Freire was a kind of patron saint of policy! It meant self-understanding and faith-sharing.

Students usually came from busy and organised work-places and it took time and energy to slow down and re-assess goals. The more workaholic the student, the more difficult the start and willingness to shift the education paradigm. However, NPI relied on processes that are enabling, empowering students to evaluate where they have come from and the baggage they bring and to express more personally the goals they want to pursue. While NPI has a program of course offerings, not everything could be followed done. Students had to choose. Again, assessment was more personalised, incorporating academic skills rather than having these predominate. Special studies, log-keeping were preferred for assessment.

I had always been impressed with NPI, even if sometimes puzzled as I came from a more obviously structured theological college. But my experience of working with MSC students put me on the NPI wavelength. I had always had a respect for Monsignor John Kelly, the first Director of NPI (despite his capacity for deeply sardonic observations), who allowed this kind of institute of adult learning to prosper, and for Jim Briglia, of the Archdiocese of Melbourne, the second Director. Working with Rosemary Crumlin, however, was a significant experience, watching her patience in staying with tense situations as students gave up their obsession with clear directives and discovered their more personal agenda. An artist, with a delight in symbols, Rosemary operated 'obliquely' at the unexpected angle and the creative tangent. She had a shrewd ability for assessment and challenge. And not only for the students. I certainly learnt a great deal from working with her (forcing, in the best possible way, me to move outside myself and comfort zones) and with such a wide range of men and women during those years.

Michael Gilchrist again! Opening his sequel to *Rome or the Bush*, called (with the same perspectives as before) *New Church or True Church*, I discovered a 13-page 'in-depth examination' of NPI. The examination was done without the benefit of interviews with the staff, a visit to the Institute, or even correspondence with us. The sources were handouts for different courses, looked at out of the context of the courses themselves, and discussions with some 'recent NPI, students'. Staff were named, but the sources were kept anonymous not a particularly rigorous historical method. As with the previous book, statements from articles or handouts were used to ridicule and condemn stances. Rosemary Crumlin and Sonia Wagner, the new director, received this treatment. Gilchrist drew the conclusion that NPI, saw itself as an agent for 'Newchurch' changes and cited liturgies, international visitors like Benedictine, Joan Chittister, and Daniel Berrigan and the notice board with its pro-Marxist advertisements as indicators of this. I was also surprised to find that in a parenthesis about the NPI, and its staff, the author quoted some recent students as saying that a 'relative exception' to this were some of the courses handled by Father Peter Malone MSC and Father David Timbs CSsR, though our courses had been named on previous pages as suspect. The style of the critique is cleveristic-caustic and the evidence is 'hearsay'. Needless to say, NPI was not the only Church institution criticised.

A high point was a pilgrimage in April 1988 to the centre of Australia, a way of celebrating the Bicentenary of white settlement by visiting Uluru. It's quite a way. Through the Murray River area, the Flinders Ranges, Coober Pedy (with Mass in the underground Church), Alice Springs. Best to go from Alice Springs to Uluru by road to experience the vastness and the distance. Best, also, as the aborigines advised, not to climb to the top (like scurrying ants so the aborigines thought) but to walk around the base, contemplation rather than rush, thinking of the biblical parallels of desert, clifts of the rock, the water pools. In the centre of Australia is an invitation to pause, reflect and experience a sense of the sacred.

Sad days at the end of 1988 with the closure of NPI, not because of the criticisms as many assumed. A sad ceremony of closure, tying yellow ribbons and tears with songs from *Les Misérables*. The way was being paved for ACU, the Australian Catholic University. The staff was interviewed in 1987 by Brother Ambrose Payne who was to be the first head of ACU. I had an affirmation moment with him, then ... He told me that my courses were not quite mainstream in style. 'But authorities prefer things in the mainstream!'

28. CHRIST-FIGURES

ON A PERSONAL note, Dad enjoyed these years in Hocknell Street and at NPI, visiting the house and the Centre, with plenty of advice on vegetable growing as well as supplying plants. He enjoyed the company of the NPI staff at lunch and kept assuring me how lucky I was to work with such an agreeable group.

Whether it was the perspective of change in my life or whether it was so in reality, I think the MSCs received a freshening boost at this period. The early 1980s had been quiet, cautious, an attempt at steadying as well as re-organising formation. Perhaps it was the 1980s reaction after the unpredictability of the 1970s.

At the Provincial Chapter of 1983, there was an attempt to reform-ulate priorities in our sense of mission. This was preceded by a marvellous exercise where we took time for the more than 50 men there to have their individual say for five minutes on how each saw the 'Spirituality of the Heart'. There was a consensus that Jules Chevalier's charism was one of gospel joy, the good news of God's love for all human beings and how this was made clear in the person of Jesus Christ and 'the desires of his heart' that met 'the desires of the human heart'. The time of writing, re-writing and editing Constitutions was over. With a more heightened consciousness, the Chapter affirmed its commitment to work with aboriginal peoples that we had been engaged in, successfully and unsuccessfully, in the Northern Territory since 1906. This was the top priority. There was also a request that at least two Australians go to India since there were men there interested in becoming MSCs. In fact, the Indian region developed rapidly.

It took more than a year for something tangible to happen about the work with aborigines. The first phase was a retreat to be held in Sydney with the title 'Listen to the Voices'. Invitations were sent to a number of aboriginal people, tribal aborigines from the Northern Territory, urban aborigines from all over Australia, men and women from north Queensland, western New South Wales, the Centre and Sydney. Those who worked full-time or part-time, whether they were diocesan chaplains, members of religious orders or lay missionaries were invited. So were all MSCs. An objection was validly made that it was a case of white people inviting aborigines to a white site. However, it seemed best to go ahead, with the proposal to have the retreat at Kensington. I am glad that I was able to go.

There were over 100 men and women attending. TAA was on strike at the time so the contingent from the Northern Territory was unable to come. Stories were told, often very movingly, especially by the grandmother-figures who gave personal accounts of oppression and separation of families, harsh treatment on missions, heroic survival. Authoritative aborigines spoke on justice issues, education, the challenges to the churches. We listened, prayed, discussed and stayed together for eight days. I am not too sure what emerged, how it affected us as a Province, what practical changes and developments have occurred in the Northern Territory as a result. But, in terms of being there, listening and learning, it was an important event of 1984.

Six months later, the MSCs were celebrating 100 years of presence and ministry in Australia. How would this be done? Not a big cathedral Mass and elaborate dinner. (But the big Mass did eventuate). Not just a spiritual spectacular but something of worth to offer the Church in Australia from the MSCs. The agreed-on idea was a 'Congress' to be held in the main capitals and open to everyone. We had a particular interest in it in our house. Brian Gallagher was to be the organiser. And organisation it took, but even that was a sign of great vitality. The motto for the Congress was taken from a 1900 statement of Jules Chevalier, 'A New Heart for a New World'.

'The Word, coming from the Heart of his Father, made the world emerge from nothing; and from the Heart or the Incarnate Lord, pierced on Calvary, I see a new world emerging, the world of those he has chosen.

And this creation, so fertile, full of grandeur and inspired by love and mercy is the Church, the mystical body or Christ, which makes this new creation present on Earth until the end of time.'

It was taken up by the Superior General and used for other MSC meetings throughout the world.

The principal overseas guest for the Congress was noted English author, US-based, Rosemary Haughton, whose books on many subjects included family, the meaning of stories and 'The Catholic Thing' have enthused many readers. One of the reasons for the invitation was her book on the love of God, The Passionate God. Unstinting, she spoke in all the centres where the Congress was held, including four days in Sydney at the University of New South Wales and a weekend in Melbourne. There were shorter sessions in Brisbane, Canberra, Hobart and Adelaide. An MSC Bishop, Joseph Lescrauwert from Holland, who had written extensively on Heart Spirituality over the years and had been a member of the Vatican's International Group of Theologians, came for the Sydney sessions. There were many local speakers, not confined to Missionaries of the Sacred Heart, giving papers, chairing sessions, responding to keynote addresses, sitting on panels, leading workshops in Sydney and Melbourne. Several hundred people participated in each centre. It gave quite some warmth to a cold July. (I do remember Les Murray's talk, reminiscing about visiting his Catholic relatives and wondering why they had a picture of Jesus with a strawberry on his chest in the hallway!)

Unfortunately, Rosemary Haughton was also subject to the Melbourne Catholic protesters. They attacked her views on the Church, declaring that she would start a new church. They caricatured her views on family as if she were determinedly trying to destroy the traditional family.

Again, it is hard to gauge what effect such a Congress has on people but the papers were published in tape and book form, *A New Heart for a New World*, and it is still spoken of with happy memories. Congresses were in the air in 1985. To round off the Centenary Year, as many MSC as possible were invited to come for five days in December to

Kensington for a first Assembly of the Province. Over 200 were there. It was a morale-booster just being present. However, there were speakers and a facilitator but, more importantly, group sessions where everyone had the opportunity to speak, a chance to speak of hurts and pain as well as joy and fulfilment. Everyone could speak as honestly as they liked, and many did, a chance to communicate and assess what had happened to us in our religious lives. Again, the effect?

One of the most significant experiences for most MSCs was the illness and death of Harvey Edmiston. Harvey had been the first Pre-Novitiate Director in 1969-70 and had then had the influential position of Novice Master over 10 years. A friendly man of principle, he commanded the respect of almost everyone in the Province as well as many members of religious orders around the country. He was almost elected Provincial in 1980 but cancer had been detected in his face and he had had some operations. Made Deputy Provincial by Frank Quirk in 1981, he spent five years doing an extraordinary job as a personnel man, helping men in crises, smoothing out diplomatically administrative tangles (or mopping up after Frank Quirk's gung-ho action), full of bright ideas and initiatives. But he continued to have operations, chemotherapy and increasing disfigurement of his face. He kept going until three months before his death, facing pain and personal discomfort, dying on 31 January 1986. The first phone call we received at the new Canterbury venue for Heart of Life, the day we were moving in, was to let us know he had died. Harvey showed us how to live with illness and how to die. The cancer was detected when he was 47. He died aged 52. But he had a significant life.

Film reviewing in *Annals* continued but by 1984, the video had become a significant feature of home entertainment and the video shops were appearing and disappearing as owners tried to get in on a good thing.

It seemed useful to offer some kind of response to films available on video, some kind of guide to families who may remember the advertising for a film but can't remember whether it is suitable for home viewing. The Editor of Melbourne's Catholic weekly newspaper, *The Advocate*, offered me space for a weekly Video Column. The series was launched in May 1984. The format used was an introduction of about 150 words to give a setting to the selection of titles; family films, comedies, westerns, R-certificate and themes like police dramas, mysteries, biblical epics, nuclear issues... Each week 10 titles were commented on in the 20-word capsule fashion. They soon mounted up (and finally found a shortlived place in *The Australian Video Guide* in 1991).

Early in 1985, The Australian Catholic Truth Society published a booklet of 31 of these columns with the helpful title, *Video at Home*. It seemed to be helpful, apparently in country areas where there were few cinemas, limited television stations and video was relied on much more for entertainment. I did get one letter earlier in the piece from a couple who took exception to my noting of some swearing in comedies and exhorting me:

> Sin is sin. We cannot bend what constitutes it around and not call it by its proper name. Swearing is a sin if done deliberately. The breaking down of its various aspects as you write in your letter, each of these is also sinful. The difficulty is the fact that because people do it, many people do it, it becomes accepted, not to do it makes people alien, unwanted. Unfortunately today, many people in the world do not want to know about sin. But the Catholic has to know and he needs to be taught and reminded. And you have to do the telling, Father.

Later that year, 1 was surprised to receive a letter from the official Family Life Committee of the diocese of Wagga. The committee had intended to recommend *Video at Home* for parents' use, but 'Several members of the committee were of the opinion that the booklet failed to make what we consider a 'Christian judgment' on the films reviewed. We consider that there is a real need for a booklet of reviews to which parents may refer quickly in selecting suitable video films for their families to watch and that your booklet was inadequate in this respect.'

Examples cited included *Kramer vs. Kramer*, considered excellent but has 'one nude bedroom scene of which parents should be aware' and Bruce Beresford's *Puberty Blues* which parents would not permit teenagers to watch 'in a fit'.

Unfortunately, the group had looked only at the film titles and the capsule comment for quick reference rather than read the material in the introductory section which, in the case of the films objected to, did have a brief explanation of traditional Catholic ways of evaluating moral worth. Again, it is the panic reaction instead of work done towards healthy preventative education. Apparently not everyone was persuaded of the validity of these arguments. That same month, the Board of Sydney's *Catholic Weekly* decided not to continue reprinting the Video Column from *The Advocate*. A Board member considered the comments too liberal for *Catholic Weekly*.

An interesting and different opportunity to check the reliability of reviews carne in 1984 when Ivan Hutchinson, an exemplary Catholic, host of movies on Melbourne's HSV7, asked me to write in his place while he was on holidays, reviews for the Melbourne daily *Sun News Pictorial*. Each week there were three reviews required, about 300 words each. Writing for a Catholic audience tends to draw on one's Catholic presuppositions and language. I was pleasantly surprised how I could write for the *Sun* readership from the sane presuppositions, although in plainer language and in shorter paragraphs. I noted that the sub-editing was efficient and kept the sense of what I submitted. Space was always a criterion. It was the period *The Karate Kid*, *The Natural*, *Splash* and of half a dozen of 1984's best Australian films which it was a pleasure to review. Some quotations even appeared on the advertisements, 'A film that can be recommended to the widest audience, Melbourne *Sun*' (for Silver City).

In fact, I was able to do another four weeks, 1985 in Ivan's absence. This was the time of Woody Allen's delightful *Purple Rose of Cairo*. There was a bit of a buzz when I noticed that Village were advertising it in the papers with the usual snippets of reviews and saw 'The word for Woody Allen's latest film is delightful, Peter Malone, *The Sun*'!

The developments in theology and story in those years led to looking more closely at films, their plots, characters and their meanings. One of the most fascinating features is the Christ-figure, the character who resembles Jesus Christ significantly and substantially and is portrayed in the pattern of the Jesus Christ of the Gospels.

For believers, there is little difficulty in recognising these patterns. For the person who does not believe in the Christian claims about Jesus, the Christian mysteries have become universal metaphors, used constantly in Western culture and the arts. The resemblance has to be significant. Not everyone tossing off a sign of the cross or using the name of Christ as an expletive is a Christ-figure. The resemblance has to be substantial for its impact. One of the arresting ways in which the Christian legacy is frequently used is in newspaper cartoons. The reporting of the 1983 election capitalised on Australians' knowledge and appreciation of these Christian references with Bob Hawke the Messiah. (John Howard opted for Lazarus in his autobiography, *Lazarus Rising*). Even in the 1987 campaign when the Prime Minister came across Sydney Harbour to the Opera House by boat, some still said that he came this way in order to avoid getting the soles of his shoes wet!

In Christian understanding, Jesus Christ has been perceived as a redeemer and as a saviour. The representation of Jesus himself, the 'Jesus-figure' has been as that tortured, suffering man who lays down his life for others or as a triumphant risen leader to a new life. Sometimes these Jesus-figures are meant to be 'realistic'. But, the history of Christian art has always relocated the figure of Jesus in contemporary locations and styles and has usually nationalised him with a Western look rather than keeping his Jewish appearance. In films, even the much-praised austere Jesus of Pier Paolo Pasolini's *Gospel According to St. Matthew* is a western Mediterranean man rather than an eastern Mediterranean man. Franco Zeffirelli has probably made the best attempt to portray a 'realistic' Jesus but *Jesus of Nazareth* is certainly not a naturalistic portrait.

Artists from the catacomb painters to Georges Rouault, composers from Bach to Andrew Lloyd Webber have been far more successful in presenting a stylised Jesus-figure in images and sound. The stylised Jesus-figure appeals to our imaginations.

This means that the Christ-figures in films can be seen as redeemers and saviours. Often the redeemers are martyrs, like Billy Budd or prisoners, from Joan of Arc to contemporary victims, or are like Job who is the innocent sufferer, someone like Alfred Hitchcock's The Wrong Man.

There is greater variety in the savior-figures. Legendary heroes and heroines cone to mind, but since 1977 with the coming of *Star Wars*, the pop legends have become the best-known saviour figures, including Luke Skywalker, Superman, E.T. and Mad Max. Robert Short, who has written books of religious insight using the wisdom of Charles Schultz's Peanuts strips, has also written imaginatively of these films and the updating of the legends and genres of chivalry, quests and heroes, The Gospel from Outer Space and its universal message. Short, tongue-in-cheek, wonders whether Luke Skywalker is not 'the Gospel according to (creator George) Lucas'! Still tongue-in-cheek, someone wondered whether, after the O.T. and the N.T., E.T. might be the 'Extra Testament'! In the post *Star Wars* decades, audiences expect the Christ parallels. Think *The Lord of the Rings* trilogy, *Hobbit* films, the *Narnia* films and *Avatar*.

There are many kinds of saviour-figures. There is the mad figure, like Peter O'Toole in *The Ruling Class* as an insane English peer who thinks he is Christ but is cured and becomes Jack the Ripper; there are good and evil strangers like Clint Eastwood's character in *High Plains Drifter* who comes mysteriously out of the haze into a western town by a lake. He saves the poor and helpless, paints the town red (literally) and puts a notice 'Hell' outside and sets it alight one night. He stands there in the middle of the flames, a demonic Christ-figure. There are variations on this in his *Outlaw Josey Wales* and *Pale Rider*.

Of course, there are the saints' biographies, plenty of clergy and nuns and, in fact, plenty of angels over the decade.

One of the questions that always comes up is that of the women who are Christ-figures. Men have predominated in films but there always have been the feminine Christ-figures, obvious ones like many a Greer Garson character or Ingrid Bergman in *The Inn of the Sixth Happiness*. One of the most striking feminine Christ-figures is Harriet Andersen as Agnes in Ingmar Bergman's *Cries and Whispers*. She suffers and dies from illness, attended by her two sisters, one imperious, one sensuously lazy, both self-centred, and by a devoted maid. Her death scene is horribly moving. The minister prays for Agnes in explicit redeemer-figure language. Agnes (like Agnes of God?) reminds us of the sacrificial victim, the Latin *Agnus Dei*, 'the Lamb of God'.

Two striking Christ-figures which were very popular are found in *The Mission* with the two Jesuits played by Jeremy Irons (the peacemaker) and Robert de Niro (the warrior). There are liberation Christ-figures.

But it is not only the Christ-figures who are present on our screens. There are the anti-Christ figures as well. Not only in the incarnations of the Divine, but the incarnation of evil. These figures have proliferated since the 1960s (the era of 'The Death of God') beginning with *Rosemary's Baby*, moving to possession stories like *The Exorcist*, then all kinds of variations of incarnate evil in humans (*The Omen*), in nature (*Jaws*), in houses (*The Amityville Horror*) and in technology, like Stephen King's diabolical car (*Christine*). There are Lucifers like Sting in *Dune* and *Brimstone and Treacle*. There are the legendary symbols of evil, Dracula, Zombies and the Living Dead. There is the mysterious malevolence that grips individuals and groups like Hitler and his Third Reich or the Corleones and the Mafia of *The Godfather*. There is also the malevolence in seemingly ordinary human beings which is more realistically anti-Christ than the powerful symbols. Shakespeare dramatised this in Iago.

1987 brought two striking Christ-figures which were very popular: *The Mission* with the two Jesuits played by Jeremy Irons (the peacemaker) and Robert de Niro (the warrior) as well as the version of Umberto Eco's *The Name of the Rose*.

Someone wanted to call this exploration Reel Redeemers or Celluloid Saviours. Eventually it was published as *Movie Christs and Antichrists*.

29. STATESIDES, MANY

WITH THE CLOSING of the National Pastoral Institute, I was out of a job, so to speak. Paul Castley, Brian Gallagher and I discussed the prospects of sabbatical leave, something which the Australian MSC province was organising for its members after 10 years of work. It was suggested that I go first, in 1989. In fact, there were delays after that, Brian going in 1992 and Paul not until 1994.

Where to go for a year, a year in which I would turn 50! It didn't seem a good idea to go for formal study. Informal study and, perhaps, auditing courses seemed a better idea. The thought also came that I should earn my keep for the year and be available to work in a parish. And how could that combine with the film ministry? Go to New York. New York it was.

Dorcas Mann and the Cabrini sisters, officially Missionary Sisters of the Sacred Heart, with whom I had done some work, were more than helpful. Their founder, St. Frances Xavier Cabrini, had become the first U.S. saint (and she was an Italian migrant) in 1946 and was buried at a shrine in the Cabrini High School chapel which was in St. Elizabeth's parish in Washington Heights. This was the area that I was later to read in Tom Wolfe's The Bonfire of the Vanities described as a frontier of New York City. I will vouch for that later. The pastor of St. Elizabeth's, Monsignor Joachim Beaumont, agreed to have me, working part-time in the parish while on sabbatical.

Before I arrive at St. Elizabeth's, I will detour to Manila as this stop had repercussions for Media Ministry. The Superior General of the Missionaries of the Sacred Heart, Kees Braun, had worked at KRO (Katol ... in Holland. He was aware of the possibilities for media ministry in the spirit of Jules Chevalier so suggested a meeting of the MSC Asian Pacific region. That region included the Pacific Islands, Papua New Guinea, Indonesia, the Philippines, India and Australia. A collection of us assembled in January 1989 in Manila at the Communication Foundation for Asia (CFA), a quite large enterprise established by another Dutch MSC, Cor Lagerwey, one of those enthusiastic, entrepreneurial types with connections. A solid brick building with audiovisual technology and a printing arm that produced Gospel Komiks in Filipino languages. As of writing now, CFA is the flagship of Media Ministry for the Missionaries of the Sacred Heart and I teach there briefly each year. And there is a bust of Fr. Lagerwey at the front of the building.

The meeting was enjoyable and we discussed and discussed but there was no immediate result except for some printing jobs done in Manila for other provinces. It was to be 10 years until we had another Media meeting, this time for all provinces, for sister congregations and lay participants in Issoudun in December 1998.

It was only three years since Ferdinand Marcos had been ousted by people power in the Edsa protests. Corey Aquino was president and there was more optimism in the Philippines. You could actually tour Malacañang Palace – and look at merely 2,000 pairs of Imelda Marcos' alleged 3,000 pair collection. And you could visit the famous tip with its scavengers at Smoky Mountain. Quite a different way to begin a sabbatical. But, before getting to the U.S., there was more.

Paul and Brian had been in Manila earlier leading spirituality renewal programs and we met for an afternoon going to the war cemetery and to Intramuros. I suppose community meetings can be arranged if you try hard enough. So Paul and I agreed to connect in Hong Kong and, if possible, go into mainland China. Getting to Hong Kong on a Friday afternoon, I was hurried by Paul to the long taxi queue and then to the underground so that we could get to the travel agent before they shut for the weekend. There were two places left for a tour on the Monday. We got there in time, though the walk from the underground to the Jesuit community in Argyle Street, Kowloon, was a trek in itself (my year's luggage and all). The 116 address seemed near enough to the station. We had no idea that at one stage there was a hospital stretching along Argyle

Street with one of the street's numbers extending from A to J. In those days, the Jesuit house was a short enough walk to the airport (where you seemed to taxi along the entrance areas of apartment blocks). As the planes were landing and flew over Argyle Street, you felt you could reach up and touch them. The then Cathay Pacific ads on television showed this in close-up – and weren't exaggerating. (The new, spacious airport is on an island where you can come into the city by car, bus or a comfortable express train.)

After indulging that memory, I should hurry, as we did, to get the train to Guangzhou. In 1989, it seemed amazing that Australians could be travelling into China, and in comfort. Our generation was brought up to fear both Red Menace and Yellow Peril. We read of the persecutions of Christians and knew that if the Chinese got to us, we would be tortured for the faith – those bamboo shoots up our fingernails. But, 40 years after Mao's revolution, here we were in a train speeding through the countryside, joining a minibus group for the sights of the city, religious temples, memories of Sun Yat Sen, and crowds in the malls with nowhere to sit down. It was Chinese New Year, so we were treated to several banquets as part of the package. Then, a night in the five-star Hotel China, where I made sure I got into bed and turned on the television to watch some of, of all movies to be looking at there, *The Sound of Music*.

Just a few of us for the return trip to Macao with an amazing young guide who had never been out of China but had boned up on travel books, guides and maps and could converse about Pitt Street and Sydney as if he had recently been there. This was four months before the killings at Tiananmen Square. We had another banquet, visited a factory which did exquisite paper cut-outs of birds and flowers (still have some) and a walk through an empty commune farm. Macao and the Portuguese style seemed paltry after this.

You might think I would be in a hurry to get to New York but, no, a stop in San Francisco and Los Angeles for old times' sake, just getting out of LA before a quake, en route to Tulsa, part of a compulsion to visit every American state. I don't recommend Oklahoma in winter. Before flying out on Monday morning I went back to the Tulsa Cathedral where I had been to Mass on the Sunday and found that we were celebrating, this time a small group of us, a 7.00 am Mass in the Cathedral crypt. The presiding priest, Peter Dally, was the one whose hand I had shaken the day before at the end of Mass. Once again he was there to greet us, mentioned remembering me from the day before and asked who I was. He immediately offered me what would two days before have been most welcome accommodation, but it was too late. But I did accept an invitation to breakfast. As I went out of the chapel with him, he beckoned to a lady near the door, 'And this is my wife, Mary.'

One of the gifts I was most pleased to receive (and unhappiest to lose among the debris of the room of, what can I say, the least tidy priest I have ever met) was a copy of Mary's book, signed by her, *Married to a Catholic Priest. A Journey of Faith*. As might be guessed, Peter was a convert from the Episcopal Church – but the lesson I learnt was that, while a priest might convert, it should not be assumed that his wife will want to become a Catholic. Mary's book showed that the wife will have her own faith journey.

Finally to JFK and Sharon Casey, a Cabrini sister there to meet me care of a pre-mailed photo, who introduced me to a man who suddenly said, 'Bmmn'. I did twig after some awkward moments. 'Beaumont'. Monsignor Beaumont, a Basque, was introducing himself.

What might be interesting about this year at St. Elizabeth's and about living in New York (where I could live quite happily, I think)?

Since this is a story about an Australian, a Catholic and priest, and a film person, those might be the best headings to indicate what a wonderful year 1989 was and how it affected me.

An Australian living in the U.S. Not too difficult. There is more than enough which is the same to make it easy – and to live with those things which are not the same or which we don't like. As with people all round the world, Australians love to criticise the Americans and then take everything they have to offer whether it is good for us or not. One difficulty I do have with a number of Americans is that they so live in the present that their good will to you while you are in front of them, 'Have a nice day', does not always carry over when you are not there. 'Keep in touch' is not something to be necessarily taken literally. Of course, there are great American friends but we overestimate the enthusiasm of extroverted politeness.

That said, the temptation for an Australian, at least for me, is travel. I made a resolution long since that I would try to find an opportunity to visit all of the American states. For 11 years, there have been eight to go. (Here's hoping!) The means for travel within the U.S. has been Greyhound buses, so before moving on to more serious things, I would like to reminisce about some of those bus trips – skippable stories unless you would like to compare notes.

I left the long trips until the fall (their autumn) although I was able to attend an international Myers-Briggs Conference in Boulder, Colorado, a chance to be in the Rockies. According to the map, Denver was not too far from Wyoming so this was a now or never opportunity. Greyhound as always. There was a story, *The Green Grass of Wyoming*, but that is not my memory at all. It was 3 July and it was, understatement, hot. I was happy to drive through Cheyenne and to get out and wander about Laramie, indulging in memories of westerns. But, it was hot. Most of my budget went on drinks which never seemed to last long enough. But, at least, I can tell you I have been in Wyoming.

The other trips were longer. Greyhound had that wonderful system of paying for seven days' unlimited travel. Perhaps I am a quantity rather than quality person, but the first seven day-er was from New York through Pennsylvania and Ohio (the first day), on to Kentucky and Tennessee with Nashville as a desired destination and seeing the Grand Ole Opry in honour of one of my favourite films, Robert Altman's *Nashville*. Then on through Alabama to Jackson, Mississippi, the southernmost intended stop. Except for Samoa where there seems to be a Catholic, an Adventist and a Mormon church on every village corner, I have never seen such a concentration of churches as along the road out of Montgomery, Alabama.

The road out of Jackson was interesting more because of the driver than the scenery. Our driver was black. So, this is September 1989. Earlier that year I had seen Alan Parker's drama about the racial conflicts, protests and murders in this state, *Mississippi Burning*. But, here we were, only 25 years later, driving along the highway with an African American driver. That seemed to me to be quite a change and I'm glad I experienced it. Then, on to Memphis. Even though I missed out on most of the early Elvis phenomenon and have no great devotion to him, I thought I would like to see Graceland. Out in the bus which was full of black people except for me. Lining up to get the shuttle across the street from the ticket box to the entrance to Graceland – and scarcely a black person in the queue. The tour of Graceland in those days was an exercise in logistics. Into a room, a clean-cut young guide with explanations. Into the next room with a new but similar guide (while the first one went back to explain that first room, over and over and over again – how could they stand it?). I enjoyed the tour, the explanations, the photos, the trophies and the potted history. Elvis' spirit has definitely not left that building.

The longest trek was from St. Louis to Fargo, North Dakota (before the Coen Brothers and Frances McDormand made it famous). This was a zigging and zagging 23 hour trip, continually crossing borders so that I could tick off Kansas, Nebraska, Iowa, South Dakota on my list. Actually, I did have a good intention. I was on my way, really, to an MSC General Conference dinner and 50th anniversary celebration of the American MSC province in Aurora, Illinois, just taking the long way round. That took me in its final stretch through Minnesota and Wisconsin to Chicago and Aurora. Come to think of it, I cheated a little. I flew back to New York.

If you can bear it, there was another trip, another seven day-er over the Thanksgiving period (which was a bit unpatriotic of me but I had celebrated an American Thanksgiving in 1978, enjoying it and its very American menu and atmosphere and the fact that they publicly thanked God). This time I spent Thanksgiving sitting at a bus station in Wilmington, North Carolina, after ticking off Maryland, Delaware and Virginia on my list. But, I think the reason I wanted to mention this trip was the visit to Charleston, South Carolina, a beautiful city, with no building at that stage more than seven storeys high (except for church steeples). The tour on the harbour ranged from USS *York*, to the locations for *Porgy and Bess* and, of course, Fort Sumter and memories of the Civil War (and the film, *Glory*, about the black regiment in South Carolina, just about the be released). I should have mentioned that bus trips do offer a great opportunity for reading. In that earlier trip I read all of John Jakes' *North and South* and had been reading Gore Vidal's historical novels that began with Aaron Burr, through the U.S. discovery of 'Manifest Destiny' to Teddy Roosevelt and the achievement of Empire.

The furthest south was Savannah, Georgia, with memories of John Wesley's mission and, soon to come, *Midnight in the Garden of Good and Evil*.

What follows might seem very short and tame with the 3,500 miles in seven days from east to mid-west and from south to north. To visit American confreres who worked in parishes in Providence, Rhode Island, included a walk along the cliffs outside the mansions at Newport and imagine Gatsby (though from New Jersey) and Vanderbilts ... Or a December visit to Boston. I would advise against it. It is fascinating to walk the city and the well-marked revolutionary trails with Bunker Hill and Tea Parties. Less interesting to find that I could not stay overnight at the YMCA (I didn't bring photo identity) or stay at the bus station as I had in the past in Columbus, Ohio, and Montgomery, Alabama. The Salesian College sign looked more than welcome. They advised me to try the big Franciscan Friary at the crossroads. After explaining that the reason I wanted to see a priest was not to go to Confession and after producing my visa card which I had forgotten said 'Father Peter Malone', I was warmly welcomed. I knew Australian friars that they knew ... I had no hesitation eight years later in requesting accommodation during a Boston International Psychological Type Conference – and, God looks after the spendthrifty, I insisted on leaving an offering (larger than smaller) which they insisted I should not give but left it with them, then went to the airport where I was upgraded to Business Class on the way home even though I was on a Qantas Frequent Flyer redemption flight. I don't know whether you really needed to know that, but I decided against deleting it!

More than by the way, the warning against Boston in December is that it is freezing. I wore a pair of gloves and the wind seemed to pierce through them. Lucky the Franciscans were so central. I could duck in occasionally and get warm.

It wasn't so cold in Philadelphia, Declaration of Independence, Liberty Bell and all that, and out past Valley Forge to the Cabrini community. Best of all was wandering around Gettysburg. It is a large battlefield, well signed so that you can re-create the battle in your imagination as you look at the hills, the paths, the memorials. And read those extraordinary 84 words of Lincoln's Gettysburg Address. I was lucky enough to come to Gettysburg again two years later with an Australian enthusiast, Peter MacCrossan, who had hired a car. We had a free afternoon from the Psychological Type Conference, this time in West Virginia. Retracing Gettysburg steps with Peter was a bonus but we returned to Richmond via Manassas, via the convent of St. Elizabeth Seton in Emmitsburg, Maryland, but, best of all, a visit to West Virginia, to Harper's Crossing, where the Potomac and Shenandoah meet in a beautiful valley. More memories of the Civil War and of John Brown's execution before his body lay moulding in the grave.

I don't really know why I have been fascinated by the American Civil War. How could they have fought one another with such passion and loss of life – and for what? Abolition, state independence, honour... ?

Phil de Rea, an American Missionary of the Sacred Heart, lived in Washington DC, and was in charge of a charity which provided motor vehicles to American missionaries. Earlier, I had worked three weekends for him, preaching the appeal, which took me to Longfellow's Portland Maine, where I was the guest of a Polish American Conventual Franciscan who had a numerological system for betting on the horses (nothing to do with form) and who took me out for my one and only lobster meal. He also gave me the run of the rectory and reassured him when I told him I was not a whisky drinker – he told me about his confrere who visited, drank too much whisky so that my host offered him another, watered it down, and the visitor never asked for another. He had a good day with the horses and gave me a bonus. Another trip took me to Durham, New Hampshire. We were in a small plane and had to circle New York before we could land at La Guardia. Our circle route was right over Manhattan flying in a north-south line almost following Broadway all the way down. You would have paid big dollars for such a flight by itself. Oh, the third mission preaching was simply across the George Washington Bridge into Montclair, New Jersey. A pleasant feature of that visit was going out for a meal on the Saturday night with a group of the area's parish priests and then going back to a rectory to sit on the porch with a drink and with good conversation. The people at all these Masses thought that the Australian accent was just lovely and could listen to it all day. Many of the men were glad to tell me that they had served in the Pacific during the war and knew Townsville or Melbourne. I hope that they gave generously to make the appeal worthwhile.

That was a detour, so back to Phil de Rea in Washington. No, sorry, another detour. After a bus trip north, back to Virginia, I decided to visit historic Williamsburg, where the whole town is as it was at the time of the American revolution, where men and women in the dress of the period go about their work and explain to tourists what it was like in those days. Very interesting and enjoyable. Now, back to Washington.

I never got to Capitol Hill (but did 20 years later) which seemed a negligent thing back then. What happened was that, after a tour of the

White House and a visit to the Smithsonian, I went into the headquarters of the FBI. I can't remember what our awareness of J. Edgar Hoover was at the time, but I stayed a long time. Lots of explanations and demonstrations of the Agency's work, the training of agents, displays of weapons, historical cases. Just as well I went then because after 9/11 apparently, it is not open now for this kind of visit. I really like the Lincoln Memorial. And there's the text of the Gettysburg Address again.

That's enough – I hope you're not thinking 'more than enough' for Be Australian, will travel.

It's time to do some reflecting on the Catholic Church by 1989.

30. BEYOND THE PATHOLOGY (ECCLESIASTICAL, THAT IS)

AS I MENTIONED, not just to be age-conscious, 1989 saw me turning 50. Gets you thinking. As regards the Catholic Church, how had it changed in that 50 years? in the previous 30 years, from 1959 when John XXIII so unexpectedly announced the Second Vatican Council? 'A great deal' is an understatement. During this year I had the opportunity of standing back from the Church at home and experiencing the Church in the United States. It was a positive experience.

But, of course, I brought with me a lot of presuppositions about what the Church should be like. Tony Kelly once remarked that each generation in the Church has its own pathology, the way it sees things, diagnoses matters, is exhilarated and is disappointed. My positive ecclesiastical pathology is that the 1960s was a marvelous time. No matter some of the consequences, they had to happen, or else where would we be, a little narrow sect hanging on for dear life, for dear old life? For me, changes could not come fast enough – that is, the changes I approved of, of course. I was happy to say 'Vale' to Latin, having paid my dues to the language at school, in seminary and in Roman university exams (always grateful that it has enhanced my knowledge of English). Standing on clerical dignity is another bane, not just because of the dress which can serve as ecclesial armour, but because of the consequences of clergy being pedestalised (further to fall when scandals like sex abuse abound) and making assumptions of superiority over laity. It does happen. The changes in religious life have been life-giving even as some congregations have served their mission well and are dying. The more scriptural and personal language of Church teaching in the Council documents has also been transforming, making theology more accessible even though I was wildly optimistic in the 1960s imagining that everyone would be studying the Old Testament within years. The perspective and language of the document on the Church in the Modern World, the theological and spiritual reflection on 'terrestria', 'things down here' – heaven's above! – and the dialogue with the world within and outside the Church is envigorating while challenging. It is mission, even evangelising, with respect, rather than presumptuous proselytising.

A friend commented on the 'siege mentality' that enthusiasts used to decry those hanging on to the past for past's sake and defensiveness would find when they looked over the parapets that the besiegers had gone away long before.

It hasn't worked out entirely that way. Pendulums swing. For every action there is an equal and opposite reaction. Truer of the Church than I would have anticipated. You see my pathology. It came home to me recently, from the time I am writing this section of the book, with the introduction of a new translation of prayers for the celebration of the Eucharist. Many, perhaps reluctantly at times, will admit the process was flawed. Initial use of accessible language was countered by those who felt that they should be loyal to tradition, that previous language was poor English (in some cases, yes, but a lot of fine prayer that contemporary minds and hearts could pray). The new translations have lost a lot of their vernacular verve and vitality. Looking at some of the translations, 'Behold' rather than 'Look'. Who says 'Behold' nowadays? Someone in a period movie perhaps. 'Endow' and 'beseech'? I wonder whether the translators acknowledged that each language has its own particular idioms and use of similes and metaphors that are not the same in other languages and can't simply be transferred in the name of translation. That's obvious, you might say. How does 'suffering catfish' translate into Latin (not that it is ever used, though an exasperated Jesus might have muttered it when Peter and the others were obtuse at the Sea of Galilee)? We need to find the equivalent in our own idioms and sayings. It's meant to be translation not transliteration – visibilium et invisibilium was rightly translated as 'seen and unseen', perfectly good contemporary English.

But it has now been transliterated as 'visible and invisible' which, in contemporary English is something different and more to do with ghosts and suchlike, or *The Invisible Man*. Some clergy were enthusiastic on Pentecost Sunday 2011 when these changes were introduced in Australia. Perhaps they had a surfeit of the Holy Spirit as they proclaimed that the new translation was more beautiful, richer and deeper. For the old, 'It is right to give God thanks and praise', we have 'It is right and just'! Just not all right! As Marshall McLuhan noted of people who sit tight, they 'live life in the rear vision mirror'.

As a confrere often says, 'thus endeth the lesson', time to get down from the soapbox. I finished up writing more than I anticipated but, as Sir Les Patterson used to say, 'You get my drift'.

So, American Church 1989, from the partial viewpoint of St. Elizabeth's in Washington Heights on Wadsworth Avenue and the corner of 187th Street, Broadway running along the back, St. Nicholas Avenue (Wolfe's Bonfire of the Vanities frontier) a block away, Yeshiva University overlooking the East River quite close as upper Manhattan narrows before the Bronx, Fort Tryon on the other side overlooking the Hudson River, the Cloisters further on, across from the New Jersey Palisades. The George Washington Bridge at 178th Street crosses the Hudson, only a 35 minute walk from St. Elizabeth's to Fort Lee in New Jersey, the other side of Manhattan having the crossing of the East River to the Bronx Expressway.

I borrowed the parish school video camera before I left and have these images still in shaky focus and with whispered commentary and the frequent sudden close-ups of the footpath (sorry, sidewalks). In 2007, retracing my steps, I now have fine digital pictures.

Having settled into a cosy area in a basement corridor, next door to the room where they counted the money each Monday morning, Mary Gleason the parish secretary and a group of parish ladies who used to be younger but were still friendly and active, the first day I went to Mass in the church. It was a requiem Mass for a young policeman,

Polish American who was known at the primary school across the street because he often visited and gave talks. He had been shot dead nearby. In the words I was to hear often, 'drug-related'. The church was packed, kids, teachers and lots of police. Welcome to St. Elizabeth's.

The next thing was to visit the personnel officer at the New York chancery so that I could be officially appointed. This was exciting, my first ever appointment to a parish even if it was to be part-time. Joaquin Beaumont further enthused me. I was to have a special mission to a parish minority. Some justice, rights issues? No, this was a bigger minority. The English-speakers. Oh.

Yes, St. Elizabeth's was a mixed-language parish. The majority of the parishioners were, as you might have guessed, Hispanic. 2000, Hispanic, 1000 English. As well so many of the latter were ageing and have now gone to heaven. Actually, it was a very active parish. Joaquin, who had been a teacher in Venezuela had come to New York City in the 1960s to study at Columbia when his religious superiors were experiencing some upheaval in the order and thought that he and another priest were running away. Cardinal Cooke took them in. Joaquin was the vicar for Hispanic ministry in that part of Manhattan. There were many Cubans but the majority in St. Elizabeth's were from the Dominican Republic. Joaquin had two parish councils, one Hispanic, the other English, but tried to honour all the traditions, Our Lady of Caridad, of Guadalupe – and St. Patrick. A few Masses in English at St. Elizabeth's on the weekend, two at the Cabrini Chapel and one at a home for the elderly, Isabella's. There were four assistant priests and, while they had their vacations in summer, two Jesuits from Spain came each year for supply. Joaquin also believed in open house. People always in and out of the place, always welcome. I might mention at this juncture that whenever anyone came to the door for money, we would offer to accompany them to wherever and buy it for them. I remember the man who wanted to travel some distance declined the offer. Another man accepted and we found ourselves at the pharmacists buying ointment for haemorrhoids.

Always singing at the Sunday masses, the leader of song was always paid. Lots of Hispanic devotions, English novenas and plenty of confessions. I liked the little boy who looked at me with a knowing look and said, 'forgive me, God, for I have sinned, less the other little Hispanic boy who, when I kindly said to him, 'Go ahead', gruffed, 'what you mean, hat?' Eventually, I was able to offer some Old Testament evenings as well as a retreat for the women of the parish.

Come to think of it, that doesn't sound so startling. Rather, ordinary in fact, but it was fine pastoral ministry.

A couple of things. I realised that a diocesan parish was more flexible in timetables and so on than a religious community. I learnt that ferrets could be pets but had to be sequestered – the young and enthusiastic curate, Rudy Gonzalez, kept them and fed them most solicitously. Another curate, Gerald Murray, was a genial traditionalist with traditionalist parents and was an associate member of Opus Dei. I should say he enjoyed watching videos (but they had to be rather more proper than not and he came in to watch Kevin Costner in *No Way Out* after the sex scene I felt I should warn him about), the more so because he told me that Monsignor, now saint, Escriva, did not allow movie-going. (The saint lacked the gift of prophecy in not anticipating video!). We had lots of table discussion about liberal Catholics and he did say that it was a battlefield – which opinion I politely rejected. My idea of church was not fighting. But it certainly was stimulating being challenged by Gerry.

But, back to videos for a moment. Each month Gerry (whom I never saw out of clerical black until I visited him when he was studying in Rome some years later and he was wearing a navy blue pullover) organised a group of similar-minded priests and seminarians to protest outside abortion clinics. One auxiliary bishop was prepared to go to gaol for this and did. But, Gerry and friends did not. They would return to St. Elizabeth's and enjoy a take-out meal of Chinese. Then they would watch a video. There was *Wild Geese 2, Rambo 3*, though they asked me for an Australian film and we saw *Breaker Morant* (my concession to their predilection for violent movies). When we had the comedy, Midnight Run, there was almost two hours of four-letter expletives resounding round the rectory. Even Joaquin looked in to see what was happening. Actually, one of the deacons counted 318 'fucks'. I mentioned to Gerry that I felt I had to mention the language in my review of the film. But, he reassured me, it was not swearing, just cuss-words. I don't think Gerry casually used these cuss-words in real life.

The group was always friendly to me, even as I sat in non-clerical clothes. But, the conversation was generally anti-liberal clergy and bishops and a fair (unfair) amount of anti-women.

Joaquin took me to clergy meetings, to visit Dunwoody seminary where he used their swimming pool. He was not a fan of the seminary staff nor of the students. 'Rather traditionalist staff and some rather 'precious' students' can do as a comment. The priests that I met when I went on the mission appeal trips were usually very welcoming. Over the years, and during the 1990s and early 2000s, I stayed in many rectories while attending Psychological Type Conferences as far afield as Richmond, Virginia, Newport Beach, California, Scottsdale, Arizona, and Minneapolis. Models of hospitality. Which meant, of course, that I saw them when they were hosts, not in pastoral action, but, at least they were consistently friendly.

Being in New York meant that we were in the archdiocese of Cardinal John O'Connor. His was another image of church. He was a man of image, a former navy chaplain and admiral, and is the best ecclesiastical worker of the popular media that I have come across. He was a kind of a non-royal prince bishop. He was also one of those dignitaries who met everyone and had a word but it was said when he was looking at the next person, already about to shake their hands, which meant that you were forgotten almost the moment he was passing on to the next person (or really the one after that).

A few words about him in the limited close-up I had. During Holy

Week, Joaquin took me to the Mass of the Oils, where the different oils used for the sacraments were consecrated by the bishop with his clergy in attendance, also a chance for a pep-homily on the theology of the priesthood. Cardinal O'Connor often gave three homilies at the one Mass, the Masses lasting 90 minutes. He did so that night – and later at a centenary Mass for the Cabrini Sisters. I was taken as well as amused by reflecting on his outreach to his brother priests, telling them that he would be willing to sacrifice every honour he had received just for the love of one of his priests. Allowing for the dramatic and well-meaning hyperbole, it made you realise that he was also reminding us of how many honours he really had.

It was the same with the press. Very soon after I got to New York, Ayatollah Khomeini issued the fatwah against Salman Rushdie for his alleged insults to the Prophet. Before you could say Koran, the Cardinal declared that he endorsed the fatwah. Splash headlines, TV interruptions, talk show arguments. Then, as quickly, he admitted he had shot from the hip (really from the lip) and that he didn't mean it as literally as it sounded. More headlines, more TV interruptions, more talk show arguments. And that is what he did, keeping himself in the news for at least a week at a time when he intervened. He did it when he decided to visit Lebanon against all political and ecclesiastical advice in April or May. On his way to the airport, he got extra photo-opportunities by going to a hospital to visit a young woman who was unconscious after being mugged and raped in Central Park while jogging. Then, at the airport, he suddenly announced that he was going to follow the aforementioned advice, and drove home again! One more. He denounced mayoral candidate with a Catholic background, Rudy Giuliani, for his stances in favour of abortion. Wouldn't be seen dead with him, let alone alive with him. But, a week later, he changed his mind for civic reasons and did stand with him on a platform for the Columbus Day parade. Headlines, TV for both. Imagine if he had lived into the Facebook, Twitter era. Yet, as early as the late 1980s, he was compassionate, visiting parishes where a priest had been accused of sexual abuse and apologised at the Masses, rather ahead of the times as we look back.

In 1991 the Vatican issued a document, *Nova Aetate* (A New Age), which urged every Catholic organisation, especially dioceses to work on pastoral plans involving media. Many have taken a leaf out of Cardinal O'Connor's book (Cardinal George Pell, for instance), but no one has been more forthcoming, more sensational and more media-coverage-successful than he.

Because of the kindness of the Cabrini Sisters, I thought I should accept their offer of working with a group preparing for their provincial chapter at the end of the year. They asked me to join the government committee, though statutes and regulations were not my forte at all. Needless to say, very interesting to have a close-up experience of a congregation of sisters looking at their works, declining numbers and changing styles of living. Interesting to have the opportunity to make comparisons with Australia, though there were more similarities than differences. However, there was one very sad side of the experience – but I am going to add an incidentally and accidentally funny side first. Though their headquarters were in Philadelphia, there was Mother Cabrini's tomb in Washington Heights and a big hospital downtown. The delegates all came to New York for a special Mass at the tomb and then we sped, yes sped, to the hospital (I was invited to come along but there was room for me only in the back of the station wagon, the luggage area). During the tour of the hospital, we were far too many in an elevator and it stopped rising just before we got to the sixth floor. Briefly, we were stuck for 90 minutes, couldn't have slid to the floor we were so packed in. One sister kept urging us not to panic, which we weren't – she seemed to be projecting on to us! It was a Saturday afternoon, no technicians on site. Thoughtful sisters suggested coat-hangers to prise open the door – then someone suggested finding a v! We did get out, the two male doctors I noticed getting out ahead of the 23 sisters (including Superior General, Provincials, matron, etc) leaving me to do the gallant act and leave last.

Then they told us, it was not so much the danger of the elevator falling but smoke inhalation if the wires started to rub with increasing friction.

The sad part concerns the Superior General who was in that elevator. She was one of those active persons who does not tolerate what she perceives as weakness of character or decision-making. The sisters, few in Melbourne, had some sisters with problems (and I would vouch for that from experience). They asked for help, for transfers. This was interpreted as weakness. But, the situation was too much to manage and, after providing more than sufficient explanation, several of the Australian sisters left the congregation, including Dorcas Mann, the Regional Superior, who had been so helpful to us in counselling our students and giving advice. But, most congregations have some horror stories from this period where authorities did not handle the problems and departures and disasters followed. The sisters were good enough to allow me to say all this at the Chapter itself after Christmas 1989 – and, after getting Amtrak back to the 34th Street Station, I found on getting up into the street that I had to lean at almost 45 degrees against the wind to make any progress forward. Obviously time to leave New York City.

I appreciated the welcome in the parish and in the Archdiocese of New York, the discovery of the Hispanic Church as well as the English-speaking minority and Joaquin Beaumont's pastoral comprehensiveness from parish service to promoting justice and human rights. It was a church I could live in.

31. IN 42ND STREET – AND IN MORE SALUBRIOUS LOCATIONS

ONE OF THE MOVIE reasons for spending a year in New York was to see the American Bishops Conference Film Office and learn from Henry Herx, the director and chief reviewer. It turned out to be more useful than I anticipated.

I have already acknowledged Henry as one of a group in Chicago 20 years earlier who had committed themselves to the values and religious dimensions of the movies, publishing discussion material that had inspired me to do something of the same back then. Henry, a bit heavier than he should have been, definitely smoking more than he should have, was a laid-back kind of man who could sit in a chair, talk quietly for more than an hour and have you enthralled as he took you back over the history of the Church in the United States and its dealing with the movies, back to the origins of Catholic reviewing and the emerging, instead, of the Legion of Decency in 1934. He had examples, anecdotes, arresting perspectives.

Henry invited me to the premiere of *Romero*. John Duigan, the director, though not religious, said that practising Christians ask the most interesting questions. In fact, under his photo portrait in Parliament House in Canberra, there is a quotation in this vein, 'It's not so much film per se that's interesting to me, it's film as a vehicle for ideas, and for exploring human psychology and personality, and love and political oppression or whatever it is.' He had made *Far East* in 1982, a story of the Philippines which featured a Catholic social worker. He had made *Fragments of War*, the story of war cinematographer, posthumous Oscar-winner for his coverage, Damien Parer, a very devout Australian Catholic. On the strength of these films, Paulist producer Fr. Bud Kaiser had asked John to direct his project on Archbishop Romero with Raul Julia (which

John Duigan noted later was until then the only film screened to the two houses of Congress). This was also an opportunity to meet the legendary Fr. Kaiser who had spent years persuading Hollywood stars and directors to make his Insight television series which ran for decades. Fr. Kaiser and Fr. Patrick Peyton in the 1950s pioneered Catholic involvement in American movie-making. After American television was deregulated and channels not obliged to make or feature religious programs, Fr. Kaiser moved to movie-making, including *Entertaining Angels*, the story of Dorothy Day (whose beatification process has been introduced, beating *Romero* whom the Vatican has ignored in terms of his becoming Blessed Oscar Romero). Fr. Kaiser mentioned that Raul Julia had not been practising but portraying the archbishop had given him a new sense of church. Raul Julia died five years later after playing the Brazilian man of the rubber people in *The Burning Season*. But most people know him as Gomez in *The Addams Family* movies!

It was always interesting to visit the office and discuss reviewing with Henry and another reviewer of the time, Judith Trojan. I also persuaded Henry to go to the cinemas in 42nd Street, something of a risky prospect that Joaquin Beaumont always cautioned me about. But, it was an education, especially to see how a real audience, usually a black male audience responded, 'cuss-words' and freely and loudly offered advice to the protagonists.

Unfortunately, we went to see the John Belushi biography *Wired*. Very little participation for this life of films and drugs cut short. The only comment we heard this time was from an old man leaving the cinema near us, 'waste of a fucking life'. Yes.

One very good turn that Henry did me was to arrange a lunch with Mike Leech from Continuum. I had given Henry a copy of *Movie Christs and Antichrists*. He showed it to Mike who published an American edition. It came out a year later by the time I got home again, but the blurb said I was an Australian priest living and working in New York City. I had added some paragraphs on *The Last Temptation of Christ* and a still from that film was put on the cover with the Australian film deleted. They had taken literally, *Annie's Coming Out*. Books published just in Australia used to be limited to the home market. The Continuum edition meant that I was read and quoted as I never had been before and some said the book was 'seminal'. A nice film beginning for the year.

One of the aims of going to New York was to find some summer courses to audit on film. The best place seemed to be Fordham with its Jesuit foundation and its links through Fr. Pat Sullivan SJ with the National Catholic Office for Film. There was a course on film comedy that didn't come up with much. However, a course on American film from 1939 to the 1950s, watching a film a night that related to the politics of the time, like *High Noon* for 1952 with the House of Un-American Activities sittings and interrogations of the period, and then discussing was a useful cinema experience – though many of those who took the course were those giant basketball players who were not particularly on the ball concerning film or politics. Better was a course at the New York New School. Richard Brown was the professor, a writer and media personality. Again we watched films, this time in preview, every Saturday morning during the course. The following Thursday night, he would chair discussion from the stage (many audited the course, 500 at least, because of its general interest). He would then introduce a guest whom he interviewed on stage for about an hour. We listened to Richard Dreyfuss and Charles Grodin who were excellent. We watched *Steel Magnolias* and Brown interviewed the writer, Robert Harlan who told us that the play and film were based on actual characters in his Louisiana home town. Most of them came to the premiere in New York. Shirley MacLaine played the dominantly outspoken Ouisa. It seems that the real Ouisa could identify most of the characters but she asked who Ouisa was based on!

Supplementing this some more courses at the Jung Institute.

I mentioned going to review in 42nd Street. This was in the ex-live theatres that by the late '80s had become ex-sleaze cinemas, playing the first releases on double-bills at half the cost of the first run movie houses around the corner and in up-town avenues. This striking economic appeal, two for much less than the price of one elsewhere, could overcome the drabness and sometimes the ugly dirtiness of these cinemas: the two Cine 42 screens, the Selwyn, the Harris, the Victory. All gone in the Disney buying and clean-up of the area!

I had better tell you that cleanliness was not a forte of most of them. We expect popcorn and soft drink (U.S., soda) bottles on the floor, but there was quite a bit of spit as well. And plenty of pot fumes. And at the Harris a perpetually wandering cat. But, it was also an education, gauging how this audience was actually alert to all the cinema trick and techniques, great movie comprehension. It was also interesting to see a film there and go back and look at the reviews that morning in the *New York Times*. Sometime a chasm between reviewers and real audience. I sat through *Harlem Nights* which Eddie Murphy wrote and directed and the audience loved, laughed and cheered. It was denounced by a white reviewer as loathsome and racist – against African Americans. Seeing Spike Lee's *Do the Right Thing* in the Bronx near Fordham also made me re-assess the African American use of 'cuss-words' which, certainly, Australian audiences were not used to. It received an R, Restricted certificate in Australia because of language. A reader caution for a moment but I learnt that just as Australians affectionately called friends 'you old bastard', African American slang could do the same with 'motherfucker'. Horizons broaden.

I was able to continue reviewing in *Annals* as if I were at home, and editing *Compass*. The first releases meant that I was sometimes ahead. And there were always the videos to catch up with home releases.

That was the film year in New York. Time to come home.

PART II

32. THE PHONE CALL THAT CHANGED THE NEXT TWENTY YEARS

I RATHER enjoyed writing that title.

But, it is true. Coming home included a Eurail visit to the Scandinavian countries from our MSC house in Tilburg in Holland. Scandinavia in winter does not lend itself to travelogue. Half of Stockholm harbor was frozen. The most northern town I have visited, Uppsala, was covered in snow. It got dark so early in Oslo. But, the luxury ferry from Gothenburg to Friedrichshafen was an eye-opener. It was huge. And then a train ride through *Babette's Feast* countryside of Jutland. When I got back, I started to answer my Dutch confreres question of where I had been but they seemed so amazed that anyone would travel from Amsterdam to Copenhagen that I did not dare reveal the rest.

The winter was more than a dampener for a bus trip to Assisi to commemorate my silver jubilee of ordination. The town was covered in fog. You had to feel your way from the bus to the upper Basilica of San Francesco. It was impossible to find the way to San Damiano. The only possibility was to go higher towards the Rocca. Suddenly a cloudless, sunny blue sky and a walk to the Carceri (and, later, San Damiano by piercing through the still thick but slightly less opaque fog).

I had been invited to visit the Australian Sisters of Mercy working in Pakistan on the way home (as one does!) When I finally discovered from what city in Europe Singapore Airlines flew – I realised that, impatiently, I had not persevered to the back of the schedules. The answer was Vienna. Thank goodness for the Eurail pass which enabled me to stop in Salzburg to commemorate *The Sound of Music*, in Linz with some memories of the origins of you-know-who and in Vienna not only for Freud's house, the ferris wheel from *The Third Man*, Cardinal Innitzer's St. Stephen's Cathedral (the Anschluss and *The Cardinal*) plus the Vienna Woods (and going to see *The Cook, The Thief, his Wife and her Lover* because it was dark at 4.00 pm), but also to Budapest and the cathedral with its memories of Cardinal Mindszenty, the American Embassy where he was sheltered, finding that there was almost nothing in the Pest McDonald's, but the ad for *Batman* was several stories high on the outside of a department story and, in both cities, the not blue Danube.

The Sisters of Mercy worked in Peshawar and Gujarat, so a flight up from Karachi and a great welcome with the Himalayas in the distance (you lift your head much higher to look at the peaks than you do when you see ordinary mountains). We were only 15 kilometres from the Khyber Pass but it was too dangerous to go (the Russians were fighting there this time). The Catholics of Peshawar and Pakistan were the lowliest, often street sweepers, but accompanying Daniel, the catechist, a 68-year-old retired tailor, to about 16 homes: one room, mats and a cooker – and a TV set – where Daniel prayed a brief prayer with them, made a deep impression. The new parish priest didn't do this preferring to drive around in his new car. Though he did drive us to Gujarat. The sisters told me that you always witness an accident on the roads in Pakistan. They didn't warn me that I would be in one. Just a simple skidding off the road as a long limousine tried to pass between our 'flying fox', a 20 seater minibus, and one of those brightly decorated trucks that frequent the highways. Anyway, we were all right (I would have joined with the other (all male) passengers clamouring to reassure out driver that it was not his fault but I had no Urdu. The limousine, however, had a long scrape scratch and (probably unnecessary detail this) it enabled me to go behind a tree, a providential break since it was so cold. We were late into Lahore but a St. John of God sister from Australia still found me and took me to the mosque and for a drive, then to an interfaith meeting. A quick visit but great for me – and I need to make a tribute to those sisters who worked in Pakistan.

Home at last.

The next day I got a phone call that meant that the next 20 plus years of my life were not going to be at all as I might have imagined them. The call was from Fr. Pat Casserley, an Irish Marist missionary in Fiji. The news: I had been elected president of OCIC Oceania (later had that changed to OCIC Pacific). Did I accept?

Well, my awareness of Organisation Catholique Internationale du Cinema (OCIC), the International Catholic Organisation for Cinema, was tidbits from Fr. Chamberlin, who mentioned it, asked some of us to provide comments on cinema and the Church for it, organised our annual OCIC Australia film award, and told me that he was going to Oceania conferences in Fiji, Tahiti, Tonga ... or to Manila, Nairobi and Quito. Exotic. I had thought that when he finished as director of the Australian Catholic Film Office, he would appoint Fr. Bill Stevens of Sydney who had done some training in the area. As it turned out, he nominated me in Kiribati (which I still have never visited, and add Tahiti to that!) and, sight unseen I was elected. Advice from Peter Thomas who had attended Unda meetings (Unda, the International Catholic Organisation for Radio and Television). Advice from the Provincial Superior, Jim Littleton – who asked, rather laconically, 'I suppose it will involve a bit of travel?' My 'yes' seems in hindsight to have been something of an understatement.

I think it best to focus first on the other aspects of the 1990s before concentrating on OCIC and SIGNIS (The World Catholic Association for Communication), because that it is what the rest of this story will be mainly about.

In fact, at home during the 1990s, things continued much as before except that, while I was editing *Compass* and attached to the Heart of Life Centre and offered seminars there, I spent a lot of time working in other places, especially in schools with the Myers-Briggs Type Indicator – which will be explained in the next section.

But, there was opportunity to do some writing.

One of the great pleasures of the early 1990s was being asked by Cathy Jenkins at Collins Dove to contribute to a series of books, A4, large print, many illustrations to reach an audience that might not be inclined to read so much. The series was called 'Understanding ...'. My allotted task was Understanding God. I would much rather have tackled 'Appreciating God'. As it turned out, I was allowed to pursue Understanding God's Presence. I re-read some of it the other day and was surprised. It's not every day that someone is offered the opportunity to reflect on God in print. I seem to have been not exactly carried away with writing the book, but there is an enthusiasm, even zeal, with a blend of the poetic with the (not too much, I hope) rhetorical. It ranged over relationships, nature, arts, science, and tried some theology, philosophy and taking up the aboriginal meditative term *Dadirri*. Plenty of quotations in the margins, plenty of anecdotes (not without some films) in the text. I am glad I wrote it.

Then I saw that the publishers had called it *Traces of God*. That I really liked, nicely evocative. I politely enquired where they got this title from. 'You used it in your introduction.'

However, the process for *Traces of God* did bring home one of the issues that I had to deal with as an editor. My personal inclination is to leave the author's voice clearly heard, even if it is idiosyncratic. Why should I smooth everybody's style into a homogeneous mass of similar sounding writers? It is worse when you are published in the U.S. and the editor assumes that your modulations and word pronunciations are the same as theirs and they alter the flow to make you sound American. But, Americanised we have to be for sales to that vast public. If you attend a Mass in the U.S. and say the Lord's Prayer, you get caught with the different rhythms and pauses and when you get to trespasses, we go speeding ahead as they slow down for tres-pass and tres-passes. I know that there are rules and styles from different companies. But, I prefer this kind of freedom of expression and leave the authors with the real voices. With *Traces of God*, I wanted to tell a story with some urgency. Staccato sentences. One after the other. Important. The sentences were all elided by the editor into a smoothly flowing cadence that was not what I wanted at all. No urgency, just a polite piece of information. Now that

I am complaining, I had better mention that you could ignore the cover if you ever see the book. It has two teenage boys sitting on a pier, which reminded me of pious seminarians about to meditate. There was one other mini-disaster, aunts-wise. The staples in the middle of the book meant that it opened on a large representation of one of Arthur Boyd's Shoalhaven crucifixion with the naked Christ catching the immediate gaze of Aunty Sheila and Aunty Mary. Not quite their devotional image. But, I suppose I was lucky that the female crucifixion was at the back of the book.

I gathered together the reviews of videos that I had been doing for *The Advocate*, collecting titles under theme headings which I thought might be a little different. But, looking back I see that video guides were a bit of a fad and I am not sure how successful the rather ambitiously titled, *The Australian Video Guide*, actually was. Thank goodness I caught the typo for *The Naked Gun*, 'Naked Fun'.

Better was a brainwave about film reviewing (OCIC already having an influence). I asked thirty Australian reviewers to write a short review (100 words) and a longer review (350 words) of a specially chosen film (*The Killing Fields, Black Robe, Cry Freedom* and the like), five reviewers per film. I also asked them to write a short essay on their criteria for reviewing, the whole enterprise and opportunity for readers to think about reviewing and assess what the critics thought they were doing. The title, *Worth Watching. Thirty Film Reviewers on Review*. I remember many of the reviewers came to a pleasant launch at the Balwyn cinema. Continuing on projects, I offered to write a book on Australian cinema for OCIC international as they had been publishing books on African national cinema industries. Taking a schema of different ways of storytelling, like parable, satire and myth, I chose some prominent Australian films of the time to explore the ways of communicating story. It was called *Cinema Down Under* ('Down Under' a phrase that I am always wary of, a blend of affection and condescension from the northern hemisphere – but I suppose it is better than that consciously/unconsciously disdainful 'Antipodean').

With editing *Compass* and the bi-centenary book on Australian Theology, then *Worth Watching*, I rather liked inviting authors to contribute to books. So many people with good ideas and arresting speculations are not as self-confident as they deserve to be but do respond eventually to a bit of cajoling. I hope that this was one of the best benefits of *Compass*, a forum for writers who might have never been. With the centenary of cinema in 1995, it seemed a good idea for the Australian Church and OCIC to commemorate it by a book on how the churches had been represented in Australian films. Even in 1995, there was substantial material. Adventists had the Chamberlains and *Evil Angels* and Bob Ellis's memoir, *The Nostradamus Kid*. The Salvation Army had been treated sympathetically in *Bad Boy Bubby* and *Kitty and the Bagman*. Plenty of protestant themes, and even more Catholic representations, Fred Schepisi for a start. Paul Cox for a second. John Duigan and Bruce Beresford for thirds. The disappointing realisation was the Anglican presence. The author, rightly, lamented that generally Anglican representation was stereotype or mockery. Jan Epstein contributed on the representation of Jewish themes. It was a modest contribution to the centenary. It was also an edition of *Compass*, *Compass* and index on the back and, on the front, a book title, *From Front Pews to Back Stalls*. One of the activities I tried to encourage for OCIC and SIGNIS was the study of religious representation in the national film industry. We had a success in 2010 in the Philippines with a collection of articles in a book, *Spirituality and Filipino Film*.

In 1993, a Latrobe University Conference explored the Australian themes in films so a contribution on priests in films – and the putting forward of a phrase which I hope I didn't steal from anyone else for the films of romantic entanglements of clergy: *The Thorn Birds Syndrome*. Actually, Australia had early examples in *The Church and the Woman* (1918) and in an Anglican context, two versions of *The Silence of Dean Maitland* (silent in 1918 and sound in 1934, the only time pioneer and prolific director Ken G. Hall treated a religious subject in his films, although the

1978 film which draw on his Newsreel experience, *Newsfront*, was very interesting on Catholic issues). There was a 1999 film, *Missing*, where a Richard Chamberlain Vatican equivalent had to return to Australia to find his child. (If you wanted to see a Hollywood-Vatican film like this, try Frank Perry's *Monsignor*, full of purple passages.)

The last thing to mention here, looking back at the 1990s in Melbourne, is a year in Sydney. I was asked if I would take on the role of Community Leader at the MSC house of studies in Drummoyne, a suburb west of Sydney on the Parramatta River. I grew up in the eastern suburbs. Apart from driving along Victoria Road towards Ryde, this area was unfamiliar. Actually, I had never been a community leader (except for standing in for someone who was away) until 1994 when the considerate Melbourne community (while I was away at an OCIC meeting) decided that it was my turn. One of the interesting features of that job was attending the annual Provincial Conference, examining policy and activities of the past and doing some planning.

When I said yes to going to Navarre House, Drummoyne, there were to be 11 members of the community. By the time I got there, there were 16 with two more joining during the year. The year was 1998 with the prospect of my becoming President of OCIC at the Assembly to be held in August that year.

I have decided that I should mention that I had something of a mental blockage about going to Navarre. This was the place where our students were moved to and the seminary at Croydon closed. With several of the staff, though I was no longer at Croydon but in our small community in Canterbury at the time, I was strongly opposed to the closure and the move. Surely we could have found a smaller house nearer the YTU. Surely we could not give up on our foundation commitment to the Union. (With his way with words, Tony Kelly thought that our Provincial Superior, Frank Quirk, was a man of 'nimble morality'!) Then I remembered an occasion, 15 years earlier in fact, when we were discussing changes in our Formation policy, moving towards that 'Formation by Association' with the staff, rather than the hierarchical model in place to that point. One of our confreres could not bring himself to agree, even when asked whether he could allow the Province to make a mistake. He couldn't. So, a challenge, could I let the Province make a mistake. I had to.

And, now, for whatever retributive providence was at work, I was being not only asked to go to this house but to lead it. It was an odd year, really. There were a number of students doing their theology. The Vocations Recruiter also lived there. Our travelling Religious Education team had their base there. A priest who had been on leave was moving back. Three of the community lived outside because of their particular ministries. Motley to say the least. But, we managed more or less – and I had to work on cooking for 20 rather than for three or four.

It was our two boarders that were a challenge.

With the 1990s issues of refugees, legal and illegal, Catholic institutions offered homes for them. The immediate gesture was to refugees from East Timor. By the time, Navarre House put in an offer, the East Timorese had all been accommodated. Tony from Sri Lanka and Ali from Iran were the two men who took up residence in 1997. They had a room each but, as with the students, there were shared bathrooms and toilets. Tony and Ali took their turns in cooking and cleaning and were on the same money allowance as the students.

Tony was in his forties, had experienced persecution in Sri Lanka and had lost contact with his family. He had been getting advice for his applications for staying in Australia. By the time I had to assist a little, he had been rejected and continued to be rejected – I still don't understand why. Ali was quite different. He had fled Iran, many thinking it was to get away from his wife. Be that as it may, he was welcomed by a Christian group in Parramatta and decided to become a born-again Christian. As far as I could see this was a ploy to stay. He was a singer and was looking for work but, at that stage, there was not a great demand for Farsi singers. He also had some drug problems, dealers sometimes coming to the door. And, he invested some of his allowance in the services of local prostitutes. He was also fairly sensitive to adverse comments and felt that one of the community was racist and insulting. I seemed to spend more time working things out with Ali than with the rest of the community.

Unfortunately, when Navarre House took in Tony and Ali, no contract was made and there was no arrangement for a review of the situation. Eventually, I asked the help of Jesuit Refugee Services who commented that Ali was an extreme case. I had thought he was par for the course.

Ali was taken to the Villawood Detention Centre and, presumably, returned home. Ali was a survivor and I would think that he would have settled back in Iran after his Australian adventure. This was a small learning experience – especially for the intensity of the issue of refugees and boat people coming to Australia and the political and social conflicts that were soon to come and would be dominant for the next decade and more.

33. SOME FOUR LETTER SIGNS

NO, NOTHING unbecoming in this section of my life.

I don't know whether you remember the letters MBTI or INFJ from an earlier time in this book (actually in 1978). I had mentioned that I would have to take them up at another time. And, this is it.

I just felt a temptation to be romantic and to use the language of falling in love. For someone with a vow of chastity, falling in love has considerable limitations. Though, as Milos Forman as the wise old parish priest in Keeping the Faith, told his young curate who was trying to sort out love/infatuation/vocation problem, he had fallen in love many times. It's how you handle the consequences that it is important.

So, continuing the metaphor for just a little longer, the initial infatuation with the Myers-Briggs Type Indicator (that's the MBTI part) in Berkeley in that November of 1978 was not just a flash in the pan (getting tangled in the metaphors now), but a love and affection that has lasted a lifetime. That had better be the end of that, but you know what I mean.

I have valued the insights into personality and traits that Carl Jung introduced as mediated by the insights and practical applications of Katherine Briggs and her daughter, Isabel, who married Chief Myers. The feminine perspective of their work and its heritage played an important role in its widespread success. I think the Quaker influence on Isabel and her family in Swarthmore, Pennsylvania, gave it some spiritual depth as well. Of course, it has taken on a life of its own in recent decades (Isabel Myers dying in 1980 after almost completing her book which, significantly, she titled *Gifts Differing* with reference to St. Paul and the gifts of the Holy Spirit.

Those other letters, INFJ, are the letters of my profile, not a box or compartment to be confined to. Rather, they indicate particular ways of dealing with life in both the inner and outer worlds. The I is for introversion, a preference for the inner life while, often, the outer world becomes overwhelming with the need to follow Jesus' advice when he was in the introverted vein, 'come away and rest a while'. It certainly did him good and out he went again extraverting at a great rate. The J at the end indicates my preference for 'let's get this show on the road' rather than waiting for yet some more information for making a decision. I rather like being decisive but know that we must develop our opposite so Jung advised for what he called 'individuation' moving towards integration and wholeness, so I try to be patient and not hurry people along too much. The N and the F? N is a symbol for a preference for Intuition or iNtuition as it is sometimes written.

One of the ways I like to explain it is the epigraph at the beginning of E. M. Forster's *Howard's End*, 'Only Connect'. I love hunches. I love making connections – it is really my favourite function (and, as in introvert, it is all 'in there'. I might look impassive at a lecture or even at a film (so I've been told), but inside it could be absolutely marvelous, making links and hunches dawning at a great rate. A bit like a birthday card I received once. There was the Mona Lisa with the caption, 'Smiling on the outside', then you opened the card and the artist had put a huge grin on her face, 'Laughing on the inside'. So, I have been a bit put out when I have shared this approach to life and work when somebody says, 'Why don't you just sit back and enjoy?'. I do, and this is how I do it.

Unfortunately, if the introverted intuition is my favourite way of perceiving reality, then a focus on sense detail is my least developed. E.g., I once admired a painting of confrere artist Patrick O'Carrigan and mentioned it to Brian Gallagher at Croydon years ago. Now, there is someone who prefers sense detail. On a Saturday afternoon he buzzed my room and asked 'What do you think?'. My hunches must have been having a rest so I asked, 'About what?'. He said, 'Raise your eyes'. I did, and there was the painting on my office wall, right in front of me. I thanked him and asked whether he had put it there that morning (Saturday). 'No, Thursday'. I have always been in danger of walking through some of the realities of life, oblivious.

Almost there. The F is a symbol for the criteria that I prefer to use for decision-making. Rather than use logic, principles and cause and effect (which we all do), I am more prone to look at the more personalised, subjective aspects of the situation. So, INFJ, and, though I discovered that it is one of the least prevalent of profiles – no wonder I can seem eccentric – I like it very much.

The reason for making it part of this story is that I found it a great help in working with students and their self-understanding and self-esteem. The MBTI is not a test but an indicator. Nor is there any judgment implied that one way is better than another, no good or bad, right or wrong. Just Gifts Differing.

Unfortunately, there was no accreditation program in Australia until 1986. Over 40 of us applied for the week-long program (the statistical part seemed even longer). But we were guided very well by Margaret and Gary Hartzler from the U.S. and privileged to have as part of the leader team, Kathy Myers, Isabel Myers daughter-in-law. So, connection with the sources.

The program was conducted at St. Joseph's College, Hunter's Hill, so I asked could I stay at the about-to-be-opened new MSC student house in Drummoyne (the one that I was strongly opposed to, the first irony staying there so early in the peace and then the greater irony when I was asked to be community leader and live there for a year in 1998!) As it turned out, most of the participants were of the NF variety – Temperament theory refers to them as idealists. While all of the Types there presented a mime, activity, with drama and/or songs, the INFJs had decided to stay in the audience and each one would go out and tell a story, explain an image or symbol or narrate a dream. That was a bit of a shock to me, a very private profile!

While I had led some seminars using material that was available in book form in the earlier 1980s, especially about ways of praying, I was now able to administer the questionnaire to determine profiles more accurately. However, unlike the American approach which was to fill in questionnaires first, get results and see how they fitted. I preferred, and found that most Australian Type practitioners preferred for individuals and groups to self-verify using explanations and a range of imaginative and visual devices, whether literary, comic strips and, you guessed it, I liked to show film clips (still do) to help people to identify with one or other of the four complementaries (not contradictories, important point), E-I, J-P, S-N, T-F. I was very pleased in 1994 when Mary McCauley, who had worked with Isabel Myers for many years, came to Australia, wondered about our self-verification process first then the Indicator but listened to us and declared that we were right for the Australian sensibilities (and wariness of the authority of unknown questionnaires).

On a personal note, that was the time I was to drive Mary around Melbourne and show her our city and take her out to the Healesville Sanctuary to see roaming kangaroos, wallabies, some koalas and a platypus ... We never got there. Mary wanted to meet Sister Margaret Dwyer, one of the pioneers of Type in Australia through the Melbourne Catholic Education Office. I was to learn that in Britain, New Zealand and Australia, Type was introduced through Catholic Education Offices. Margaret was directing retreats and so could only spare an hour. I believed her, and shouldn't have. One of my regrets was not having a tape recorder. They talked for three hours, most insightful stuff as you might imagine. The upshot re tourism was Mary's choice of a meat pie (the local touch) sitting on the banks of the Yarra at Warrandyte and then a walk through the tall gum trees in Sherbrooke Forest. And Mary kept remembering the meat pie at the river.

As it turned out, I spent a lot of the next 12 years conducting Myers-Briggs workshops, earning a lot of my living with it. There were seminars at the Heart of Life Centre. For three years, I went out in the name of the National Pastoral Institute. After its closure in the name of Heart of Life. Most of the bookings came from Catholic schools. Looking back, I realise how much I enjoyed this work and am always pleased when I meet someone who attended a seminar and even says the Type insights changed their lives, and sometimes their jobs. There were some groups from religious orders, some nursing staffs, some other Christian denominations. But that was a lot of my life from 1986-98.

What I particularly liked were the follow-up workshops. There is far more to Type than merely discovering your profile. There are applications to education and learning skills, to leadership, to business. There is a lot of academic research. The Type community has always welcomed religious and spirituality interest as well.

We did workshops on different styles of prayer. How about taking a psalm and praying it with two sides of the chapel as religious communities do. Very sensing, here and now. Pray it as at Mass, the Leader up front and intoning, 'Response' and we repeat an antiphon. Very thinking, objective, formal. The mode that drove some Sensing types momentarily berserk (some of them gripping a table to control themselves!) was my priming some of the group to read verse 4, then an indeterminate pause followed by verse seven, longer pause, then another person read verse 13. Very intuitive. Then we sang it. Very feeling. Another exercise well worth doing – and very revealing – was to divide the group into thinkers and feelers and then ask them to go away and prepare a retreat day program. The first time we did it, two women thinkers got the giggles as the feelers described their day. Listening to the diversity within the two groups, it is a wonder that any retreat day is a success. The feelers wanted a lovely day. I had to ban the use of the word 'lovely' as it put off the thinkers who wanted something 'appropriate'. The feelers had name tags, cups of tea, some chat, the possibility of an outdoor lunch by the river and, after Mass, a group hug. The thinkers wanted a clear theme, a timetable, the name of the visiting speaker, a clear stating of the cost and, after Mass, an evaluation discussion. Gifts differing!

One of the Type things I did in the 1980s was to follow a lead from Stephen Hackett, one of the MSC students at the time who understood Type well. He had been looking at a book of *Hagar the Horrible* cartoons and recognised a confrere in the joke in a panel. The upshot was that I went through all the Hagar books I could find and selected panels to represent all the aspects of type and add some introduction and some captions. I first put some in *Compass*, then asked Kathy Myers whether she approved. We published them as a book in 1987, *Let a Viking Do It, Hagar and Family Illustrate the Myers Briggs Type Indicator*. It did well. The Americans lurved it, declared it was 'cute'. (To get the full benefit of Americans saying 'cute', have a look at Monty Python's *Meaning of Life*, the segment where Michael Palin and Terry Jones as husband and wife go to a restaurant where they serve philosophical conversation menus instead of food. They try Schopenhauer. John Cleese plays the waiter whom Terry Jones as the wife declares with a sweet emphasis that he is 'cute'.)

It was only in 1984, watching Michael Douglas as a judge in *The Star Chamber* working with other judges to kill off criminals who had eluded justice in the courts. Somehow or other, the writing and the performance suggested ISTJ. (I hope the explanations so far have enabled you now to appreciate how an ISTJ functions – if not, don't worry). This led to a book, finding movies to illustrate each of the 16 possible combinations of Type and explore their development. I tried it out in poster form at the international conference in Boulder in 1989. That encouraged me to put it in book form (checking with Kathy Myers whether it was appropriate or not, especially the title the publishers suggested, *Myers Briggs Goes to the Movies*). It did well too. This time the Americans decided it was 'furn'.

An American author who had looked at this book, suggested it might be a good idea to do a book with longer Type studies of films. So, I did that. From *Citizen Kane* and *Grapes of Wrath* through *Vertigo* and *Lawrence of Arabia*, *The Sound of Music* and *One Flew Over the Cuckoo's Nest* to *Interiors* and *Thelma and Louise*. I really like my title this time, *Mirror, Mirror on the Screen*. Some copies were printed in folder form but it never received much circulation and is still sitting on my C/drive. Maybe one of these days.

To finish these book excursions into Type, I had been impressed for years by Margaret Dwyer's work in retreats according to Type and her Berkeley thesis which included noting how the Gospels, centuries before and without the benefit of Jungian theory, could be seen as corresponding to the four different functions (but always the same Spirit). There was a tradition that Mark's Gospel was, perhaps, from Peter's eyewitnessing the events and passing them on to Mark, a Gospel with lots of (sensing) detail. Matthew's Gospel was always considered the 'sayings' of Jesus, lots of sermons and teaching and, with parables and other incidents, very much plain talking, a 'no frills' (thinking) Gospel, rather confirmed by lots of Catholic men responding in prayer days to its matter of factness, how good Catholics ought to be. So, no prize in remembering that Luke's Gospel was considered the Gospel (feeling) of the heart and love. John and signs and wonders, symbols and meditations, an intuitive Gospel.

I thought it would be interesting to look at each Gospel in its particular narratives and styles and see how true this was. The result was *The Same as Christ Jesus: Gospel and Type*. It was published in London. Not sure that it had great sales, I'm afraid, but I liked working on this one.

Before moving away from the Type part of my life, there are three more aspects I would like to write about. The first brings me back to the books on film and Type. When the Australian Association for Psychological Type (more on this next), was launched in 1991, we started a journal. I have been contributing an article to every issue on so many different films and exploring them in the light of Type. A quick count indicates almost 60 over almost 20 years. For the last 10 years or more, I have tried to concentrate only on Australian films and Type. In 1998, I received a kind invitation from Ken Green, editor of the *U.S. Bulletin of Psychological Type*, to contribute to that magazine. So I did that until 2004. In the meantime, Gill Clack, editor of *Typeface*, the magazine of the British Association for Psychological Type, offered her invitation, which has continued from 2002 to the present and still continues. I thought the collection, around 120 by this might make an interesting book, *The Type and Movie Book*. Thanks to Trischa Baker of and Geraldine Corridon of

Melbourne and their Inkshed Press, this became a reality in 2012. The subtitle of the book was 'Personality through the lens of film'.

I mentioned the Australian Association. One of the Australian distributors of Type materials, David Freeman, was in Boulder for the 1989 conference. At a meeting of international members, that is non-Americans, it was suggested that local associations be formed since the official Association for Psychological Type (APT) was expanding around the world. David was commissioned to establish the Australian Association. Because I was in Boulder and lived in Melbourne as he did, he invited me to be part of a committee to sound out members in Australia, work on the feasibility of an association with state members and prepare statutes. This eventuated in many meetings in 1990 and a consensus to establish the association. In the meantime, I was a kind of inaugural president and represented Australia at the 1991 APT Conference in Richmond, Virginia. A meeting was called under the auspices of Mary McGuinness and her Institute for Type Development in Sydney. This led to an initial national conference and the formalising of the association and I spent some years as President of the Victorian association.

At this stage, we decided to have a national conference every two years, in the alternate years to the years of the APT Conference.

I would like to say that I think we made great successes of our conferences, states taking it in turns to organise – in Victoria we did the one where Mary McCauley was guest in 1994. Sydney and Brisbane organised others but since I left Australia in 1999, I was able to resume first hand attendance in 2010. The tradition had held very well: keynote speakers, plenty of concurrent workshops, activities, sales of an ever-increasing number of books, how to ... and devices to assist Type comprehension and develop skills.

Concerning the international conferences in the alternate years in the US, they moved across the U.S. from east to west. God bless Frequent Flyer points and Qantas, which enabled me to attend from 1991 to 2004, Richmond, Newport Beach, Kansas City, Boston, Scottsdale,

Minneapolis (Kansas City was in Missouri, but Greyhound enabled a trip into the state of Kansas and another on the list of U.S. states 'been there' (the intended conference outside the U.S. but still in North America in 2003 was to be in Toronto and was postponed for a year because of the SARS outbreak). I would have to say that some of those conferences were among the best I have ever attended. People were friendly (the Type community at its best), you got to know some of the authors you read and the lecturers you admired, and I found that presenting often on the film and Type themes, a ready audience who were eager to discuss and make suggestions. The religion and spirituality interest area always provided plenty of stimulating workshops. After 2004, times for conferences clashed with previously accepted commitments, so that was the end of attending. But, as support and challenge for those years of working with Type, the conferences and the friendships were, to use the cliché, invaluable.

I continue to do some Type workshops, some follow ups on Type and praying as well as write the movie columns and will do so as long as I can. You may not have been expecting this section of the story but I hope I have persuaded you that it has been integral to my life.

A very nice postscript. Psychologist, Meredith Fuller decided to do a series on people involved in the type community in Australia and I spent several afternoons living in reminisceland, enjoyably so, being taped for an article she was writing on me. We finished and that was that.

I went back to our national conferences in Sydney in August 2010. Watching my purse strings carefully – I had had to pay a fair price (no, probably too much in the event) for a dinner for the centenary of the MCD – I thought I would give the Conference dinner a miss. Phil Kerr, the president and long-time editor of the Journal in Australia, checked with me about going, then kindly said that I should be a guest. Let me say the dinner left the MCD dinner for dead. Halfway through (and they kept the hotel music on during the speeches), it dawned on me that Phil was talking about me. It was a plot by the committee – interview article and now I was being made a Life Member of the Australian Association. That was something I was very pleased and honoured to accept. If you live long enough, some very good things happen.

And then the 20 years of columns were published, *The Type and Movie Book*.

34. FAMILY

THE MALONE family. Very little to report in terms of drama. And not a film in sight.

I have mentioned that Dad was one of the most agreeable of men – the only point of disagreement with that is if you were pun-intolerant. He wasn't. Rather, he was something of an addict. He enjoyed words.

In 1990, he turned 80, still playing bowls, still driving. Still joking. He used to like coming up to our house in Kew, always arriving far earlier than you intended, even driving as slowly as he used to. He was still down at his little fibro house, just the three rooms, and his veggie garden. He loved walking around Chelsea, strolling along the beach, beachcombing and finding a mini-income. Chatting to all and sundry, generally instantly, and regaling shopkeepers and parishioners with the achievements of his sons. (A bit of dread walking with him and going into the shops – so this is one of Joe's sons that he's forever talking about!) He enjoyed chatting with nuns, visiting the Daughters of Our Lady of the Sacred Heart at Bentleigh, Christmas Eve and other meals with the Sisters of Our Lady of the Missions at East Kew, pals with the sisters who worked in the parish.

Dad was someone who liked the changes in the Church, from the way Mass was celebrated, especially the Children's Masses for Holy Thursday and Christmas, to the accessibility to nuns, freer than when Aunty Lucy and Aunty Mary were younger. I noticed that back in the early 1990s, he changed from referring to his Sunday morning task of preparing the altar for Mass to 'preparing it for the Eucharist'. My guess is that he picked that up from the Brigidine, Sister Pat, who worked in the parish – and with whom he went to Sizzlers once a month for lunch where I sometimes joined him. What a pity Sizzlers closed down. Great for older people like Dad – and I didn't mind it either.

When I celebrated 25 years of ordination in 1990, we went to the local parish church of Our Lady of Good Counsel at Deepdene, and I have the photos of him standing by the altar sharing with Philip and myself in the Offertory prayers.

Things went on like this until the middle of 1996, except for his first visit to hospital, a hernia operation at Frankston hospital. I wondered what it would be like to find him in hospital. When I rang to find out how the operation went, the nurse who answered the phone said she would check. She came back and told me he had commented on how attractive the nurses were, so I knew he was all right. When I got there, he knew the names of the other five men in the ward and their life stories as well. As we talked, I noticed his eyes darting to the door, taking in everything that was happening and everyone who passed by.

It was a bit of a shock, however, when I was called back from a Saturday morning Mass at the Cluny community down Sackville Street because Dad had rung and said he was hungry and had no food in his house. As it turned out, his kind neighbour, Gordon, had taken ill and was in hospital. I rushed down to Chelsea, realising that this could be the beginning of something different for Dad. Gordon returned but was also anxious. It looked as if Dad needed to go into hostel care. When Philip and I went down to see him the next month, his car wasn't there. We thought he had lost it as he had, for a time, earlier. But, it had been put in for servicing. He had also bumped the gutter with the car, at another time had fallen because of an upraised bit of concrete in the footpath. These had dented his confidence.

But, he needed to be assessed for going into a hostel. With his dislike of doctors, that was not going to be easy. It wasn't. But, yes, he could go into care. I had always thought that he would go to the MSC Sisters at St. Joseph's Tower in Kew. They were full-up at the time. Providence kicked in with some vacancies at Cluny. So, on 7 August 1996, he left Chelsea and moved to just down the street from us into Cluny. No praise too high for the sisters, especially Fran who seemed to take him on as her special guest-friend.

When I was first packing up at Chelsea, I came across a video cassette and remembered that Peter Thomas of Catholic Communications who had known Dad for quite a while, suggested he might like to take a small role in a program they were making on the homeless in Melbourne. By all means. And he used his own clothes and a (very) aged suitcase as costume and prop. One of the photos I have of Dad in my room is of him standing outside Catholic Communications dressed down for filming. And we still have the video as a living memory.

Speaking of the homeless and the needy, Dad led a simple life but he always loved following stocks and shares, always did with his quick mathematical intelligence. He had stopped the pension when he had lost confidence but Gordon and I put him back on. And his bank book. I looked and saw that he had $105.00. Not bad for a simple man. The next day I noticed I had misread the dot. He had $105,000.00, which meant that I (he) could pay the full entry amount at Cluny and prepay his funeral. I mentioned to him that he had two fixed deposits of some thousands of dollars which he thought wasn't bad and would cover things. I didn't have the heart to tell him about the $105,000.00. The pension paid for his board at Cluny and the odds and ends like haircuts. When he died, he left $96,000, not bad for a frugal man.

On my birthday, the day after Dad moved into Cluny, I went down to his house for a final clean up. When I got back to Cluny for the 11.00 Mass, Fran hurried into the sacristy upset: Dad (she always referred to him as Dad) was dismayed and confused, was in prison. Thanks very much. The Gospel (for the Mass of Blessed Mary MacKillop) was about providence and not worrying about what to eat or what to wear. After all … the birds of the air, the lilies of the field. I decided that this was the best faith to have. The next day, Uncle Maurice's second son, Adrian, called in, had a chat, took photos, cheered Dad. Adrian was visiting all his family, coming over from Western Australia where he and his wife, Heather, had lived for almost 30 years. He had a terminal cancer and died some months later. By Monday – the crisis was on Thursday – Dad had settled down completely. Despite offers of drives, he never went out again. He had been there and done that.

In fact, he never went to Mass again. The old legs! Fran and the sisters regularly and diligently brought him Communion. I used to go round to see him after the morning Mass and sometimes in the afternoon if I had not been there in the morning. If Dad was still in bed, then I learnt to know that all was well. I would knock. 'Thought it'd be you.' But, if he was sitting on the side of the bed, he had been wandering and needed settling. Breakfast came round – tea and toast, but cold toast. He had always liked hot toast and we often tried to warm it a little next to the teapot. Then he used to say that he should not groan because he was all grown/groan up.

We got a phone for him so that he could talk to Philip in Sydney, usually on a Saturday morning. He had a couple of close friends who rang or visited. They were from his wardsman days, Margot who had TB and with whose parents he boarded for many years, Joan his matron in Frankston, Anne, a nurse at Greenvale whom he might have married. Philip visited when he came down from Sydney where he was still teaching Moral Theology at St. Paul's Late Vocations Seminary. (Philip also had a most interesting Sabbatical in 1993, travelling and visiting moral theologians around the world, talking and picking their brains on current issues, then a personal time at Herrenbrook House outside Birmingham. He boarded at Nazareth House at Hammersmith – preparing a way for me to live there for almost 12 years.)

Our Benedictine aunt, Lucy, died in September 1993 while we were both in England. She had been a nun for almost 55 years, at Rydalmere, then moving to Pennant Hills when Rydalmere became industrialised, then to the south of Sydney to Jamberoo, on a beautiful mountainside. She had also spent some years in Melbourne helping a little local order for women who could not enter more established congregations because of age or health, the Sisters of Reparation, co-founded by our cousin Fr. Darcy Morris MSC. I never expected Aunty Lucy to be living over the back fence at Croydon. A couple of weeks in 1972, then three years from 1975 when she came with Sister Joan Maloney who stayed some years longer. Eventually, the local sisters died and only two were left and it all came to an end. Very nice for Dad that his sister was unexpectedly in Melbourne for three years. One of the interesting things was that they decided to buy a car and Joan got her licence. Some of them came to courses at YTU, including Aunty Lucy. I'm afraid I had a delegation of students come to ask me to transfer her to another Old Testament tutorial group as she was taking over! Some of the students took to calling her Aunty Lucy – and still do. She was a great singer in choir, something of a historian, and always had an open ear for all who come to see her.

Now that I have mentioned Aunty Lucy, I had better mention the rest of Dad's brothers and sisters so that you have the proper picture: one priest, two nuns, one a former seminarian and one member of the Third Order of St. Francis – and Dad who always liked to introduce himself punningly as 'the real Father Malone'.

Fr Maurice Malone (Uncle Phil), the Franciscan, died in 1981. Aunty Mary, the second youngest, was a school teacher who joined the Presentation Sisters in Lismore, New South Wales, and spent her life in school until some hospital work in later years. She always reckoned that she was a subject when they did all the work and was appointed a superior when the Council seemed to indicate that the superiors should do all the work. She was a short, lively woman, always encouraging, always. We had hope that she would be able to be in Sydney because, even in her early seventies, Aunty Sheila was beginning to show signs of dementia. To our shock, at the beginning of 1996, Aunty Mary went to Lismore, was diagnosed with cancer and died very quickly, aged 78. It became clear that Aunty Sheila could not manage by herself, so her brother Maurice arranged for her to stay in a nursing home in Terrigal, north of Sydney, where she lived for several years and died at the age of 80. One time that Philip and I went up to see her, she was sitting in a common room, looked up, saw us and smiled. But, no real communication after that.

Another time, Maurice and his wife, Dorothy, brought Aunty Sheila out to their place where we could have some afternoon tea and she would be more at ease. She was, but again no real communication though she did say some words. As you can imagine, it was very, very sad to see someone who had helped bring us up as boys finally so helpless.

Which leaves Uncle Maurice, a great man. He spent years in the MSC junior school but did not continue on for the novitiate. He had a lovely wife, Dorothy, and they had seven children. Maurice was a gentle man, a gentleman. For some early years he was a photographer. He was also very deaf, but if you wanted interesting conversation on all kinds of topics, he was the man. I thought I should try to visit him at the beginning of 2009 because he would soon turn 93. His oldest son, Paul, had been very good to his father. As he got older and Dorothy died, he moved from his house to Paul's home. An office outside the main house was transformed into a flat for Maurice, very comfortable and only three metres or so from Paul and his wife, Kerry. I enjoyed the visit, chatting with him and Paul and Michael, who was also there, and seeing how happy his last years were. He died in August 2009. He had so many grandchildren (the first 14 of whom were girls) and who knows how many grandchildren. I did baptise one of his grandchildren, Catherine, Mary's daughter in Acton in 1965 and conducted her wedding, but their world does not cross ours in Melbourne.

I have already mentioned how we lost touch with my mother's side of the family.

And, that's it, not The Malone Saga. But, it's mine and I have liked it.

So, back to Dad and his final days. He lived at Cluny for only 16 months. They were comfortable and warm. He liked to carry a water bottle. And that was one of my tasks when I arrived to see him, 'Could you fill up the water bottle.' Nana was a great water bottle person. Dad may have had more reason, living in Melbourne, while Nana was in Sydney but she often said that she was 'perishing with the cold'. Which reminds me of a strange episode. A visiting doctor to Cluny was doing research so I said that it was all right if she talked with Dad. A mistake. He never liked doctors and may not have been at his most genial, especially when she asked about the water bottle. She told me that she thought he needed psychiatric care because she considered this bizarre behaviour. Then I made another mistake and told the doctor about Nana. 'So, she needed psychiatric help too.' I ask you!

As the months went by, Dad became more passive. Towards the end, he would go round and round asking about getting up, going to the dining room at 11.00 am and whether someone would help him. It meant continual reassurance. He didn't like the old ladies, who well outnumbered the men there, fussing over him and telling him he should eat more. Not too keen either, after 50 years of living alone, for others to wash him. At the beginning of December 1997, the sisters thought he was declining and moved him because he had started calling out. Denis Rebic, our doctor, saw him and said that he thought he had some melanomas, but Dad had always been stoic concerning pain. It was time for Philip to come down to Melbourne and I think he was shocked to see how Dad had deteriorated.

The sisters arranged for him to go to Henry Pride hostel at the other end of Kew. Their care for Dad was the best you could want, very personal, one of the nurses even asking us if we would like to call a priest. I had to whisper we both were. Dad had a quietly comfortable day. Since Philip had been travelling, I was to stay the first night. I noticed about 4.00 am that the pace and sound of his breathing changed, so I stood by the bed, speaking, praying, singing some verses of hymns for him. At around 4.10, he simply stopped breathing. As quietly and as peacefully as that. By the time, I went and brought Philip, they had taken away the drip, smoothed the bed and put a flower in a vase beside him. I'm going to opt for understatement now and simply say it was a joy, a sadness and a privilege to be with him as he died. 12 December 1997.

A big crowd in the Cluny chapel for the Rosary. Even more at the Requiem at St. Joseph's Tower. We put mementoes on the coffin. Dad's friend Margot placed a picture of our mother, Eileen, Peter Thomas placed that video cassette, Paul Castley placed one of his bowling trophies and Sister Fran the water bottle. Philip and I moved between us for the prayers. At the graveside, the small group of us sang the *Salve Regina*. Just right. He is buried in a lawn cemetery at Cheltenham and his grave faces the road. I thought he would enjoy looking at all those who pass by!

His gravestone reads:

IN LOVING MEMORY

OF

JOSEPH WALTER MALONE

DIED 12TH DECEMBER 1997. AGED 87 YEARS.

BELOVED HUSBAND OF

EILEEN

LOVING FATHER OF PETER AND PHILIP

R.I.P

He always used to sign his letters, 'Your proud Dad'.

35. THE PACIFIC

FROM 1991 TO 2000, I went to meetings of OCIC Pacific almost each year. This was very new for me. While I had flown over the Pacific three times and we had touched down one early morning in 1966 in Nadi, I was hardly prepared to be president of OCIC Pacific. I did have one very pleasant week of preparation though I did not know it was. It was on Rarotonga in the Cook Islands. Cluny Sister Elizabeth Russell was having a sabbatical at the National Pastoral Institute in 1986. Peter Thomas and I were presenting material for the Diploma in Social Communications and discovered that Elizabeth was the representative of Unda and OCIC for the Cooks. When she returned in 1987, she invited us to come for a media seminar. Peter's forte was radio, so a radio seminar it was to be. And I was invited to offer some religious input. I hadn't had a passport for nine years, so ... back in the air, again.

Obviously, the trip was exotic and enjoyable. Rarotonga, the centre of the many Cook Islands is volcanic, a high mountain in the centre. It is only 32 kilometres all round. Some old vehicles but travel was mainly on the back of a motor bike. There are beaches, rather coral sand, and the reef surrounding the island out there. Tropical – and if I reached out the window of the room I was staying in, I could pick a pawpaw. I don't want to give the impression that this was just an island holiday – though the pace, even with the seminar, was not what you would call hectic.

So, learning a bit more about the Pacific Islanders. And about Pacific time. It was school time, September 1987, so our course was an evening course. Scheduled for 4.00 pm. If we got started before 4.30, that was something special. However, there is something to be said for the traditions of European missionaries. No matter what time we got started, the bell rang for the 6.00 pm Mass at 5.55 and you have never seen such sudden and rapid down tools even in a wildcat strike. That Mass was sacred. Everyone attended. And it started right, right on time.

The islanders let themselves go at Mass with their singing, rich, powerfully loud, breaking into polyphony spontaneously, the congregation a choir.

Then, more course, some reflections on religious aspects of media and God's communication, and lots of hands on, script preparation, recording, assessing. In an interfaith gesture, the Baha'i leaders lent us their radio equipment and attended the course.

Then, to an astounding experience of hospitality – eating. What poet referred to tables groaning under the weight of the food? Our Rarotonga tables were beyond groan. A literal feast every night. The Polynesians can be mighty eaters and often have the bulk to prove it. Our meals were prepared by the Catholic Women's League and they showed us the way, digging in. I mean that in the literal way. It was real hands in. I do remember talking with the ladies about video which was beginning to be much more available. No television at that stage, but the Catholic Women had seen all the current mini-series that were on Australian television and enjoyed comparing notes. They had helpful relatives and contacts in New Zealand for their supply.

I was thinking that this was my life's visit to the Pacific so wasn't psyching myself up as to working with people in the Pacific. But, it was a providential preparation.

As we left on a Saturday morning at 8.00 am, we were, within the hour, at almost 8.00 am Sunday morning. The dateline. The pilot then announced that our flight would take an extra hour since we needed to fly close to an international airport in case of emergency. That morning it was to be Nadi 'because today is Sunday and the Kingdom of Tonga is closed'. Speaking of the dateline, I remember going once in the opposite direction. It is only an hour or so's flight from Tonga to Samoa, but you go back 23 hours. Didn't Kiribati alter the dateline so that they would definitely be the first place in the world to greet the new millennium? And in 2011, Samoa decided it wanted to lead the world again.

My first meeting with Unda and OCIC Oceania was the early morning after arriving in Bangkok

in November 1990 for the International Congress and Assemblies. Chairing our meeting even as I was introduced to the group. Sister Dasko Williams of Pohnpei (where?, I hear you ask, as I asked long ago), one of the Caroline Islands as you travel back from Guam and Truk towards the Marshalls and Hawaii, was the president of Unda Oceania. OCIC and Unda did everything together in the Pacific – and there really was no so much OCIC activity in the region, the media work being that of Unda, radio, television and video production. So, we combined agendas, reports, finances, applications for media grants via Unda and OCIC from the Vatican's Congregation for the Propagation of the Faith. From the Cooks, I knew that informality was the order of the day (of all the time), that we did not stand on ceremony (and we sat for the Kava drinking, Kava being affectionately called 'grog', and giving something of a buzz and literal tongue numbing I-don't-know-what). Bill Falakaono, my successor as President of OCIC Pacific, from Tonga, played the guitar, had a powerful voice (still has) and could lead us in song, though the Australians always had to fall back on Waltzing Matilda. At these international gatherings, with jokes and stories, song and a beer, we found that lots of other delegates from Europe and Asia quickly turned up. By the end of the meeting, we were well met and I was made to feel a hail and hale fellow.

Over the years, we had to assert ourselves in the face of the bigger powers. Most did not know where we all came from, some even (as George W. Bush did in his visit) mixed Australia up with Austria. You had to search hard on the map to find the Pacific countries. After all apart from Australia, PNG and New Zealand, no country had a million people, not even Fiji. Rather, some of our islands were far flung and sparsely populated. At times, maps were used which bisected the world into Americas/Europe/Africa and Asia, eliminating most of the Pacific Ocean since it was easy to bisect the globe vertically, cutting through empty water. I found myself over the years becoming more aggressively defensive about our mostly water part of the world.

In the coming years, we met in various local countries, our budget being carefully caretaken by Peter Thomas as treasurer who managed to get us to the regional meetings and the international assemblies.

Where did we go in the 1990s? They included the year we went to Pago Pago (American Samoa and a landing base for transports on their way to Antarctica), volcanic, 32 kilometres round and in many parts smelling of the fish canneries, and when we held a long seminar in a very finely appointed conference centre on the issues of censorship, film classifications and consumer advice. During a scene from Steven Seagal actioner, the women cringed in the front seats of a very nice theatrette, the violence not appealing. However, the married deacons were also attending the seminar and one of them, Francis, with more than an American twang, reassured us that Polynesians could watch and appreciate this kind of film because they too were warrior peoples. Not sure that that really justified it all, but a salutary caution of simply importing our own sensibilities and sensitivities and making assumptions.

The trip to Pago Pago required going to the then Western Samoa first and on return because you either went from Apia by boat or flew in small planes for which they weighed both you and your luggage, deciding how many hefty locals could go on the plane for safety. Only a 40 minute flight. In Samoa, a chance to visit Robert Louis Stevenson's grave and see the Gary Cooper hut at Aggie Grey's – he was in Apia for the filming of *Return to Paradise* in the early 1950s.

So, that was an OCIC focused meeting. Unda and practical workshops for the next two, one at the Jesuit High School on the island of Truk (not pronounced Truck, as Anglos and Yanks rendered it, but, with local consonants, more like Chuuk with an R sound in there somewhere). The New York province of the Jesuits staffed Guam, Palau and the Carolines and the Marshalls. At the High School on Truk there was still evidence of a bomb that had struck the school decades earlier. And Truk Lagoon was the safe anchor for the Japanese navy. At meetings like this you realised more and more the difficulties of flying in the Pacific (let alone the prices). We were lucky coming from Australia because Continental flew direct from Brisbane to Guam (where, on the huge banks of TV monitors in the airport, song proclaimed that Guam began America's day!) Fred Chamberlin and I saw *Sister Act* that afternoon in a Guam cinema. There are many Catholics on Guam and they delighted, as we did, with Sister Whoopi and her choir. Many Catholics in the Pacific and Asia will begin singing, 'I will follow him, wherever he may go ...' and we are back with *Sister Act* and the Pope tapping his feet and applauding, not unlike Pope John Paul II joining in rocking and swaying with the youth music at Randwick Racecourse five years later. Continental stopped these flights only three months later (but transferred the frequent flyer points to our Qantas tally; now that's professional courtesy).

The Continental ticket plus allowed us flights to and from Guam to Saipan where we sat on the southern edge and looked across at Rota and Tinian. Bishop Comacho told us that as children they watched the Enola Gay and the other planes take the bomb from Tinian to Hiroshima. Saipan too is one of the main places where the Japanese soldiers hid in caves for years not knowing the war was over. You can drive (actually, the only time I have driven on the American side of the road) past an abundance of tourist hotels and flats to the crags where the Japanese jumped to their deaths as the Americans took over, or go up to the high cliffs where Japanese families lined up from the youngest to the father, each pushing the one in front over the cliff until the father fell, not heeding the appeals of the Americans that they would not be harmed.

We did a day flight to Yap with its stone money (one of the Caroline Islands and only about 1400 kilometres from Guam) and then an overnighter in independent Palau with its wonderfully exotic stone formations in the sea, the place where Damian Parer was killed while filming the war. There were a lot of photos there of what Palau looked like in the 1930s under Japanese rule. It looked a lot better than it did in 1992. So, that was how we were able to fly to Truk for the meeting and then on to see Dasko's home in Pohnpei. This was certainly a trip to remember.

Delegates from Kiribati came via Nauru but then couldn't board the island's one and only plane as it was commandeered for a political figure. Oh well, just another couple of days' delay.

Maybe this is the moment to mention a strike on New Caledonia in 1994. I had used Frequent Flyer points to visit Pierre Demurger and Nicole Constans in Noumea for OCIC and Unda work. New Caledonia is so very French. I got to know this better after the strike. Nicole took me to Tontouta airport to leave and I told her not to wait. I would be all right. No such luck. The luck was that Nicole stayed, so back the 53 kilometres to Noumea and Pierre's house and three more days because the French airline had struck and Qantas always used their steps to get passengers on and off and this was forbidden during *un grève*. The next day was Bastille Day and I was able to see the procession and its French military style, the presenting of Legion d'Honneur medals. In those days, audio programs and videos were flown in daily from France. This was part of France, 'metropole'. There was so much François Mitterrand on television that you would not have known Bill Clinton was alive let alone President of the United States. We did go back in 1996 for our annual meeting to Noumea. Henk Hoekstra, the then president of OCIC, was there and we did a workshop on spirituality and cinema. That was the year we published a combined statement against nuclear testing in French Polynesia.

Regular delegates to our meetings were from the Solomon Islands so that was where we went in 1993. And arrived in National Malaria Week. We had our tablets but it was a bit off-putting to see at once a float of a giant mosquito, as well as the real ones. For an Australian it is important for war memories to visit the Solomons and Honiara and Guadalcanal, only a few hours flight from Brisbane. As The Thin Red Line reminds us, the fighting in the Solomons was crucial for Australia's safety and we were indebted to the Americans. I suddenly felt resentful when at the Berlin Film Festival in 1999, after the press screening of *The Thin Red Line*, a European critic marched down the aisle and yelled out against the Americans, 'One, two, three, four, we don't want your fucking war.' Even some of the Protestant pastors from northern Europe wanted to exclude the film from consideration and discussion for an award. I found that I felt I should explain what this battle meant for us but it seemed too hard for them to comprehend or they thought it irrelevant.

When we arrived and assimilated the malaria focus, we saw many locals watching a rugby match on TV – and they were all loudly cheering Australia against South Africa.

One of the values of going to a country is the support that the group can give to the local church and the local church media workers, meeting the authorities, doing some PR work, visiting the studios, looking at the equipment, so hard to keep cool and clean with the humidity, supporting the programs. I remember we were shown a 90 minute video production made in Honiara, Peter the Rock. And I still remember the scene where Jesus chose Peter and the apostles. It was filmed on the beach. Peter and co were so exhilarated at being chosen that they literally kept leaping into the air with joy. The 1990s meant that this kind of production could now be made, equipment being handier, cheaper and exciting for so many to use.

In the meantime, having become friends with our members in the Pacific, I was invited to several countries for specialised workshops. In going to Fiji a number of times, I was the guest of one of the fine missionaries of the Pacific, Fr. Larry Hannan. Larry, at the time of writing, is an Irish Marist priest in his late eighties, his eyesight failing. He arrived in Fiji in 1948, had been parish priest, vicar general, rector of the seminary twice. When he finished the second time, in his late sixties, he was asked to take care of an ecumenical video library. I don't think that Larry had had much experience of movies before this. But, he was nothing less than thorough in everything and quickly built up a detailed knowledge, studied catalogues and reviews and bought wisely, became involved in OCIC when the organisation had begun to languish in Fiji, attended meetings internationally on children's film, a benignly modulated quiet manner of speaking earnestly that encouraged everyone. One year, we did seminars for Pacific Regional Seminary, for religious, and for mixed groups of teachers and parents in Suva and right around the north west in Lautoka. A tourist hint. You wouldn't be sorry to go by bus around from Nadi to Suva, a couple of hours, some buses a bit open air, but time to absorb the transition from dry tropical round Nadi and the west to the wetter east and Suva.

Larry and a group of interested parties had begun Fiji Media watch, not as a censorious watchdog but as an observer group, both positive and challenging. I was invited to meetings on changing legislation with the introduction of television in the early 1990s. I still send movie reviews once a month and Larry unfailingly acknowledges them, always alluding to how useful they are to *Media Watch*. Speaking of government, in 1995 and 1998, we had workshops with the Censorship Board. Now that was interesting. Many of them were older than they used to be, grandparents in fact, who had been appointed officially because of some position in government in the past or some good repute, especially religious. Many said their grandchildren wondered what they were doing on this Board. They were paid, but, were they to take a taxi to work and back, they would run at a loss.

They certainly watched the films, but their work lacked a little finesse, to put it politely. Excising a longish shower scene from *The Specialist* with Sylvester Stallone and Sharon Stone still left about 20 seconds before and after so we all had some images of what we missed! We looked at issues of sensitivities and the perennial question of what is presented and how it is presented to help gauge the intentions of the film-maker. We decided one year to test our approaches and our ethical, values and religious systems by looking at the abortion-themed, *If These Walls Could Talk* but did not get far as it was a too hard basket issue. Still, the members took their job seriously and tried to judge the films. They had been hacking into a *Highlander* film the day before the workshop.

Bill Falekaono, himself a former student at the Pacific Seminary in Suva organised a week of media studies for students in 1998. As part of our research, we were able to go as a group (though found it hard to get in because of the crowds) to the newly opened Village Six multiplex and tested ours and audience reaction to *Lethal Weapon 4* and *The Negotiator* (still the overtones of Polynesians as warrior people).

The visits to Fiji were also important for the MSCs working there and the establishing of a novitiate, out of Suva on the side of a mountain with a farm and then, moving out of the PRS building (where, I was told John Paul II had stayed, in the room next to the one I always seemed to get) to new buildings, again on hills with a group of separate buildings and with vegetable gardens at Wailuku. The Pacific Foundation had become a Union with candidates from Fiji, Kiribati and some from Futuna and Samoa.

Of the islands that just leaves Tonga of places where we met in the 1990s. Bill had invited me to Tonga several times and we did quite some extensive courses for teachers and other church workers there. They were substantial now that I think of it, appreciation, media literacy (and visuacy) with a lot of screenings and a lot of discussions. Since Bill owned a video store we were not without plenty of cassettes to choose from – and even a special event, a screening of Baz Luhrmann's *Romeo + Juliet* at the local cinema (which Bill tells me has burned down). You may remember that Tonga closes on Sundays – well, not exactly. We decided to have the Sunday off from our OCIC Pacific meeting. After a magnificently sung Mass (Bill was choirmaster at the cathedral), we went a short boat ride from the jetties of Nuku'alofa to a little island where it was lawful to swim all day. In Nuku'alofa, not. At another time, I went with Bill and the Bishop for a pasta meal at a restaurant on a Sunday night – because the Italian owner took in guests, he could serve meals for them (and others and us). Tonga has been a kingdom not a colonial fiefdom and proud of it, but struggling with attempts at democracy in recent times.

Oh, add a week in PNG. Somehow or other, invitations to PNG

in the past had lapsed for lack of funding. My confrere, Tony Arthur, with whom I had been at school at Chevalier all those decades ago, was Rector of the seminary in Port Moresby. After I was elected as OCIC president, he thought that, as such, I needed some Papua New Guinea experience so invited me for a week's teaching for the seminarians. And the Melanesian experience within two months of the Polynesian was instructive on different approaches and styles of learning. So much of my education about the Pacific has been by experiences, comparisons and contrasts.

The next paragraph is an indulgence I invite you to share. Saturday was a day off – no classes on Sunday but a chance to visit parishes, meet the OLSH sisters working in Port Moresby and concelebrate Mass in Pidgin. The MSC community bought me a plane ticket. The advice was simply, go to the airport on Saturday and take the first flight whatever its destination because, at least, it has taken off and is going somewhere. Options were Fane, where some of our men worked, or Kokoda. I thought a little prayer urging providence was in order: Lord, Kokoda. As the Psalm says, 'The Lord heard my prayer.' Off we went to Kokoda and memories of the Australian troops confronting the Japanese approaching from the other side of the Owen Stanley Ranges and the help they received from the locals, the so-called Angels of War, the Fuzzy Wuzzy Angels. (Not sure you would get away with that these days.) But, the best was landing and taking off in the mountains. Fourteen seater, I think, with a Papuan woman co-pilot (making me realise I have seen very few women as commercial pilots even now). The landing was on a mountain slope, cut for an airstrip, the up-hill slowing us down. Then a turn (in front of the cliff face) and park. Then the fog came up. More than thick. Enough sun or warmth to break it up? After an hour or so, yes. Then, and I think this is the best part: taking off. I have never and will never hang-glide. This is the closest I will ever get. Speed down the slope, then out over the thousand feet high cliff, gliding, swooping, engine throttle, and there we were. Terrific. In the valleys, a long way down, you could see trails – many of the French Missionaries of the Sacred Heart who pioneered in the mountains got workers out from Switzerland to use their alpine experience in this tropical setting. Glad to say, we had several stops, including one like this and another stop at Kokoda. On the Sunday afternoon, we drove up to the start of the Kokoda Trail. It was wet and thick muddy. We drove a couple of kilometres but had to turn back. Brought home the conditions of the soldiers up there, back then.

If nothing else had happened to me except this Pacific experience, it would have been well worth it. In fact, I found I could be a missionary, however briefly, the kind that collaborates with the local church, brings some experience, shares it with the local people, no imposing, experiencing both teaching and learning, finishes and goes home, keeps in touch, offers help when needed, at the service of the local church.

But, more did happen, and even further afield from Australia.

36. 'I SUPPOSE IT WILL ENTAIL SOME TRAVEL?'

THAT WAS Jim Littleton's question when I asked him about OCIC. Yes. I was amused when our gung-ho former Provincial Superior, Frank Quirk, was 92 and I wondered if he would know who I was or whether I was Philip. 'Here's the man with the eternal air ticket.' (Perhaps that what I should have called this section – though it continues well beyond this section!)

Fred Chamberlin's nomination of me for the presidency of OCIC Pacific was not his only nomination. He put me forward as a member of the International Board of OCIC. In fact, this meant that I spent from 1990 to 2006 on the Boards of OCIC and SIGNIS. If I had to learn from experience, comparisons and contrasts in the Pacific, it was also true at the international level, and requiring something of a devious mind at times, learning diplomacy (for some reason, many nationalities consider us direct, even blunt, while we think we are the essence of considerate thoughtfulness), adaptability and, above all, decent respect for everyone, no suggestion even of any superiority. Maybe the Australian egalitarian tradition and not always taking authority too seriously are an unexpected advantage. In fact, it often seemed rather funny, even absurd, being so deferred to by more hierarchical societies, ushered in first, stood back for, called *il* and *el presidente*, presented with souvenirs, and various other forms of kowtowing. But, even this required respect for the traditions that took this way of acting for granted. Though it was always a bit much to be stood attention to and saluted by the Swiss Guards as they looked through anyone accompanying you who was not wearing a clerical collar (which was the case with the laymen, laywomen and sisters going to Pontifical Council meetings) and oneself the next day, going in without a collar where you were just one of the unsalutables. You see what I mean.

The first experience was that OCIC-Unda Assembly in Bangkok 1990 which I have already said was my introduction to OCIC Pacific. And to the Thais. They do say Sawasdee a lot, smile and mean it. Chainerong Monthivienchinchai (I defy you to get that right the first time – and Archbishop Foley could always say it with such smooth ease every time) was president of Unda World and organised this Congress and Assembly to perfection. In fact, no Congress could match it for organisation, courtesy, and introduction to the world of the Thais – until he organised one in Chang Mai in 2009 with the same panache and success.

We certainly did a lot of work, but I found I could relax a little at the back of the hall because, though I was president, I had no constituency allowing me to vote. Fred was still the delegate for Australia. I could observe proceedings, meet and get to know people I would be working with for many years to come. Ambros Eichenberger OP from Zurich was finishing 10 years as president of OCIC. Henk Hoekstra O.Carm was about to succeed him. Robert Molhant from Brussels had already been Secretary General of OCIC since 1979. He and I were both to finish together leading SIGNIS in 2005. Very impressive was one guest, Cardinal Carlo Martini of Milan, a great speaker, full of stimulating ideas, former head of the Biblical Institute in Rome and often talked about as papabile', a possible pope. That would have been more than very interesting. I also met Jim McDonnell, Director of Catholic Communications for the Bishops Conference of England and Wales who would become a good friend. He gave a talk on Christ-figures, on science fiction, fantasy and storytelling. At last, someone I could share ideas and insights with.

I hesitate to write this but there was one drawback, the accommodation. It was at a University. That was not bad. But, we discovered there was a PA speaker in each room and, with that Asian penchant for beginning the day before the day begins, our host Fr. Haberstroh would boom into the morning an irritating good morning and welcome to the day and play music – and you couldn't turn him off. Not so important, I suppose, but it is one of the main things that comes to memory.

We were taken to floating markets, to what was really a theme park, 60 kilometres from Bangkok where we had a beautiful meal, saw an elephant parade and kickboxing – amongst other entertainment. And, after the congress we went on a bus ride to the resort, with sometimes dubious sex tourism reputation, Pateya, where we visited an orphanage run by a Chicago Redemptorist priest (who first showed us his *60 Minutes* interview with Jana Wendt for Australian television). Fr. Brennan, who seemed a cross between Mother Teresa and Al Capone, explained what was what in Pateya before we wandered round, now noticing all the elderly European men with young Thai girls on their arms. This made up for our timidity when, after visiting the beautiful Buddhist temples and the museums where we learnt that Thais and Burmese had never been the greatest of friends, we looked into a Pat Pong bar (had heard about them, of course, during the war in Vietnam), but quickly exited for a nearby McDonalds.

If this was OCIC and Unda, it was a different world from what I had been used to.

Being on the international Board meant an annual meeting, usually in Belgium where the General Secretariats were located. The 1991 meeting was in fact in Leuven at the American College. So, international agendas dwarfed our small concerns in the Pacific, even the finance, rather modest I realised, that we asked for projects. The Board meetings reviewed the past year (that first one looking at the costs of Bangkok, in a word, 'wow') and planned for the coming year, film festival juries to be considered, conferences in different parts of the world, legal matters and liaison with the Pontifical Council for Communications, whose representative (Monsignor Enrique Planas from Spain for many years) attended. That's probably enough about most of the Board meetings to come, except for one of those devious attitudes I mentioned. In 1992, one of the Latin American delegates had had some sexual misconduct problems and was asked not to come. He did, and then, as not infrequently happened, the group from that continent began to exhibit hostility, blaming Europe for refusing to pay for his fare. I happened to be chairing so decided I would make a point on behalf of all non-Latin Americans present. 'I have no background on these matters, so I yield the chair to the president.' This was a new one for them, and for the poor president, Henk. Monsignor Planas told me that if I was chairing, I should know. I (courteously, of course) indicated that he might not know too much detail of Pacific matters. Anyway, this changed the dynamic and the question was discussed differently, the money not forthcoming. In case this sounds like a touch of paranoia about some Latin American tactics, it is, not without reason as I found over the coming years. But, that's the risk for international organisations.

And, that is probably more than enough about Board meetings but, at least you know it was not like a community meeting at home.

One of the advantages of going to Europe each year (apart from the chance to see a play or two in London on the way) was staying with a Jesuit community in London involved in media research. Very interesting to be there and to talk with these experts. Unfortunately, after 1992 the English province of the Jesuits wanted the accommodation back and the Centre moved to St. Louis which was the beginning of its end. As regards accommodation, some MSCs had contacts with the Sisters of Nazareth in Australia and had stayed at the sisters' headquarters and home for the aged in Hammersmith. In fact, in 1993, Philip spent five months of his moral theology sabbatical based there. This was to be my refuge from 1993 to 1997 and, when I was to move to London, the sisters kindly took me in for eleven and a half years.

Members of OCIC and Unda in Eastern Europe during the Communist times received financial and moral assistance from the international organisations. After the collapse of the Soviet Union, they offered to hold an assembly in one of their countries to express their gratitude. The choice was the Czech Republic. Which means that everyone was excited at the prospect of going to Prague. This was September 1994. For many, it was easier said than done. At the airport, many of the delegates from the Pacific were held up for long periods. The officials had never seen such people before. A number of Africans had the same problems. Black people confused the officials. They kept re-checking the names of the countries they had never heard of.

During the time in Prague, we were taken on a tour of an animation studio. As the guide explained procedures, it was clear that the administration of the studio was very cumbersome. Our delegate from Peru made some derogatory remarks. The guide, rather patiently, reminded us that it is difficult to change ways of doing things over night – and beyond. He asked us to imagine that a new government ideology was introduced in our country, how long would it take us to adapt. I was reminded of this later as we traveled by car from Prague into Poland. There was only one official checking passports. It took two hours to cross the border, allowing for plenty of pitstops. It was faster walking than driving. But, this was the Soviet bureaucracy at (slow) work.

Actually, it was a bit like that at the Agricultural University where we stayed. Basic accommodation, basic food and a surprising lot of impatience from people who should have known and behaved better before moaning. That sounds a bit judgmental. But true.

The main keynote speaker I remember was the delegate from Burundi. Remember it was September 1994, not long after those dire months of the Rwandan genocide. Listening to the priest, who was explaining the role that Church radio stations played during these tragic events, with Burundi able to broadcast into Rwanda, was a dismaying experience, even more dismaying as more information came out, as more evidence was accumulated and the indictment of participants in the massacre, including priests and religious.

The OCIC assembly went well. We prepared for a possible merger with Unda. Henk Hoekstra was re-elected as president. And we had a good number of interesting workshops on cinema and religion and spirituality. Unda became embroiled in a dispute. One of those messes which ecclesiastical behavior brings on. Church politics. While the

OCIC names which were sent in for Vatican approval came through unscathed, two of the Unda nominees did not. Washington Uranga was from Argentina, already a Vice-President, but not approved. Neither was Peter Thomas, with no explanation from the Roman authorities and no communication with Peter's boss of Catholic Communications, Melbourne, who was, of course, the archbishop, Frank Little. Years later, I was to hear at a meeting in Aachen that there had been complaints about some of Peter's productions at Catholic Communications and Peter was not approved because of 'ideological differences', Bishop Pell not approving! The ban simply happened and that had to be that.

Except that the Latin Americans have a revolutionary history, so why not one now! Unda spent a long time going to and fro – with the upshot, Washington and Peter being elected as the two vice-presidents.

One of the great features of these Assemblies was the celebration of the Eucharist organised by the different continents, especially the rhythmic Africans and the colourful Asians. The Pacific rhythms and colours received a lot of attention (and we plain Australians got some kudos by association).

At that time, air tickets to and from Australia could get you to Europe via Asia, North America, South America or southern Africa. Everybody has their thoughts on the effect of traveling a different route. Here are some of mine on coming home via Africa twice in those years. But, just before that, getting into Poland after that two hour border crossing mentioned earlier.

With all respect to John Paul II, Krakow tended to mean to me the road to Auschwitz. My OCIC Polish host, Zygmunt Gutowski (and old Solidarity man who took me around Warsaw and to the church of the murdered priest, Fr. Popalawski), organised me to Krakow which was beautiful but paled a bit in comparison with Prague. A family who had lived in Australia were to meet me – and then told me that Auschwitz was about 70 kilometres away, which rather dashed hopes in terms of time and transport. They told me they had not been there for some time and would drive me. They did and it was an experience I think I had wanted to have for some time. I wrote it up not so long afterwards, so I thought I would include some of that reflection.

It was the sight of the gate with *Arbeit Macht Frei* over it which brought back the memories, mainly from reading and from the movies, which meant that Australia was a whole world away from the suffering and the brutality and the dying that took place here and in other camps like it. As I walked through that gate on a sunny and peaceful Sunday afternoon in 1994, I knew that I had had to come here.

What can one say about the rows of brick buildings, some now overwhelming as you wander in and see the remnants of those interned and gassed so long ago? What comes to mind now is that awesome (precisely awesome) sequence in *Life is Beautiful* when Roberto Benigni as Guido suddenly comes upon that mound of shoes, that mound of glasses ... They are still there.

While Auschwitz is rightly famous and notorious for its extermination of the Jews, they were anticipated by many Catholics, gypsies and homosexuals. In the last block we visited, we were shown the cell where Maximillian Kolbe died, where, in total darkness, in a space that confined any real freedom of movement, he spent some of the last days of his life. Watching the news at the Mikruts before I went back to Warsaw, we heard that there had been special celebrations at his birthplace. It was his hundredth birthday.

I had visited Dachau in 1966, walking the distance from the station, wondering why directions to the camp were not clearly marked, walking the distance back overwhelmed by the images of the ovens and what they meant. The liberation of the camps had taken place only 21 years earlier. Now 28 years later, with all that we have learnt about the Holocaust, with all the images we have from photos, from newsreel footage, from the movies, a Sunday afternoon in Auschwitz is both shocking and sobering.

Within 48 hours of visiting Auschwitz, I had the surreal experience of remembering where I had been and marveling where I was, sitting on a tour boat on the Zambesi River. I was coming home via Zimbabwe and the travel agent had booked me unexpectedly on this river cruise. Worlds away from Poland. It seems a bit banal after the Sunday visit to be doing a Tuesday look at a hippopotamus in its natural habitat. Victoria Falls, of course is beautiful, somebody telling me when I said the park was very hot, that I saw the falls at the best time, no heavy spray obscuring the view.

With OCIC, there was accommodation everywhere through members. Staying with the Jesuits in Harare and listening to stories about the changes after Ian Smith and Robert Mugabe (who was in favour in those days in what seemed a prosperous country) meant discovering more about a continent that seemed remote from Australia. Two years later, the return was via South Africa and staying with the Irish Missionaries of the Sacred Heart who worked in and around Johannesburg. This meant a more personalised visit and longer explanations and recounting of experiences from confreres. The first night, I went to a restaurant in Brakpan with the superior, Jimmy Mitchell. That doesn't sound startling. But, we went with a priest from a diocese near the border with Namibia. He was black. Nelson Mandela had been released from Robben Island only six years earlier. It was only two years since the breakthrough elections. I hadn't imagined in the past that I would be having a meal with apartheid officially over. One of the things that had brought home the unjust restrictions was the curfew on Christmas Eve for black South Africans. We took for granted freedom to go off to midnight Mass if we wished. Sounds a small thing in a way, but it made an impression (along with films like *Cry Freedom*).

Johannesburg (apart from those huge ugly mounds of earth around it from the mines) meant great care when walking around the inner city – and observing the elaborate security systems in the house of one of the relatives of an MSC brother. Locked doors against carjacking. But, also a visit to the township of Ivory Park, the shantytown result of apartheid, which is an MSC parish. Going to Pretoria and walking along the calm streets of the city with its beautiful jacarandas was a complete contrast. Then, off home with some more memories and a lot to think about.

A peak experience of 1995 was going back to India and having the opportunity to go to Agra to visit the Taj Mahal. One of the most beautiful buildings I have ever seen. Our deluxe bus coach sailed grandly past crowded roads, old cars, bikes, people, skirted Agra to take us to a five star hotel, with many fashion shops, for lunch, more than a shock. Then the vista of the vast pure-white façade, the paths and the water, the interiors. On the way home, we were delayed for some minutes. A dead cyclist on the road – more shock at the bland and unfeeling tone of the guide who seemed to take it as a personal affront that someone would inconvenience our progress by dying and lying on the road.

'I suppose it will entail some travel.' As you might guess, there is a great deal to come, but I will give it a rest for now.

37. OCIC AND CINEMA

BECOMING a part of an international Church organisation means not just going to meetings but to become involved in conferences and events which were interesting learning experiences, as well as the opportunity to become more aware of the range of Catholic research and writing on film, to meet more people in one's field.

Speaking of conferences, this is probably the best place to consider some of those of the 1990s. Two of them were the Cavaletti Conferences, held outside Rome in the Alban Hills (definitely a plus) and sponsored by Fr. Bob White SJ who conducted communications courses at the Gregorian University for overseas students. In 1993, the focus was completely on film. I volunteered a paper continuing the Movie Christ exploration. Accepted. But, it was interesting to hear two German speakers on the topic – and researching and speaking Germanically, thoroughness personified in lists, themes, treatments. There can be moments when one wishes one was more Germanic rather than pragmatic Anglo-Saxon-Celt. Of course, it's my limitations but I get easily distracted when there is an indulgence in, what can I call it, 'thought for thought's sake'. I was rather smug when it occurred to me that 'I was not enthralled by the aesthetics of abstraction'. Fred Chamberlin had told me years earlier that a reviewer should be open to the widest range of films. He was right, of course. But, I am not sure how open I could ever be to Hegelian theses in the light of Heidegger's existentialism in analysing *Cats*. Of course again, that never happens, but you know what I mean. On the continent, let's say, there is a predisposition to abstract reflection on cinema. And, *Cats* once taught me a lesson that is relevant here. I was disappointed at the interval when I indulged a desire to see *Cats* on Broadway. Apologies to T. S. Eliot but some of the poems are as silly as some of the dialogue in a Gilbert and Sullivan play. I enjoy hearing 'Memory', but we went into the second half of *Cats*, then I blushed. One of the first lyrics in that second half is 'to have the experience but miss the meaning'. Maybe that's what happens during those abstractions.

But, I did learn a key idea and phrase at that 1993 Cavaletti Conference where I did have the pleasure of meeting so many OCIC film people who would become friends and from whom I would learn. The particular learning concerned films which were dark, even seemingly despairing. How does a religious person interpret and deal with this kind of film? Should a film like this receive an OCIC award? Is such a film a denial of grace?

At this time, American director Abel Ferrara made quite some impact with his *Bad Lieutenant* (not to be confused – or compared – with Werner Herzog's newer 2009 version which omitted all the religious elements). I wish I could remember who it was who introduced this phrase which has become so important to me – and to SIGNIS as many will testify who hear me quote it so frequently.

Somebody referred to *Bad Lieutenant* as a De Profundis film. In later years, this is how I have explained this idea:

The discussions about De Profundis films can be seen as a significant example of OCIC consciousness raising. German theologians and OCIC have held annual discussions on film and theology. In 1992-93, the issue of dark films, films presenting evil in sometimes sordid and frank plotlines and treatment came to the fore. At some festivals, jurors were wondering whether such films should be given awards. The theologians came up with the tag, De Profundis films. The reference is to the opening of Psalm 130:

> Out of the depths, I cry to you
> O Lord, hear my voice.

One of the main films that led to this terminology was Abel Ferrara's *Bad Lieutenant* (1992). Director Abel Ferrara has a Catholic education background. There is explicit Catholic imagery in the film. A nun from

Poland has been raped in the sanctuary of a New York church. Harvey Keitel plays the bad lieutenant of the title. He is a corrupt man, alcoholic and drug-addicted, a gambler who is in debt to criminals. Frustrated when the nun will not name her assailants, he comes to a peak moment of desperation. He hallucinates in the aisle of the church, howling his despair in four-letter frankness. He sees an image of the crucified Jesus (whom the audience has seen when the crucifix moves into live action during the nun's rape ordeal, clearly showing her as a suffering Christ-figure). The lieutenant demands to know where Jesus was in all his troubles, screaming and whispering, 'Where were you?' He crawls towards Jesus, weeping and repeating, 'I'm sorry.' It is a hallucination because the figure is actually a church cleaner. It is a cinematic equivalent of Eduard Munch's 'The Scream'.

The De Profundis film has been a way of OCIC/SIGNIS exploration of films which portray evil and the cry for redemption. In 1999, this approach received some authoritative backing: 'even when they explore the darkest depths of the soul or the most unsettling aspects of evil, artists give voice in a way to the universal desire for redemption'. (John Paul II, *Letter to Artists*, 1999.)

In more recent times, some other thoughts on this topic have arisen:

Not all films are as dark as *Bad Lieutenant* or, say, the *Godfather* trilogy or some of Martin Scorsese's films like *Cape Fear* or *The Departed*. People do live their lives, which can have many miserable moments, in a less profound way. This is not to underestimate the pain and suffering, but it is a reminder that so many lives are lived in the shallows rather than the depths. But, from those shallows, there is a similar cry.

The film that suggested this distinction between depths and shallows was *Waitress* (2007). It is a film about women who worked in local diners. One of them, played by Keri Russell, is subjected to physical abuse by her husband (Jeremy Sisto). Again, she was the innocent victim who needed salvation rather than redemption. It seemed useful to include, 'Out of the Shallows' with 'Out of the Depths'.

A further development of these considerations came with the very grim film from Gaspar Noe (who had made one of the most De Profundis French films, *Irreversible* (2002)). His long and tortuous drama, *Enter the Void* (2009), made reference to the Tibetan Book of the Dead, the Japanese belief in ghosts and a pessimistic view of life. *The Void* was the name of a Tokyo nightclub where much of the action takes place. *Enter the Void* was a reminder that some films are so pessimistic about life and human nature as to be nihilistic. Characters do not get out of the depths, they are not redeemed. Their destination is the void or in Graham Greene's *Brighton Rock*, Hell.

A significant figure at the 1993 Cavaletti Conference was Irish Jesuit Michael Paul Gallagher, writer on faith and culture. I asked him about theologians and films. He reassured me that doing theology without knowledge of film was like doing theology in a bell-jar.

We ventured further afield from film to the range of media at the 1997 Cavaletti conference. While the papers of 1993 were edited by John R. May as *New Images of Religious Film* (1997), the even better papers of this next conference never found a publisher.

The same year that John R. May's collection was published, a similar volume came out in Britain, *Explorations of Theology in Film*, edited by Clive Marsh and Gaye Ortiz (who would become a vice-president of OCIC and of SIGNIS). This was a book with contributions from the English-speaking world, a readable book on the whole, able to present theory but in the context of real audience response and a belief that cinema spirituality was to be found in popular film, that it was not the preserve of the respected master-directors (Bergman, Fellini, Tarkovski, Kieslowski). Because I had been invited by my friend, Maggie Roux, to teach some sessions at Trinity and All Saints College at Horsforth, outside Leeds, I was in Yorkshire at Gaye's campus of St. John's Ripon and invited to one of those pally meals after lectures and chat, which led to this book and a chapter examining some Christological themes in Tim Burton's *Edward Scissorhands*. I have always been bold enough to think that films can be a theological source/resource (Latin: *Locus Theologicus*) and am happy to quote from an Ecumenical Council that fell out of favour, the First Vatican Council, 1869-70. When discussing the role of faith and reason and theological investigation, the bishops noted three ways of deepening theological understanding: the connections between the different mysteries of faith themselves, the connection of these mysteries to our final destiny and... wait for it (they actually didn't say that) – analogies. Metaphors, stories, the arts can offer analogies for faith seeking and expressing understanding. So, film and theology – which in recent decades has proliferated, especially in the United States.

Speaking of the United States, the 1995 annual OCIC Board meeting was planned for Los Angeles, the reason: celebrating the centenary of cinema in LA/Hollywood. It was a great idea, better in the planning than in the execution. We had some interesting screenings but some mixed meetings with film makers and PR people. The best was a screening of *Mi Familia* and discussion with the director, Gregory Nava. I was commissioned to present a paper on our juries with clips from our prize winners for discussion about our criteria for awards. Something of a fiasco – so many of the participants had not seen the films or even heard of them! We collaborated with WACC (The World Association for Christian Communication) and Interfilm. But we have had better and more fruitful meetings since!

I found the experience (along with that of the discussions in Australia seven years earlier concerning *The Last Temptation of Christ*) very helpful in showing how reasoned proactive statements on the part of the Church and thoughtful reviews led to more light and less heat in the ensuing conversations. I followed it for the next years for The Australian Catholic Film Office which I now headed as Fred Chamberlin had retired to Justin Villa for the clergy, though he still did reviews. He died before his time at the age of 74 in December 1996.

Less than a week before he died, he rang me as he was reviewing *Hamlet* and could not remember Kenneth Branagh's surname. It was the last time I was talking to him. I was visiting a confrere the next Sunday and asked at reception at St. Vincent's Private for the number of Fred's room. There was a man at the desk, which was unusual. His reply to my enquiry about the room number was a quick and emphatic one word, 'Deceased,' I have had a thing about that word ever since. I asked him, 'When.' Equally abrupt, 'Just now.' Fred had bequeathed his many books and periodicals to us and I stored them at Cathedral Hall but they disappeared into a library and that was that. Archbishop Pell presided at Fred's funeral and the future Archbishop of Melbourne, Denis Hart, gave the eulogy, including quoting one of Fred's brisk reviews of something he didn't like, 'Bloody nonsense' but not the other, his judgment on characters that got on his goat, 'needs a good quick kick up the backside'. He had been ordained 50 years, had been dean of the cathedral for 20 years and had worked for the Church and film all his priestly life. During his lifetime, he received little credit from many Catholics, 'it's just his hobby'. Fred was diabetic but enjoyed an ice cream or chocolate at the movies. Not long before he died, I met him at a preview and we went for lunch to Pizza Hut. I hadn't been before so I asked him the rubrics for getting the pizza: 'You pays your money and go for your life.' I made sure when I was elected president of OCIC to acknowledge all that he had been and done for me.

In subsequent years, I put out some Film Office statements on films like *Breaking the Waves*, *Crash*, *The People vs Larry Flint*. I had noticed that Henry Herx, soon after the *Priest* controversy got rather stuck into the Richard Gere legal thriller, *Primal Fear*, where the Archbishop of Chicago had indulged in reprehensible sexual voyeurism and had been murdered. It was – and still is – a powerful courtroom drama. The statement on *Primal Fear* had a Melbourne paper ringing Richard Gere for quotes and cited the head of United International Pictures Australia praising the Film Office for its mature comments! The statement that received a bit of notoriety, but positive, was that for Larry Clark's *Kids*. Here was an opportunity to be proactive and positive even while appropriately critical with reference to the film itself rather than hearsay. There was an enjoyable post-script.

The press release for *Kids* was the first of my press releases, issued as 'A Statement from the Australian Catholic Film Office'. A reporter for the Melbourne *Herald Sun* had made contact with a number of Christian offices, inviting representatives to a preview screening of *Kids*. Its director, Larry Clark, a photographer, allegedly had a history of drugs. His film was about kids in the New York streets indulging in drugs and sex, running the risk of HIV infection.

At the discussion after the screening, it appeared that all the Church people the journalist had invited were not going to condemn the film at all. Instead, a number of pastoral care and social workers who belonged to more evangelical churches, especially the Baptists, while not enjoying the film, said that it was a fair representation of what they found amongst some kids on the streets of Melbourne. The journalist was not impressed, left in a huff and no article ever appeared.

In the meantime, *The Age* (Melbourne) asked the Communications Office for a comment. It was the week before Christmas with *Kids* due to be released on Boxing Day. A bit of a slow week for stories, but someone had heard of the preview we attended.

I wrote the following statement. *The Age* headed the report, 'Support for *Kids* from unexpected source' (or words to that effect) stating that the Catholic Church had lent its support to *Kids*. That was not exactly the case! *The Age* journalist faxed through the article and changed a couple of things at my suggestion. (I have found when journalists realise you know what you are talking about, they pay attention.)

The ABC's *7.30 Report* had some footage of interviews with Larry Clark when he had promoted the film some weeks earlier. They had a brainwave to make a seven minute feature, going to cinemas to ask patrons, especially the young, whether they liked it or not. The interviewees tended not to have liked it. There were bits of Larry Clark.

And some fair bits of me sitting at home trying to say that these were issues we had to face whether we liked it or not but that not everybody needed to see this particular version of kids and drugs.

As always, I sent my releases to Brussels. Guido Convents printed it early in 1996. It was the period of the centenary of cinema and the publication of the list of movies recommended by the Pontifical Council for Social Communications (and, therefore, according to journalists, by the Pope).

The British Film Institute's magazine, *Sight and Sound*, published an editorial on Church interest in cinema. The editorial was initially taking a shot at the doyen of British reviewers, author Alexander Walker, of the *Evening Standard* (though they did not mention him and his condemnatory remarks about *Kids* by name). The editorial then went on to praise the Catholic Church and its stances. At the same time, Derek Malcolm, veteran reviewer for *The Guardian*, asked about 10 representatives of the churches in England for their lists of excellent films to compare them with those from the Vatican. He was impressed by the Catholic list enough to make one seriously think of becoming a Catholic!

However, the *Sight and Sound* editorial, 'Fallible Judgments', included these paragraphs:

> *Kids* has prompted this moral controversy partly by raising the troubling issue of adolescent sex, something society's Moral Guardians, especially the Church, have traditionally felt the need to deplore. So it is ironic that certain elements in the Catholic Church are demonstrating a far more generosity towards *Kids* than these secular commentators. In a forthcoming issue of *Cine & Media*, published by OCIC (Organisation Catholique Internationale du Cinema et de l'Audiovisuel), Father Peter Malone writes in *Kids'* defence, noting that 'while the treatment is graphic (more verbal than visual) and the behaviour of the teenagers will shock many audiences, the film reflects a part of today's society and its

moral problems and makes a plea for change (especially to parents).'

The editorial then refers to the Vatican's 100 films for the centenary of cinema and (rightly) notes that the list did not come from the Pope but from Monsignor Enrique Planas in a booklet distributed to Italian schools to encourage media literacy.

Then another mention:

Nevertheless the Pontifical rubber stamp indicates (in the words of the *Catholic Herald*) that 'the Vatican is now acknowledging the beneficial effect that films can have on the lives of their audiences', a view already endorsed by such open-minded clerics as Father Malone. This is in marked contrast to the Christian fundamentalist groups in the United States who have lobbied against films deemed offensive to their principles. One group even runs a hotline which anxious filmgoers can ring and find out how much swearing, violence or sex a particular film contains. *Kids* was a notable recent target of these groups ...

As the abuse of *Kids* gathers momentum over the next few weeks, it will be interesting to see whether British religious groups jump on the banning bandwagon or show the intelligence of their Catholic brothers and sisters.

Alexander Walker was not impressed by their treatment of him, 'even trimming a film like *Kids* in order to sanitise a censor's conscience and make possible a distributor's profit cannot remove the way in which almost the whole emphasis of interest is placed on apparent minors aping the lasciviousness and debauchery of adults'. The editorial did not refer to him by name, mentioning only *The Evening Standard*. He immediately penned a reply. *Sight and Sound* headed it 'Ego te absolve':

Your editorial (*S&S* April) gives a source for the adverse quotation you use (*Evening Standard*) but names no author for it. This is sloppy journalism and, since the passing of the Copyright, Designs and Patents Act, an unlawful denial of the writer's right to be named when his or her work is being cited in a text. In the film's defence you quote (and this time name) one Father Malone. You clearly place great faith in the heterodoxy of Roman Catholic clerics. You will therefore understand my surprise at the anathema my own name continues to cause you when you quote from my writings as you again did several issues ago without any authorial attribution. I suggest you discontinue this practice, lest it blind you to the requirements of scholarly discussion, and I shall absolve you from this sin of omission, imposing on you only the penance of three Hail Mary's [sic] to be said on your knees when reading the review of *Kids* which, *deo volente*, shall appear in the *Evening Standard* when the film opens.

So, for the fun of it, a letter to the editor:

20 July 1996

Dear Editor,

I thought I would make myself known after reading your kind words in the editorial of April on the Catholic Church's approach to films and your quoting me about *Kids*. My June copy of *Sight and Sound* has just arrived and I see a rather detrimental comment about heterodox clerics from Alexander Walker so I thought I would send you a 'Letter to the Editor'.

In fact, I am the director of the Australian Catholic Film Office for the Bishops of Australia as well as the President of the Catholic Film Offices of the Pacific and a member of the International Board of Directors of OCIC (International

Catholic Organization for Cinema and Audio-Visuals). So, 'heterodox' sounds somewhat over the top. But before that I have been a regular reviewer of films since 1968 in religious publications as well as newspapers and Cinema Papers and written a number of books. In fact, in the post yesterday was an invitation to write the entry on 'Religion' for *The Oxford Companion to Australian Film*.

I have appreciated *The Monthly Film Bulletin* and, now, *Sight and Sound* for my work.

Sincerely,

I had the opportunity to go to the Venice Film Festival a month later and wondered whether I would meet Mr Walker. David Stratton of *The Australian* and *At the Movies* mentioned that he had seen the letter and added that Alexander Walker was not attending the festival as he had had a car accident, knocked down by a taxi and was in hospital!

On moving to England in 1999, I made myself known to him and he wished me well in my work, always chatting at previews, he always calling me with prim precision, 'Father Malone'. Once he quoted me (about an erroneous scripture reference in the final credits of *The Body*) as his 'theological adviser'!

In interviews with the media, I have found a positive response 99.9 per cent of the time. If you discuss professionally, not defensively, and join in a conversation rather than an argument (which still allows for some controversy), you get media respect. And that 0.1 per cent? When Madonna had given up her sex phase in the 1990s and was into repentance, Catholic Communications Melbourne received a phone call, 'Would we comment?' When I explained that Madonna had a Catholic upbringing and knew her symbols, they hung up. All they wanted was an intolerant Catholic rant.

One last thing, interviews with film directors. I don't know why I didn't think of it before but, when *Black Robe* was released in 1991, I was offered time with director, Bruce Beresford. It was a great opportunity to hear him on why he made such a Catholic film, his interest in and reading of the French Jesuit missionaries' letters from Canada in the 1630s and his recreation of the way of life, the mission effort and the clashes with the Iroquois. That set in motion one of those obsessive plans, to interview as many Australian directors as possible. By 2000, the total was over eighty. All of them, the famous and the independents, were welcoming and forthcoming – and many with the reassurance when they realised that I was a priest-reviewers that they were not really religious (most) but that they were spiritual (all). There was a disappointment with Peter Weir who promised me an interview, urging me to see *Fearless*, but then decided that he would let his films speak for themselves, then wishing me good luck for the project.

Getting the interview with George Miller was an enterprise. All set to go at the end of 1998 before I went off to London. But ... he was so upset by the response to *Babe, Pig in the City*, that there was no go. He was on the jury in Cannes in 1999, but I thought it better not to approach him. Then, his agent contacted me in July. He was ready. We had a good phone conversation though he wanted to talk about the awards from the Ecumenical Jury. But, I got the interview.

Nick Parsons who had directed *Dead Heart* and was manager of Currency Press agreed that they would publish 15 of the interviews. The selection was five of the most famous directors. Five best known at home and five less well-known. Amongst the directors were Rolf de Heer, Scott Hicks, Fred Schepisi, Simon Wincer. Nick was able to break through PR barriers that I could not. One was Gillian Armstrong. We agreed to meet in Balmoral. I turned off Pittwater Road on the wrong side. Tracking back, I found there was no right turn to the other side for more than five kilometres. She was still waiting when I arrived. A good long interview after a lunch. At the end, I offered to buy a coffee. She said she should pay since I had covered lunch. A nice gracious memory. Several of the directors said they were happy to talk about themes in their films rather than budgets and temperamental actors.

Nick thought my introduction was not punchy enough. Then he came up with an idea, that he would interview me about why I was interested in talking to the directors. An epilogue rather than an introduction. The book was called, Myth and Meaning, Australian Film Directors in their own words (2001). Quite a number of the reviews appeared in magazines like *Eureka Street*, *WomanChurch* ...

There were some interviews with overseas directors like Kevin Reynolds, in the aftermath of the dismissal of *Waterworld* and Paddy Breathnagh and, a special, with Renny Harlin for *The Long Kiss Goodnight*. Half a dozen of us sat around a table with him, then 30 minutes with Samuel L. Jackson, then, best of all, 30 minutes with Geena Davis who looked even more glamorous than her photos! One of the downside results of being out of the country for so many years meant that it was not possible to keep up with the so many directors who emerged in the 21st century.

38. THE OCIC EXPERIENCE, 1998-2001

FROM SUMMER to winter. Christmas Day, 1998, reached 38 degrees and the Melbourne Community celebrated Christmas dinner in the garage of the parish ministry house in Sunshine. Next day, always the opening of the fourth cricket test at the Melbourne Cricket Ground, it reached 13 degrees and poured with rain, which did not deter 65,000 fans from going to the MCG – and not seeing a ball bowled. I flew off to London on 1 January 1999 to a new life and a home away from home in London, for almost 12 years.

Actually, my first months as president of OCIC saw me back home and at the 1998 MSC Provincial Chapter, a great event held at Downlands College in Toowoomba, a chapter open to everyone as well as to a number of invited sisters and lay participants. Not only a great get-together, but lots of discussion about key issues and the future. One of the pleasant things I do remember was that a number of confreres, who had probably shared that old opinion of 'Ecclesiastical Peeping Toms', were happy with my new ministry and congratulated me. John Northey could rest in peace.

There had been a visit to Europe at the end of 1998 to set in motion the workings for the merger of OCIC and Unda. We had given ourselves three years to achieve it, which we did. I am leaving the details to the next chapter for those who would like to know how it all progressed. Just after our first joint executive meeting in Luxembourg, there was a Chevalier Family conference in Issoudun, a belated follow-up to the regional meeting on the Media Ministry in Manila in 1989. Here we were in Issoudun, France, the town in which the Missionaries of the Sacred Heart was established, 42 participants, eager to talk about media and planning. I would like to say that it worked. It wasn't a failure but it wasn't really a success – though eventually, in 2000, some further meetings got going. Let me put those aside for a moment. I'd like to get to London.

Let me tell you a bit about Nazareth House in Hammersmith, perhaps an odd place to live for so long, although I was in and out of London twice a month during those years. It is a home for the elderly, about 95 residents. The congregation, the Sisters of Nazareth, manages several Nazareth Houses in the UK, Ireland, South Africa, Zimbabwe, Australia and New Zealand. It was founded by a Frenchwoman who is buried at Hammersmith, Victoire Larmenier, Mother St. Basil. Hammersmith was the main foundation and celebrated 150 years in 2007. There is a community of sisters and, in another house on the property, the international administration of the congregation. There was a steady stream of visitors. In my earlier years, there were many visitors who had been orphans in Nazareth Houses and visits were financially supported by the British government.

And there was another boarder, Fr. Ron Fennell, a convert to Catholicism, to the right of Margaret Thatcher (one of his heroines) politically speaking but to the left of Hans Küng, ecclesiastically speaking. Plenty of interesting, provocative discussions there. He enjoyed ribbing people in a very British (pronounced Briddish) manner and decided early on that I was corrupting the Church by promoting that evil medium, cinema. If I had a pound for every time Ron repeated this to me, let alone to all the visitors, I could live in luxury. But, Ron was also very welcoming to my Australian confreres and members of OCIC who came to stay. I tallied up that I had 33 Australian MSC stay at Nazareth House over the years, not including repeat visitors.

I had a room which served as bedroom and office. After six years, I was urged to ask the superior if I could use the adjacent visitor's room – granted. So, for half the time, a little more space and comfort. Though my desk was small, with only tight spaces on each side of the computer, I got a lot written – with reference books open on the bed and my being able to swing round on my mobile chair to consult them! The rooms overlooked the busy Hammersmith Road, above the tops of the passing buses. I would do a TV add in praise of double glazed windows!

One of the features of Nazareth House that appealed to me, from the times that I had stayed there during London visits from 1993-97 when I came to Europe for OCIC Board meetings, was that it had an extensive garden at the back, one might say a mini-park, beautifully green, space for the residents, quiet despite the Hammersmith Flyover just over the fence and the flight path to Heathrow not all that far away. Worth a fortune now, of course!

A word about the sisters who welcomed me (though there were a few who, if asked, might have agreed with 'Ecclesiastical Peeping Tom'). The sisters have been rather traditional in their community life style, ways of prayer and wearing of the habit. I remember when I visited in 1994 there had just been a first-time decision for the sisters to have a day off. Some time later, they agreed that they could choose ordinary clothes for going out on their day off. They had a fair amount of tolerance for Ron and myself who did not look clerical at all. Over the years, there was a succession of full-time chaplains. Fr. Geoff Sweeney, a White Father, was a friendly Bradford man who had worked for almost 50 years in Tanzania. For my last seven years, there was Fr. Jim McGuire, an Irish Salesian priest who had worked mainly in England and Malta. He began his ministry at Hammersmith after a hip replacement at the age of 87 – and retired as he turned 95. Not the easiest man to get along with (and visitors found his accent very difficult to follow), strong-willed and definite but absolutely devoted to visiting the elderly every day. Unusual community, unusual community living, now that I come to think of it.

The sisters asked a small rent and I was able to repay in kind as supplement, so to speak, by celebrating Masses which put less burden on the chaplain and to offer a scriptural conference once a month when I was at home.

But, I was always glad to be on the Underground from Heathrow, come out on Hammersmith Broadway and walk along Hammersmith Road, though when I got my Freedom Pass, glad to be on the bus – the 9, 10, 27 and 391 all stop outside Nazareth House and, over night when the Underground does not run, the N9 stops at the door and takes one to Heathrow in the early hours. We were only about four miles from central London. In the days when there were bus strikes – not many at all in recent years – I found it took 75 minutes to get from Nazareth House to the 20th Century Fox theatrette in Soho Square.

Mention of Fox leads to remembering my years of reviewing films in London and going to previews.

When I stopped doing the reviews in the *Annals* at the end of 1998, I thought that it must be time to let go of seeing all new releases. I wasn't prophetic about this. I asked a friend, Tom Aitken, who reviewed for The Tablet, what were the procedures to get accreditation to review. To cut a short story shorter, I applied to the Film Distributors Association, was accepted (not at the top level, that was for the dailies' reviewers and those with important magazines). That meant that for the 12 years, I was a member of the UK national press. The preview system was to see new releases on Mondays and Tuesdays. If there were extra films, then on Friday was well (and occasionally back to Thursdays). In Australia, previews were more spasmodically scattered throughout the week, and still are.

This meant that I spent a lot of my time in Soho where most of the preview theatres were. This also meant that my day-by-day view of London was rather drab, but I have to say that I enjoyed going to the previews, generally in the theatrettes, Columbia, now Sony, United International, now Paramount, Fox and Mr. Young's, soon to be the Soho Screening rooms. Some companies hired freelance preview screens or hired small theatres in hotels, more than I would have thought. For the big ones, we often went to cinemas in Leicester Square like the Empire where the sound for *The Matrix* or, especially, *The Transformers* series, would batter the eardrums. The Odeon in Leicester Square has a huge screen, good for *Narnia* or for enduring *Mamma Mia!* One of the things I noticed over the years is how many cinemas closed in central London and how many interiors of surviving cinemas were divided up to make mini-cinemas while out in the suburbs, the number of multiplexes increased. Virgin cinemas (taken over by UGC, then taken over by Cineworld) introduced membership cards around 2000. Because I was away a great deal and missed previews, the card (which, if you saw three films a month covered its cost) enabled me to catch up (or repeat) when I needed to. There is a Cineworld 4 in Hammersmith itself and they have a 15 cinema complex at Wandsworth shopping mall, a quick ride (sometimes) in the 220 bus.

This did mean that I kept up to date, filed the reviews for OCIC and then the SIGNIS site, for the Australian Catholic Film Office site and for the Australian Catholic Press. In 2000, I was invited to do a weekly review for the British Catholic paper out of Manchester, *The Universe*. This lasted for four years until editorial decided to review only family friendly films. However, in 2005 I was invited to resume the reviews weekly until 2008 when financial difficulties arose. I was also able to contribute some articles to *The Catholic Herald*. These reviews meant that I was acceptable as a reviewer of the national press, and the income enabled me to pay rent to the sisters (and to pay for my luggage, the 46 boxes, getting back to Australia).

The National Press group of reviewers is not so large, consisting mainly of older male reviewers. By the time I came home, I was the third oldest! For a while, Alexander Walker, whom I quoted earlier, was considered the doyen of the reviewers, a man of strong views, many books and television appearances, and a long life at the *Evening Standard*. He was a fussy man and was not afraid to voice his dissatisfactions – for instance, that the company whose film we were to watch would take the liberty of screening trailers, trailers!, before the feature. He was succeeded by Derek Malcolm, formerly of *The Guardian* for many years, but then taking over at the *Evening Standard*. Derek had been a jockey in his younger days and was short and fit (despite smoking). He was on the board of FIPRESCI, the international association of film critics, and spent a great deal of time at international film festivals, often doing the daily comments for Screen International. An expert on foreign language films, he helped the Bangladeshi Rainbow Association in London and, because of my work for Rainbow and the Dhaka International Film Festival, I found myself at many committee meetings with him, trying to do our best to help the director, Moustapha Jamal, to entice the Londoner Bangladeshis round Whitechapel and Aldgate to come out to see their films. Despite some good choices, the exercise was fairly futile. But it introduced me to a world I was little aware of. In later years, as he grew older, Derek was inclined to nod off fairly instantly.

The critic I admired most was Philip French of *The Observer*. Philip was a gentleman and a good friend. He loved film, had an encyclopedic knowledge and something of a photographic memory for scene detail. He wore his expertise lightly. And he was one of those, sometimes rare, critics who did not treat films he did not care for with disdain. We had plenty of those in London, especially in the back row where they could scoff or mockingly laugh out loud. One day, we were invited to watch a collection of French pornographic films of the 1920s and 1930s. At the end, when we sitting there more than a little sheepish, Philip told us that one of the short pieces was mentioned in a short story by Graham Greene who had gone to see it. Philip was a literary man as well. And his son and daughter in law were the prominent novelists who wrote under the name, Nicci French.

I was used to the friendliness of our group of reviewers in Melbourne and our founding the Melbourne Film Critics Circle. We enjoyed each other's company. The publicists were friendly as well. In London, I got to know some of the publicists, but not so many. The publicists were polite but tended to be on guard, more interested in getting us to make sure we signed in. Much more congenial were the caterers who, sometimes, provided food and drink to buoy us up. You could chat and talk things over with them. Actually, food became a greater issue over the years. Older reviewers thought they had entitlement to be fed at previews and complained when there was nothing – not minor complaining either. If you were to go to a multi-media preview in the evening, you were often more likely to get plenty of sandwiches, rolls, cakes, fruit, alcohol or soft drink. Don't know why there was this discrimination.

Alan Frank, who used to write for the *Daily Star* but also, under another name for the *Jewish Chronicle*, became a close friend. His wife, Gill, was the daughter of Harold Schuster who edited *Sunrise* and directed films like *My Friend Flicka*. Alan could be sardonic, even cynical, and had his pet peeves (Michael Caine, Annette Bening, George Clooney's self-regard and Tom Wilkinson's American accent which he never failed to mention). But, he loved films, had been an extra on many a movie over the decades, their union rep, and had a fund of anecdotes. He was always conscious of the targeted audience when he wrote rather than just dwell on cinema as art. He had been a governor of the British Film Institute and secretary of the Film Critics' Circle. But, he always had an adverse comment on reviewers who wrote no longer (or very little) but still fronted up to screenings, suggesting that if they did not mark a preview off for each night, they would have no social life and/or starve to death. His word, which I was not familiar with, was 'liggers'.

The friendliest of the reviewers were those who wrote for smaller papers or websites. By contrast, there were some reviewers, from the British dailies, who never gave me the time of day over the whole period.

All in all, I am glad that I had this experience, got to know this professional world, enjoyed the company and conversation of film experts, had the opportunity to keep up to date with new releases. Interestingly, I met them first as an Australian, a reviewer, then they got my name. It was only later that they discovered I was a Catholic and a priest. It made me more credible than if they had got to the priest part first. After a short time, many, including Alexander Walker, could talk about films, Catholic themes and ask me questions. I was happy to count artist and reviewer Jeff Sawtell as a friend. He was a Communist from the old days and reviewed for the Communist paper, *The Morning Star*. I finished up sending Jeff my reviews and he used quite a number of them in his paper, especially when he couldn't get to a preview.

One of the main advantages of living in London instead of in Brussels where the General Secretariat of OCIC was located, was speaking in English. But, it also meant being able to go up to Trinity and All Saints in Leeds to contribute to film and spirituality courses, to take on one-off seminars, to help out in parishes, especially in Brook Green, the parish Nazareth House belonged to.

You might be wondering about the OCIC Secretariat. And, even if not, a word or more about it and how it worked.

Because OCIC was established in the 'Low Countries', Brussels was chosen for the headquarters. At the outbreak of World War II, the Secretariat was taken over by the Nazis. But, at the end of the war, the energy revived and, under the leadership of Fr. Jean Bernard of Luxembourg who had been secretary before the war and was president from 1947 to 1972, OCIC flourished and then spread all over the world. Yvonne de Hemptine had worked at the secretariat from 1935 to 1979 (bequeathing her house to OCIC at her death in the 1990s). In 1979, Robert Molhant, from Brussels itself, became the Secretary-General, remaining in that position until the merger of 2001 with Unda, and then serving as Secretary-General of SIGNIS until 2005. He was a man of energy, a good organiser and something of an entrepreneur in finding funds for projects. I was on the OCIC board with him from 1990 and for the eight years I was president. We travelled a great deal together, shared many experiences. We could compare notes with some of the unlikely happenings. He had one of the best. While I was interned at a police station in Argentina for six hours after opening a car door and hitting a couple on a bicycle, relieved that the frail girl was not hurt (and that she was not pregnant), being fingerprinted nine times, finally let go ... he had been in Burkina Faso at the festival in Ouagadougou in the 1980s after a coup. All the visitors had to join in the chant in support of the president before screenings – and one day, they were all rounded up and put on a bus (no windows to keep out the dust) and were set to work for some hours on building a railway line. Then back to the hotel, a wash and the festival.

I like to think that Robert and I made a good team and that we were creative in many projects and that we got to know and be friends with as many of our members worldwide as we could.

Amongst the other members of the secretariat, the one I worked most with was Guido Convents, a Belgian from Limburg, who joined the office in 1988. Guido is a born researcher. He can't help himself. He is forever burrowing into documents, immersing himself in archives, with a wide range of interests from his rather left-of-centre perspective. His main area of expertise was the Belgian silent movie era. His (huge) PhD thesis was on this topic, 1896-1908, hundreds of pages and many hundred footnotes. But, he has always been interested in Africa, co-managing an African Film Festival in Leuven where he lives, and producing large tomes on the cinema of Rwanda, Congo, Mozambique.

Guido and I always got along well and have shared a great deal, especially in Brussels and at festivals. He can be over-extraverted – going round the festival film market stands in Berlin can take a long time since he knows everyone. And he loves to joke. Which means that you have to be cautious as he greets the female attendants checking badges at festivals so that they don't think he is harassing them. Through Guido, I wrote a lot for the OCIC magazine, *Cine y Media*, during the 1990s and the years in London.

So, the Secretariat is busy co-ordinating programs around the organisation, co-ordinating the applications for grants from the Vatican's Office for the Propagation of the Faith and from other funding agencies, being present at festivals and conferences, involved in publications. That said, I feel a little guilty about not liking the city of Brussels more. I used to visit several times a year and got to know several of the areas well. Perhaps, it was because my visits were for work ... but, still, even touristically, I don't find the city so attractive or interesting. And, in winter, it was still dark at 8.00 am. Though, one morning I stood and watched the snow falling because that was a new experience for me – though walking and sloshing in it soon cures any romantic fantasies about snow. But, I was glad to visit Ypres with its memories of World War I and the museum of Flanders Field, as well as a war cemetery outside Mons where allies and Germans were both buried, and to see Bastogne and be reminded of the Battle of the Bulge (and the tanks still there as mementoes of that fight).

I think I will stay with the ecclesiastical side of things for the moment. One of the duties of the president of OCIC and then SIGNIS was attendance at the annual plenary meeting of the Vatican Office for the Media. Its official title is The Pontifical Council for Social Communications. For over 20 years, it was presided over by an American archbishop (Cardinal when he retired), John Patrick Foley from Philadelphia.

In February 1994, Robert Molhant had called an Executive meeting of OCIC in Rome to prepare for the forthcoming congress in Prague. As a bonus, we were permitted to sit in on a session of the Pontifical Council and to attend the papal audience for the members. I had an anti-clerical temptation and succumbed to it: to be photographed meeting Pope John Paul II while wearing a sports coat and tie. Mission accomplished and I have the photo to prove it. Later in the day, John Foley was asking whether I was a priest or not.

No ties for further visits to the Council. I went each year from 1999 to 2006. There is really not much to say about them, but that probably signifies a lot. They were held in the old Synod room in the Vatican. But, while the Swiss Guards saluted the clergy and ignored the laity with us, as we went into the vestibule to climb the steps up to the Court of St. Damasus and then went down the stairs or in the lift to the meeting hall. The meetings were usually very, very ordinary. Much of the time was taken with the reading out of reports which we actually had in front of us. There was not much discussion although this improved around

2002 with a move to let go some of the reports and raise some relevant media issues for conversation. There were discussions about documents on the internet, many members pressing for a pastoral approach while the person who wrote the drafts, American ethicist Russell Shaw, tended to emphasise the philosophical and the abstract.

This was the case with a project that was dear to me. I thought that if I were to do something in the Pontifical Council, I could promote a pastoral booklet on movies (especially those films that people saw in the multiplexes) and spirituality, to make the Church credible in its approach to movie entertainment as well as to more serious themes. Archbishop Foley agreed and asked me to be the 'architect of the document' while Russell Shaw would write the draft. In the event, his draft bore little resemblance to my outline. He started with the word, caution, and told me that he couldn't include the title of popular films (like *The Matrix* or *The Lord of the Rings* at the time) as the Pontifical Council would not accept them. He quoted the usual art house suspects, Bergman, Kurosawa and Tarkovsky.

A number of consultors were critical of the draft. The Council discussion tended, as Fr. Bob White SJ, told me, to vindicate my approach. I took notes, gave them to Archbishop Foley. Next day, he simply announced, no fanfare, no explanation, all briefly blunt, the project was shelved. Maybe one day ...!

At the papal audience, John Paul II was slower and slower, year by year in entering the Sala Clementina. The first time I had been at the Council meetings, in 1994, he had just slipped over in the bath. Some wag remarked that, while he was infallible, he was not infallible! By 2004, he was being wheeled in. He was taken to hospital in February 2005 just before the scheduled audience. Looking at the photos, they look exactly the same year by year: the pope leaning over, Archbishop Foley introducing me at the side, me on my knees shaking hands, later standing and shaking hands. I don't know how to spell this, but, after the introduction, again year by year, all I ever got from the Pope was 'ungh' or something sounding like that. For women and children, he was more than 100 per cent attentive. For men and clergy, 'ungh'!

A postscript to these Council reminiscences is the audience of 2006. Robert (who attended as a consultor – they had to pay for travel and board, whereas members, as I was, were covered by the Vatican!) and I should not have been there since we had finished our terms. However, the Secretariat of State, after the death of John Paul II, had not got round to officially approving our successors, so they came as guests while we had an unexpected swan song opportunity. When Pope Benedict XVI arrived at the door, he walked so quickly to his chair that we were taken aback, so used were we to John Paul's slow trudge. And, after Archbishop Foley's introduction, no 'ungh' but a pleasant question, 'Where are you from?' When I answered that I was from Australia, the Pope said that he was to go there in 2008. A pleasant papal finale to Council meetings.

I should have mentioned that we had an opening Mass in the German church in the Vatican each year. It bore little resemblance to any renewal of liturgy that was advocated. Then a dinner at a hotel, a chance to chat with the head of the Knights of Columbus or Cardinals from Taiwan, Montreal or Rio! There was always a film at the Council offices each year, so media-wise, we were in the 21st century. We saw 2001 in 2001, *The Emperor's Club* and in 2004, *The Passion of the Christ*.

To be fair to Archbishop Foley, he was a newspaper editor, a pragmatic American, who was most courteous and had got to know most people in Catholic Communications around the Church. He was not really a policy person but journalists, especially at the time of Pope John Paul II's death and the conclave, found that they were welcomed and treated well. He should have been made a cardinal much earlier but his predecessor died after he did and there is a rule (which could be and has been overlooked) that the incumbent could not be named a cardinal while the retired head was still alive and had not turned eighty. I mentioned this at one Council meeting to his friend, Bishop Joe Galante, who had worked in the Congregation for Religious for years, that it was a bit of a humiliation for Archbishop Foley not to get the red hat. Bishop Galante replied that the Curia members were afraid of him. That didn't seem likely. The bishop remarked, 'He tells the truth and believes in fair play.'

Speaking of Bishop Galante, he was for some years, the Media bishop for the American Catholics Bishops Conference and attended the Unda USA annual conferences (which by 1998 incorporated members of OCIC on the board as the merger moved towards reality). In 2001, we gave him a copy of the first volume of a project that I worked on for several years, *Lights... Camera... Faith*. His enthusiastic response was, 'I hope *The Godfather* is in it'. Not that volume but the next. By the way, that meeting was in San Antonio, which meant a visit to The Alamo and meeting Vikki Carr who co-hosted the awards. Previously, we had been in Las Vegas. You have to be a gambling enthusiast to go to Las Vegas if you want to enjoy it. After walking up and down the Strip and gawking at the casinos and their glitzy imitations of pyramids, Eiffel Towers and Venetian canals, what else is there to do? Though I do remember the homily by the Archbishop at the conference mass. He defended Las Vegas with the words from St. Paul, 'Where sin did abound, there grace did more abound.'

In my early years in Hammersmith, *Lights... Camera... Faith...* occupied a good bit of my time. Frank Frost, a good friend from Maclean, Virginia, and a great supporter of Catholic film involvement in SIGNIS, suggested that it would be an interesting idea to find a movie that would correspond to each Sunday gospel. Working intuitively, I became eager to find those films. The idea was to take the three cycles of the readings in the liturgy and find those films which would illuminate the Gospels and the other readings for each Sunday and major feast day celebrations and create a dialogue. The Gospel and readings would offer meanings for appreciating the films. The films would open up the Scriptures. But, who would be interested in publishing such a project?

Fortunately, there was only a short wait. For some years, I had been a friend of Sister Rose Pacatte, an energetic American sister, a member of the Daughters of St. Paul, who had studied media in England, was a great proponent of media education as well as enthusiastic about films. She proposed it to the editorial board of Pauline Media in Boston and off we went. I was rather keen, because of the Scripture readings, on calling it 'A Movie Lectionary'. Boston was not so keen and suggested *Lights... Camera... Faith...* But, to my delight, they did include 'A Movie Lectionary' on the cover. Boston also suggested that Rose contribute in some way so that her name could also appear on the cover – good marketing in the US. The Daughters of St. Paul certainly took the project to heart and sold quite a number of each volume. Many parishioners actually bought it for their parish priests for a Christmas gift – and hint. I enjoyed some of the surprise expressed about my choices: *Terminator 2, Judgment Day* for the feast of Mary, the Mother of God (wasn't John Connor a messiah figure?) or *Edward Scissorhands* for the Sunday of the Passion (people turning against the kindly Edward and wanting him dead).

This meant over two hundred films in the books, a substantial enough a resource. Thank God for video and for DVD, which means that the films are still more readily available than they were in the past. In 2006, we published *Lights... Camera... Faith... The Ten Commandments*, three films for each commandment, one for general interest, one for adults and one controversial. You might like an example. For the commandment on honouring father and mother, we used *Finding Nemo, On Golden Pond* and *Ordinary People.* We were able to use some more discussion-challenging titles than in the liturgical cycle books, like The Cider House Rules for 'Thou Shalt Not Kill' or Glengarry Glen Ross for 'Thou Shalt Not Covet'. A manuscript, *LCF... Beatitudes and Deadly Sins* has been ready for some years – living in hope for its eventual publication.

The Daughters of St. Paul were generous in offering opportunities for promotion, Rose and I travelling to launches and conferences and book signings in New York, Chicago, Los Angeles, San Diego and, best of all for me, Hawaii. Actually, we had the biggest attendances at our sessions in Honolulu. I had always been interested in Fr. Damien (after listening to John Farrow's biography, *Damien the Leper* in the novitiate) and am grateful for the plane ticket the sisters bought for me. It was only a short flight across to Molokai though, in Damien's day, it meant exile from Oahu and beyond for life. We were able to walk around the former leper settlement, with a recovered leper driving us around in one of those orange American school buses. He was the sheriff and welcomed us, guided us to the old church, the old school, filling in the history for us. I had seen Paul Cox's *Molokai* with David Wenham as Damien (and a poster was on the wall in the classroom) and been moved by it. Cox filmed there, capturing the isolation as well as the beauty. I realised it was one of the places I had always hoped to visit but had thought it unlikely.

The first promotions for *Lights... Camera... Faith...* took place in October 2001. That means saying something about September 11. Everybody has some 9/11 stories.

I had been in Montreal at the end of August, a member of our Ecumenical Jury at the festival. Got back to London on the sixth. The ninth was just an ordinary day in London. It was a Tuesday and we were at the regular national press previews. The afternoon film was *Greenfingers* with Clive Owen and Helen Mirren, at the Fox theatrette. As the final credits rolled, without warning, the screen (cinema size, not just TV) showed planes crashing into the Twin Towers. Was it a promo for a disaster movie? Why were they showing this? And then I noticed that the time indicator on the Fox News coverage was real time, that we were watching what was happening on this New York morning. We are now so familiar with the images that it is hard to remember that immediate and shocking impact. Out in the foyer, the critics started to ring their newspaper offices – some receiving alarming messages that there could be a terrorist attack on the offices at Canary Wharf. What were we to do? The decision was that there was little else except to go on to the next preview. Would you believe it was actually called *Pandemonium* (a story of Coleridge and Wordsworth)?

But I did go, as I mentioned, to the U.S. in October – and was singled out at every airport (San Antonio, changing at Dallas, La Guardia, Chicago, LA) for special security checks, almost causing me to miss connections. Of course, the information given was that I was chosen for the procedures, 'Computer generated selection'. The main impact, however, was walking along 6th Avenue in New York, looking up above the skyscrapers and trying to visualise the planes flying over, so close to the ground, on their deadly mission. Not as dramatic as so many people's experience of the final months of 2001, but we all have our stories.

While the advantage of being based in London was easy access to meetings for the merger (outlined in the next chapter), the ease of travelling to other parts of the world compared with starting out from Melbourne enabled me to visit many members of OCIC. They also opened my eyes (and heart) to a wide range of men and women trying to work creatively in media.

Let me take Africa as the first illustration of this.

When I was elected president of OCIC, I was rather overwhelmed by all those who came up to congratulate me. Jim McDonnell, a wise friend, advised me to be cautious about all my 'new friends' – and what they might be after. I was amused that Benedict Assorow, longtime member of the Unda Board, and quite a successful wheeler dealer in his home Church of Ghana as well as beyond, got in early to invite me to visit his country. As providence would have it, within a year there was a pan-African meeting to celebrate 25 years of the African Bishops media offices and all the secretaries were to attend a special conference – in Ghana. So, there we were at Accra airport being welcomed by Benedict, who, of course, was a wonderful host. Before we could say 'Bishops Conference', he had the five of us who were visiting from Europe in a car and hurtling out of Accra to the west. Instant local exposure.

We visited Cape Coast where we were welcomed by the local bishop, Peter Turkson. He was a very impressive man to meet just as a man, but also as a pastoral bishop with a knowledge of scriptures. Morning tea with him. I was not surprised when he was appointed to the Vatican curia with a responsibility for Justice issues and made a Cardinal. He has navigated Vatican and world waters with skill and insight. Then we were off to Takoradi for lunch with the Italian Franciscan Conventuals from Padua who had a printing press which served the Church in Ghana. Before hurrying back to the capital we were taken to Elmina Castle. Now, that was an experience. It was one of the slave castles in West Africa, where the slaves were crowded into dark (many completely dark) cells before going on board the ships to be transported into exile. My knowledge of the slave trade tended to come from the movies (and the then recent *Amistad*), but it is an altogether other sobering experience to wander the dark of the castle, discover the lightless outlets to the ships sidling up to the castle and imagine (as far as one could) the devastating experience of those slaves. One reassuring thing. Matters can improve. Our guide around the castle was a local man, free, educated and able to communicate the history of his ancestors. Elmina appeared in the film, *Little Senegal*.

I know it has little to do with OCIC, but on the way back into Accra, we experienced the worst traffic jam I have ever been in: five ways in the dusk – and no give ways at all. Time and the traffic stood still. Whether we approved or not, Benedict once again showed his ingenuity by skirting round vehicles, pedestrians, stalls and shops, veering towards gutters and getting by on what seemed to be basic footpaths and liberating us. He told us some years later that they had installed traffic lights at that crossroads. Not before time.

The next day at the opening Mass, lots of music and song. I looked rather delightedly at the collection ritual. Everybody went up, no, danced up, swaying to the rhythms of the music to drop their gift into the basket. Now, that's a different aspect of liturgical participation. I kept trying to imagine it happening in an Australian or in an English church.

The conference was a long one, Sunday to Friday but offered the opportunity to learn how communications and media had developed in sub-Saharan Africa, East, West and Southern Africa. At times we were sent out to visit media centres and radio and television stations, to be hosted by government ministers who were interested in dialogue with the Church. I had to give some thought as to what one should say in speeches of welcome or speeches of appreciation or votes of thanks.

Accra was not the most spick and span city at that time but it functioned well, the heritage of empire and British orderliness and bureaucracy. We were to find the following year in Abidjan that the city could look good, thanks to French style, but did not function well, civil war breaking out three months after we were there.

Accommodation for the Accra conference was at the seminary, about twenty kilometres out from the city centre. The staff had had to buy some mattresses and towels for the visitors, for the wooden frames (and low springs) that constituted the beds which some guests could not fit into and who had to go next door to the Society of the Missionaries of Africa. Showers consisted of a concrete floor with a pipe high up on the roof with a hole in it where some cold water dropped out on us. The next year at the conference centre in Abidjan, I was ushered into a room with an en suite and hot water in the efficient shower – only to discover that I was the only one who had such luxury. There was some advantage to being president!

The other lesson I learnt was important. After I had sat in on all the sessions for the week, the general secretary, from Togo, thanked me for being so constant in attendance. I told him that that was why I came. He then pointed out that several of the other visitors from Europe kept skipping out, going into town to check emails, to go shopping, or just to go out. He told me that Europeans expected Africans to be in attendance at all sessions when they came to Europe but had no scruple in giving sessions in Africa a miss. Later in the day, several of the visitors returned just as there was some local dancing (which had included dragging me up to try to develop a sense of Ghanaian rhythm and body gyration) and they all went immediately up to the front to take photos. Unwitting vestiges of colonial attitudes and behaviour. I was glad I came from Australia. We had experienced colonial downputting – and, of course, we are still learning how Australians have been colonial towards our indigenous people and towards populations of neighbouring countries.

The main thing that I wanted to add about the 2000 trip to Abidjan, Cote d'Ivoire, (three security checks to get out though an upgrade from British Airways to compensate!) was the opportunity at the end of the conference to go by bus to a place that, like others unusual destinations, I never thought I would visit: Yamoussoukro. Yamoussoukro is up country from coastal Abidjan. It has become the capital but at that time it was developing its facilities for hosting international meetings. But, the main reason was to visit the new basilica there, a scaled down model of St. Peter's in Rome. It might have been smaller but it was still large, impressive, much of it beautiful. But, what was it doing out there in what, as we first drove in, seemed to be the middle of nowhere? John Paul II had come to bless it and there was a two storey, solid residence adjacent to the basilica – to what purpose? We were told that it had not cost the people any money, all paid for by the previous president. But where and from whom did he get his money? It was an impressively beautiful enigma out in the bush. It probably now seems more significant as Yamoussoukro itself has developed. Civil war broke out three months later.

If you are still in the mood for travel and discovering people – otherwise a break might be in order – I would like to go to Latin America. We are, sometimes vaguely, aware of the dictatorships of South America, oppression, poverty and 'the disappeared'. The Generals in Argentina may come to mind, or Pinochet and Chile. Whether that affected the way the Church worked in Latin America, some would say yes, that the Church adopted the secular patterns of governance, of control, of secrecy. The reason for mentioning this is that I would have to say that the delegates to assemblies and boards from Latin America during the 1990s and into the 21st century (though less now as younger members come up who don't necessarily have the oppressive decades in their lives or memories) could be very hard to deal with. I would have to say that they were not against intrigue, either. They were not against claiming poverty for not readily paying their dues – though not against travelling around the continent for meetings (and taxis and meals).

So my first visit, with Robert, to Latin America was against this background. We were invited to Ecuador where the combined office for Unda, OCIC and the Catholic Union of the Press (UCIP) were located. In fairness, I should say that we were welcomed heartily, well looked after, shown the range of activities of OCIC Ecuador and taken to visit churches and universities, acclimatising to the altitude and all. The central square had largely been taken over for the filming of *Proof of Life*, but no sign of Russell Crowe or Meg Ryan, though one of our members was the sound engineer. So no problems, except when I got out of the minibus in front of the office (and many eyes watching) and tripped over one of those small concrete barriers to indicate where the vehicle should stop. Flat on my face, observed by all. (I had tripped less than a month earlier on a higher step than expected going into the chapel where we had our meeting in Munich and a month later, with three of us walking down to the accreditation office in Cannes, my left leg went down the side of a drain hole which was open, the grate moved to the middle. That required visits to hospital and watching all the films with my leg propped up. I have tried to be careful ever since.)

OCIC was trying to foster young talent in film-making. In 1999 we held a competition which resulted in a dozen or more young directors receiving a grant to study for a weekend with Kzrysztof Zanussi outside Warsaw. Zanussi was the head of Polish film production at that time. He was a friend of John Paul II, member of the Pontifical Council for Culture. He had suffered under the Communist regime but had continued his career outside Poland during those years. We went to his country farm (actually only 15 kilometres from the centre of Warsaw) where he lectured, coached and critiqued their work. It was interesting, of course, to sit in as an observer – and to be taken to the local church for Mass on Sunday (somewhat traditional) and to meet his friends and acquaintances. Zanussi had been a tour guide in an earlier incarnation and did the honours for us in Warsaw itself, explaining that the city had been destroyed by the Germans and completely rebuilt, one of the largest movie sets in Europe, he suggested.

In the middle of the following year, I found myself in Poland again, this time to celebrate the 2000 Jubilee, especially the media ministry of the Church. We were in Lodz, which I discovered was pronounced Wudj, the home of Polish film-making with such directors as Roman Polanski and Andrej Wajda and the film school. We visited the city, the film studios and museums, celebrated Mass with some pomp, participated in seminars where, I noticed, that the paper I gave in English took up twice as many pages when translated into Polish. One insight into the changing Church. Speaking to the bishops gathered there – Italian. Speaking with the seminary professors – French. With the younger clergy – English. It was 1 June. The weather was sunny and cloudless. And the priest showing me the city thought the weather was sweltering and complained of the heat wave.

Best to get back to more 'ordinary' adventures!

The other area of OCIC where I had become more and more at home was Asia. While English was not the first language of most of our members from Asia, it was the common language. This made it easier to participate in regional assemblies – and venturing into some countries never previously visited. In 1999, we went to Taiwan, not as interesting and attractive to visit compared with Hong Kong. But, its history of separation from mainland China, its sense of independence and its sense of prosperity made an impact. Unda Taiwan also had an outstanding reputation for its production and training centre, Kwang-chi, inaugurated by the Jesuits and developed by Fr. Jerry Martinson who began to have an influence on China itself with his television programs and his screen persona of Uncle Jerry.

Actually, the main memory from Taiwan is the visit to the memorial hall of Chiang Kai-shek. It seemed the length of a football field or more, vast open spaces, some artwork along the walls and, in pride of place ... several of the automobiles that Chiang Kai-shek was driven in. More than a touch capitalist and consumerist. I remember being most impressed by the absolute immobility of the soldiers who were standing on guard, despite the chatter around them, and the photo taking.

The next year, the regional meeting was in Korea. It was held outside Seoul, though we went into the city for several excursions, to see the venues under construction for the Asian Games, to visit the historical area and to visit the Catholic Cathedral, the diocesan centre – and the Samsung organisation. I would not be hurrying back to Korea. Our experience was, shall we say, over-regimented, which caused one of our participants (herself German) to remark that the Koreans were the Germans of Asia.

This contrasted with a visit to Japan earlier that year which, sadly, lasted only 30 hours, flying from Fiji to Hong Kong (as one does!). People were friendly, offering help to bewildered visitors, guiding me to the train for Nagoya (and wanting to practise their English as they did). The bullet train swept past Mt. Fuji – lucky to glimpse it as it was covered in cloud the next day. Nagoya was the destination as it was the headquarters of the group of Missionaries of the Sacred Heart who had gone from Australia to work there after World War II. I was proudly driven around Nagoya by our Japanese confrere, Makino, guiding me through 'my city'. And, then, off to Narita, and no return.

I'm not sure whether all this adequately shows what OCIC was like in those years or what I was doing. But the next chapter will take you to the more formal side of things.

39. MERGER: OCIC AND UNDA BECOME SIGNIS

MONTREAL. 1998. Summer. August. Not the Montreal of snow ploughs and the frozen St. Lawrence river – that would come in another four months – but now a rather hot and sunny city. The two Catholic audiovisual media organisations were holding their international assemblies, assemblies that were to take a vote that would bring them to some closure after seventy years of activity for each of them and move them to a new phase of their life and work: together, as one organisation.

I am now going to plagiarise. But, that's all right. I will plagiarise from myself. At the SIGNIS Assembly in Chang Mai, the history of the merging of OCIC and Unda was launched. The first part, the history was based on memory and the documents published by the two organisations. Since it was my memory, since I contributed to a lot of the documents, and since I was the author of *The Emergence of SIGNIS*, (and since you are not likely to read that book), I am taking the liberty to draw on, in some detail, the description of the merger. For those who might be wondering about the history of the Church's audiovisual media journey through the two organisations, here it is. I will try to make it as easy and as interesting a read as possible.

From 1945 to 1980, the two organisations had developed their particular mission and service in the Church, Unda focusing on radio, then incorporating television and production, OCIC on cinema. The 1970s saw an interest in small media, media at the grass roots, like street theatre, and this offered new challenges to the organisations. The 1970s and early 1980s also saw the development of video production and the wide distribution of programs, movies and educational, on cassettes. In Munich in 1977, it was decided that there be a division of labour, so to speak, with Unda concentrating on production and OCIC on distribution.

This reflected something of how the two organisations were coming closer as well as an indication that many of the media workers in the Church were operating in both Unda and OCIC fields.

This was recognised in 1980 with the two organisations holding their assemblies together in Manila. This pattern continued for the next 20 years in Nairobi (1983), Quito (1987), Bangkok (1990), Prague (1994) and Montreal (1998). Many members frequently asked the question: should the two organisations become one? There were persuasive arguments on both sides. Each, for instance, had their particular focus and their particular media, a sense of identity which could be lost. On the other hand, with the technological developments of the latter part of the 20th century, more and more members of each organisation found themselves working in multimedia, or cross-media communications. These changes meant new communications identities for most who worked in the media.

To employ a useful cliché, moods in both OCIC and Unda blew hot and cold concerning a merger. At times, as in the early 1980s, it seemed a good ideal to pursue. By the late 1980s, there was less enthusiasm. Again, as the 1990s went on, there were new moves for a merger. In fact, the executives of both organisations met in Rome at the time of the annual Pontifical Council assembly in February 1994 to prepare for the Prague Assembly later that year. They looked at what was particularly characteristic of their organisations and what that would mean for the future. The decision was made to present these ideas to members in Prague and to hold a straw vote concerning a merger. When the discussion was held in Prague and the vote taken, it was a straw poll against a merger.

The move towards one organisation was at a standstill.

Some of those in favour of a merger felt that there was more to life than spending time at endless meetings, toing and froing about the issue,

Merger: OCIC and UNDA Become SIGNIS   365

and thought that the discussion should be put on hold for a time. Some of the reasons for this hesitation are found in the thesis on OCIC by the then-Vice-President, Gaye Ortiz, quoting a paper that I had written when things seemed negative which emphasised the then lack of meeting of minds and the need for OCIC to maintain its identity and tradition.

However, it was the force of the two secretary generals which moved matters ahead. Robert Molhant, secretary general of OCIC since 1979, was strongly in favour of a merger. The new secretary general of Unda, Victor Sunderaj, assessed the realities of the situation, the cross media work, the financial situations and the interest of funding organisations in streamlining their grants through having one organisation. Surprisingly to many, each Board voted in favour of moving towards a merger at the meetings in Brussels in November 1997. The decision was to put the matter to the vote to each Assembly in Montreal in 1998 with the members of the Board speaking in favour.

During 1998, the executives of the two organisations, Angela Ann Zukowski (President) and Victor Sunderaj (Secretary-General) for Unda and Henk Hoekstra (President) and Robert Molhant (Secretary-General) for OCIC, consulted the members and prepared some documentation to present in Montreal. They held a special meeting in (unexpectedly and disappointingly wind and rainswept) Malta, producing a Malta document.

The stage was now set for a merger.

Preparations for the 1998 assemblies were not easy and, at one stage, it was thought that the meetings would have to be held in Rome. However, the efforts of Pierre Belanger and Jacques Paquette, representing Unda and OCIC respectively, enabled the assemblies to be held in the first week of August as planned. The venue was the University of Montreal.

A tradition had grown up of both organisations sharing study days prior to the actual days of each assembly.

So, in August 1998 we had the opportunity to see the complexity and rich diversity of our members' insights and interpretations on the theme, 'Creativity in the Mediasphere: A Spiritual Opportunity', a very American title. The World Congress Study Days created a paradox and a challenge for us. How can we present experiences and information that trigger a global sense of connectedness among our members as a world association? How can we present themes and experiences that have a longer life span than two or three days?

The message that emerged called us to transcend our own cultural boundaries and perceptions to embrace the global scenario. We were challenged 'to be sentinels and advocates for equality and accessibility for all women and men to the opportunities of the new media age'.

A speaker from North America emphasised Al Gore's hope that every child would be linked by the web to the National Library of Congress in the audience were representatives of small Pacific countries, like Sister Tettayrua from Kiribati who had experienced going up in a lift only once in Fiji before testing them out in Montreal!

One episode that probably stayed in the mind of many participants was from the European presentation. Maggie Roux from the UK was speaking of 'epiphanies'. In her words: "The final part of our exploration into the power of the image is very personal. This is particularly so when out of the artist's expression of imaginative transformation the image speaks to our deepest selves. This is what many of us experience as an Epiphany. So far, so good – and theoretical. Then ...

The Full Monty was a British movie set in a small city in the North of England. This film had done incredible repeat business many people have gone two and three times to see it in quick succession. It has (in England at least) spawned imitators in pubs and clubs. *Full Monty* Nights where the men dance and remove their clothes in front of their family audiences are extremely popular (who says the English are reserved?). Oh dear!

'But how might such a film express Epiphany? There are no wonderful scenes of nature pointing to the glory of God or the majesty of the created universe. The director has not painted a canvas full of colour and light. There is no intention to explore spiritual yearnings or moments of wonder when the transcendent breaks through.' OK, but ...

'But what *The Full Monty* does is explore everyday human concerns. Beneath the light-hearted comedy is a powerful story of broken dreams and broken lives. And it is a story about a loving way of living. Through the love of family, friends and community the characters finally live life as a celebration ... It was in that triumphant naked dance that epiphany was expressed. We are not broken people on the scrap heap of life. We are God's creation, and like David in the Old Testament, we can dance in joy before the Lord.' Then she showed it!

When Maggie screened the last five minutes of *The Full Monty*, not everybody was looking directly at the screen for their epiphany! And Archbishop Foley, head of the Pontifical Council for Social Communications, fiddled with his briefcase and later did mention in the OCIC Assembly proper that juries (and *The Full Monty* had received an OCIC award in San Sebastian in 1997) needed to be aware of vulgarity.

While the assemblies attended to ordinary business and reports, there were elections. 'Angela Ann Zukowski was re-elected president of Unda, with Washington Uranga (Argentina) and Peter Thomas (Australia) re-elected as vice-presidents. Pierre Belanger succeeded Victor Sunderaj as Secretary-General of Unda. Peter Malone (Australia) was elected president of OCIC with Augie Lourdusamy (Malaysia) and Gaye Ortiz (UK) as vice-presidents. Robert Molhant continued as Secretary General of OCIC.' The names are important because this was the group that had to lead the work for the merger, with Angela Ann and I presiding.

The significant votes for the merger: Unda, OCIC: 95 in favour, 1 against. I abstained.

The morning after the end of the Assemblies saw the first meeting of combined Executives and the first official discussion about the merger (and the French word 'fusion'). It was decided that the first meeting would be held in Luxembourg in December 1998 – and, with a basis in the Malta Document, everyone would go home and think seriously about how the merger could actually be effected.

If you are not attracted by a process for a merger of two Church organisations, give the following a miss. But I thought it useful to offer an overview of the process towards the merger. It was new to me. And it worked.

When the presidents, vice-presidents and secretary-generals, along with some seconded members, met in December 1998 in the seminary in wintry Luxembourg, even the intended date for the merger was not yet established. The assembly opinions were that it should be achieved within four years. In fact, it was accomplished in three. This is in no small part due to Angela Ann Zukowski's practical American know-how in establishing a timeline for the process and the detail for each stage of the timeline. And the timeline was followed exactly for the three years.

The basic chronology for each year consisted of:

> An end of year meeting of the Executive which would establish the parameters of the goals to be reached over the 12 month period, the specific details of what was to be achieved, the ways in which the Executive, the Boards and the total membership could be involved in every stage of the process.
>
> A Joint Boards meeting in the European spring to discuss the proposals of the Executive which each member was to receive in sufficient time before the Boards' meeting; the Boards' reworking of the material would be sent to all the members around the world.
>
> A meeting within two or three months of the presidents and secretaries general to fine tune the material of the Board to be sent out to all members.
>
> Regional meetings of the continents in the second half

of the year with feedback in time for the next Executive meeting, so that the consensus of the world membership would ratify what had been achieved during the year and the process could start for the following year.

Approval of the documents by the Joint Boards' meeting of the following year.

This timetable was followed, not without difficulty, especially in such demanding areas as legal wording for statutes. It was the responsibility of the two presidents to chair the meetings, which they did, though delegating the vice-presidents and other members with a flair for chairing meetings to preside at particular sessions.

The first Luxembourg meeting opened up the realities of the structure of the new organisation. One of the key questions was whether the geographical model be retained or a model be considered which looked at the different fields of media and the range of networks they could develop. The structures of UCIP, the Catholic Union of the Press, and The World Association of Christian Communication (WACC), with its 'desks' for the different media, were studied. Ultimately, the geographical model prevailed, though the networking idea was incorporated into what ultimately came to be called 'priorities' and 'fields of action', and, even, 'desks'. In November 1999, Alvito de Souza (Kenya) from Vatican Radio was appointed as the secretary for the merger, preparing the documents and co-ordinating responses. He continued this work during the succeeding two years.

The Joint Boards met in 1999 in Rolduc, Holland, near the borders of Belgium and Germany, in 2000 and 2001 in Munich (where 2000 saw the boards having a couple of hours off on Shrove Tuesday and being amazed at the instant meticulous clean up of central Munich after the Mardi Gras celebrations and where 2001 saw many Board members not leaving the building for five days!).

The mid-year Core Committee (presidents and secretaries-general) meetings were held, in Brussels, then Angela Ann Zukowski hosted a meeting on her campus at the University of Dayton. In 2001 the meeting was at the Cenacle Retreat Centre in Chicago. Another 2001 meeting was held in October in Madrid to put the finishing touches to the documents for the assembly which would vote on the merger. The decision was made that this would be done in Rome in November 2001.

In order to ensure that the process was open to all and that the executive were attentive to the views from around the world, the presidents and secretaries general were present at as many of the regional meetings as possible in order to listen at first hand to opinions and difficulties.

The Rolduc Joint Boards' meeting was a big challenge to everyone there – at least 50 people. The members of each board numbered twenty or more.

The main elements discussed in Luxembourg were the Nature of the new organisation (incorporating the vision), the Aims and Objectives (the elements of a Mission Statement), the range of membership and the consequent structures needed. And, as you can imagine, there were also initial discussions on the financial issues for the new organisation.

Participation in festivals seems to be one of the strengths to be preserved. It is one of the essential functions of an international Catholic organisation for audio-visual media to be a meeting place for professionals, to develop a dialogue with those who 'make' television, radio and films to be aired or projected all over the world. This is the kind of challenge we are facing when we are told, sometimes bluntly: 'Create a new organisation that will play a role in the public forum and will not confine itself to the sacristy'. This was from the two Secretaries General. As was this:

> It is a perpetual challenge to 'go beyond the border, over to the professional world'. This world, indeed, is in fear of interventions from churches that would try to impose moral values that are less and less universally agreed upon or censorship that no one accepts anymore. A long

companionship with the professional milieu is necessary to base our credibility as representatives of Catholic media. At first, you feel suspicion. You must be a priest or a religious. If you are a lay person, the question you hear is 'is it possible, at the same time, to be professional and to work within a Catholic institution? Leave the sacristy and come out to the public square!'. There is, then, a strong challenge for the new organisation to face: to cross over better than OCIC and Unda have been able to do it the border of the professional world.

We thought this was good stuff, the Church in the Modern World. No siege mentality.

This is what was starting to emerge:

> 'X' [Name yet to be chosen] is a Catholic world association of dedicated and professional media communicators (who work in fields such as video and television and cinema, information technology and other emerging (or future) forms of mediated communication).
>
> It respects all cultures, and builds community through the service and promotion of human, social, cultural and Christian values. ('Christian' specifically articulates a preferential option for the poor in a way that 'spiritual' does not. We include other faith perspectives in the phrase, 'it respects all cultures'). It is a 'gathering place' (a 'virtual' or metaphorical (i.e., not literal) term which connotes the ethos of the association as open, welcoming and supportive of communicators working within the media industry as well as those who work within the Church) for communicators to feel at home and to inspire each other through dialogue and the sharing of experiences (through education and training initiatives as well as through networking in world assemblies, film festivals, video markets, etc).

The association aims to promote the development of women and men of all cultures through communications in order to respond to the issues and concerns of society. This is realised through research, education, productions, service and protection of human rights:

1. To promote and coordinate the work of the association in communications, education, research and productions by means of communication technologies.
2. To offer professional formation opportunities, particularly promoting education for communications that will develop critical and active minds and contribute to healthy public opinion.
3. To program activities motivating and encouraging participation in a continuing dialogue of the transformation of the communications culture.
4. To facilitate inter-religious and ecumenical collaboration in communications activities.
5. To contribute to the pastoral care of communication professionals.
6. To position the Church to be an active voice in the world of communications.
7. To encourage the members of the association to be living witnesses to the Gospel values.
8. To protect human rights and justice in addressing communications issues and concerns.
9. To represent its members at the international level.

Now I am going to quote from myself, from a President's message in mid-1999:

> The ... dynamic of thinking new and thinking creatively. It is of little value simply taking the concerns of Unda and

the concerns of OCIC and adding one to the other. That would not be a 'new' association for the next century, just an amalgam of the two old organisations. If the mentality of simply merging the two organisations is still part of our thinking, then we have to move on. After all, we speak of multimedia. We also speak of our individual involvements in our work as being 'cross-media'. The desire to merge was to acknowledge this cross media reality, to acknowledge the ever-changing and quickly-changing technologies and to be at the forefront of these developments as Church. This would mean that the Church was credible on the level of international and of changing and challenging media.

But, the second dynamic is equally important and could sometimes be in danger of being overlooked. It is this: the specialist areas that have been developed in each organisation for over 70 years must not be downgraded or lost. The new technologies are coming, but they often facilitate the practical use of what are now becoming 'traditional' media. From the OCIC perspective, we will need, in the new association, to continue the focus on cinema culture, liaison with the industry and the presence and awards at film festivals.

In that vein (with some final pessimism about this experiment), I will mention a venture that sounded good, started well and then the bishop responsible went back on his word. He became the archbishop of Brussels and found himself caught up in the Belgian abuse scandals, especially with what might be gently called 'infelicitous remarks and statements', Archbishop Leonard.

The diocese of Namur was selling its printing press and other media enterprises. It was suggested that the new worldwide Church organisation would a good place for programs that fostered communication and media. Money was set aside and the enterprise was given the name Futur Talent. The go-between was Brother Ferdinand Poswick, a Benedictine monk of Maredsous. There were some interesting activities, after a press conference with the bishop, and international think tank meeting, some awards to films including at Cannes, some gatherings of reviewers, women and film. Whatever the reasons, pressure from the diocese about funds leaving, the bishop's own decision, within four years, Futur Talent had not present or future.

'The ability to authentically listen to the winds of change calls for nimbleness. Nimbleness enables us to continually identify and implement critical changes more quickly and efficiently. Nimbleness is fitness to change.' I rather liked this notion of nimbleness from Angela Ann Zukowski.

Our 'buzz words' (the American influence!) for 2000 were 'programs' and 'services'.

And a sigh of regret: one of the elements that still eluded us was the name of the new organisation. What sounds good in one language does not necessarily sound good in another! many suggestions had been made – and rejected. This was a perennial item on the agenda and a great deal of time was spent in the discussion and quick time in the rejections. With the languages of the organisations being Spanish, French and English and nouns and adjectives not appearing in the same order in each language, acronyms seemed to be impossible. Eastern Europeans understandably were reluctant to have a name with 'Com' in it no matter how much they believed in Communication. The suggestion, Communicom, was therefore shot down. There were translation ambiguities in other suggestions. It seems that Signum is like the Thai word for breast. And having Spanish and French speakers saying Cathcom meant that it sounded too much like 'caca' to be acceptable.

Since there had been jokes about OCIC and Unda for decades, it would seem that it should not matter too much – 'members of O-sick'! and were members wearing their 'Undapants'! Even SIGNIS did not eventually escape since someone suggested 'sickness'!

Key to programs and services was the decision that the future

Merger: OCIC and UNDA Become SIGNIS 375

Catholic association would have its secretariat in Brussels. The general secretariat's role will be of course to coordinate; it has already been agreed upon that all activities would not necessarily have to be dealt with from Brussels. A flexibility in the organisation, thanks to the possibilities electronic communications offer today, is part of the organisational landscape.

For one year now and in the context of the consultations related to the setting up of the future unified Catholic association that we are creating together, we, the Secretaries General, have given high priority to our participation in regional meetings. In Suva for the Pacific, in Beirut for the Middle-East sub-region, in Vilnius for Europe underlying the special attention we would like to give to Eastern European Abidjan for Africa, in Orlando for North America, in Seoul for Asia and soon in Curitiba (Brazil) for Latin America, we have the opportunity to listen to our members, to be the privileged witnesses of their initiatives and projects. We also carry a message: OCIC and Unda are meeting at an important crossroad of their history: you are all invited to contribute to this moment of creativity.'

Progress was interrupted by a sad event. Soon after he finished his service as President of OCIC for eight years (1990-98), Henk Hoekstra became unwell. He was unable to accept an invitation to come to Rolduc for the Joint Boards' meeting. He was in an out of hospital during 1999 but, fortunately for so many who knew him, he was able to come to Munich in 2000. It was the last time that most would see him. He died on 12 September 2000.

A significant development was that at this time a pervading sense of justice increased amongst members. It was expressed in the aims and objectives and was to permeate programs. The final English word that was adopted for this social justice emphasis was 'Advocacy'.

It was in Aachen that we found the name SIGNIS. Not exactly what people were expecting. I sent a 'brief' on the name and the reasons for it to all members:

One theme that seemed powerful was that of 'fire' (with its evocation of light and energy and the Spirit). *Ignis* is the Latin word for fire. At the beginning of the session on the name, Robert Molhant wrote the prospective names on the white board, but slipped when writing *ignis* and, in fact, wrote 'signis'. When the executive looked at this, SIGNIS found favour and was voted in unanimously.

The 'sub-title' of SIGNIS in English is 'The World Catholic Association for Communication'.

In discussions about the website, net was preferred to org as we are a 'network' association. We have registered signis.net for our website. For regional and national sites, it is possible to use, for example, signis-Asia.net or signis-Zimbabwe.net

At last! And, now, you know.

2000, the Jubilee year was now over. Robert Molhant, Pierre Belanger and I had attended what was the final celebration for the Jubilee year, the December Celebration of Entertainment. This consisted of a number of liturgies in different Roman churches. A planned procession to the Church of San Ignazio failed to materialise but a presentation of circus acts at the film studios on Via Tiburtina was very entertaining. Pope John Paul II found this to be the case when some of them, including an extremely dextrous young boy juggler, performed for him during the offertory procession. While Pierre and Peter were among the concelebrants, Robert proclaimed one of the readings in French in St. Peter's Square.

In the next president's message, there was something of an *apologia* for my not being of legal mind!

> Statutes. How many of you have participated in that most gruelling of occupations: writing statutes? For some it is an exhilarating experience, making sure that every 'i' is dotted and 't' crossed and, of course, more importantly, that meanings are clear and formulations are as exact as possible. For others who don't have a legal mind, it can be protracted

Merger: OCIC and UNDA Become SIGNIS

agony. Well, after thorough discussions, our joint Unda OCIC Boards have voted favourably on a framework for our SIGNIS statutes as well as satisfactory expressions that can go to our lawyers for the legal precision that is necessary for the final version.

A line of emphasis that had constantly been raised by members over the three years was the deep desire to open SIGNIS, at all levels, not only to Catholic media institutions but also to Catholic professionals active in the secular media. It was noted that this would not be easy. In certain countries professionals in the secular media do not want to feel 'confined' by an organisation that they feel is too 'clerical'.

Interesting to look back at the status of email and internet at that time:

> The development of email and the internet will evidently lead to the question of which of the publications will continue to be printed and which of them should be distributed by email. The present OCIC site is regularly updated and which seems to be appreciated by our members, also receives visits from surfers who, in discovering the organisation will obviously be open to a SIGNIS site. On the other hand the general point of view of the Director's Committee was that the printed publications should be continued as email and internet access is not universal. The cost of internet access is also still unaffordable across a vast number of countries on this earth.

Almost there!

One of the problems I have had with Church organisations is that many agree how wonderful they are but their main preoccupation is what can I get out of it – at least possible cost. This was also taken up in the preparations by the Secretaries General: 'It is only human nature, so it is said, to ask what benefits we can receive from SIGNIS. We hope that the statement of nature and objectives, of membership and services give indications of benefits that of members can receive. But, one hopes that the spirit of a Gospel-inspired association leads members to ask what benefits we can give to others, what benefits we can share with others, especially those still struggling to establish media and communications in their own area.'

September 11, 2001.

Two months before the Congress and Assembly in Rome, the American tragedy of September 11, 2001, scarred the consciousness of people around the world. In the immediate aftermath many were afraid to travel and fly. However, by the time of the Congress, most delegates decided that they would come.

The presidents' message acknowledged the events and the death and suffering, written with heartfelt American emotion by Angela Ann Zukowski:

> What we originally set out to communicate to you in this last Unda/OCIC newsletter has been overshadowed by the events of September 11, 2001. The domino effect of the tragedy is unveiled each day. We wonder if it will ever end. We wonder what position, tactics or strategies are best for humanity. We find we cannot escape the flood of information that penetrates the mass media. We discover ourselves face to face trying to understand the moral consciousness of peoples and nations. Yet, it is not simply a matter of looking around us we must look within us. We ourselves must be rooted and live from a moral consciousness that respects the rights and dignities of all women and men.

Despite world apprehensiveness after the events of September 11 and despite the fact that the process of merger had been in action for what seemed three rather rapid years, the delegates and a number of observers arrived in Rome in November 2001.

With several hundred people present, participants stayed at Domus Mariae where the plenary sessions were held, others at the Fratelli Cristiani

Merger: OCIC and UNDA Become SIGNIS 379

close by. However, prior to the assemblies, there was a Congress which focused on the range of media and technologies. It was ambitious but not an unmitigated success. With the involvement in the merger process, there was not enough time and energy available to ensure that the Congress ran smoothly and met the needs of those who attended. And some Italian bureaucratic tangles meant that all the space promised was not available. The venue was the Fabbrica di San Michele a Ripa, an old 18th century children's prison – renovated! – near the Tiber in Trastavere.

The Congress had small rooms, former cells, for screening of video productions, especially those selected for competition. Another room had 50 computers for a Cybercafe. In the large conference room, there were presentations of websites (and competition) as well as several symposia. The workshop on the internet and the website competition drew substantial numbers. A nearby cinema provided venue for film screenings of some films which had won OCIC awards.

What turned out to be the most important feature of the Congress were the five workshops on Media Education, Theology of Communication, Promotion and Distribution of Religious Programs, Professional Training, Film Review and Critique. The minuted reports of these workshops formed the basis in the first SIGNIS assembly for defining and clarifying the priorities of the new association.

One of the highlights of the time was to be a group audience with Pope John Paul II. It was to be on Thursday, 22 November (the American celebration of Thanksgiving), scheduled for the day after the vote for the merger. However, just prior to the participants' arrival, it was announced that the Pope could not meet the Unda and OCIC members because on 22 November he was to promulgate the document from the Pacific Synod of 1998, making a click on a computer that would send his address all over the world immediately. This was a touch dampening to spirits! A Vatican official suggested we simply join the general audience on Wednesday, 21st.

However, Archbishop Foley worked behind the scenes and the Pope dispensed with his custom of not having audiences on Tuesdays and received the delegates in audience, making an address (the text of which follows) and coming to sit in the front row with those present for a photo opportunity. He was heard to clarify with Archbishop Foley that there was Unda and there was OCIC and now there is SIGNIS. In one of the frescoes at the front of the Sala Clementina where the audience was held was an inscription which contained the Latin word *insignis*, which means 'outstanding'. Archbishop Foley brought this to the Pope's attention. The two presidents were given a minute each to introduce the delegates to the Pope and to tell him (so to speak) what the Church's policy was on cinema and on radio and television!

A bit immodest thought it be, I am going to include my Papal moment, captured in photo and later, I discovered, on video. Archbishop Foley suggested that Angela Ann and I introduce our members to the Pope – just for a minute, though I noticed Angela Ann's minute was much longer than mine! It is not every day you get the chance to tell the Pope what you think the Church's cinema vision should be:

> Holy Father, I would like to present to you the international members of the Catholic Organisation for Cinema in my role as president, Peter Malone, an Australian Missionary of the Sacred Heart. In our 73 years history we have tried to be a bridge between the Church and the professional world of cinema and, within the Church, a bridge to all people for education, critique and the promotion of human and spiritual values.

The actual sessions for the vote were preceded by the final discussions on the draft of the Statutes. By one of those strokes of fate (or providence or just bad luck), a press conference hosted by Vatican Radio (and unduly long-winded if memory serves me right!) had been postponed to the day of the vote and Pierre Belanger and I had been committed to attend. By the time they returned to the Assembly, the vote had been taken. We missed it!

In preparation for the leadership elections for the first office holders for SIGNIS, the candidates presented themselves and their vision. Although

Merger: OCIC and UNDA Become SIGNIS 381

two of the candidates for president, Bob Bonnot (who had not been approved by the Vatican as a candidate) and Jim McDonnell, had withdrawn their nominations, they were invited to speak about SIGNIS and its future. President of Unda USA, Frank Morock, also spoke but later withdrew. This left me as the remaining candidate and I was elected President with the two OCIC Vice-Presidents the new Vice-Presidents of SIGNIS, Augy Lourdusamy and Gaye Ortiz. (There had been much discussion at Joint Board meetings about the presence of women in significant positions in SIGNIS and there was satisfaction that Gaye had been elected). Robert Molhant became the first Secretary-General of SIGNIS and Pierre Belanger was to return to his Jesuit province of Montreal.

After the election, presided over by Angela Ann Zukowski, Archbishop Foley presented the retiring presidents of Unda and OCIC with the medals Pro Ecclesia et Pontifice. Archbishop Foley told me it was a 'oncer' and not to expect another when I finished as president of SIGNIS!

I am going to finish this part of my story with parts of my first message to members:

> A warm welcome to the first edition of SIGNIS Info. It brings home to us that we are now living in a new reality, an association which is concerned with the variety of media in the world today and tomorrow.
>
> As I write this editorial, it is two months to the day since we had the first SIGNIS Assembly. In many ways it seems a long time ago. In other ways it seems only yesterday. I would like to take the opportunity to thank all those who came to Rome for the Congress, who made it a world Church event. So many people came for the Multimedia Forum. But it is to those who came to the OCIC and Unda Assemblies to vote on the new statutes for SIGNIS or who came to witness these votes that our gratitude is due.

Three-and-a-half years after the Montreal votes and just under three years since the first Executive meeting in Luxembourg, SIGNIS was a reality.

40. THE FIRST SIGNIS YEARS, 2002-2004

OF COURSE, it was only after the merger between OCIC and Unda had been achieved that the magnitude of the establishment of SIGNIS dawned on us. Two organisations had become one and, while the staffs of the two organisations in Brussels now were to work as one, there was now only one executive for SIGNIS and all that it hoped to achieve. Quirk of fate or whatever it was, the main office-bearers for SIGNIS had been the office bearers for OCIC. Augustine (Augy) Lourdusamy and Gaye Ortiz had been and were now the vice presidents. Robert Molhant was the Secretary-General.

The biggest challenge, it seemed to me, was acknowledging and supporting the central ministries of Unda. The other challenge was not to communicate an impression that cinema was more important than the other media fields.

One of the best developments here was the establishing of a television desk and, in 2003, inaugurating what has become an annual conference of SIGNIS television producers. This was the brainchild of Robert who took to this new activity with his usual enthusiasm. When OCIC had been given the mandate to handle video promotion and distribution in the 1980s, it had organised Video markets, the first in Lisbon in 1987, followed by Driebergen, Holland, in 1992, Cologne in Germany in 1996 and Vilnius, Lithuania, 2000. There was a final market in Rome during the Congress at the time of the merger, 2001.

The first meeting of the new group was held in conjunction with an Assembly in Cape Town in November 2003. Since then, the meetings have moved around the world though held mainly in Europe. But there have been gatherings in Buenos Aires and Nairobi ... This continued one of the key elements of Unda but focused not just on vision and policy but on production, co-productions, promotion and the establishing of a website which allowed for streaming video. Since television was not my area, I was pleased with how well this annual meeting was able to lead to a SIGNIS TV producers' network. There had already been co-operation between Unda, OCIC, SIGNIS and CRTN, The Catholic Radio and Television Network, based at the headquarters of Aid to the Church in Need in Konigstein, outside Frankfurt. Mark Reidemann had built up studios, international productions and a database catalogue. Mark had been able to negotiate distribution in Russia and the countries of the former Soviet Union of many Catholic productions for the emerging television channels. Larry Rich, who had spent years in Latin America, worked for Maryknoll productions in New York, was a significant player with an emphasis on justice and missionary productions.

Peter Thomas had been vice-president of Unda (1994-2001) and was elected Vice-President of SIGNIS in 2005. He had been director of Catholic Communications, Melbourne, and had made a substantial number of videos which were screened on Australian television. He became a central member of the television desk, experimenting with a SIGNIS television magazine, SIGNS, which could not be sustained because of costs. However, there was collaboration with Vatican Television, Italy's *Sat 2000*, a video news magazine, H20 and a liaison with the ecumenical network covering countries from Iran to Mauretania, Sat 7.

The meetings and network continue with Ricardo Yanez, the assistant to the Secretary General in Brussels, taking on the responsibility. He also took on the responsibility of another television initiative for SIGNIS, the SIGNIS junior reporters. At the congress in Chang Mai in 2009, local youngsters filmed interviews, events and edited programs of their work. This involvement of the young was part of the policy of SIGNIS, with its slogan, Media for a Culture of Peace, and continued for such events as World Youth Day in Madrid, 2011. SIGNIS Asia, with its president, Laurence John, has been a major contributor to the young journalists' work.

For many years, SIGNIS Europe in collaboration with WACC, have hosted a well-respected television festival with entries from major producers, including the BBC.

Perhaps I have just written this to make sure I acknowledged that we had begun SIGNIS by supporting television interests. There were also radio meetings and conferences and networking. But that might take me too far away from this story.

One of the results of the merger was a more streamlined Assembly, six members from each of the geographical areas of the world and six representing the international members. This also meant that the SIGNIS Board was even more streamlined than before, two from each of the groups just mentioned plus president and vice-presidents as voting members, 17 in all.

After the first meeting in Rome at the end of the merger Assembly, we first met in Mechlin (not recommended as a tourist attraction, especially the rather spartan diocesan centre where we met) which enabled all the Board members to go to Brussels to visit the General-Secretariat and meet the staff to get a feel for the organisation and the process of re-organisation. The next year we ventured far further afield to acknowledge the Latin American contribution to SIGNIS. We went to Lima.

Going to a new country has meant many visits – to Church authorities, to production centres, to television channels and, sometimes, some political gatherings. The most interesting visit in Lima (while we had those just mentioned) was to go to a new diocese in the outlying suburbs of the capital, a mixture of city, nearby desert and the approach to the Andes. We needed to get back to our meeting to get through business – an idle thought in Peru! However, to my delight, I discovered that the bishop was an MSC confrere, a German missionary who had spent several decades in Peru. As regards media, his diocese was exemplary and heartening: radio station, press officer and programs for distance learning, a great example of progressive media inculturation.

At the end of the meeting, six of us had a bargain ticket to take us up into the Andes. The immediate destination was Cuzco – and the altitude. Maybe it was the quick flight from sea level to more than 3,000 feet but breathing was laboured and one could sense the pulsing of one's heart. We did the touristic visits which seemed like going back to the Spain and the churches of the 17th and 18th centuries. Very baroque. But, our main destination was Machu Pichu. With the conscious heartbeat and the lack of desire to eat anything much (though we did the obligatory chewing of coca to acclimatise), I wondered just how we would feel as we visited one of the wonders of the world. The first reassuring factor was that to get to Machu Pichu, a rattling train trip of several hours along the top of the Andes (something one never imagined doing), we went down rather than higher. A little more breathing space.

A van took us to the entry of the historical area – and then 100 steps up! As I sat resting after 30 steps, the director of the Rome SIGNIS Missionary Services, Canadian Jean Paul Guillet, went striding past me. What else could pride do but force me to my feet. Actually, we were all right once we got on our feet and spent a couple of hours following a guide (and discerning her heavily accented English), clambering over rock ruins, up and down mountain paths, amazed at these long-hidden remote remnants of Inca culture, and admiring (the sometimes literally) breathtaking panoramas of towering peaks and the deepest of valleys. There's something to be said for having Board Meetings in Lima.

Which means something of an anti-climax for 2004: Strasbourg. A pleasing city to visit, connections with the television channel, Arte, but the main reason for choosing Strasbourg was SIGNIS' interest in connecting with international political and cultural organisations. We have had representatives at UNESCO in Paris. Fr. Gabriel Nissim OP represented SIGNIS at the Council of Europe, based in Strasbourg. In the discussions for the establishment of SIGNIS, justice and media rights had emerged as very significant issues. Gabriel was able to link us to policies and projects (including grants for projects outside Europe) that opened our awareness of problems around the world. SIGNIS members themselves sometimes experience extremes of opposition (bombing of Catholic stations in Bolivia in 2003, in Beirut in 2005). These concerns led to the establishment of an Advocacy Desk in Brussels, managed by Jim McDonnell of the UK. These issues can arise when regional or national meetings are held. I remember our Pacific meeting of 1996 in Noumea where we signed a statement protesting the nuclear testing by France in Tahiti (one of our member countries) and, more positively in 2011, requesting Pacific governments to open up modern communications technology to all and to the smallest of countries like those scattered over the Pacific.

The new statutes specified that there should be an Assembly every two years – we were to find that financially this was unrealistic, not helped by the global financial crisis let alone the precarious nature of European Union fiscal management. But, we did do one biennial assembly, this time to acknowledge SIGNIS Africa. We went to Cape Town. Robert and I traveled to Cape Town in June 2003 to prepare the Congress for November since we had no permanent SIGNIS representative in South Africa though radio presenter and manager, Fr. Emil Blaser OP, contributed to the preparations.

An old prison on the waterfront has been transformed into a conference centre, Breakwater. It seemed the place to go to, prices reasonable, an interesting location, away from the centre of the city (which seemed to be ageing, part dilapidated, and becoming less populated), near the bustling (very) markets and shops (and a cinema multiplex which we did try out!). We discovered the ferry to Robben Island, went on the tour, saw Nelson Mandela's cell, the quarries where the prisoners worked (and shared ideas and study) and listened to the impressive guides who themselves had been prisoners. One of the enigmas of Robben Island is that you can stand on the rocks and look across to the beauty of Cape Town and Table Mountain while realising how trapped the prisoners were. For Nelson Mandela, 27 years. Robert and I decided that this would be the first activity for the congress, that we all go to Robben Island for this South African experience of what apartheid meant. At the opening Mass, the Archbishop of Johannesburg offered his reflections and did a Q and A with delegates along with Fr. Peter John Pierson who served as liaison between the Catholic Church and the South African government.

Prior to the Assembly, the first of the television conferences that I mentioned earlier took place as well as a conference of people involved in radio throughout Africa. This was the first of the SIGNIS congresses, more modest than the election assembly and congress.

Touristically speaking, one of the highlights of this visit was the opportunity to travel south of Cape Town, beautiful countryside and finding ourselves at the bottom of Africa and the Cape of Good Hope. I can also mention that we were in Cape Town on 21 June, the shortest day of the year in the Southern hemisphere. No cable cars working! After the congress in November, I stayed a day at Nazareth House for the ceremony of perpetual vows of one of the African sisters. So, a spring visit to Table Mountain (camera forgotten). On the return, we watched the Rugby Union Grand final on television, the even match between Australia and England until Johnny Wilkinson kicked a field goal in time on. That was the time when Prime Minister, John Howard, pinned on the medals for the victorious England team who towered over him as he did his duty with a stern, unhappy face. One of the sisters watching kept calling out that the Australians needed taking down a peg while the kindly superior sat next to me offering reassurance. Five years later, in Pretoria, I visited the sisters and found Sister Ligouri, the commentator, the only one home. I reminded her of the match and Australians needing to be taken down a peg. Quick as a flash, she retorted, 'They still do.' She won.

On a more positive note, I will mention an occasion where I was very pleased to be present. German director, Volker Schlondorff, made a film of the Dachau autobiographical story of OCIC secretary general (1935-46) and president (1947-72), Fr. Jean Bernard from Luxembourg.

The story of *The Ninth Day* tells of Fr. Bernard (called Abbe Henri Kremer in the film), who had been arrested by the Nazi regime for his writings against the Third Reich, his time in Dachau and his being sent by the Nazis back to Luxembourg to persuade his archbishop to speak out in favour of the regime. If he did not return to Dachau in nine days, all the priests imprisoned in Dachau would be executed. Fr. Bernard did not try to influence the archbishop, who did not speak in support of the Nazis. Years later, Fr. Bernard spent a lot of time discussing OCIC and its policies with Vatican officials when OCIC gave its award to Pasolini's controversial *Teorema*. Perhaps, after surviving Gestapo interrogations, he did not find the Church questioning so difficult.

But, the premiere of *The Ninth Day* in Luxembourg was memorable for me, amazed to be listening to Schlondorff and his praise of Jean Bernard and to realise that I was one of his successors.

In the first four years of SIGNIS, it seemed important to foster the network by going to regional meetings where possible, something which had been very important in the years leading up to the merger. So, in 2002, to the Asian meeting, a meeting I always liked attending. This time we were in Manila, with veteran Jesuit missionary and adviser to presidents, Fr. Jim Reuter, despite his age, waiting at the airport to meet us. Jim Reuter went to work in the Philippines the year before I was born! A very friendly meeting although Fr. Reuter always exercised a considerable control over Church and media matters in the Philippines. He belonged to the generation where the individual was the organisation and gave all the directions – Jim could announce the result of an election, a euphemism for his nominating the results.

2004 saw us in Kuala Lumpur with the excellent organisation of Laurence John. This meeting was quite serious as it was a preparation for the international congress and assembly for the following year, raising issues of elections and boards. It seemed important to me that we follow the spirit of the new statutes which stipulated a two terms maximum for office bearers. Since I had done one term as president of OCIC and one as President of SIGNIS, I wanted to give an example of relinquishing one's role at the proper time and for younger people to come up. I had said I would finish at the end of 2005. How shall I put it? Not everyone agreed when it came their turn ... but this seemed to me to be very important, letting go at the right time.

The Malaysia meeting reminded me of diplomacy with the local church. Usually, we are heartily welcomed, especially if the national members work well in collaboration with the hierarchy. At the opening Mass in KL, Archbishop Murphy Pakiam seemed to suggest that media was like playing with toys and that there were other, more prayerful, occupations that we should be involved in. He hosted charmingly at meals but I remember sitting between him and his predecessor at a concert for peace (the SIGNIS motto at the time that slogan 'Media for a Culture of Peace'). Archbishop Pakiam was formally gracious but the old man on the other side offered me a commentary, a translation and his version of the jokes.

We did the right touristic thing, going up the world's tallest building (remembering Sean Connery and Catherine Zeta-Jones in *Entrapment*) were able to visit Putrajaya, the new development for a capital beyond Kuala Lumpur. The new mosque there was one of the most beautiful I have seen.

While there were European regional meetings (in Holland where we focused on making and performing in video productions, and in Rome), they were less dramatic and picturesque than the Asian meetings. The other meetings I was able to get to were those in North America.

In the history of OCIC and Unda, there is a clear demarcation between Quebec, French-speaking Canada, and English-speaking Canada (which extends the breadth of the country). The two Canadian organisations (which took turns with each other as well as with the U.S. to nominate Board members and official roles) met in Winnipeg to talk about collaboration after the merger. I was glad to be there to explain the process and to answer (many) questions from the English speakers since there had been quite a dominance in OCIC and Unda from the Montreal based Catholic organisation, Commaunite et Societe. One still wonders how the two Canadas do work together.

The 2002 meeting for the United States in Los Angeles was important because the Americans agreed to call SIGNIS US, The Catholic Academy of Communications Arts Professionals. One of the difficulties with the Academy and its establishing of interest groups is that most of the members are diocesan directors of Communications which focuses meetings on more local issues. At the 2002 conference, besides establishing the Academy, attention was given to the U.S. experience of the Church and sexual abuse, 2002 being the key year for revelations, for discussions about zero tolerance in the United States Church. A day was set aside to reflect on how the media handled the crisis as well as how the Church communicated with the media, especially dialoguing with a journalist from the *Boston Globe*, the city which was at the centre of attention, and the transfer of Cardinal Bernard Law to Rome as well as the imprisonment of priests like Fr. Geoghegan, a notorious offender.

Three years later, Showtime U.S. made a feature film called *Our Fathers*, with Christopher Plummer offering an interesting interpretation of Cardinal Law, plus stories of abuse, court sequences based on the Boston experiences. It is worth looking at to appreciate feelings in the U.S.

But, the U.S., while congenial for most Australian visitors, can certainly be a mystery. At the 2004 conference of the Catholic Academy, there was a special panel on the SIGNIS theme, Media for a Culture of Peace. The members of the panel were a film director from Palestine who worked with Israelis for peace, a member of the Catholic international organisation, Pax Christi. Archbishop Foley was delayed so I found myself taking his place. It was about 10 days before the presidential election which saw the re-election of George W. Bush. The presentations were encouraging, a challenge to Americans concerning issues of peace – the invasion of Iraq had taken place only a year-and-a-half before.

With the discussion, I can't remember how it happened, but within 10 minutes many of the group were involved in vigorous discussion about pro-life and the condemnation of abortion and where 'liberal' candidates stood. I decided to take a risk and make a strong comment on how we had guests, a significant topic that needed discussion, and that so much of the anti-abortion advertising and articles in the Catholic media was something of a waste of time and resources since it was preaching to the converted. We wasted an opportunity, participants getting more and more worked up. The U.S. president of the Academy was reassuring that I had done the right thing and that the discussion had got out of hand and had degenerated into partisan politics.

I want to say something pleasant now about the U.S., mentioning a man who became a good friend, one of the finest men I have met. He came to stay at Nazareth House in Hammersmith in 1999 on the recommendation of a Catholic friend who had made a video program on the sisters. He was a Baptist minister, Ken Curtis. Ken was a film and television producer – some of the films he worked on included the Joss Ackland-Claire Bloom version of C. S. Lewis's *Shadowlands*, the BBC series of short films on characters from the Gospels, *Tales from the Madhouse* and, later, *Amazing Grace*. Ken was educated in theology and, especially, in Church History, visiting Asian countries for lectures and publishing magazines featuring Church History. Ken soon became at home at Nazareth House, attended daily Mass, and brought me into an awareness of the vast amount of religious media production by the wider range of churches, inviting me to ecumenical media conferences. I stayed with him once on the way home to Australia, outside Philadelphia. He was a great ice hockey fan and took me to a match whose rules I did not understand but was amazed at the energy of the cheering crowds, the long and long pauses so that TV commercials could be inserted. But, I found it almost impossible to see the puk and follow it when the teams scored – and that was on the television monitor as well as in eyes-on fact.

Ken had established a video distribution company, Vision Video.

When Catholic distributors fell on hard times at the end of the 1990s, he set up a Catholic catalogue drawing a number of Catholic customers. I visited the offices – and was asked to lead the day in prayer, something the staff did at the beginning of work each day. Ken's son, Bill, worked with his father and took over the firm when his father retired at the outset of discovering his cancer. Ken combined treatment of the traditional kind as well as homeopathic methods, but always with prayer and exploring spirituality of illness and health. During some remission periods, Ken and Bill went to Israel and filmed Ken meditating on The Lord's Prayer and produced a DVD for those with cancer as well as their carers. They did the same with Psalm 23 and with The Beatitudes.

When it seemed that Ken would not have many years to live, I made another visit, welcomed as always, taken to a Lutheran Mass on the Saturday evening (not all that much different from the Catholic Mass – at first glance, with vestments, sacred vessels, even the church itself, it could be taken as Catholic). He then took me to a Catholic Mass the next day.

Oh, one quaint thing to add. Ken wondered if I would write some reviews of the films on the Vision Video catalogue – plus a photo in clericals which is what their clientele expected and the title, Fr. Peter's Picks!

Knowing Ken and meeting Bill and his staff was one of my best ecumenical experiences.

One of the features of Los Angeles at that time was The Festival of the City of Angels, a religious festival which was established by a group of churches after the riots over the attack of the police on Rodney King. The religious leaders wanted to offer the city something positive, especially through film. I was able to go to the festival for six or seven years. At the first one I went to there was a challenge. Would I agree to participate in a panel discussion? The topic, 'What can Protestants learn from Catholics; what can Catholics learn from Protestants about cinema?'

Now that's a question. Without much time for preparation, and listening to co-ordinator Protestant, Rob Johnstone from Fuller

Theological Seminary, and his pointing out the strong Catholic image tradition compared with the Protestant suspicion of images (thinking of Cromwell's iconoclasm), as well as Catholic emphasis on the incarnation, the human-divine, I was even more challenged. My refuge was commenting on Catholic reticence on proclaiming personal faith (apart from Charismatic Renewal) and how pervasive it was in American films to hear people comfortably proclaiming Jesus as their personal saviour.

Some years later, another panel: 'Are horror films Catholic?' We assumed that the subject focused on the classic horror films rather than the contemporary slasher, chainsaw, 'torture-porn' exploitation films. We decided the answer was 'yes', given some of the traditions, for example, the Catholic Vlad (as in the prologue of Francis Ford Coppola's *Bram Stoker's Dracula*), the satan imagery in cathedral gargoyles, the traditions of the antichrist.

While in America, I had something of a surprise experience. It was a visit to the Eternal Word Television Network (EWTN) in Irondale, Alabama. This is the network founded by the, how shall I put it, entrepreneurially eccentric Poor Clare sister, Mother Angelica. Never a fan of ETWN, I nevertheless did go to hear her speak when in New York in 1989. But, she didn't turn up – was establishing EWTN distribution in Russia! I did buy a bargain biography, fascinated by this old-fashioned, motherly nun (whose own mother eventually joined the order) who began with print, moved to radio and then her television, well, empire.

She was full of that old style religion which does appeal to a lot of viewers, especially traditional Catholics with money. She was never short. Dutch philanthropist, Piet Dirkson, gave her $25,000,000 for her transmitters. When she lost six million, he supplied that. Just as well a photo of him and his wife acknowledges this debt just inside the entry to the building. Mother Angelica fell out with the American bishops over satellite television plans in the 1980s. EWTN withdrew from Unda USA. However, by the end of the 1990s, with mother ageing and not so well, the management decided that they should associate again with Unda.

At the Unda USA gathering in San Antonio in 2001, the month before the merger for SIGNIS, I found them circling me, offering extensive documentation, wanting to be active in SIGNIS. This did happen with Scott becoming the first president of the international group and member of the Board.

So, when we held the SIGNIS U.S. meeting in St. Louis in 2003, there was no reason for Robert and myself not to accept the invitation to visit Irondale, Alabama. The hospitality was most genial. We stayed at the old convent compound which had become studios as Mother and the community had moved forty miles away to a new convent (modeled on an Italian Chiesa, Castle and forecourt) all paid for by donors, not by EWTN. Unfortunately for us, Mother was unwell and we did not meet her.

Mass was televised each morning from the chapel, celebrated by a group of young priests, Franciscans of the Eucharist, which Mother had established. How shall I put it? The homily espoused a pretty exclusive vision of the Church and salvation. Later in the day, I had a rather ascetical supper with the Friars and a Capuchin who had been nominated their superior though they belonged to the archdiocese of Birmingham. He had worked in PNG and knew many MSC missionaries. They asked me what I thought of their programs. I hope I diplomatically skirted the issue so that they knew I admired the effort but had great theological and media difficulties with the programs.

I first saw Mother in discussions during my year in New York. She was tut-tutting as Monsignor McKenna was denouncing David Coffey, a theology lecturer at the Sydney seminary in Manly, for denying the Resurrection of Jesus. That was libelous. But, that's what can happen on TV: say anything. When she was told that a recent book would contradict scholarship that Mark's Gospel was the earliest and that the author had proved that Matthew's was the earliest, written in AD37, so close to Jesus' death, she really enthused (I was about to say gushed): 'Isn't that wonderful, Monsignor, we'll know so much more about Jesus!'

The First SIGNIS Years, 2002-2004 395

Who should be visiting Irondale when we were, Monsignor McKenna! One of the amazing aspects of the visit was going up to the transmission centre. Mother had bought a hill and constructed such a mammoth building for state of the art broadcast, more than a dozen towers literally towering. She had sliced the top of the mountain. She had paid for double glazing for houses in the valley below. If this was EWTN what would the Pentagon be like!

Mother had retired from fronting the camera (though the constant repeats of the rosary, where she featured – a distracting prayer as we watched the camera watching the nuns rather than the images of the mysteries of the Rosary) and Jesuit Mitch Pacwa had taken her place. I had heard a lot about Fr. Pacwa who had visited Australia in the 1990s. His traditional stance books were quoted by members of Charismatic Renewal. A series of tapes had been produced, 'The End of the World, The Enneagram in Queensland'. He had also been banned from speaking by some progressive Australian church leaders – a bad mistake, it has always seemed to me, especially when you think of the outraged hullaballoo when a liberal visitor was banned, something Archbishop Pell was prone to do in Melbourne.

Here we were immediately after arrival in a restaurant in Irondale sitting next to Mitch Pacwa. I found him gracious. He advised when asked to drop the tie and just appear in open-necked shirt. I found that he had never heard of the Enneagram denunciation tapes. When I asked about the Enneagram, I discovered that he had visited Esalen, so prominent a centre in the 1960s and 1970s for new age kind of movements and sex therapy. He did not like the Enneagram but argued his case from experience and rationally. You could discuss with him without acrimony.

So, an 'official visitation' by SIGNIS to EWTN. Quite an interesting experience and an immersion in a kind of Catholic Church I was, in practice, unfamiliar with.

The next chapter will give some information and background to the presence of OCIC and SIGNIS juries at international film festivals.

There were several new juries in this first term of SIGNIS. The most significant was the Muslim-Catholic Interfaith jury at the Fajr festival in Tehran. I think it is better to write about this jury at greater length in the next chapter and simply mention here that we were invited to form a jury in the Italian city of Alba where the Infinity Festival was inaugurated in 2002. It was billed as a Film and Spirituality festival sponsored by a Capuchin Friar and the Catholic television production company, from Turin. Alba is the home town of Blessed Alberione, the founder of the two media-oriented religious orders, the Pauline Missionaries, the Daughters of St. Paul. The program was well chosen, films as well as discussions and press conferences. Head of the international jury was U.S. director, Jerry Schatzberg – who still remembered that he had won the OCIC award almost 30 years earlier for *Scarecrow*. The festival survived 10 years but the explicit spirituality element has gone.

I have noticed over the years that the direction of festivals outside of Europe have been quite lavish in their welcome of our juries and providing us with great hospitality. This has been true of Zanzibar, the festival of the Dhow countries. More of that later when I was able to go to Tanzania in 2005 and 2006. It was the same in Hong Kong where we welcomed in 2004. The festival acknowledges our particular focus on human values and has made a list of films they recommend for our jury – interesting to discuss sometimes why one film or other has been chosen and how the festival sees us. The auxiliary bishop of Hong Kong fronted the press conference about the jury and was present on stage for the presentation of the awards. SIGNIS becomes part of the cultural life of Hong Kong through this high-profiled jury. Bishop Tong became archbishop of Hong Kong and in 2011 was named a Cardinal.

A one-off was the 2003 Galway film festival. The opening film was *Conspiracy of Silence*, directed by John Deery whom I had met in Cannes when invited to a screening of his film. He asked me if I could come to Ireland and be part of a panel for a discussion after the screening. Once again, sensitivity to local issues. When I contacted the media officer for the Irish Church, he thought it would be better not to go. Already, the crisis in the Irish Church in the aftermath of revelations of clerical and religious sex abuse, meant that not only controversy but bitterness were in the air. But, then he changed his mind and thought it was better if I went and was considered as representing the Irish Church. I did check out the bishop's office when I arrived in Galway (after driving through Ennis in County Clare where the Malones and Madigans migrated from). The vicar general said that they had received the invitation to the screening only the day before and could not get there.

It was a funny kind of panel discussion but quite a turn-up for a Wednesday afternoon. John Deery himself was part of the panel as was Gay Byrne, the well-known host of the Irish late night television show who appeared as himself in the film. The other member (we were all men) was actor Sean McGinley who appeared as the rector of the seminary in the film. The opening comment from a lady in the audience was, 'The Church robbed me of my sexuality ...'. I learnt more first hand of the Irish Church and the current ethos in the short time than in the years before. Many complaints, some fiery comments. I thought I should mention that we had problems in the Australian Church but, in listening to the comments, I was glad that my ancestors had moved out of Ireland. Despite everything, there was still an underlying sense of belonging to the Church. I presumed that the original questioner, who also spoke about seeking spirituality elsewhere, had long since stopped churchgoing. But, during the cuppa afterwards, her friend said to her, 'But you go to Mass more often than I do ...'. Sean McGinley told us that he and his family went to the 10.00 am Mass because some of the children were in the choir.

In the years since, the standing of the Church has been under continual fire, the scandals revealed appalling, the need for some kind of healing and reconciliation imperative. But it was surprising and fascinating to be inserted, however briefly, into this Irish occasion.

At the end of 2003, I was inserted into another occasion, The SIGNIS Salutation, the annual Sri Lankan media awards presented a theatre in Colombo. The SIGNIS Salutation was a far bigger civic event than I had anticipated. Dignitaries, formal dress, procession into the theatre preceded by Buddhist rituals. I found that I was a guest of honour, so managed to acquire some aplomb and dignity befitting the occasion. With Catholics only 15 per cent of the population in Sri Lanka, most of the awards went to Buddhist film and television productions as they did each year. Certainly, a fine interfaith media occasion.

The ceremony, televised, was moving along at a fairly stately pace, when veteran director, Lester Pereira, moved on to the stage. There followed a solemn speech in Sinhalese. Suddenly, I found I could understand two words, Peter and Malone. It was a tribute to my work for OCIC and SIGNIS. And it was the reason that Gamini was so anxious that I be there. So, I am up there on stage receiving a trophy that looked like a little monument, globe on a pedestal, media and SIGNIS symbols as well. On a leaden base. Heavy to transport back to London and causing some curiosity at customs checks. But, as I turn round to look at it now on the top of a chest of drawers, I remember the inscription that rather undermined the solemnity, an award to Fr. Peter Melon.

Going to Sri Lanka was possible as I broke my journey to and from Heathrow each year with stop offs to visit SIGNIS members. The stop at the beginning of 2003 was in Dubai – which has a most absurd airport terminal based on the principle more money than sense. It looks like part of a sheikh's palace. Others tell me that it has grown more lavishly since I saw it. We had meeting of SIGNIS Dubai, managed by an energetic man from Sri Lanka. In fact, energy is a word that describes Catholics in Dubai. There is only one Catholic centre, established by Italian Capuchins but later staffed by an international group of Capuchins. There are all kinds of offices and ministries in the Catholic compound as well as the school and the large church. Because 85 per cent of the workers in Dubai are foreign workers from India, Pakistan, Sri Lanka and the Philippines, there is quite a large Catholic population. And weekend Masses begin at 2.30 on Friday afternoon and continue through Friday afternoon and all day Saturday and Sunday. I attended one of the Friday afternoon Masses. I think I am right in remembering that there were about 1,500 attending.

While I am telling stories about these countries I was able to visit, I will stay with that theme for a bit more time. Anyone beginning to feel travel overload, might like to take a coffee break, or turn some pages to find some more stable material.

The first of these episodes takes us to Africa. Returning home at the end of 2001, after the merger, I was able to visit Zimbabwe and South Africa, staying with the Sisters of Nazareth in Harare and Johannesburg. Matters seemed rather dicey in Zimbabwe, more tension in the streets and in people's attitudes than when I had passed by seven years earlier. But, staying with the Sisters made me more aware of where Robert Mugabe seemed to be leading the country. While one could go to shops and even to a restaurant, it was clear that everything was becoming scarcer and that worse was to come. We could not have guessed at the time for just how long it would get worse. As I write this (July 2012), Prime Minister Morgan Changerai is on an official visit to Australia, something one would not have dreamed of four years ago. At the airport in 2001, there was a hefty departure charge – paid up fairly willingly!

Then, on to Johannesburg, having recovered my luggage which had been left at Heathrow (the same for about a dozen other travellers who lined up for a British Airways handout to buy some supplementary cloths. I still have the two shirts, but Sister Lorraine took me to the bin at Nazareth House for some pyjamas, which didn't stay in my cupboard. It was just before Christmas. At the airport at Johannesburg, the passport control officer saw that the address I had listed was. He asked me had I been there before. I hadn't. He just raised his eyebrows and wished me good luck. We were sheltered inside the walls of Nazareth House but one of the sisters did drive me round that part of the city, where she had grown up, which was in decay, a drug dealing area, the synagogue abandoned and some murders in the street outside Nazareth House the day before. But, inside Nazareth House, an opportunity to share the work of the sisters for a few days, the care for the little orphans, hearing the confessions of a group of mentally disabled women, just being around the day-to-day life of the range of residents, young and old.

One more story from Africa in this period, courtesy of Qantas frequent flyer points. Philip and Ben, from our community in Melbourne, were to go to southern Africa on their points as well. Could I join them in Namibia? Why not? We were to stay with some MSC sisters in Windhoek. Because Namibia had been a German colony, South West Africa, the German sisters had gone there as missionaries and to set up a hospital in Marienthal, south of Windhoek. They had welcomed local women into the congregation from the 1950s and had built up a Namibian province of the congregation. Going to Namibia seemed rather exotic, though it is not a very long flight from Johannesburg to Windhoek. Providence was on our side. Philip asked, rashly I thought, how far it was to the Atlantic coast. 400 kilometres or so. But, it proved possible because Sister Crystal had driven in from Swakopmund with some women to attend the funeral of the late archbishop of Windhoek. That was Saturday. They were returning on Sunday. We could go – and Sister Crystal would drive us back so that Philip and Ben could catch their plane at 1.00 on Monday.

I still like to look at a photo of the three of us climbing the huge dunes outside Walvis Bay. I regret that I have no photo of our stopping back at the coast after the dunes to look at the vast array of flamingos in the water. It gave new meaning to pretty in pink. Then back through Walvis Bay which was South African territory during the apartheid years when Namibians had to go through passport control in and out of the resort town. We stayed at Swakopmund over night then back through the desert (where we saw litter bins at wayside stops with a table, seats and a roof, all neat – after all there was an imported German sensibility!) A great and unexpected trip.

I stayed in Namibia for a week, visiting the SIGNIS offices and offering support, learning more about the Church in the country and going down to Marienthal to lead a retreat weekend for the sisters. The sisters told me that they had pulled out of their hospital in 1976 as a protest against apartheid. But, here the sisters were in 2002, still at the service of the people, with two thirds of the sisters in the province local.

2004 saw the release of *The Passion of the Christ*. The build-up mounted the year before, different opinions on Mel Gibson's kind of traditional Catholicism and that of his crusading father. There was the issue of Mel's alleged anti-Semitism (with his alcoholic outbursts later confirming many people's suspicions). I accepted an invitation to see a preview, work still in progress, in October 2003. It was at Mel's office, late Friday afternoon. He would probably not be there, although the other three people were from Newmarket who had accepted the U.S. distribution the day before. But, at the end, in he came. My first faux pas was to say that I was from Melbourne. He was certainly Sydney-focused. Then I had some good words about his film. 'Anyone who thinks otherwise is an asshole.'

He fidgeted on his feet like his Martin Riggs in the *Lethal Weapon* films. Second try. Archbishop Foley had liked the 12 minute show reel. 'The bishops are all gutless!' Then he made an exception for Cardinal Castrillon from Colombia, head of the Congregation for Bishops, who was, I think, promoting his cause as a papal candidate, celebrating Tridentine Masses in St. Peter's, working with the conservative Lefebvrians to come back into the fold. He has achieved world headlines when he stated that every Catholic priest should see *The Passion of the Christ*. Mel had definitely appreciated that endorsement.

Actually, after a while, he quietened down and talking interestingly about the film, praising his writer, Benedict Fitzgerald, whom most reviews and comments ignored.

Mel does know how to make a film. Much of *The Passion*, whether one likes it or not, is very striking, very cinematic. Everybody has an opinion on the violence, especially the scourging – though many forget the range of 'humane' inserts throughout, from the playful scenes at Nazareth to the Last Supper. It is very much a passion, rather than resurrection, emphasis – though, he increased the brief resurrection scene to Jesus standing up and beginning to walk from the version I saw where Jesus was seen briefly alive and sitting in the tomb.

Because of the rediscovery of a spirituality of the Resurrection in recent decades, some spiritual writers and spiritual directors have felt that many people have not developed this aspect of spirituality, that they are stuck in the Passion. There must always be the challenge of the Resurrection for spiritual growth, but it sounded during discussions in 2004 and seemed reflected in much religious writing that those who have had the benefit of a deeper education in biblical theology took a superior and sometimes intolerant stance over those who were less religiously sophisticated and who relied on a very personal faith, whatever its limitations. Some of the articles and comments sounded elitist – that this Passion spirituality was for the less spiritually developed. Some of the comments also sounded intolerant: that their more comprehensive spirituality was what people should follow, that they should not have a Passion of the Christ spirituality.

Some comments were colonialist. When told of the popularity of the film in countries like Poland or the Philippines, many European commentators did not notice how they looked down their noses at this inferior Catholicism to their own.

I wrote a lengthy 'SIGNIS Statement' offering background and giving praise where praise was due. A number of Bishops Conferences thanked me and put it on their websites. (This included the Spanish Bishops Conference who six months later were objecting to my Statement on Almodovar's film about sexual abuse, *Mal Educacion*, complaining that the director was attacking the Church so that I had to reply that I was commenting on the film and its impact worldwide rather than on Spanish Church politics). This also meant a number of radio and television interviews. A leading Jewish commentator from Oxford told me that he thought the film was not anti-Semitic but insensitive to Jewish sensibilities at the time. I was invited to ITV where the host showed the trailer and then an attack on the film by MP Gerald Kaufman, definitely not in favour. I acknowledged the critique, agreed with some of it but when on to offer a point of view. The interviewer let the program go on for thirteen minutes, a confirmation that, while polemic is popular, a sensible discussion can also be good television.

I had to see the re-cut version of *The Passion* a year later and be available for BBC radio and the regional outlets who all wanted to discuss the film (except for Belfast). Some of the interviewers asked key questions. Others just alighted on Mel and violence. You can try, but the limitations of the interviewer set an agenda.

I want to add just a little about teaching in some different institutions and comparisons of attitudes of students.

Since 1995, I had been doing some lecturing at Trinity and All Saints College, just outside Leeds at Horsforth, the Catholic College of the University of Leeds. The initial invitation came from Maggie Roux whom I had met at the OCIC-Unda Congress in Prague in 1994. I should immediately say that Maggie is one of the best teachers I have come across, one of those people that are referred to as a dynamo. She is short, originally from Scotland, an extrovert, an organiser, with a passion for film. Her course on 'Movie Myths and Meaning' has introduced undergraduates for almost 20 years to a deeper ability to really look at films and to reflect on their meanings. In more recent years, this has become a little harder than before. The visual generation is more attuned to social media and the immediate and short attention span and no real feel for a bit of cinema history. But, by and large, the scope of assignments undertaken by the students and the enthusiasm of those who 'got it' impressed me a great deal. Over the years, talking with students about what they wanted to see and explore was also impressive. My contribution each year was a day on archetypes and movies, using the Jungian basis, but drawing on the system developed by Carol S. Pearson in her *Awakening the Hero Within* (1991). Having been in workshops with Carol at Psychological Type Conferences, I found that her categories were most helpful in appreciating archetypes – and finding film clips to dramatise them. That was the main British experience backed by some similar lectures at the Anglican university, St. John's College of Ripon and York.

I wish I could say something the same about an American experience. Unda President, Sister Angela Ann, asked me several times to offer a summer course at the University of Dayton, Ohio, which was her base. The students for these courses tended to be older, doing supplementary work for degrees or out of interest. The Americans seem to get up earlier than we do and classes were starting at 8.00 or 8.30 am. We explored the Jesus movies and the Christ-figures. Since many were studying for accreditation, I wanted to be as helpful as possible. At the Melbourne College of Divinity, we used the categories of HD, High Distinction (85+), D, Distinction (75-84), C, Credit (65-74) and Pass. I thought I would be more encouraging and suggested a numerical figure along with the category. Big mistake, especially for the middle-aged women doing the course. One was so upset with the mark for her HD that she wanted to write the assignment again to get a higher mark. Another who had been given HD, 91, complained, humiliated, that it was the lowest mark she had ever received. Compared with essays I had read from Trinity and All Saints, these assignments were good but not that good. Lesson learnt. No more marks and being on the receiving end of woes. But, the University kindly gave me their Daniel J. Kane 2001 award for Religious Communication.

We didn't have marks for the assignments at Crec Avex in Lyon. Crec Avex was the brainchild of French priest, Pierre Babin. He had become world renowned in the 1960s and 1970s with his insights into religious education, aided by his friendship with Marshall McLuhan. Eventually, Pierre was to call his approach to a holistic education, The Symbolic Way, grounding his education in experience, senses, emotion, symbolic experiences. His centre in Lyon worked in collaboration with

OCIC and drew students especially from Asia and Africa. Many of them were working in Communications offices and the course in Lyon was a qualifying sabbatical.

These were students who were sent by bishops or religious superiors and were keen to study. No problems there except for the year when I had to teach in French (usually there was lecturer for English-speakers and one for French-speakers, discovering the words Anglophone and Francophone). Plenty of advice on word choice and pronunciation from the students. In 2003, Pierre told us that the Vatican's Congregation for the Propagation of the Faith had decided there were to be no more scholarship for this kind of student to come to Europe. They preferred students study in their own countries. But, I am glad that I was offered this kind of different experience for six years.

Since 2005, Crec has offered courses in different countries in Africa. Robert Molhant has been the Director of Crec since he finished as Secretary General of SIGNIS. He could draw on previous lecturers. The courses have been mainly in Francophone countries. I was invited to join a team for the seminary of St. John Vianney in Pretoria which served most of the dioceses of South Africa. It was a great experience, Robert and myself working with Sean Patrick Lovett; director of the English language programs of Vatican Radio, very interactive, which I liked. We had the senior year of 24 who had the course sprung upon them, we discovered, at the last week of the academic year with the prospect of exams the next week. They were very co-operative and we covered all kinds of media experiences, theoretical and practical. Pretoria is a very attractive city, away from the bustle of Johannesburg. The main excitement that week, the first week of November 2008, apart from our course, was the election of Barack Obama as U.S. President. Not a Republican sentiment within cooee!

So, that is something of how SIGNIS began its life, how it affected me and something of what I hope I contributed.

41. FESTIVALS AND JURIES

'CANNES must be glamorous.'

Well, it depends on what you are doing there.

What OCIC was doing there from 1952 was offering to the direction of the Festival de Cannes, a specialised jury which would make an award to a film dramatising human values. The festival direction accepted. Until 1973, the jury was Catholic. An agreement was made that year between Interfilm and OCIC with the festival that, from 1974, the jury would be Ecumenical, three Catholic members and three nominated by Interfilm (Protestant, Anglican or Orthodox). The first Ecumenical Prize was given to Rainer Werner Fassbinder's *Fear Eats the Soul*. Fassbinder would not be the first director that came to cinemagoers' minds for such a prize. But, there it was, and it indicated the broad tastes and interests of the jury. This was to continue.

And, as for the glamour, I suppose there is a great deal if you want to look for it. Crowds meander along the Croisette then stand for hours and crane their necks to glimpse the arrival of the limousines, the stars and other celebrities in fashion magazine dresses as they alight and walk on the red carpet up the Salle Lumiere steps. The Ecumenical Jury and officials do this once each festival as well, the men, as all men must, putting on black suit and bow tie, called in French, 'Smoking' attire which does not sound particularly politically correct. There are press conferences, as at other festivals, but the least glamorous part is the interminable queuing to get in, waiting in crowds for the previous session to empty, shading head and eyes from the wonderful spring sunshine – it is May and getting through plenty of books before the plentiful security personnel let you through in batches to race up the stairs to have your bag searched, be warned and then have your bags and camera put in the cloak rooms. The price of glamour, I suppose.

In many ways, such juries do not find the limelight. And, in many ways, neither do film festivals. Of course, the major festivals like those of Cannes, Berlin and Venice, receive a great deal of media attention but it is usually more in terms of glamour, gossip and controversy. The awards made by the official festival jury often get a publicity plug. In more recent years, advertising has taken to indicating that a film was chosen for competition in such and such a festival. But, except for the trade journals and the reviews published by the thousands of reviewers accredited at the festivals which may or may not be read and which may or may not have something substantial to say about the films, the festivals are very much social and public relations events.

You will not be surprised that many observers ask why the churches field so many juries – and to what purpose.

The quick answer is that they indicate that the churches have always been interested in the arts and are keen to promote worthwhile films. And the work of juries is one of the most important contacts with the professional film industry where the churches can contribute to cinema culture.

While I had gone to screenings at the Melbourne International Film Festival – one of the oldest in the world, established in 1951 – I did not take part in an OCIC jury until 1993, in Venice. Once I became president of OCIC, Festivals were an important part of the work, and of my presence at them. I was invited to be a member of the Melbourne Festival Jury in 1994 and, having to watch up to 200 short films for the awards, meant some hard and constant work and concentration.

Mussolini had set up a festival in Venice in the 1930s but it lapsed – as did, eventually, Mussolini's power in Italy. After World War II, the festival began a new phase in 1948 and OCIC was there. Other film federations wanted another European festival which did not have a history like that of Venice, which led to the establishment of Cannes. On a personal note, I have enjoyed Venice perhaps the most of all the festivals. It was my first. Even the trip from the airport in the Vaporetto across the lagoons via Murano to the Lido is a tourist's dream. The Lido (where there are buses and cars) is filled with colourful old mansions, side streets for attractive short cuts to the venues, and views of the Adriatic. It is the end of summer (usually rains once and heavily) but it is a most enjoyable experience, and better now that they have some dividing barriers for queues to prevent the old stampedes to the doors and seats. Speaking Italian, I was always on the jury, liaising with the Church and festival officials, so easy access.

By 1952, the Festival of Cannes had begun. Many festivals followed in the next 20 years. Berlin grew in prestige. There were festivals in Valencia in Spain, Mar del Plata in Argentina. They had their vicissitudes and not every festival survived. Some died and rose again, Mar del Plata being a case in point. With Latin America's strong cinema culture, many festivals developed there. Asia and Africa introduced festivals later. Melbourne led the way in Australia, followed by Sydney. In North America, it was Canada and Montreal which set the pace rather than the United States. But, it was in Europe that festivals began to proliferate. By the end of the century, there were thousands of festivals, some international, some national and any number of local festivals. Not all of them included competitions but most did in one way or another. Melbourne and Sydney offered prizes only for short films. Cannes, Venice, Berlin, Montreal, Locarno, Karlovy Vary in the Czech Republic stipulated that the festival films had to be the world premiere. Other festivals gathered their programs from premieres as well as films which had screened elsewhere.

Some personal touches about some of these festivals. Berlin is in winter, often with snow, once the whole 10 days with ice, and we all had falls at one time or another. We used to be in West Berlin, moved to the new venues around Potsdamerplatz in 2000 (it is like a movie set piece with the skyscraper look, and faux New York street angles and the huge Sony dome that tries to proclaim 21st century). There are no leaves on the Tiergarten trees, with rugged up tourists wandering Unter den

Linden and the Brandenburg Gate across to the Angel. Berlin is orderly, reviewer-friendly – and what else is there to do but watch films!

It is much the same for Montreal though it is the end of summer. Not a greatly touristic city, though interesting, there are lots of films, good venues and easy access. But the beautiful locations of other festivals are well worth it. There is the Alpine beauty of Locarno, mountains and lakes and an open air screening space. Come to think of it, some of the halls are a bit ordinary and, come to remember it, the seats were very hard. Best to go back to thinking about the scenery and films.

But, the place for scenery is the Czech Karlovy Vary, the old Carlsbad, a picturesque spa town with mountains dotted with colourful classic buildings as is the town itself. And you take a little chugging electric train for 80 minutes and arrive at Marienska, the famous Marienbad of Last Year at Marienbad (though it wasn't actually filmed there!). More spacious but, again, classically attractive.

The two oldest organisations which had juries were OCIC and FIPRESCI, the International Federation of Cinema Critics. Both still have juries, FIPRESCI, drawing on a membership of world film reviewers has a considerable number. SIGNIS, with its more specialised juries, has of 2012, around 30 plus the Ecumenical Juries.

That's a bit of factual background and tribute must be paid to the president of OCIC after the war, Fr. Jean Bernard who supported the growth and work of juries and to Andre Ruszkoski who did the initial negotiations in the 1940s. Dr. André Ruszkowski (1910-2001) was present in the first FIPRESCI jury in Venice in 1934, and became a very active member in the board of OCIC. When the OCIC general secretariat in Brussels organised its first international jury at the Festival Mondial du Film met des Beaux-Arts in Brussels in 1947, Ruszkowski was among the five international catholic jury members and he became in the ensuing years a driving force for the work of OCIC in international film festivals and he became in the ensuing years a driving force for the work of OCIC in international film festivals. The first award in 1947 in Brussels was to *Vivere in Pace* by Luigi Zampa because, according to the jury, the film contributed to the spiritual and moral revival of humanity: peace, spirituality human understanding, hope and dialogue beyond racism.

The first jury awards in Venice 1948 went to two American films. The prize went to John Ford's version of Graham Greene's *The Power and the Glory*, *The Fugitive*, with Henry Fonda. A commendation (the SIGNIS translation for the French 'mention' which sounds a little off-handed in English) was awarded to Fred Zinneman's story of a mother's search for her lost son in Czechoslovakia after the war, *The Search*. Off to a reputable if surprising (not everyone appreciated Graham Greene's whisky priest) award start.

Which still doesn't explain what the Church was doing at film festivals in the first place. Having had to answer that enquiry often enough, I can suggest that these awards are in the best traditions of the Church's patronage and sponsorship of the arts (not without some critique over the centuries, some enlightened, some cautious, some condemnatory). On the whole, the Church can boast of a strong record in recognising and promoting the arts. There have been some rocky moments during the 20th century when Church people, ordained and lay, didn't see the point – or disagreed with the point. While it was called 'The Seventh Art', many saw cinema as just popular entertainment rather than an art, especially in the early decades. Many authorities thought that popular art was something that everybody had access to, and they were right. But the access they were thinking about was along the lines of censorship and prohibition. You might like to glance back at earlier sections of this story to see the kind of puritanical fears that many critics had and the thinking behind the establishment of the Legion of Decency which set something of a negative attitude in the minds of many devout Catholics.

Think also of the U.S. Production Code which was applied in the 1930s. It would be foolish not to acknowledge that problems increased with readier access to media and the availability of material that was not dreamed of by the Legion's classifiers. There has to be critique at all times, but informed and intelligent critique rather than an often sight-unseen crusade. We have also seen that from the time of Pope Pius XI, there has been constant encouragement from officials in the Church to appreciate cinema, to enjoy movies, and to explore the values and the spirituality that underlie so many of them.

It was in that spirit that OCIC established its juries. Over the years, criteria were developed for assessing the films. Ultimately, it came down to good film-making which portrayed human values (which are in accordance with Gospel values). Justice-focused values have been emphasised in recent times. The films should not be so confined to a local culture that audiences from other cultures could not relate to them. This came up in Berlin in 1995 where the vote for the award in the Forum section was divided. The Western European jurors greatly admired Luposhansky's *Russian Sympathy*. Those from other parts of the world (myself included) found it too difficult to appreciate. Of course, that can be a challenge as well. The other jurors proposed a documentary on Tieneman Square *Moving the Mountain* by Michael Apted. The prize (a cash prize) was divided between the two but it brought home the point that jurors must have a broad cinema culture but that there were films which did not travel well beyond national borders.

One of the first tasks I had was to prepare a booklet giving background to the work of the juries, giving examples of winners and offering a rationale for our criteria, including an explanation of how we could give awards to grim films (some jurors thinking that Church awards should go only to sunnier films), the De Profundis films. With an introduction by Robert Molhant on the history of jury work, it was published in 1999 and accepted as a basis for juries by Interfilm as well. A few years later, Hans Hodel of Switzerland, secretary then president of Interfilm, worked with his national thoroughness on writing official regulations for Ecumenical Juries, starting with the old OCIC statutes and re-formulating them for our times and current cinema. Nothing like having official regulations when asked tricky questions about jury decisions.

The culture of the jurors is evident when so many of the SIGNIS or Ecumenical Awards are made to films honoured by the official festival juries or, as happens not infrequently, FIPRESCI and the Church's juries made their awards to the same film. More recently, our awards and those of FIPRESCI are sometimes co-hosted.

Since 2000, the number of juries has increased, both SIGNIS and Ecumenical Juries. While the invitations have been forthcoming, festivals have experienced financial difficulties. There used to be 10 jurors in Berlin but, rightly, that had to be reduced to six in 2003. Cannes, Montreal, Locarno and Karlovy Vary have six members (three for each organisation, Interfilm and SIGNIS) as do a number of other juries. But, new juries consist of three members, usually one for each of the organisations and one representing the country where the festival takes place, taking it in turns for this member to be from Interfilm or from SIGNIS. This is the case in such newer juries in Kiev, Yerevan, Warsaw.

I made mention of the United States. SIGNIS did not have a jury there, despite many attempts, until 2009 and this courtesy of the DC Fest in Washington DC. Film-maker and reviewer, Frank Frost, negotiated the award and hosted the two jurors at his house, where we could watch DVDs of competition films at our leisure during the day and attend the screenings at night in the cinemas where many people come after work. And, we availed ourselves of the luxury of seeing the city in the spring, political sights, the memorials (really worth seeing the World War II garden with the soldier statues and the moving wall in memory of Vietnam). One can even be photographed standing on that Georgetown flight of steps that featured in *The Exorcist*.

While there had been a jury in Fespaco in Ougadougou, Burkina Faso, since the 1980s, then a short-lived presence in Cape Town, the main SIGNIS festival presence is in Zanzibar, the festival of the Dhow countries, those bordering the Indian Ocean. Zanzibar seems more than a touch exotic: Muslim culture, Catholic churches, an island with lovely coast and some lush jungle – and a cinema, open air in an old fort, and some screenings in the basement of a hotel.

The Asian development was in Hong Kong – where nothing is too much trouble to care for jurors and the custom has grown up for the auxiliary bishop (who became the cardinal in 2012) to present the awards on stage.

Probably this is the best place to talk about Interfaith juries. This takes us to Iran and to Bangladesh and, for a few years, to Brisbane. And, I am glad to say, I was personally involved.

In 2001, a delegation from the Iranian government and the Iranian film industry made a visit to the Vatican. They brought some Iranian films which were screened at the Festival of the Third Millennium held annually at the Gregorian University. Iranian films, by the way, have been a constant for several decades for winning Catholic and Ecumenical awards, many of them. These films, fine cinema art, are also great stories embodying basic human values.

The delegations paid the courtesy of inviting Cardinal Poupard and Archbishop John Foley, the respective heads of the Pontifical Council for Culture and the Pontifical Council for Social Communications, to come to the annual Fajr Festival in Tehran.

When I got back to London at the beginning of 2002, just after the establishment of SIGNIS as the World Catholic Association for Communication, and the merger of OCIC and Unda, I found a handwritten note for me at Nazareth House reception. It advised me to go to the Iranian embassy to get a visa for a visit in 10 days' time. You would think it a joke, wouldn't you? I forget how I found out that Archbishop Foley had rung and said that because of SIGNIS and the film work, I should go.

The week before my first visit to Iran, just over four months after 9/11, President George W. Bush declared that Iraq, North Korea and Iran were the axis of evil. That raised, at least, some hesitations. But, off I went, arriving at 1.00 am, a long trip through passport control and customs – in recent years, we are met at the plane and whisked into the VIP lounge while passports are taken care of – festival car into Tehran, to the Laleh Hotel and into bed by 4.30 or so with the prospect of screenings at 9.30. Walking the streets of Tehran at that time didn't indicate a feeling of axis of evil – much safer than Port Moresby or Johannesburg.

The international group has always been welcomed to the Fajr Festival, even the Americans who come (only a few admittedly). Fortunately, I had met some of the officials at other festivals receiving our awards, so it was quite easy to suggest to Amir Esfandiari, head of the film distribution Farabi Foundation that we might create an Interfaith Award for Iranian films which best dramatised human values. I think he took only 15 minutes to agree that it was a good idea. And it has continued, with two SIGNIS international members guest of the festival each year to work with a local Muslim. Come to think of it, I am very pleased that we accomplished this.

Even in recent years where the government has been more repressive, we are still welcomed, an opportunity, despite the jailing of several prominent directors, to try to see at first hand what it is like. Not always easy for the people, especially the young people with their hopes for greater freedom.

One of the interesting features of the presence in Iran was Fajr's establishing of a Spirituality section in 2005, which continued for the next five years. I was invited to be part of that jury in both 2005 and 2008. I don't think that a lot of the international jurors agreed with the local criteria for 'spiritual'. Each year there were some Japanese, Korean or Thai ghost stories and a slasher movie or two which also featured ghosts. Different kind of spirits – which Polish director Kzsrystoff Zanussi (friend of Pope John Paul II and director of films about him and by him) denounced quite definitely. But, t here were some beautiful films with backgrounds of Islam, Russian Orthodoxy and Japanese Shinto traditions. The first film we saw in 2008 was Luther! A number of people express great surprise to hear that Iran should have this kind of official section. And why not!

One of the jurors in 2005 was Ahmed Zamal, director of the Dhaka International Film Festival. He is a member of FIPRESCI, served on many of their juries and had known Guido Convents for some years. We became friends and I have tried to help with programming and some finance over the years. Not easy in Bangladesh, films not turning up (disappearing), not released from the censor's office requiring an extra bribe. With the change of government, the festival of 2010 was much better organised, with a better program, though visitors spend a lot of time waiting for vehicles, stuck in vehicles in bumper to bumper traffic (no wonder there are banshee like speed capers when it is possible, as well as when it is impossible) — and eating!

Lia Beltrami of the Trent-based Religion Today Festival was a frequent visitor to Fajr, which led to Ahmed entering his documentary on Shariah law and music (for which I was persuaded to give a small donation — actually, the persuasion was for a bigger donation, with money from ministry for the Sisters of Nazareth; both they and I receive a thanks credit!). Religion Today became more involved in Dhaka and, with SIGNIS, make the Spirituality awards.

In Iran, I thought it might be good to call the prize 'Fajr-SIGNIS' but Amir Esfandiari told me that he liked what I had first said, 'Interfaith Award'. And so it is, a small but significant moment in the Islamic countries of Iran and Bangladesh.

There is an Australian postscript. Brisbane International Film Festival director, Anne Demy-Geroe, like the award at Farj so arranged for an Interfaith Award in Brisbane. SIGNIS was always to have a member of the jury but the other two appointed by the festival in consultation with us could be of any other faiths. While the award lasted for only six years, lost when a new director was appointed in 2010 and cut out all competitions, we had Jewish, Hindu, Buddhist, Muslim, Bahai, Protestant, Aboriginal jurors along with the Catholics, a model that would be fine for other festivals but which has not yet been possible.

You might think that with this story, all has been plain sailing. I'm afraid not.

The most celebrated controversy began in Venice 1968. Pier Paolo Pasolini had won the 1964 OCIC award in Venice for his Gospel According to Matthew. In 1968, the jury gave him the award for Teorema. When we remember that it was in the mid-1960s that the Legion of Decency was changed in name and perspective for reviewing to The National Catholic Office for Motion Pictures and that the Motion Picture Association of America came into being in 1968, we are still at the beginnings of a more considered way of looking at films, especially those which raised moral issues. Teorema raised issues when a stranger came into an Italian home and tested the lives of the family, with sexual overtones, an allegory of modern living, seduction and moral choices. The award was denounced. Pasolini sent back his award. Pope Paul VI was quoted as condemning it. Vatican officials questioned the values of OCIC and whether it should be abolished. It is to the credit of Jean Bernard, who was coming to the end of his 25 years as president of OCIC that he spent months and months discussing the issues – and enabling OCIC to continue. There was a complication when the OCIC jury in Berlin 1969 gave its prize to John Schlesinger's *Midnight Cowboy*. But OCIC survived that one too.

With the first Ecumenical Jury in Locarno 1973 (and the prize going to Kzrysztof Zanussi), the rest of the 1970s and the 1980s were years of steady consolidation. A glance at the list of prizewinners and commendations indicate the quality of the awards and the growing reputation of the juries' work.

I mentioned that my first OCIC jury was in Venice, 1993, at the ripe old age of 54 – which I offer as consolation to those who have only been on one or two juries by their thirties. It was an initially unpleasant experience (which I never had afterwards). There was tension about the use of English, though I speak Italian, some edge of antagonism towards English and the British tradition. Then, we had an elderly Salesian priest, Ettore Segneri, who had been on the OCIC Board, represented the Vatican at the Council of Europe and was a fixture in Venice. He was, how shall I put it, 'old school'. In 1991 he had denounced the Belgian film Daens about a 19th century worker priest as unhistorical and anti-Church until another juror checked with a historian in Rome who vouched for its accuracy. In 1993, we saw Rolf de Heer's *Bad Boy Bubby* (which ended up winning the official festival jury prize). Don Segneri went at once to Gillo Pontecorvo, the festival director, to denounce the film as beastly and unethical. Our jury wanted to discuss the film and were divided three-three about giving it the prize. It is an Australian film, so I was being cautious. Ultimately, some jurors declared that they could not give it the prize (which went to Kieslowski's *Three Colours: Blue*) but could give it a commendation. And so it was. I still have photos of our making the award to Rolf de Heer and who should be standing near him? Don Segneri. Nothing quite like this, but he did throw several spanners in the works each year.

Home from Venice, I had to defend *Bad Boy Bubby*. Fr. Chamberlin said it was 'indescribably vile'. We agreed that it showed vile things but not vilely. Interestingly, in view of the OCIC action, I was asked by Currency Press to write the introduction to their published screenplay, an opportunity to justify myself and OCIC!

We did have another crisis in Venice in 1998, after I was elected president but it was handled by Henk Hoekstra. Claudio Siniscalchi, who had been on the Jury several times, a member of Ente Dello Spettacolo, wrote to the Italian Bishops Conference as well as the Pontifical Council for Social Communications, denouncing OCIC awards and that for 1998, L'Albero delle Pere (which I have yet to see). The president of the jury was Leo Bonneville, an 80-year-old Canadian veteran of film reviewing who had just been honoured by the Pontifical Council at the Montreal Assembly – who had nothing to lose with his strongly-worded reply. The matter blew over and the Bishops Conference took over Ente Dello Spettacolo which, under the direction of Don Dario Vigano, has become a well-respected Church-cinema organisation with excellent review magazines and website. Dario has since become the head of Vatican TV.

Sensitivity to local sensibilities is important and juries keep this in mind. But, you never know. In 2004, the jury voted Mike Leigh's *Vera Drake* their choice for the SIGNIS award. Then the Italian members of the jury recommended not giving *Vera Drake* the prize. Because of its topic, abortion, they thought that the Church would be crucified by the Italian media if the SIGNIS jury gave *Vera Drake* the award. There had been an article in the media that week by a Vatican spokesperson who thought that Mike Leigh had made a fine film that offered a story that gave food for thought. The only thing I could do, as chair of the jury, was to accede to the Italian advice, our award going to a modest Swiss film (which was able to capitalise on the prize to get further Swiss distribution). As was the custom by then, I wrote a SIGNIS statement on *Vera Drake*. Then a surprise comment from *Variety* a month later:

> Oct. 17, 2004, 'Inside Move: Leigh pic plays both sides'
>
> 'Vera' hoping to ride controversy to success"
>
> By Gabriel Snyder
>
> With 'Vera Drake', helmer Mike Leigh may have accomplished the impossible: making a film about abortion that both sides of the debate can admire.
>
> Fine Line hopes the pic – about a homemaker and abortionist in postwar London – will be the next film to ride controversy to success, a la 'The Passion of the Christ' and 'Fahrenheit 9/11'.
>
> It's even enlisted pro-choice groups like NARAL and consultants who worked on 'Fahrenheit', to push the pic. But so far there hasn't been any controversy. Pro-life groups,

such as the U.S. Conference of Catholic Bishops, have only had positive things to say about the film.

Harry Forbes, who classifies films that are considered morally offensive for the USCCB's Office of Film & Broadcast, actually gave 'Vera Drake' a rave review.

Noting the story doesn't 'proselytise for abortion,' he wrote, 'Leigh's script has all the subtle nuances of "real" people reacting to a domestic crisis.' Imelda Staunton's performance, he says, 'is acting of the highest order.' Forbes echoes other official Catholic voices on the film.

Shortly after 'Vera Drake' won best film honors at the Venice Film Fest, World Catholic Assn. for Communication prexy Peter Malone praised the film despite its subject matter. 'It is not simply, or simplistically, moral judgment by unnuanced application of moral principles.'

In this shrill season, how refreshing.

It's the only time I have ever been called a 'prexy' in *Variety* talk!

Just one more controversy to indicate you never know where the ground is going to open up under your feet. In 2009, the Cannes Ecumenical Jury invited Jewish Romanian-born, Paris-based director, Radu Mihaescu, who had won two Ecumenical awards, to be president of the jury. So far, so good. He attended the films, came to the prayer ceremonies, led good discussions. (Ken Loach won the prize for *Looking for Eric*, Michael Haneke the commendation for *The White Ribbon*). 2009 was the year of Lars Von Trier's *Antichrist*. Lots of hostile press and it was difficult to get into a screening. I had been warned a little beforehand, but I thought it was just a brief tongue-in-cheek stunt. Radu announced a special anti-prize to *Antichrist* for its hostile depiction of women. It passed by, except, director Thierry Fremaux was far less amused than Queen Victoria about anything and was reported as being furious. Later, he avoided meeting SIGNIS and Interfilm personnel. Would we survive?

We did, but after the festival, had you Googled, there were at least 40 pages of French items and 40 pages of English items reporting the fury and furore. (Those who benefited were Ken Loach and Michael Haneke who were always mentioned as the award winners).

Perhaps I should have mentioned before this some of the explicitly religious aspects of some festivals. Cannes once again leads the way. On the Sunday, there is a Mass at Notre Dame de Bon Secours (where Napoleon bivouacked on his way from Elba), sung High Mass, crowded church, the jury introduced and a homily that reflects on the Church's presence at the festival. At the same time, the Protestants assemble at the Reformed Temple (a room at the back of the church serves as a jury meeting room and the headquarters for the PR and the website which features daily reviews (for many years I had the 'English Corner' since the site was French). After the services, everyone comes into the same street and there is an ecumenical aperitif. The SIGNIS Cannes personnel and Interfilm Cannes, along with the jury and invited guests adjourn to the festival market building where there is a SIGNIS stand, a rendezvous point and an opportunity to explain to passers by what the jury does and why. The mayor of Cannes hosts a reception for the jury and the officials. He or his deputy also attend an Ecumenical prayer service, alternating between the Catholic Church and the Anglican Church. The awards ceremony is also an ecumenical and public social, especially for the media. It is shared with FIPRESCI.

In Berlin, there is an Ecumenical reception on the Sunday evening with church leaders, including the Catholic bishop for media, speeches (always substantial with Peter Hasenberg from the Bishops Conference Cinema department writing them). In 2011, to celebrate the 20th anniversary of the Ecumenical Jury in Berlin, I was able to write a retrospective booklet with lists of winners and citations and observations on the choices with Peter adding material in German. In Berlin, money awards are made to the winners in the Panorama and Forum sections, provided by all the churches.

There is an Ecumenical Reception in Karlovy Vary, a Mass and an Ecumenical Prayer service in Locarno. The Ecumenical Jury winner receives a cash prize provided by the churches to promote distribution of the film in Switzerland.

In Venice, the Jury and Catholic workers in the Church cinema associations (there are more than 600 parish cinemas in Italy and a number of periodicals) are often received by the Patriarch and then share one of those multi-coursed, wonderful Italian meals. At the festival, Ente dello Spettacolo hosts a function to honour a director who has contributed to values in world cinema. Recipients include Wim Wenders, Manoel de Oliveira, Aleksandr Sokurov, Daniel Burman and Walter Salles. This is the Robert Bresson prize, widely international and embracing many faiths and denominations.

Not necessarily best of all, but very special is the religious atmosphere in Yerevan (that's the capital of Armenia). Proudly letting all know that this was the first Christian nation, and the country grateful to the Apostolic Church for its support during the Soviet era, the explicitly religious element is to the fore. The opening and closing are in the open, in a central city square. Hierarchy and clergy are there in some numbers, and very colourful mitres and copes. The festival's name is that of the Golden Apricots (and you have never tasted juicy apricots if you have never eaten this Armenian fruit), so there is a ritual blessing and distribution of apricots to the big numbers attending, a bit of a variation it looked like of the distribution of communion.

There is not always something so religious at other festivals but it is something desirable to mark the particular character of a Church film jury.

Enough about festivals? Probably. I hope this gives a clear enough rationale for the juries and some of the activities.

42. 2005

AT OUR AUSTRALIAN Provincial Chapter in September 2004, we voted to support the new foundation in Vietnam, difficult though it might be given the recent history of the country, the Communist past and wariness about the Catholic Church and its activities and policies. Fr. Thoi Tran, one of the founders of this new community invited us to visit should we be in the neighbourhood. With a stop in Asia on the way back to Europe, it was a good opportunity to take up the invitation and gain a little awareness of Vietnam, and to visit the very active SIGNIS members in Cambodia. The visit to Pnom Penh (unfortunately, not Ankor Wat) meant meetings and workshops on media, an opportunity to see what missionary Fr. Omer and his group were able to do with very few resources and the belief that the way forward was to train young workers in print, radio and video production. There was time to visit the museum of the killing fields and be appalled at what Cambodians suffered under the Pol Pot regime.

I had never seen so many motor bikes and push bikes on streets as in Ho Chi Minh City (or the continual concern, can we say Saigon?). At the beginning of 2005, the first three MSC aspirants were ready to begin their novitiate in Manila. One of my happy memories is being asked to give the special blessing to the three, two of whom made their vows and whom I was to meet six and a half years later. Apart from the opportunity to visit the presidential palace and go into the war bunkers and see where the helicopters took off in April 1975, to get on the back of a bike to be part of the city traffic, to visit families who had lived through the war, we made a day trip to Vung Tau on the coast. That is where the giant statue of Christ the King is. You can climb up inside (and take some fine photos of the coastline). Then there was a large new church dedicated to Mary, with its own big statue. Christ the King and Mary had been built after the (very) large statue of Buddha some kilometres along the coast. Some rivalry? Perish the thought.

Vietnam and Cambodia were exotic enough countries to visit, but I will take this opportunity to bring in East Africa, another destination in 2005 and 2006. With our SIGNIS jury at the Festival of the Dhow countries in Zanzibar, it meant that I should go there as well. The trip was via Nairobi, staying at the Secretariat of the Conference of East African countries (and discovering that Kenya was a country of tribal loyalties in all areas of life). It was a rather ecclesiastical kind of visit. Off to the Cathedral, the Daughters of St. Paul's bookshop (one of their biggest and best from what I saw), driving around the central business district and finding myself the only white face in the area, then going to a more upmarket area and a shopping area, more white than black. And, a drive along a road where there must be more seminaries in the one area, except for Rome. But, one congregation which does not have a seminary there is the Missionaries of the Sacred Heart. More Church memories in the Resurrection Garden that Pope John Paul II blessed.

Flying in to Zanzibar is an entirely different matter. It is an island that now belongs to Tanzania. It is a Muslim city with old forts and relics of past trade activity. One of the forts is used in fact for screenings for the festival and for the making of the awards. During the day, jurors watch DVD copies of most of the films in the basement of the Hotel Africa. While SIGNIS gives prizes for quality, there is also a cash prize for the best film from East Africa. Another activity in 2006 was conducting a workshop for young film reviewers.

Zanzibar certainly looks exotically beautiful, especially looking out to sea, the yachts, the dhows.

Wandering along the old streets on 7 July 2005, deciding whether we were going to go to what had become a favourite Indian cafe, one of a great number of small and simple places for a meal, we heard some comments from a television set and then saw some images of the explosions in the London Underground and the blowing up of the bus.

A shock that an attempt to target London had been so devastating (not all that long after the attack in Madrid). Confreres emailed about my safety and I had to tell them I was secure a long way away. And yet, back in London two weeks later, I travelled in the Underground, Victoria line, to visit a friend. When I tried to return, I was told the line was closed, so took a series of buses back to Nazareth House and discovered that more bomb attempts had been made but had not succeeded. In the late 1990s and early 2000s, I remember that London tube stations were not infrequently closed for bomb scares. I realise that as the years went by this decreased considerably despite these terrorist attacks. Not the kind of experience we are used to at home.

Since 2005 was a year of significant activity for SIGNIS, I thought I would now do what I did before with the section on the emergence of SIGNIS, go back to the history I wrote and plagiarise myself again. Not only was there to be a Board meeting in Prague in April, preparations were ongoing for the Assembly of Election for the next president of SIGNIS and my finishing in the role. The plan also entailed holding a conference on Media for a Culture of Peace in Beirut to be followed by the Assembly.

As it turned out, 2005 did not unfold predictably.

As regards the administration of SIGNIS International, I had let members know when I was elected in Rome in 2001 I thought it appropriate that I serve only one term in the spirit of the statutes, since I had served a term previously as president of OCIC. The statutes speak of two terms maximum for presidents and vice-presidents. I sent out some reflections and guidelines for members' considering nominees to be presented given the experience of the previous seven years. I just glanced at the list and see there the fact that the president is not an employee of SIGNIS and does not receive a salary though travel and accommodation for SIGNIS work is paid for by the organisation. While I was available full time, that was not necessarily the case. A number of previous presidents of Unda and OCIC had full-time jobs. But, there are plenty of meetings they have to find time for, Board meetings and Assemblies, their membership of the Pontifical Council for Social Communications, regional assemblies. Which means reasonable health as well and a travel-tolerance! Then there is the issue of language: the three languages of the association are English, Spanish and French. Around the world these days, the majority of meetings are held in English. Spanish is also dominant, Spain, Latin America and the United States. Being able to understand some of these languages is important while speaking them is desirable. Not always possible – and English is becoming ever more prevalent at international meetings. Then the president needs to be able to write official reports, overviews of meetings and activities and contribute to the website and to the publications and needs to be available through email for particular (and frequent) enquiries and requests from members as well as those seeking information about SIGNIS.

With the merger, the president needs to be available for each of the media that forms SIGNIS while being able to contribute worldwide expertise from his/her own specialisation. Well, looking back on it, that is what I tried to do.

Since Robert Molhant was to retire at the end of 2005, notices and advertisements were also placed for submissions for the new Secretary General. There was not a great number of applications but interviews began in March. The decision was made to present Marc Aellen to the Board for confirmation. Marc was Swiss French from Geneva and had trained as a journalist, had also written film reviews in France for some years and had recently been spokesperson for the French Swiss Bishops conference which gave him a familiarity with Church language and ways of doing business. He began work in the office in June, to shadow Robert Molhant to experience the work of the secretariat before taking up his office at the start of 2006. He travelled to some of the regional meetings of SIGNIS and participated in the preparations for and the running of the General Assembly.

A major difficulty emerged in February with the assassination of Rafik Hariri, former Prime Minister of Lebanon. This raised the atmosphere of tension for the region and put into question the possibility of holding the General Assembly in Beirut in November. During the Pontifical Council meeting in Rome in March 2005, Robert and I met with the Lebanese media bishop, Roland Abou Jaoude and his assistant. The bishop expressed the hope that the assembly could go ahead, but graciously insisted that SIGNIS must feel entirely free about the decision. The plan was that the Board would vote on the matter at the Board meeting the next month in Prague. Many were willing to go to Beirut but Monsignor Maniscalco from the U.S. Bishops Conference sent a message threatening to withdraw financial support if the meeting were to go ahead. Fr. Sami Bou Chalhoub CM came to the Board meeting to make the plea in favour of Beirut. However, with a number of members uncertain as to safety issues, it was decided that the Assembly would be held at the fallback location: Lyon.

As an acknowledgement of the preparations that the Lebanese had made, especially for a pre-assembly conference, with talks, screenings, student film competitions, on Media for a Culture of Peace, organised by the think-tank, it was agreed that this meeting would go ahead in Beirut with the president, secretary general, treasure and other Board members attending. The situation worsened in Lebanon and, reluctantly, the decision was made to hold the peace conference in Lyon as well.

The Board meeting was scheduled to begin on 3 April with a special SIGNIS celebration of the Eucharist in St. Vitus' Cathedral with Cardinal Vlk (a member of the Pontifical Council for Social Communications who welcomed the 1994 Unda-OCIC Assembly in Prague) on the Thursday evening. This was to be followed by the third SIGNIS producers' meeting. However, John Paul II died on the night of 2 April. The Board meeting and the producers' meeting went ahead. However, a number of members, especially from EWTN and from news services, had to stay at home or go to Rome for the Vatican broadcasts. There was a Eucharist in the Cathedral on the Thursday evening. It was a requiem Mass for the

Pope – but SIGNIS members were placed in the front of the Cathedral and acknowledged by the auxiliary bishop who presided!

Though many other events took place in 2005, I think I will stay now with the Congress and Assembly in Lyon in the November.

Media for a Culture of Peace was the motto for SIGNIS activities for the first years of its existence. I want to offer a fairly full report of the conference in Lyon and the text of its declaration. It gives and indication of how SIGNIS was not only concerned with the various media but also about a Catholic perspective on media and contemporary justice and human rights issues.

More than 150 delegates and visitors to Lyons participated in the Culture of Peace conference. The basic material had been prepared by the SIGNIS thinktank headed by Gabriele Nissim OP. The core of the preparations remained but the wide range of activities planned for Beirut had to be let go. However, after an introduction by Gabriel, the conference got off to an excellent start with a keynote address by Oliver McTernan. He not only had fine material and reflections to present, he had the gift of powerful persuasion that engendered a strong enthusiasm for the theme and for the workshops which followed.

The conference aimed to produce a SIGNIS Charter for Peace. Already in 2004, the Asian region and, particularly, the Casuahara Centre in Kuala Lumpur under the leadership of Lawrence John, had produced a fine document on peace. During the Saturday afternoon, groups met to discuss the most significant elements for such a charter. The reporting back enabled a committee to work diligently into the night and produce the draft which was approved by the conference members. After several presentations on peace themes on the Sunday morning, the first major liturgy of the conference and assembly provided the occasion for the proclamation of the charter by representatives of three continents: Annamaria Rodriguez from Latin America, Sherry Brownrigg from North America and Magali van Reeth from Europe. The president of the Liturgy was Bishop Roland Abou Jaoude from Lebanon, the conference's acknowledgement of the contribution Lebanon had made in preparations as well as an expression of solidarity with the people in their suffering.

As we know now, even worse was to befall the country in July 2006 when Israel attacked after the conflict with Hezbollah and bombed Beirut and the south.

The Peace Conference

The media have an important role to play in the construction of peace and, in spite of all difficulties, they do so more often than one might assume. We must not forget all those media professionals who themselves suffer violence and opposition in their work. Many of them have lost their lives. In putting themselves at the service of truth and justice they have been prophets. And like the prophets, people want them to be quiet, 'he is telling the truth, he must be killed'. The effort that we want to promote is one way of honouring the memory of their sacrifice.

After the Peace Conference, those attending the congress and assembly participated in two days of workshops.

The four major fields of activity in SIGNIS conducted these workshops: The Media Education group worked to develop a SIGNIS Media Education policy; the Television Producers continued their series of meetings; the Radio workshop developed themes from the 2003 workshop in Cape Town and the follow ups, especially in Africa; the Cinema group looked at themes of women in cinema as well as aspects of spirituality and continued the conferences on juries and their work in festivals.

The final board meeting before the Assembly was held prior to the Conference on Peace, 4 November. Its function was to ensure the smooth running of the Assembly. 190 people had registered for the Conference and 55-60 delegates for the Assembly. Augy Lourdusamy, the only nominee for president, was absent as he was ill in Malaysia.

The Board agreed that I would 'stand in' for Augy until he recovered his health. The Board also unanimously accepted the nomination of Marc Aellen as the new Secretary-General.

So, 2005 came to an end. SIGNIS was moving into its second term. I was to stay in Europe to help with the transition period and head up the Cinema Desk.

44. INTO SOME CONTROVERSIES

NOT EVERY reader agrees with a film review. That is to be expected as are letters that take a reviewer to task. The first *Harry Potter* film, for instance, led to a six page letter from an irate mother from Wales who was quite clear that she wasn't going to let her six children see this witchcraft and magic: 'Satan has entered into Harry Potter's heart and now he has entered into yours.' However, being a reviewer for a religious organisation, automatically means being involved in some public controversies.

In 1983, my name appeared in *Truth* and I realised that, as most people might guess, truth is the last thing that paper wanted. 'Church row brews over sadist film.' That was the headline of a piece of non-news. Journalist Peter Olszewski had rung the Catholic Communications Office. Fred Chamberlin was overseas. I received a call. Had I heard of *Viva La Muerte*? Yes, a Spanish film made in the 1970s and due for a short season of specialist release at the Valhalla Cinema. Did I know what it was about and how anti-clerical it was with scenes of sex and violence, including the castration of a priest? I had read some reviews of the film. Was I going to see it? I explained that, if I received a preview invitation from the Valhalla, I would go, otherwise I would see it at an ordinary session in the usual round of reviewing. 'Church row brews over sadist film' and the piece began: 'Catholic authorities are expect [sic] to protest against a savage and controversial anti-clerical film to be screened in Melbourne later this year. The Church's official spokesman on film, Father Peter Malone of the Monastery of the Sacred Heart in Croydon, said the Church was aware of the film, *Viva La Muerte*, and hoped to vet it during a special premiere.' The article spent the rest of its words on rather graphic descriptions of the film, calling it one of the most ferocious violent films ever made. An example of the *Truth* style is a short paragraph in bold print: 'The most gory and contentious scene depicts a Spanish priest being attacked and castrated, forced to devour his own testicles and then thanking God because they tasted good.' I continue to wonder about a man or a woman building a career on this kind of thing or simply having to spend ingenuity and energy making the sensational out of nothing. When Fred Chamberlin returned home, his words of comfort, 'Better you than me!'

When *The Life of Brian* was released in 1979, many audiences took offence. This was especially the case in North America where humour on religious issues is not easily accepted or understood. In fact, there were a number of local government authorities who banned the film. It was not screened on British television until 1999. There were some protests in Australia, mainly letters to the editor and letters to Fred Chamberlin. Once again, he was away at an OCIC meeting. When he returned, he told me that he slipped down to the Russell Centre and laughed unashamedly. The Australian sense of humour was on the wavelength of what the Pythons were sending up, the solemn religious movies rather than the Gospels. One has only to look at the Sermon on the Mount sequence in *King of Kings*, with crowds and crowds on distant hills to appreciate the listeners in *The Life of Brian* who were wondering why 'blessed are the Greeks', let alone The Cheesemakers ('not specific, but referring to industry in general'). When I mentioned the 'laughed unashamedly' in an article for the UK *Catholic Herald* in 2001, an indignant lady wrote in to say that the priest I cited should have been ashamed of himself'.

In 1986, there were complaints about Jean-Luc Godard's *Je Vous Salut Marie/Hail Mary* and devout groups and the Blue Army took to the streets outside the State Theatre in Sydney at a Film Festival Screening, some muttering death threats. Fred Chamberlin bypassed the theology and the claims of blasphemy by simply stating that it was 'boring, boring, boring'.

Looking back, I see several films and controversies which might give some idea of what happens when Catholics become militant about the release of a film and move into action. The first major controversy for me occurred in 1988 for *The Last Temptation of Christ*.

In Australia, the distributors, United International Pictures, thoughtfully conferred with the Chief Censor, John Dickie, who was, in fact, a Catholic. They decided to invite heads of all churches to a preview to discuss the classification for the film and how they saw its religious content and treatment. Fred Chamberlin should have attended the screening in Melbourne but there he wasn't away again at an OCIC meeting. He deputed me to go to the preview screening for representatives of churches in Victoria. This collaboration led to an M 15+ certificate everywhere except in Queensland, which chose the R 18+ classification. Only one leader, the well-known campaigner and politician, Fred Nile, declared the film 'blasphemous'. Fr. Brian Lucas, the spokesman for Cardinal Clancy of Sydney thought the film somewhat boring, but not blasphemous. The film was released with minimum fuss and a good deal of fruitful discussion especially among theology students.

However, I was not able to avoid some of the fuss. We were photographed at the screening and I jokingly suggested to my neighbour that we should all have our hands on our cheeks, our mouths opened in shock (just like the later photos of Macaulay Culkin in *Home Alone*). When a group of us were invited to a discussion during a working-lunch at the office of the *Herald and Weekly Times*, I found that this neighbour belonged to the National Civic Council and had already taken a dim view of the film before it started, quoting at the lunch that an early version of the screenplay indicated a homosexual tongue kiss between Jesus and John the Baptist after the Baptism (which, I thought at the time was a misunderstanding of a reference to the cauterising of the prophet Isaiah's lips in Isaiah 6). Of course, that was the quote from him that accompanied his picture. I was quoted with the Old Testament references. The first to offer an opinion was television personality, Bert Newton, who seemed to think that he ought to be against the film on behalf of the Church. The most helpful contribution came from ABC broadcaster, Terry Lane, who explained clearly that the last temptation was not concerned with sex (as so many of the worldwide complainants claimed) but it was the temptation to give up on what God asks of us, for Jesus to get down from the cross, his being willing to die was enough. The last temptation was to ordinariness.

Because I had agreed to go to the screening and be seen in the *Herald*, I felt I could not refuse to do an interview on ABC Gippsland. The federal member for the area was the Catholic, National Party member, Peter McGauran. We were to discuss the film and take talkback. The politician had not seen the film and said he had no intention of doing so but was vehement in his condemnation of it. Then he said on air that I was the kind of priest who was 'emptying the churches these days'. When I explained that the film subscribed to the basic tenets of faith in Jesus' humanity and his divinity in the one person, he backed out, 'I'm a simple Catholic, Father'. The producer then let me know that they were not taking talkback calls since all those phoning in were pro Peter McGauran, certainly not for me. A number of hostile letters followed and my being reported to the local MSC superior as well as the Provincial Superior who, before they let me know, defended my orthodoxy and explained, from the Letter to the Hebrews, that Jesus was tested in every way that we are but did not sin.

I was invited to write the review for *Cinema Papers* – but the sub-editor spelt Martin Scorsese's name with a 'c', Scorcese. When my article has been quoted in bibliographies, it is with the title and its spelling with 'sic' after it! Peter McGaurin might have taken some relish! Years later, I was asked to evaluate a university thesis on the reception of *Last Temptation* in Australia (including my own). The writer and his supervisor did not notice that Scorsese was spelt Scorcece all the way through. I hope they had not taken the lead from the *Cinema Papers* heading.

The letters from Catholics in Gippsland were loyal to Peter McGauran but were a mixture of blame and sadness (with some invective) about my alleged championing of the film. Soon after its release, I used *The Last Temptation of Christ* in seminars in Jesus on film and groups usually wanted to watch the complete film over night and found it stimulating. When I was elected president of OCIC, Peter McGauran was Minister for the Arts in the Howard Government. I wrote explaining that an Australian had been given this world position. No answer. Perhaps he remembered that radio conversation.

One lesson I learnt from the worldwide protests against *The Last Temptation* was that, if you are going to make a point seriously, you have to give the protest some thought and not be open to ridicule. One story from Los Angeles concerned 25,000 people under the leadership of Jerry Falwell driving to Universal Studios to ask the head, Lew Wasserman, to burn the negative. He didn't. But, the protestors arrived in their cars (thousands) and paid for their time in the Universal car park (several thousands of dollars). On a slighter scale, this was true of some Greek Orthodox protesters outside the Russell Centre in Melbourne. To the annoyance of the manager, they came into the complex foyer to use the toilets. He was a little more tolerant when they were hungry and bought refreshments from the cinema candy bar. Then there was the story about the protestor in Sydney from the Monty Python Club. His placard read, 'This film is blasphemous. Brian is the Messiah!'. It's a wonder he survived!

The next controversy I would choose which involved me quite a bit more was that around the British film, *Priest*.

This film was directed by Antonia Bird and written by, at the time, recovering Catholic, Jimmy McGovern (later to write *Cracker*, *Liam* and *The Street*). I hadn't been aware of it until it screened at the Berlin Film Festival in 1995. Robert Molhant had called an executive meeting of OCIC in Berlin, February. He then invited two of us, Hugo Ara, from Bolivia, and myself, to be members of the Berlinale Ecumenical Jury. OCIC president, Henk Hoekstra, was the president of the jury and Hans Hodel, then the Secretary of Interfilm, later its president, was also a member. Quite some experience there.

Priest immediately raised a lot of questions but not so much controversy. That was to come. After we saw *Priest*, we decided that we should have a meeting. Peter Hasenberg of the German Bishops Conference had an appointment to interview the director but had to return to Bonn, so I was happy to step in. She explained some of the background of the film, including Archbishop Derek Worlock's unwillingness to have any Catholic Church in Liverpool used for the film. Antonia Bird had very good memories of the Liverpool priests she consulted and their inviting her to join them at Mass around the altar. In the event, the film-makers used Anglican churches in London to stand in for the Catholic churches.

I was able to join Henk in writing a statement on *Priest*. Best to quote it:

> *Priest* is a picture of priestly life and ministry in a Liverpool parish. Jimmy McGovern's screenplay shows an authentic and detailed experience of British Catholic life.
>
> It is undeniable that clerical celibacy and homosexual relationships of priests are a real problem of the Catholic Church in different countries and continents. All media in these countries deal openly and at length with these questions. *Priest*, from filmmaker, Antonia Bird, also raises these issues and thematises them in the form of a dramatic story. A number of aspects of sexuality and sexual relationships are shown discussed. The treatment is frank, sometimes explicit but not sensational.
>
> The issues as well as the film, are provocative and controversial. The Church shouldn't avoid or deny these issues, but confront, reflect on and clarify them. Many positive Christian themes and values are strongly present in this film: the search for God, the involvement of the faith community, prayer, the Eucharist, solidarity, forgiveness, reconciliation.
>
> The lively response of the large audience at the festival at the festival at the festival at the screening of the film and during the

press conference afterwards that there are a clear interest in and need for dramatising these religious values. The Church still seems to have great opportunities, when it is aware of and involves itself in this complex and controversial area. (Berlin, 17 February 1995)

We thought we were being proactive and we were. At the ecumenical gathering for the festival, the Catholic media bishop read out the statement, which was received well. In fact, the German bishops, as did other European bishops conferences, arranged for screenings and discussions for clergy in the following months. Robert and Henk also decided to publish a supplement to *Cine y Media*, with reviews both favourable and unfavourable, the statement and the interview.

When there were reports of bombs being thrown into New Jersey cinemas at screenings during Holy Week 1995 and Cardinal O'Connor of New York, without benefit of seeing the film, condemned it as 'as bad as anything that ever rotted on the silver screen', it was time to release the statement in Australia. The cardinal had said he based his comments on reviewers' advice including that of provocatively conservative Jewish critic, Michael Medved. Later I visited Henry Herx in his office in the American Bishops Conference building to find him labouring over his review to say something positive as well as meet the demands of growing vociferous complaints, especially from the Catholic League. He did a good job in the circumstances, not rating it is 'morally offensive' but using the A-IV category to classify it as unobjectionable with reservations:

> *Priest* – Flawed British drama probes the conflict between religious ideals and human frailties in a story set in a working-class Catholic parish where a young curate tries to live a life of celibacy, yet initiates several homosexual encounters, partly out of torment at his helplessness in stopping a case of incest revealed in confession. Director Antonia Bird provides a credible picture of a lonely priest in a busy parish,

though its emphasis on his struggles with his own sexuality strangely lacks any notion of sin and the ambiguous ending in an emotionally powerful scene of reconciliation leaves matters unresolved. Serious treatment of a very troubling subject, depictions of homosexual acts and occasional crude language. (A-IV)

Later that year, *Priest* was released in the Philippines, condemned by Cardinal Sin on the advice of Fr. James Reuter SJ to whom I had explained the OCIC position. On a personal level, I had been invited to speak for a celebration of the Centenary of Cinema at the MSC media centre, CFA, the Communication Foundation for Asia in Manila, but received a phone call from the director telling me it was more prudent not to come.

We fared better in Australia. The film was programmed for the Melbourne Film Festival, but after the U.S. bomb-throwing, I thought it best to issue the OCIC statement. The result was a lot of good radio discussion and talkback, a segment on ABC television with interviews (and my being filmed walking down a Collingwood street into a presbytery that I had never been into, but it looked good, even authentic) and clips. The story goes that Archbishop Little advised the Melbourne clergy not to frequent the film but, as the lights went up at the Rivoli Cinema on the afternoon of the Queen's Birthday holiday, they shone on him and about thirty of the clergy. There was some thoughtful comment from psychologist and reviewer, Ronald Conway, who did the testing for the diocesan students. He explained in the press and in Catholic papers how much truth underlay the film. And was condemned by a number of outraged Catholics who did not believe him and did not believe a film should portray let alone explore these issues. (The sex abuse issues were just around the corner, becoming more public that year and the next. We were not able to use *Priest* in the discussions in *Lights... Camera... Faith*, published in Boston in 2002 because of the scandals that had surfaced in that archdiocese.)

As with *The Last Temptation*, *Priest* has been well used in seminars on films and the Catholic Church.

The main controversy while I was president of SIGNIS came from the Philippines.

In October 1999, I was invited to Tagaytay City for a regional conference of the Daughters of St. Paul. Sister Consolata, secretary of the Bishops Conference Office of Women had been asked to set up a new Church board for movie classifications. There had been a reaction against permissiveness at that time and against President Estrada and his chief censor (a producer and actress, Mrs. Aguillon, whose son was a well-known director). When I was explaining to Sister Consolata the ways in which I would do a workshop to help people establish such a board, she asked could I actually do it. Because of being able to stop over in the Philippines at no extra cost on the ticket from Australia to Europe, I agreed.

So, in January, 2000, about 130 people, mainly women, quite a number of sisters, and the chief censor (whom *Newsweek* had just branded a 'moral terrorist') participated in a three day workshop on movie classification on sensibilities, sensitivities, criteria, being positive and proactive rather than being negative and merely reactive. We watched a number of Tagalog movies, including a number of R-rated movies. Many of the upper and middle class Philippine woman had never seen a Tagalog movie before. People seemed happy with the plan (much of which was based in practice on the Australian Commonwealth system). The group called itself CINEMA and held other seminars during the first part of 2000 to build up a group of trained reviewers. Bishop Yalung of the Office of Women was president, Fr. Mario of the Society of St. Paul was deputy. They first published in August 2000 (some reviews a bit pious, some a bit censorious, others very good). The material that I used for the workshop was combined with some other material that I had on film appreciation and it became *On Screen*, published by the Daughters of St. Paul in 2001.

When I was able to visit Manila on a similar kind of ticket in April 2001, CINEMA decided that we would have a prayerful recollection morning (it was Holy Thursday) and then quietly assess their work thus far. That was not to be!

In the meantime, President Arroyo had been persuaded to ban in cinemas (only not video release) a film which I had seen at the Berlin Film Festival in 2000. It was called *Toro*, released as *Live Show*, and was about young poor men and women in Manila who performed live sex acts in clubs and homes to make money. The director, Jose Javier Reyes, had criticised the Church in his introduction to the screening in Berlin for its narrowness and the fact that his film would not be released. I tried to see him to discuss the matter but he had returned home, so I wrote to him telling him about our group, CINEMA:

> 28th February 2000
>
> Dear Mr Reyes,
>
> I attended one the screenings of *Toro* at the Berlin Film Festival and listened to the question and answer session following it. On the following day, I tried to arrange to meet you and have a discussion, but it was not possible as I had to return to London. It was of particular interest to me to see the film and to hear you speak because during January I visited Manila to do some work on movie classifications ...
>
> You mentioned the controversies late last year concerning censorship and various groups which took to the streets. However, the Bishops Conference Office of Women took a different approach. They want to set up a Classifications Board to supplement consumer advice available from the government's board. They are not trying to set up a censorship board in the old style but rather something that will help people to know what films are available and give advice.
>
> I was asked to lead a three day seminar in Manila in

January and over 100 people attended. We were trying to look positively at movies and values and to understand how cinema works (as different from literature). I also presented a working model for classifications, that used by the Australian government which, I think, has sufficient categories and consumer advice for the Australian public.

We also watched some movies during the seminar to gauge how we might classify and give advice. One of them was, in fact, *Phone Sex*. Hence I recognised your name when I saw that *Toro* was screening ...

I find the social concern of both your films very strong and was interested to hear your comments on those who tend to deny that there are such problems in Manila. I told the group that I thought that *Toro* and *Phone Sex* would be passed for Australian audiences with Restricted (18+) Certificates. With *Phone Sex*, we discussed, according to the Australian system, the frequency, intensity and judgment on whether treatment of themes was justified or gratuitous, with quite interesting and some varied results.

One of the reasons for writing to you, especially as it was indicated that you are now the President of the Movie Directors in the Philippines, is that it would be good for the group responsible to the Bishops Committee to meet you and discuss the issues with you. An important aspect of OCIC is dialogue with the cinema industry rather than merely staying a service within the Church. This happens in many countries. (I have been told that Lino Brocka was in communication with OCIC Philippines in his last years.)

I have written to the secretary of the group to tell her that I would be writing to you. I hope that the Church, through this group, can enter into positive discussions with the directors. With every best wish ...

Mrs. Aguillon wrote back saying that Mr Reyes welcomed my comments that I did not think his film was pornographic the subject was but the treatment was more restrained though explicit at times. He was happy to dialogue with CINEMA.

A number of vociferous Protestant groups in Manila denounced *Live Show*. The head of Catholic Laity from the Bishops Conference, Mrs. Sonia Rondi, had joined with some fundamentalist Protestant groups, especially that of Brother Bishop Eddie Venezuela, and was lobbying Cardinal Sin against the film. He quickly issued a condemnatory letter, stating that he was a man who liked to shoot from the hip. Mrs. Rondi summoned Fr. Mario and threatened CINEMA. She said it should be turned into an anti-pornography organisation or be shut down. She complained that when CINEMA was started, 'you brought in a foreigner'.

Cardinal Sin's recommendation for chief censor, Dr. Nick Tiongson who had been in the position only a month and who, in fact, had not passed *Live Show* for exhibition that was done under Mrs Aguillon then stated the film was not pornographic. The Cardinal turned on him and he resigned (offering a press kit of opinions about the film which included my letter to the director, Mr Reyes).

The members of CINEMA, in their regular weekly review, had voted to classify the movie as R-18 and not 'to be banned'. The campaign turned on them, with threats that CINEMA might be abolished. Individual reviewers, mainly middle-aged women, were subjected to personal attack and disdain from some of the clergy.

We spent Holy Thursday discussing these matters and watching the film again on video (though the head of CINEMA, Dr. Rotera, had a hard time finding a copy since the video stores were doing strong business with it). The members of CINEMA, even those who found *Live Show* distasteful, decided they should stand by the R-18 classification.

Live Show is, in fact, far less explicit than a number of films available. It is motivated by anger about the lack of social justice in Manila. It runs for about 105 minutes and the total number of 'explicit' sex scenes throughout the whole film adds up to 11 minutes. I timed them. These are 'softcore' rather than 'hardcore'. Many of them show the faces of the viewers watching these shows and most of them are accompanied by a voiceover from the central character commenting on how hard life is and how he does not want his younger brother to have to earn his living in the same way. One of the questions asked by CINEMA members was 'where is the Church in these troubled, poverty-stricken areas of Manila?'. The only traces are holy pictures on the walls of the family home where the mother, a prostitute, is dying. When some of the members commented on the gutter language of the film, one of the Daughters of St. Paul reminded us that she grew up there, that they had only one meal a day and that this was how people talked. The film was reflecting the harsh realities of life there.

During our reflections on Holy Thursday morning, I mentioned to the group that their situation was reminiscent of that in the United States in the early 1930s. At that time, a group of laywomen were seeing movies and offering what we now call 'classifications and consumer advice'. They were The Catholic Alumni. However, by 1933, some of the American bishops were coming out with individual condemnations of particular movies, the Archbishop of Philadelphia using the sanction of 'under pain of mortal sin' in forbidding Catholics to see them. In the ensuing discussions and the concern about the lowering of moral standards in the movies, the Legion of Decency was born. The Legion, with its oath for the faithful to promise not to see condemned films, used the model of 'watchdog', influencing Catholic opinion in the United States to take a negatively critical approach, seeking out what was objectionable first, rather than a more holistic and positive approach to film appreciation.

That could have happened in Manila but it did not. Bishop Yalung's recommendation was to continue quietly with the work and that the concern would blow over. And that is what happened. CINEMA continued and improved the quality of its reviews and classifications.

Dr Nick Tiongson's statement of resignation and a newspaper interview included some strong declarations about cinema, the Church and protests:

> TODAY I submit my irrevocable resignation to the President as chair of the MTRCB because I refuse to be an instrument for the repression of freedom of expression, a basic human right guaranteed by the 1987 Constitution. In a meeting held last night, three instructions were given by Malacañang which will lead to the transformation of the MTRCB into a board that will suppress or inhibit responsible cinema artists from making their contributions to nation building, even as such a board wages its war against what they call pornography. All these developments are to be attributed to the pressure applied on Malacañang by a noisy group of ultra-conservatives from various denominations who cannot seem to distinguish between films with integrity and those which merely pander to prurient interest.
>
> First, the President gave instructions to the Chief legal adviser to prepare the memorandum recalling the permit of the film *Live Show* because the ultra-conservatives want it withdrawn from moviehouses. The film has been showing since 7 March and no protest has been heard, except from this group which hardly constitutes a majority. This, I believe, is because if one bothers to watch the film, one discovers that this is not a cheap skin flick but a powerful expose by a respected director of the way live sex performers are dehumanised by poverty, exploited by their own kin and kind, and driven by desperation to seek a more humane life abroad. Amidst such abject surroundings, however, they still manage to shed tears of redemptive pain and to give care and succor to each other. If anyone gets titillated by this film, he must be sick. The film was rated R-18 by the MTRCB in

May 2000 and even by Peter Malone, media specialist of the OCIC (Organization Catholique Internationale du Cinema). According to Joey Reyes, director of the film, Malone was the media specialist that our own Church leaders invited over to help provide guidelines for censorship during the Sutla controversies of October 1999.

I never sought this position. But Cardinal Sin nominated me to it 'we thought you were a good person, you are an ex-seminarian,' without even having spoken to me about convictions and their expectations of me. At first, the ultra-conservatives could not protest my appointment because I was nominated by the Cardinal, but when *Live Show* was shown, they found the perfect excuse to prove to the Cardinal that he was mistaken in 'choosing' me. As they pressured the President to withdraw *Live Show*, they convinced the Cardinal through Sonia Zaldivar Ronda and others that I was the devil incarnate and I believe he was convinced. At a meeting in his office, the Cardinal berated me, in the harshest language that showed no respect for me as a human being, that I was not doing my job and that I could actually recall *Live Show* if I wanted to. To my explanation that that would be breaking the law, he replied that I was just making excuses. He said that I was clearly 'ineffective' and I had 'no backbone' and therefore he was withdrawing his support of me.

The big controversies of 2006-2008 concerned Dan Brown and his conspiracies. How so many millions could read and enjoy *The Da Vinci Code* is one of the mysteries of modern pop culture. And how so many people could believe these stories of Jesus and Mary Magdalene in an alleged age of scepticism and reason goes beyond belief. Prior to the release of *The Da Vinci Code*, there were articles, critiques, debates. When the film version was finally released, the opening film for Cannes 2006, it was something of an anti-climax. In fact, the producers a year or more earlier had called in publicist and distributor, Jonathan Bock, a practising Presbyterian, to discuss how Christians would respond to the film of *The Da Vinci Code*. With his explanations and the setting up of a website during the making of the film, the screenplay was written with Christian sensitivities in mind – at times, it seemed, bending over backwards to highlight that these were all theories. The English-speaking members of Opus Dei also took the opportunity to be more open about the organisation. The film was OK, not particularly provocative. My SIGNIS statement had very little on the film – there was no need but more on the background. *Angels and Demons* provided even less controversy. The Catholic League with its director, William O'Donoghue, and its aims of defending the Church had taken aim at both films. When *L'Osservatore Romano* reviewed *Angels and Demons* and didn't find anything to comment adversely on, the Catholic League backed down.

However, the Catholic League did have a significant victory in 2007. It is the only Catholic protest that has succeeded in putting down its target, at least in the United States. The film was the adaptation of Philip Pullman's *The Golden Compass*.

For the Catholic League, or any Christian group, to attack *The Golden Compass* offers no surprise. Novelist, Philip Pullman, seems to have enjoyed being his own one man anti-Catholic League. His remarks were intended as provocative, his criticisms of organised religion, of the Church and its teaching authority often trenchantly expressed. With word of the film version going into production, so did the League. A booklet, criticising the novel rather than the yet unseen film, was published in the U.S. and distributed worldwide. I received my copy through the Australian Catholic Film Office. William O'Donoghue has described himself on his CV as, among other things, 'chat show guest'. So, a concerted media attack, word, radio, TV for the latter part of 2007.

While that may be well and good for the consideration of the novel (though it is attack rather than discussion, let alone dialogue), it may or may not be apt for the film version. It may not have been Jonathan Bock this time giving advice, but it seems (I was advised) that the anti-Church tone and the use of the Magisterium (certainly a sensitive issue for the Church) less aggressive than in the novel.

My judgment in writing the SIGNIS statement was to offer an elaboration on what you have just read and to move into conversation mode rather than mere crusade. Some told me that my words were measured. But, it led to some comments that surprised me by their tone (and from someone I knew and thought was friendly). Some samples indicate what happens in polemic rather than discussion.

I had asked a question:

> Do books and films like *Harry Potter* or *The Golden Compass* actually provide opportunities for parents and teachers to communicate with their children on a different level from teaching and doctrine and raise key questions about the nature of God, the nature of faith, the need for redemption?

The reply:

> Malone. Please stop writing. Please!!!! You are one of the voices that I'm fighting hard to quiet in our battle for the souls of our kids, and the passions of parents for the faith. You have no clue how misguided that question is. Your ignorance is astonishing. I talk with parents every week who are CLUELESS about anything you suggest, and yet they come to Mass. I meet with parents that are just fine with not speaking to their kids about Christian ideas because, to quote them, 'My kids are not interested in that kind of stuff.' IS THAT WHAT YOU'RE ADVOCATING?
>
> He's advocating a religion where the self determines what is right and wrong. It's called moral relativism ... If you are right about what Pullman has said, then you have been taken in by the dark-side, and that is why you are not in a collar now, and you hide behind religious anonymity. Which I'm glad

about. Now, just stop pretending to write with any authority from a Catholic organisation. You've totally discredited any 'Catholic' credentials that Signis might have had.

A mutual friend defended me and the writer offered some kind of apology. But this tone of attack comes into the next controversy.

The last film I thought of considering here is *The Kids are All Right* screened in 2010. The initial criticism of my review was handled with his customary wise aplomb by Richard Leonard SJ, my successor as Director of the Australian Catholic Film Office. It was taken up by the editor of the online *CathNews*, Christine Hogan, where the review appeared (originally reviewed on the SIGNIS site after its screening at the Berlinale, 2010). The easiest thing to do is include the blog entry by Christine Hogan since it states clearly the policies I believe in for the Church and cinema:

CathBlog What's in a film for Catholics? Published: 22 September 2010, by Christine Hogan.

> Sometimes outrage extends to the film reviews and comes from readers who wonder why on earth a particular movie has been reviewed. This was one such recently, posted by 'POB' of Cairns, about a film reviewed on September 3 by *CathNews*' film reviewer, Father Peter Malone MSC: 'I read *CathNews* occasionally and was shocked by this review. Why is *CathNews* reviewing *The Kids Are Alright* [sic] (pictured) and not connecting it to our Catholic faith? I can go to other film reviews if I wanted a world view of a movie. What is the point of reviewing movies, books, dvds, etc, ... if (the review) is not related to how as Catholics/Christians we should view them? *The Kids are Alright* is definitely not the sort of movie that I would recommend viewing by any Catholic. Where is *CathNews*' Christian responsibility in terms of subject matters?'

It seemed to me that POB raised important questions, so I sent a copy of the comment to Father Richard Leonard sj, Director of the Australian Catholic office for Film & Broadcasting, for his response. This is what he wrote to POB, but it is informative to many who sometimes wonder about why a particular review is on *CathNews*:

'I am sorry you are sometimes shocked by our film reviews, but I thank you for raising some important issues and which enables me to reply to your concerns.

There seem to be two issues: Why does the Catholic Film Office review films that do not have a connection to our Catholic faith? And in what ways do our reviews vary from other more secular outlets, especially in regard to the film *The Kids are Alright*?

We take your concerns very seriously and I shall pass on your email to Father Peter Malone MSC, who was the reviewer of *The Kids Are Alright*.

For now, let me deal with the questions.

Why does the Catholic Film Office review films that do not have a connection to our Catholic faith?

The short answer is that very few films offer an explicit connection with our Christian or Catholic faith, and when they do it is often quite negative. Films in recent years where this is true include: *Stigmata, End of Days, Lost Souls, Bless the Child, Dogma, Possession* and *The Magdalene Sisters*. I am delighted to report that there have been outstanding films on religious themes as well, which have been generously reviewed by our office as well. *Molokai, Mary, The Green Mile, The End of the Affair, Looking for Alibrandi, Keeping the Faith, The Bank, The Man who Sued God* and *The Third Miracle* come to mind.

The readership of *CathNews*, however, is diverse and there

are two groups in particular at whom the film reviews are aimed: parents of teenagers and young adults, and teachers in our Catholic schools. There is an argument to say that films like *The Kids are Alright* [sic] should not be reviewed in the Catholic press, but if we accepted this argument, where would Catholic parents and Catholic teachers go when they need to find out what a film is like, and how they might best respond to their children or students who are seeing these films, or wanting to do so? One thing is for certain, as the Holy Father has said on more than one occasion, we can no longer ignore the film and television culture, or that by ignoring it pretend that it is not influencing us. What this office tries to do is to bring the values of the Gospel and our Catholic tradition to bear on the material on the screen, which many of our children will see, whether we like it or not. If all young Catholics hear from the Church is that we find nothing of value in the secular world, including the cinema, then how will we help them find God there? We hope that our film reviews offer an intelligent, informed and Catholic response to what the secular world is putting on our agenda. The feedback from parents and teachers on this point has been especially encouraging. I am sorry you do not agree with them.

In what ways do our reviews vary from other more secular outlets, especially in regard to the film *The Kids are Alright* [sic]?

To be fair to this Office and Father Malone, I think we fulfilled our mandate to offer an intelligent, informed and Catholic response to what the secular world is putting on our agenda in the review of *The Kids Are Alright* [sic]. I doubt you saw the film, so there was enough information there to alert you that this would be the last film you would want to or need to see. So the review enabled you to make an informed decision.

From the outset, we told you it was rated MA 15+ for strong sex scenes and infrequent drug use. Father Malone said that the film was concerned with a lesbian couple who have been in a long-term relationship within which they had two children through artificial insemination. Father Malone goes on 'The son (Josh Hutcherson) wants to find out about the sperm donor for his and his sister's conception. The daughter makes enquiries and quite easily discovers Paul (Mark Ruffalo) and they meet.'

I do not know any other secular reviewer who explicitly outlined the plot in this way and in this detail. None of our readers were left to be shocked after they had paid their money at the box office. There would many Catholics would never want to see a film about this subject matter.

Father Malone told our readers that this was a 'serious comedy' which offered reflection on contemporary issues and that 'Audiences who have previous views may not alter them one way or the other. But, while the kids are all right, the presence of the male father-figure sometimes makes them better.' I doubt there would be a secular reviewer in Australia who would write that last line, and, if they did, I doubt they would get it published.

While the review does not directly condemn same-sex couples and their families as you might like, it does have a gentle admonition, and provide viewers with ample information to make an adult decision about seeing this film.

This film is number eight at the Australian box office. You and I might not like that, or we may hope that the issues this sort of this film presents would just go away, but that would be to hold on to our Catholic faith in a vacuum. Respectfully, if we stayed away from the world outside the Church for fear of temptation and being led into evil, then our greatest missionaries, martyrs and saints would have stayed at home. The modern media is now a mission field for the Church, one we ignore or fail to evangelise at our peril. I invite you to pray for us in what is sometimes a difficult endeavour on behalf of the Church. Yours sincerely in Christ, Rev Dr. Richard Leonard.

Thanks, Father Richard. Your lucid explanation about why this movie, and others like it which raise the hackles of some readers, make it into the Film Reviews of *CathNews*, is very timely. *CathNews* is about informing and alerting our readers to what is in the marketplace, so they can make educated and responsible choices. The fact that Fr. Peter and Fr. Richard make that education so pleasurable is an added bonus. Happy viewing to everyone!'

It was interesting to read the blog comments on *CathNews*, all but two being favourable to the review. However, a Catholic organisation also wrote to me urging me to alter my review as well as sending me statistics on suicide and children from single parent homes.

Actually, in 2011, there was an increase of critical letters, some of them invoking 'mortal sin', one correspondent saying that to enter the cinema to see *Sleeping Beauty* (not the fairy tale but an Australian feature which offered a psychosexual narrative) was already a mortal sin. Some of the letters were personally insulting, suggesting that Richard and I went to see pornography.

Three letters will suffice to indicate what can happen.

Our correspondent wrote to *CathNews* after the editor referred him to Richard Leonard's views quoted above:

> The article you referred me to claims to alert parents to the contents of films that may or may not be suitable for children.

There is nothing in the review of *Hangover Part 2* that would alert parents to the extreme profanity (including bestial oral sex) depicted in the movie. One has only to look at the Internet Movie Database (IMDb) to see what kind of perversity is being presented by the show. At most your reviewer warns of 'nudity' and 'sexual references,' but this does not quite capture the picture. My complaint therefore is not only about what movies *CathNews* chooses to review, but of your lack of honesty is presenting an objective review. Of all movies out there, why review this one in particular? The impression that *CathNews* gives to readers is that actually chooses to promote such movies, irrespective of any disclaimers. Anybody can make up an excuse for their errors, but to be dishonest about it is not Catholic or Christian to say the least.

Richard Leonard wrote to him about the work of priests. The reply:

None of those profane situations you list are even remotely sinful in themselves, whereas watching pornography is, as is promoting it (you, or at least *CathNews*, do promote it whether or not you realise it by the very fact that it appears without sufficient warning material, and not objectively stating what is wrong with the movie). Malone's review is really not that much different.

Your assertion that the Mass, etc, protects priests from the evil effects of engaging in sin is therefore tantamount to putting God to the test and making a mockery of the sacraments.

I am totally with Popes Benedict and JP2 and have nothing against engaging with contemporary culture; my point is that by reviewing perversity in this way you do nothing to enlighten secular culture with the gifts God has given to his Church and to priests. How is your methodology challenging

Catholics not to watch the movie? Would you ever challenge those responsible for its promotion with the Gospel call to repentance? Christ was always very clear in his condemnation of evil, but I see none of this in your film-work.

You may recall a basic principle of moral theology, which is that an evil means may never justify the end, no matter how noble.

A final letter from Richard:

Until now I have been pleased to discuss these issues with you, but as with so many righteous Catholics it does not take very long for a lack of charity to mark the correspondence. Wasn't it the Angelic Doctor who said, "Charity is the mother and the root of all the virtues" (ST I-II.62.4).

Most of your wild and offensive assertions in your latest email seem solely based on Fr. Malone's review of *The Hangover Part 2*, and *CathNews* capsule summary if it. From there you conclude that we never challenge or condemn any films. On this, as on many points, you are wrong.

Furthermore, it is not my 'assertion' that the Mass and our prayer protects priests (and all who pray and go to the Sacraments) from the evil effects of entering into what could be compromising situations, it the Church's ancient tradition.

Accusing us of 'watching pornography', however, is a very serious charge to make against two Catholic priests in good standing with the Church. If you have evidence of Fr. Malone or me watching pornography you need to write to our respective Provincials (MSC and SJ) immediately, and to Bishop Ingham, the Bishop of Wollongong, through whom this Office is accountable to the Australian Catholic Bishops Conference.

So, from your most recent email, Fr. Malone and I are accused of watching pornography, putting God to the test, making a mockery of the sacraments, not condemning evil and making the ends justify the means. You need to be very careful here. *The Code of Canon Law* #220 states, 'No one is permitted to harm illegitimately the good reputation which a person possesses nor to injure the right of any person to protect his or her own privacy.' Under the Church's Law, every Catholic is guaranteed a right to their good name in the Church – Fr. Malone and me included.

Even calling Fr. Malone 'Malone' tells me all I need to know about the courtesy with which you are now prepared to discuss these issues, so, at least from my end, and after a very long day preaching, teaching and sanctifying (yes, doing what most priests do every weekend), our conversation is at an end.

The most vitriolic comments came from a Scottish site associated with Archbishop Lefebvre's St. Pius X Society after an article on Lars von Trier's *Antichrist* in The UK's *Catholic Herald*:

Priest Praises 'Antichrist' – can you believe?

My first thought on reading this review of the film, *Antichrist*, penned by Father Peter Malone – is ... we must pray for Father Malone.

Should the *Catholic Herald* be publishing this kind of review? Did Fr. Malone's review make YOU want to see this film? What would you say to Fr. Malone, if you had his email address? Click on 'comments' to tell us now ...

21 comments (some selections), almost all written on the night of 2 November:

No, I don't think the *Catholic Herald*, or indeed any Catholic paper, should be reviewing a film which is, judging by the content reviewed, an occasion of sin and therefore to be avoided. I stopped taking the *Catholic Herald* some years ago as I felt I couldn't leave in lying around (like one does to encourage the children to '*tolle et legere*') because I never knew what heresy might be contained therein.

Secondly, why on earth is a priest reviewing any films, yet alone a pornographic one? Has he no parishioners to visit or Confessions to hear? Or could he not supply in one of those many priest-less parishes we keep hearing about? I, a married woman with a big family, was actually embarrassed when reading that review so surely a priest, a celibate, should shun such explicit sexual scenes? (From semperfidelis).

Fr. Malone puts way too much effort into presenting the rather worrying thought processes of Von Trier, the film maker, as some kind of subject matter for serious discussion.

The truth is that Von Trier is a very troubled soul. Such darkness and filth does not emanate from a soul in the state of grace. Nor should any soul in the state of grace risk losing that grace by watching or discussing such a grossly sinful production.

The Church tells us that we are all weak human beings capable of falling into very serious sins by means of the senses. Hence, we are forbidden by the law of God from placing ourselves in an occasion of mortal sin. To do so, as Fr. Malone has done, is an act of presumption before God. (From Athanasius)

Fr. Malone clearly believes that he is strong enough to resist images of a sexual nature, and strong enough to avoid the consequences of discussing such matters as he has viewed. St. Paul says: 'Let those who think they stand take heed lest they fall.'

No Catholic, let alone a priest, should be viewing such dark and pornographic films under any pretext whatsoever. The very simple acid test is this – Would Our Lord, Our Lady or any of the saints have sat down to watch and then discuss such a vile production as this? The answer, I believe, should be quite obvious.

No, I'll say it before you do, you really couldn't make this stuff up.

Powerful comments Heather Priest. I hadn't heard of this film before I saw this thread and can safely say I have no plans to see it. Whilst I am obviously now a practising Catholic, I was a very liberal nominal Protestant for almost 19 years and without going into unnecessary detail, I was just as exposed to all the things of this world as anyone else my age. Therefore, as much as I now deplore many aspects of modern secular culture, I'm not easily shocked by them. However, when I read about some of the content of this film, which Fr. Malone refers to as 'art', it turned my stomach.

Not so long ago, the U.S. Catholic Bishops had such an influence over Hollywood that their studios turned out films like *The Song of Bernadette* and any film containing content even a fraction as vile as that of *Antichrist* would never have had any success.

Having said all that, I think it speaks volumes that I found the Wikipedia article about the Ecumenical Jury more unsettling than reading about the graphic sexual violence in this film. According to Wikipedia, the objective of the award is to "honour works of artistic quality which witnesses to the power of film to reveal the mysterious depths of human beings through what concerns them, their hurts and failings as well as their hopes." I don't know what gives Satan more glee: this vile film or groups of apostate Catholics whose criteria for judging the spiritual merit of films sounds like something you'd hear in a hippie commune.

'The ecumenical jury at the Cannes festival gave it a special "anti-award" and declared the film to be "the most misogynist movie from the self-proclaimed biggest director in the world".'

Since I never pay any attention to the fetid sewer known as the film industry, I was not aware that there was such a thing as an 'ecumenical jury,' (6 Protestants and 6 Catholics). Apparently the members of this ecumenical jury have not only lost their faith, they are trying their hardest to make the rest of us lose it as well.

No, Father Malone, I rather think our attentions should be directed at the fidelity of your faith, not at this piece of twisted cinematic garbage.

Fr. Malone, may God help and forgive you. This film is sadistically pornographic and no decent person should view it, let alone a Catholic priest. I am not a traddie, just an ordinary Catholic (I'm not saying that traddies aren't ordinary Catholics!) and I say to you REPENT, before it is too late! I will pray for you. (from Catherine).

And nobody needs to see this film to know it's awful any more than we need to see the German concentration camps to know how awful THEY were.

It's an awful film.

Let's hope Fr. Malone reads and reflects on our comments here, although how on earth he will make reparation for the damage he must have done by recommending this pornographic film, beats me.

I hope that in reproducing some of the opinions that it makes clear there are differing views in the Church and that one way of confrontation is polemic. But, the response should not be just joining in polemic.

So, surviving for another day, another movie – and, perhaps, in the words of Hagar the Horrible, another dragon.

44. THE SIGNIS CINEMA DESK, 2006-2010

1 JANUARY 2006. Terms completed. Well, not quite. Augy Lourdusamy was elected president of SIGNIS in Lyon. However, he was ill at the time, not present at the Assembly. So, I was asked to care-take until Augy was better. That meant chairing the initial Board meeting and keeping in contact with the Secretariat until the Board met in 2006. It was held in Brussels again so that new members would have the chance to visit the Secretariat and gain a feel for the organisation. And, the Secretariat was soon to be on the move.

Augy arrived, hale and hearty and, as always, boisterous, for this Board meeting. I have to thank him for inviting me to subsequent Board meetings. He believed in the U.S. principle, once a president, always a president! The great benefit of being able to be at the heart of SIGNIS for the four years of the second term, especially since Robert Molhant had also finished his time as Secretary-General, was to be able to watch the transitions, decisions and actions, close up. The important thing was not to be intrusive but rather to be able to see that SIGNIS was continuing and how it could change and develop.

As a Board, we visited the new premises for the Secretariat. It is in the north of Brussels, Rue Royale, up the hill (which somehow or other over the coming years seemed to get steeper and steeper) from the Gare du Nord. Not the most salubrious area of the city, more than a touch of the sleazy when you turned left out of the Gare (instead of right which led towards the new, smarter-looking glassed office buildings). The new Secretariat building is from the 19th century, five floors (and a basement), not the most convenient of buildings, though it has a spacious conference room. And, it has two visitors' rooms right at the top. I presume that staff fitness has benefited by constant walking up and down those flights of stairs.

Another observation. Staying in Brussels during a weekend and looking for a local church for Mass is not too difficult. Near the old Secretariat, just across the street from a marvelous Pizza restaurant which we patronised regularly, is a church – but, at the Saturday vigil Mass, about 30-40 people, elderly (who still formed a choir) or migrants from Africa and the Caribbean. It was the same at the new Secretariat. A baroque façade crosses Rue Royale, making it look something like a stage or film set. But, the church is shut and the Masses (same numbers, same demographic) are conducted in the crypt. By comparison, congregations in London seemed enormous. Brook Green (the London parish for Nazareth House) had several hundred at each weekend Mass. It seems that Catholicism in Belgium, or practice, is deadish.

The Secretariat move cost more than anticipated and helped bring to consciousness the fact that SIGNIS' financial resources were limited and seemed to be dwindling. The European funding agencies, including the Vatican's Congregation for the Propagation of the Faith, have been downsizing their contributions – one of the factors being that the dwindling mass attendance in Europe means much less giving, agency coffers not having some of the largesse of the grants of previous decades. Somehow or other, providence helping out, SIGNIS has survived the succeeding years – perhaps we have got used to living precariously!

Robert' successor was the French Swiss Marc Aelen. He managed a year and a half but, at the beginning of 2007, he resigned. Ultimately, at the end of 2008, the assistant Secretary-General, Alvito de Souza, was named as Secretary General. It reminds us of how Europe, in many Church organisations, plays less and less a leadership role. Already in 2000, of the three international Catholic media organisations, Press, Radio and Television and Cinema, the presidents came from Brazil, Australia and US, the Secretaries General from India, Canada – Robert, from Belgium, the only European. Since 2008, SIGNIS is led by Augy who is Malaysian, the two vice-presidents are from Australia, Peter Thomas, and Cuba, Gustavo Andújar (who was elected President in 2014). Alvito is from an

Indian family from Kenya, his assistant is Ricardo Yanez from Argentina and the Rome Services Director was Bernardo Suate from Mozambique, succeeded by an Italian. There is always complaint of the narrow view of many in the Vatican (who don't visit Asia enough to realise that there is a vital Church beyond Europe) but SIGNIS does not share this narrowness.

In the field of film festivals, while most SIGNIS and ecumenical juries are in European festivals, there is a greater attempt to go beyond. In 2007, Hans Hodel and I were able to go to Armenia for the first Ecumenical Jury at the Golden Apricot festival, a warmly hospitable festival where the principal screenings were at the Moscow cinema, a Soviet-style building from the bad old days. While there had been no SIGNIS jury in the United States, in 2009, the DC Fest offered an invitation where, announcing our awards, many said that they now realised there were international prizes, when they heard my accent! More recent developments have taken place in Latin America, the Dominican Republic, Ecuador, Brazil. Warmly welcoming also is BAFICI, the festival in Buenos Aires, which I was able to attend in 2008, an opportunity to see more Hispanic films than usual and, in between, being able to wander the wide European-style boulevards of the city. I recommend the ferry across the Rio Plata to Uruguay, at least the quiet colonial town of Colonia del Sacramento. As you wander leisurely through the streets, it is not hard to imagine the old days.

My last new festival before coming home was that in Cuba. Again, one of those countries one thought was never going to be on the travel list. I think it is worth pointing out that OCIC, then SIGNIS, has had a Jury in Havana for over 25 years, with Fidel Castro himself giving a speech (or a long harangue) to assembled visitors.

The accommodation for visitors was five star in the Hotel Nacional, right on the water, comfortable, spacious rooms, a marvelous spread for every meal. Just as well we travelled round the city in ancient and broken taxis which belied the allure and somewhat unreality of the good life. The Cardinal was most welcoming and good to discuss issues with.

There was a screening of the 1917 film about Our Lady of Guadalupe, a blend of the pious history and devotion with a story of society at the time of World War I. Equipment for the screening came from the Polish embassy.

This was in 2009 and, while there were lots of decrepit buildings, the minister for planning at the time had inaugurated an extensive program of restoration. The screenings (with no sub-titles or simultaneous translation) were held in venues all around Havana. For outsider visitors, we were taken to the Charles Chaplin cinema (looking a bit old now) – and not always with sub-titles or simultaneous translation. But there were full audiences who were, to say the least, very enthusiastic!

Meanwhile back in Europe, there has been Jury expansion in Eastern Europe, especially in Hungary and Poland with Ecumenical Juries. My experience was in Kiev, the jury established there in 1999. It is ecumenical. Once again, a hearty welcome. One thing distinctive is that accommodation for festival guests is on a boat moored in the river, in little cabins (where the shower sprays over the basin) not designed for large passengers. Breakfast is monitored, harking back to Soviet days, perhaps. Four at a table. Four pats of butter. Four rolls. One visitor from the capitalist west asked the waiter for another roll and was ticked off. Four at the table. Four roles. Speaking of Soviet times, it was clear that the younger Ukrainians had travelled widely and had absorbed a lot of Western ways. Not so, many of the older generation. Even in the very fashionable restaurant where we were invited to meals, you not infrequently were served with soup, dessert, salad – in that order. Some waiters did not take kindly to the implied (and sometimes) explicit criticism. You could be punished by being kept waiting (and waiting) for the next course. But, it was interesting to see so many hoardings in the streets – everywhere for a local magazine with a completely unsympathetic picture of Vladimir Putin on the cover.

The films, including a day and a half of short films, were interesting enough. Lots of students in the audiences. Enthusiastic, but not yet at the stage of not talking during the screenings.

One of the advantages of festivals like those in Yerevan and Kiev is that there are a lot of invited guests, especially directors, whom you are able to meet and talk with. This is not something you can do at the big festivals. They come with everybody on the local tours. Since getting a camera, I have been making up for all the opportunities in interviews in the 1990s, not asking for an autograph. I ask if it is possible for a picture with the director, so now I have, for instance, Jafar Panahi (the Iranian director in house arrest), Wim Wenders who was Interfilm guest for their 50th anniversary in Locarno, and Catherine Hardwick when she was getting a U.S. Catholic award for *The Nativity Story*. In Kiev, Leos Carax (Holy Motors) sat at a corner table by himself at breakfast in Kiev, continually smoking. No, he didn't like getting his photo taken! By contrast, with Bruno Dumont (Camille Claudel 1915), we had five attempts where the lighting failed and we had to try at another venue. I tried to be apologetic for such ineptness. His reply as we posed again, 'That's what film-making is like: many takes.'

With the new century and the establishing of SIGNIS, there was new collaboration with Interfilm, not just in the Ecumenical Juries. During the first decade (before it became too expensive by 2008-9), there were a number of conferences which indicate the possibilities for continuing dialogue. A beginning was made in Mannheim during the festival in 2002, what can Catholics and Protestants learn from each other about cinema. More ambitious was a meeting in Romania, in Iasi in the northeastern part of the country (not Transylvania). Outside the city were the churches with their frescoes on the outside, not only well-preserved, but isolated and walled off during the Communist regime. Iasi was chosen because the metropolitan of the Orthodox Church in the area had worked for the World Council of Churches in Geneva and had an open attitude towards cinema and the arts. Delegates and visitors met in a monastery, watched films and discussed storytelling and symbols and their religious dimensions. For me, this was unexpected, to be in this, to me, remote country, to be talking cinema. But, only a month before, I had been in

Belarus for the establishing of SIGNIS Belarus, at a Divine Word retreat centre, more than a 100 kilometres west of Minsk, a group of 40 amongst whom we were assured were several spies for the government. We visited the site in the forest where several nuns had been killed during World War II (and had been beatified by Pope John Paul II). We visited the expanse of fields and crosses at the edge of Minsk, site of the executions by the invaders in 1941. We went to the cathedral where our guide told us he had gone as a boy because it was a gymnasium. Now restored.

These eastern countries were so different – and, from Iasi to Bucharest, the landscapes were so ugly, industrialised and industrially devastated. Ana Boriu, SIGNIS Romania, then took an initiative and for three years, 2005-7, she organised a festival of films dealing with children's rights and the abuse of children. It was held in central Bucharest, an ecumenical venture and an international occasion. Bucharest looked a bit different each year, a touch more spick and span – and it had recently become a member of the European Union. SIGNIS held its annual Board meeting there in 2007 during the festival.

It is developments like these which are important for Europe that we do not hear of on the other side of the world.

A couple of examples more to fill out something of this international, ecumenical dialogue on cinema. Peace themes were the focus of a gathering in 2007, sponsored by the University of Edinburgh. A local group in Norway inaugurated a series of conferences in Oslo, starting in 2009 with films portraying different world religions. SIGNIS had been contacted for help with getting Iranian films because of our jury work in Tehran. It was one of the best conferences in terms of film selection and speakers, and it ran like clockwork, or even better! I was allotted a task of looking at an American documentary highlighting racial and religious prejudice in American films and presenting a paper on stereotyping and demonising in films. Not sure about living in Olso, interesting as the rather small city was. This was early November and it was dark by four in the afternoon, rather gloomy and depressing.

A friend invited me to give a paper at the University of Vienna where he lectured. It was in English, explaining the involvements of the churches in the world of cinema and values in films. Interesting visit, though dark at four as well. However, a quick train trip, under an hour, from Vienna to Breslau and adding Slovakia to the list of countries visited! At this time, 2007, there had been complaints from the Slovakian government about the slasher American movie, Hostel, with its seeming message that Slovakia was a sinister place, a coven of secret torture chambers, dangerous for the unwary (and stupid) young American visiting students. But, on arrival at the station in Breslau, there in very prominent view are signs and advertisements proclaiming: 'Hostel.' Not sure they were getting so many takers – and then there were two movie sequels!

A comment on the Catholic front of conferences on cinema and religion. The Cavalletti series of meetings outside Rome in the 1990s were revived in 2007 and have continued, finding a home in the United States. However, the topics have moved from cinema and culture to cinema and theology, moving to more intellectual and academic considerations, to the theory of religion and cinema, more abstract reflections for theologians where frequently the theory becomes more interesting and dominant than the films themselves. Theologians dip into some of the high art films which means that they can have their cake without eating it. Come to think of it, it may be tangled metaphors like this which put them of watching and discussing the films that people to see.

Sister Rose Pacatte and I had collaborated on the series, Lights... Camera... Faith, Cycles A, B, C. The next in the series was published in 2006: *Lights... Camera... Faith: The Ten Commandments*. Discussion starters on faith and film with films that people do see.

Which leads to Manila.

The Catholic Communication Foundation has featured earlier in this story. During 2006, Terry Hermano, who had previously worked there before spending 18 years with the World Association for Christian Communication (WACC), had returned to CFA and suggested we run some courses there on film and faith – and we did, from 2007 to 2012 – principally for religious educators and pastoral workers. In those six years, we worked on the basic principles I had worked on in the book, *The Film*, back in the late 1960s. Terry suggested I might update the book, not something I wanted to do. But, looking through the book, I was surprised (and saddened) that, by and large, what I had written then was still relevant and applicable (except for the exclusive language of the earlier time). So ..., making the language inclusive and adding over 100 references to films since then, it made its appearance as Film and Faith (2008). Gathering together a number of articles and SIGNIS statements, the 2009 book was *Film, Faith and the Church*. We moved a little differently in 2010, with writer-director Doy del Mundo (whose first screenplay was for the classic Lino Brocka film, *Manila in the Claws of Light* (1975)) editing a book on *Spirituality in Filipino Film*. The last two books, 2011, 2012, were more catechetical, *Films and Sacraments*, using the *Lights... Camera... Faith* method, three films for discussion for each sacrament as well as for symbols and storytelling, and *Mary and Film*, an overview of the Virgin Mary, Gospel films as well as Apparition films and 'Mary-figures'.

Most of the seminars were at Communication Foundation for Asia, but we branched out for a more extensive experience with more Filipinos, going to Cebu, up country in Luzon and finally venturing, beyond apprehensions about reports of uprisings in Mindanao. We went to Davao City which was a calm city, aiming to be up-to-date as possible with malls, restaurants ... There is an exuberance about Filipinos which means that the seminars are lively and people participate and you learn a lot from them. Stephen Cuyos MSC and Bob Lopez from CFA always ensured we had power points and clips all ready for exactly the right moment in the seminars, something I could not possibly do myself. Sometimes seminar organisers baulk at setting up the technology and look to me, while I explain I am not a hands on cinema person – I am an armchair observer.

But, Manila days seem to be over as funding agencies consider the

Philippines a country that does not need the same amount of funding as before.

The mention of books brings up a project that was in the gestating for almost eight years. At a conference in St. Deiniol's Library, the home of Prime Minister, William Gladstone, near Wrexham in Wales, critic and writer, Tom Aitkin, gave a paper on Luis Bunuel's basic Catholicism even in his atheism, 'thank God, I'm an atheist'. Taking Viridiana, he made a sound case for Bunuel's Catholicism permeating his films. What if we found significant directors who, though not practising their faith – or over-practising, like Mel Gibson at the time – could be called 'Catholic Directors'? Friends said yes to contributing. Nineteen directors chosen (spread all over the world) and included Terence Davies, Denys Arcand, Eliseo Subielo, Fred Schepisi, Gaston Kabore, Lino Brocka, Louis Malle. After lots of Limbo experience, Through a Catholic Lens, was published in 2007. And, the World Association for Christian Communication (WACC) commissioned a reflection book, *Can Movies be a Moral Compass?*.

Perhaps this is the moment to slip in something of which I am happily proud.

Some pleasant machinations were going on at this time, with Philip, my brother and Michael Kelly CSsR, at the YTU, myself unaware. The surprise was that the Board of The MCD had decided to award me an honorary doctorate in Theology. The ceremony was at the Wilson Hall of Melbourne University where gowned and bonneted, the honoree had to stand alone on the stage while a eulogy was read, mine by my friend, Mary Scarfe. While standing alone and stared at, I was reminded of the woman taken in adultery, standing 'in full view' of everyone. However, the eyes were friendly and I appreciated the honour which, the president of the MCD said, was in view of contribution to theology and at an international level. (One of the great successes of the MCD was is establishment as a specialist university, MCD University of Divinity, 2011. In 2014, this was simplified to University of Divinity.)

Some good things happen if you live long enough!

I didn't have to go to all those meetings of the past, for the merger of the world Catholic organisations, to board meetings, to lots of planning meetings. But I did try to follow through on the work for my congregation, especially on media and communications, Chevcom. That was the name I proposed, after years of meetings in Rome to discuss our media ministry, to the councils of the MSC and the sister congregations. In 2005, they approved Chevcom. But it has been slow progress, so many other issues rising and pushing it down the pecking order. I was invited to the MSC General Conference in the Philippines in 2007. We organised talks to all the provincial superiors at CFA, a tour, display of products. I went for several days to Tagaytay City with the group. Lots of polite interest but nothing concrete. The sex abuse scandals have risen to the top of the pile of urgencies, media going down.

There was a meeting of lay members of the congregations in Santo Domingo at the end of 2008. Paying my own way and registration. Warm reception to explanations, hopes and dreams. Lots of DVD production, especially from Latin America. Lots of enthusiasm. But, it's like those retreats, peak experiences which are wonderful. Then it's down from the mountain. Ordinary life resumes with its busyness. Then it's 'oh yes, we must do something about that'. And it doesn't happen.

Well, I suppose we have websites now. And we didn't have them before!

Almost time to return home to Melbourne.

The thing was to make sure that the knowledge in my head that this phase of my life was coming to an end was to make sure I was emotionally ready to come home. Psyching myself up, so to speak, for a couple of years. And it worked. Of course, there was the packing, doing it gradually for over six months, taking books and papers, then clothes, down to the basement of Nazareth House and collecting boxes to put it all in. Six months of this kind of thing has a definite psychological effect: I am going home, leaving this behind.

Another thing was the realisation that being busy in London means that, unless there is a visitor, one doesn't go catching up on places one hasn't been to. My main piece for visitors, however, was to walk them round the London I was usually in. Start a walk at Piccadilly Circus and through the streets of Soho where they might get lost. See the squares, the churches, the film preview venues, to Leicester Square and down to Covent Garden and the Strand and back to Trafalgar Square, something visitors might not be able to do easily by themselves.

Bear with me for a moment as I not that I had to get on a couple of bus tours in the last month before leaving. Better to visit Stonehenge than not! Then off to Salisbury Cathedral. I had been to Bath, but pleasant to go there again – and see the grave of Arthur Philip and the Australian flag in Bath Abbey. Another day up to Oxford (after 44 years) and to Stratford on Avon (the same) and relive the memories and on to Warwick.

And off to the SIGNIS office in Brussels.

The last time for a meeting in Brussels, delayed because of the volcano in Iceland in 2010, stopping all air traffic in Western Europe for many days. I had missed the planning meeting I was invited to so thought not to go. Urgent request to go. It was for the farewell prepared by the staff – and glad I did go, emotional, definitely an end of a phase of life. And happy to have some kind of immortality with two photos on the wall amongst past presidents secretary generals of OCIC, Unda and SIGNIS: one for OCIC (looking younger) and one for SIGNIS (looking older).

And a wonderful small computer as a farewell gift – on which quite a deal of this book has been typed.

Then I turned 70!

I initially spent the evening of my 70th birthday in something of despair. Before coming home, a visit to Russia – and the realisation that this was not something one did alone. Which meant investing in a 14 day tour of Finland, Russia, Belarus and the Baltic countries. Off to Helsinki, to the hotel, to meet the guide and guests. My allotted room companion was an interesting character in himself: a Belgian who had migrated to Australia, worked on the Snowy River scheme and then all around Australia, from Mt. Isa to the west; he then went back home, married and returned to Australia, all this in the 1960s. He and his family lived happily in Glen Waverley in Melbourne (not far away from here at home); he and his wife travelled until she developed MS in the late 1990s; he took remarkable care of her but each year, for some weeks, he went on tours by himself. So, plenty in common and to talk about. But, he snored (upper case volume). After an hour that first night I did wake him up. It must have done the trick for me, some kindly self-assertion, because I was able to live with it for the fortnight.

While there have been lots of travels, this is not a travel book, but I can't help saying that St. Petersburg is an extraordinarily beautiful city, that we stayed in Novgorod (which seemed a long way from home), that one could be overwhelmed by Moscow and Red Square. I had been to Minsk and the Baltic capitals before, except Riga, when I had been turned back because I had no visa. The main difference was the visit to the huge hill of crucifixes in Lithuania, a vast testimony to persecuted people and to the power of faith.

To end this chapter, it remains only to say that as I went home, retiring from front line work for SIGNIS, we celebrated a congress in Change Mai in October 2009, where Augy Lourdusamy and the two vice-presidents were re-elected. Chang Mai is Asian exotic, but also a draw for European tourists. I pity the poor elephants who parade on show thinking my great grandparents didn't have to put up with this kind of thing!

Once again, the Asian Church excelled itself as it had for the congress in Bangkok in 1990. Over five hundred people were enrolled for all or part of the congress, not many Europeans or Americans. One hundred local schoolchildren took part in workshops on communication and art, performing what they had learnt and prepared for the assembly on the third day. There were also some young people being trained as journalists who made and showed programs on the Congress. There are only half a million Catholics or so in Thailand but they have great energy and faith.

45. BACK HOME, 2010-

HEATHROW. The by-now usual stopover in Hong Kong to see the people in the diocesan media office. Melbourne. Home – and in winter, a winter I had not experienced for 13 years. They were telling me it was the usual very cold, old winter. Nothing of the kind. After London in winter, Melbourne has seemed so much milder, and always far more sunshine.

Back home, back to 1A Mountain Grove, Kew, which the Australian government had let me have as my address while away. When they gave me the age pension in 2004, they still allowed me that address, only asking that I let Centacare know that I was travelling, when I came home and when I left again. No complaints on my part.

And, did I have any regrets in leaving Europe? As already mentioned, I had spent several years psyching myself up to be ready to go, to be detached, that leaving things behind, missing people left behind, was a big part of real life. Some of the reviewers in London wondered why I was returning to Melbourne. I had to tell them that I had a life before coming to England! Then when the 46 chests, so carefully and gradually packed over the months at Hammersmith (only to be transferred to the transport company's official chests) arrived at Kew (all collected if they were emptied by the next day – and they were) and all the stuff was carried upstairs to my nicely spacious room, I was back. Easy travel from the UK, participation in festivals, possibilities for conferences, these I sometimes miss, but there is more to life than missing things.

What was I supposed to do? The then provincial superior, Tim Brennan, sent a letter: media, adult education, Province matters. That's a reasonable order for remembering what being back home was like.

Media? Not too difficult. Back to reviewing for a start, meeting old reviewer colleagues, meeting new ones, being more active in the Australian Film Critics Association (having kept my membership while away). Reviewing is not so orderly as in London with Mondays and Tuesdays set aside solely for reviewing. Ours can be any day of the week, any time of the day, and are. Smaller number of reviewers, but good friendships with many of them. And, the benefit of having a pass with entry to ordinary screenings when one couldn't get to the preview.

Outlets – the same old: the SIGNIS website, the Australian Catholic Film Office available to all the Catholic outlets, print and online, in Australia. We were/are a small team headed by Richard Leonard, with Jan Epstein, Peter Sheehan (former Vice-Chancellor of the Australian Catholic University and one time member of the government classifications board) and myself as associates. A the time of this writing, it is my 46th year of reviewing!

There was still membership of the SIGNIS Cinema desk, email correspondence making it easy to discuss issues arising, whether they be matters with Interfilm (though I continued to attend the annual meetings

during the Berlin Film Festival). Some of us are the same old faces but in 2013, a new president of Interfilm, Julia Helmke, who had written the history of Interfilm for her thesis; a very good choice. Always some tensions with Interfilm, like presence at Venice, or an Ecumenical Jury. They infiltrated a bit, starting with small seminars during the festival, then a special jury and now a downright Interfilm jury – with both SIGNIS and Interfilm juries giving their awards to the same film in 2013, Stephen Frears' *Philomena*.

In 2011, dispute between the SIGNIS Board and the Board of the SIGNIS Foundation meant mediation. Both sides agreed that I should do the job, and we met, discussed, went to the annual Board meeting, wrote some documents which seemed to resolve the problems. Actually, they didn't. Solutions still pending!

On the brighter side, the SIGNIS executive had their annual meeting in Melbourne in 2011 – and came to dinner at our house. Always nice when others get to know your world and understand it a little more. In

2012, Jos Horemans and his wife, Lieve, stayed with us at the beginning of their tour of Australia. Smaller world.

We had the SIGNIS Pacific meeting in Noumea, with some wonderful touristic moments as well. Here we were in 2011, last visited for such a meeting in 1995. Just noting the developments of information technology between those two meetings. At the former, we lamented the isolation of the Pacific Islands. When would they have the communications privileges like those of affluent countries? At the latter, everyone had their mobile phones (except me, still don't), computers, etc, and, of course, power point presentations or video clips from their video cameras. And we all had to become members of Facebook – and that included such distant countries like Kiribati.

Three months later, I was in Suva to take part in a media week for the seminarians at the Pacific Regional Seminary, the program Bill Falekaono, from Tonga, had established in 1998. How much easier to carry DVDs than VHS cassettes, as happened in 1998. Now, of course, USB sticks containing one's clips. The 2011 seminarians thought our reminiscences were rather prehistoric.

But, the good old days (the very good old days) of festival attendance were over, except for the annual pilgrimage to Berlin. There was a last visit to Tehran – and the government of Iran changed the management of the festival for 2013, so no more jury until a further change. There was still Bangladesh and collaboration with Religion Today. The Dhaka festival runs on begging and a shoestring. But in 2012 there was the interest in stopping off in Kathmandu on the way back to Hong Kong. SIGNIS had just held its annual conference outside Kathmandu and Nepal had become the latest member of SIGNIS. A chance to talk with some of the new members about what might be possible – and some attempts to see the Himalayas which were mostly covered in cloud! (The traffic in Nepal you might find somewhat hairy but, compared with Dhaka, it was mild and orderly).

And Adult Education? A bit of the same old as well ... One good thing at the Heart of Life Centre was the introduction of a four day course on Storytelling and Spiritual Direction. The basis was film. There were the usual sessions on Jesus and Christ-figures. But, we wanted the participants to connect their direction work with response to stories and films. We looked at Neil Jordan's *The End of the Affair* with its Graham Greene God, sex and conscience torment and the group took it in turns to have a roll-play direction session on their response to the film, to the spiritual issues that touched them. Another film screened was Mike Leigh's *Vera Drake* a challenge of how to handle the personal and moral issues, especially the abortion theme, and of finding the sacred in the secular. Confrere Chris Chaplin was a co-worker, with some sessions on visual art and drawing and gestalt responses.

For the rest, adult education meant seminars on Jesus in film, some Myers-Briggs sessions with one thing that was a bit different. The Melbourne archdiocese Ministry to Priests began a series of film-watching and discussion for the clergy. I was asked to join and facilitate discussion. Great idea. Each first Monday of the month we gathered at the Nova cinema in Carlton, watched a film and then adjourned to the Ministry to Priests centre for lunch and discussion. We average about 10 – and the lunch is good – and, depending on the film, discussion works well. We had success with *Carnage*, *A Dangerous Method* and, particularly, *The Sessions* with its theme of a quadriplegic journalist and his desire for sexual experience, the work of a surrogate and his discussions with his parish priest. A year later there was *Thanks for Sharing* which dramatised sexual addiction and a 12-step program which raised the issue that we hadn't thought of, of celibate clergy and the possibilities of sex addiction (especially with internet) and pastoral care.

And 'Province matters'? Once again, being on a list of people to ask to run days for school staffs, parish talks – and workshops of Jesus in films! But, the main focus was finding myself editor of the website. Having been an enthusiast for the development of the site, I was at a meeting on how this could be achieved. I think it fair to Tim Brennan to state the he inveigled me into the job. He suggested we try a sample entry. I followed instructions – and then he said that now that I had put one item on the site, I could take over.

I have to say that I have enjoyed this work, finding an item of MSC interest but also national and local stories, Church stories that would be of interest to visitors to the site. It makes me realise that I would not have minded being a journalist. It's a matter of being alert, checking some regular sources, following leads. It's putting an item on every other day, often every day. With illustrations. 1500.

Here is a paragraph or more that I could not foresee when I started this manuscript. It is now 2013 and the year began with the resignation of Benedict XVI as pope, something I think we hoped he would eventually do. And he did – as the cartoon showing St. Peter's and the piazza said in the bubble coming out of the Vatican, 'You gave up what for Lent!' Which facilitates greater freedom for future popes.

And then they elected Cardinal Bergoglio: southern hemisphere, Latin America, Jesuit. And then he took the name, Francis. And then he travelled in the bus back to Santa Marta, where he paid his bill (another cartoon with an open-mouthed clerk and the Pope saying, 'I checked in under another name') and decided to live there and meet visitors at meals and at mass; and then he … the litany goes on. He rang and cancelled his paper in Buenos Aires; but he kept the same shoemaker. He washed the feet of women on Holy Thursday, in a prison, and the feet of a young Muslim. He celebrated Mass on the island of Lampedusa and the altar was made from a boat on which refugees from Africa had drowned. Cardinals began to put their cappas magna in mothballs. Cars were more low-key in the Vatican as were liturgical trimmings and vestments. He called himself Bishop of Rome. He took to calling people on the phone, giving impromptu press conferences on planes as well as lengthy interviews to Jesuit magazines. He attracted millions to his Masses on Copacabana (Popacobana) beach. He started reform of the Vatican

Bank and set up a group of eight cardinals, representing all continents, for advice on curia reform.

And so on.

And that was only in the first six months.

The point being that suddenly we had a leader who embodied and preached the poor in spirit, whose favourite words in speeches have been joy and mercy, who has urged Catholics out of a 'small church' to embrace all world issues and not to focus principally on sexual ethics. 'Who am I to judge ...?' He has attracted approving headlines worldwide, has encouraged Catholics and non-Catholics alike. In fact, those he has disappointed are extreme rightwingers ('I have never been a rightwinger', he declared) whose websites have been vitriolic – but they also call John Paul II and Benedict XVI heretics and declared that John Paul's reign was the worst in the recent history of the Church. And they said that before Francis arrived on the scene.

The Church must stop being 'too cold, perhaps too caught up with itself, perhaps a prisoner of its own rigid formulas, perhaps the world seems to have made the Church a relic of the past, unfit for new questions'.

I rather liked part of his text from World Youth Day in Rio:

> We need saints without cassocks, without veils. We need saints with jeans and tennis shoes. We need saints that go to the movies, that listen to music, that hang out with friends. We need saints who put God in first place, ahead of succeeding in any career. We need saints who look for time to pray every day and who know how to be in love with purity, chastity, and all good things. We need saints, Saints of the 21st century with a spirituality appropriate to our new time.
>
> We need saints that have a commitment to helping the poor and to make the needed social change. We need saints

to live in the world, to sanctify the world and to not be afraid of living in the world by their presence in it. We need saints that drink Coca-Cola, that eat hot dogs, that surf the internet and that listen to their iPods.

We need saints that love the Eucharist, that are not afraid or embarrassed to eat a pizza or drink a beer with their friends. We need saints who love the movies, dance, sports, theater. We need saints that are open, sociable, normal, happy companions. We need saints who are in this world and who know how to enjoy the best in this world without being callous or mundane.

We need saints.

Now, there's an ambition, 'we need saints who love the movies ...'.

We can breathe easy, breathe more easily – and hope that this trend will not be reversed. This has been an unanticipated feeling for us all, especially those who sparked with Vatican II and have felt much disappointment since.

So, in that vein, moving towards the end of this book, something on the current trends that I find, or have been invited to participate in, as we are getting used to the 21st century.

Despite coming home, there have been several conferences that I have been able to go to, indicating the diversity in interest in religion and cinema. There was an international meeting in Oxford in 2011 with invitations to contributors to reflect on the presence and the influence of the Church in cinema in their countries. The heritage of the American Legion of Decency, of course. And widely diverse experiences in, say, Italy, Ireland and the low countries. Guido Convents and I did our bit for the importance of OCIC and SIGNIS. You may not have heard of Opole, let alone go there. It's in western Poland, not far from the German border. In 2012, Marek Lis from the university convened a conference on representations of Jesus on screen. A number of Polish clergy analysed popular films in the way we used to in the 1960s and 1970s. The papers were interesting and well-argued. I was able to present humorous and irreverent portrayals of Jesus, including *Don Camillo*, Mel Brooks' version of the last supper, 'Separate cheques?', in *History of the World Part 1*, as well as some of the bizarre images, from Ken Russell and *The Devils* to those weird shorts and clips on YouTube, *Starsky and Jesus*, on police patrol in New York City!

More sober was a conference sponsored by York St. John's University where I had given some lectures in the past. The conference was held in Jerusalem in November 2012 and it was on peace and reconciliation and whatever could contribute to this. I was invited to speak on the theme with film. Not difficult to find films on that theme. One of the difficulties was holding the event in Jerusalem. A group of British academics protested that the conference affirmed the occupation of Palestine stances of the state of Israel. What about the presence of Palestinians? Not welcomed by some Israelis? Or criticised and shunned by Palestinians for participating? The conference was held, some few Palestinians attending, but an attempt to contribute to peace consciousness.

After the conference I was able to stay for a day or two with a confrere doing a course at the Tantur Ecumenical Centre. Here is a contribution to reconciliation and peace right there in Jerusalem. But, it is situated on a hill looking across at the apartment blocks which are some of the settlements in East Jerusalem. But at the bottom of the hill is the wall, something I wanted to see and experience – a Jewish friend in Australia, who sees it as a necessity, always refers to it as 'the fence'. There it is, long and winding, and so high. We went through the checkpoint to go to Bethlehem. The checkpoint reminds you of lanes for separating and pushing cattle forward. OK leaving Israel, but no smiles with the passport demands on the way back. And lots of images, graffiti, portraits on the wall.

The night I left, the rockets started landing on Israel again, rockets on Palestine, mutual retaliation.

I am not sure whether Omaha is one of the religious centres of the

United States, but the University of Nebraska, April 2014, is hosting a conference on religion and cinema.

Actually, that reminds me that in these years, a lot of film scholars and film buffs are being invited to write for book collection of essays or for on-line publications and Encyclopedias. Because of SIGNIS, I am on a number of lists. Two books emerged from Omaha in 2009, both named *Companion to Religion and Film* (one published by Routledge, one by Continuum). Since I was a Catholic contact for these ecumenical publications, I wrote on The Catholic Church and Cinema since 1967 for one. The other asked for images of the Catholic Church on screen, 5,000 words. A brainwave came to the rescue as I had used for seminars, Avery Dulles models of the Church, which include Institution, Sacrament, Herald, Prophet. By giving some explanation of each model and adding some examples, the topic and the 5,000 words meshed.

One mammoth task in the U.S. is editing an *Encyclopedia for the Reception of the Bible*, 25 volumes intended. Once again, I was on the list and have stayed on the list, from Cain and Abel, Celibacy, Demons, Devils, Fallen Angels, Franciscan Order, Frogs ... with Holy Week, Joseph of Arimathea and Jairus on the current list to do. An invitation to contribute a new article on film iconography of Jesus for the *New Catholic Encyclopedia*. I was sent an audio copy of the article but recorded by a machine voice which included the page number in the text and always pronounced Fr. as fur!

The good thing about these contributions is that they are for an ecumenical, even interfaith, readership. I have previously made a number of references to De Profundis films. Another book, *Light Shines in Darkness*, contained a full article on that theme. I wrote for *An Anthology on Spiritual Direction* an article on images and storytelling.

No worries about getting older and wondering what to do. Plenty to write. A book that took several years to write was published in the U.S. in 2012, *Screen Jesus*, portraits of Christ in television and film. I had wanted the quote from the foreword by my friend, Maggie Roux, 'from celluloid to digital', but the company board said no. I suppose I like collecting data as well as reflecting on it. So, *Screen Jesus* covers all the Jesus films, moving through the decades and looking at the development of Jesus films (and wondering why there was a commercial gap to full portraits of Jesus in English-language films from 1927 (De Mille's *The King of Kings*) to 1961 (Nicholas Ray's *King of Kings*)? Nothing during the Depression or World War II. Audiences in 1961, not all that long ago comparatively speaking, saw their first widescreen, colour, speaking, face-on portrayal of Jesus by Jeffrey Hunter.

One of the annoying but creative realities of data-seekers these days is the internet. One reference leads to another, to another, to yet another, with the possibility of watching a whole film or clip on the Internet Archive or on YouTube, so that the book gets bigger and bigger. It's not an academic analysis of the Jesus films, but rather, theologically speaking, using Bernard Lonergan's method which he used when he taught us Christology at the Gregorian University in 1964, a Via Analytica, gathering as much information so that the Via Synthetica will solidly grounded in that data.

In 2003, I began a similar approach to the portrayals of priests on screen, but had to leave it for many years. Well into it now. And getting larger by the week with more discoveries – the internet again. Recently, I was checking on Henry Travers, Clarence the Angel in *It's a Wonderful Life* and the businessman in *The Bells of St. Mary's*. Looking in the familiar pages of the IMDb, the Internet Movie Database, my eye caught 'Fr ...' in his performances list. I checked on the film, *None Shall Escape*. Never heard of it, but it looked interesting, a film about a war crimes tribunal in Poland, made in 1944 before the war ended. Next question, is it on YouTube, a quick look. It is and I had watched it within two hours of discovering it existed! I'm not sure when it will be finished, but I'm getting there.

Last thing on books. I finished my contribution to the new volume of the *Lights... Camera... Faith* series in mid-2005. Rose Pacatte was still finishing hers. And the years rolled by, sometimes an indication that it would come out. We took out six films in 2008 and substituted more recent titles to give some impression of being up to date. More rolling years. The manuscript was on the tarmac ... And more years (that's eight in total). Suddenly, in mid-2013, it was a goer. Another six films out, more recent ones in. It's to go to the editor. At this moment that is where it is at. Here's hoping.

A final thought, seriously, for this chapter.

Any story about a priest would require some consideration of sexual abuse. When I was informed in 1994 about the major MSC case in Australia, concerning Peter Chalk and his offences in the parish of Park Orchards, I never dreamed that I would spend so many days of my life in discussions on this issue. Most of us didn't. Yet, year by year, more and more accusations and revelations have been part of our lives. One of our first reactions was dismay at such crimes. Because we know the perpetrators, our automatic attention is on them and, generally, wondering how we could not have known.

What we have learnt to do is to draw on our compassion for the victims. For many this has been gradual, hearing some victims' stories and realising their suffering so that we try to empathise with them. Court cases, state inquiries in Victoria and New South Wales and the ongoing Royal Commission into institutional abuse have meant that there is a constant challenge for victim compassion. There is also the shame that clergy and religious, in such numbers, have been criminally abusive.

There has been a lot of writing and media reporting on the inadequacies of bishops' responses, of leaders of congregations and institutions – which were exposed early in Australia compared with some other countries, including the United States. Revelations are ongoing.

With my cinema ministry, it has been important to note the feature films, fictions and documentaries, and to make SIGNIS statements that indicate the issues of the films and the treatment. For many not directly connected with abuse crimes, the films open up awareness and compassion. The award-winning documentary, *Silence in the House of God* (2012) is one of the best, principally focused on Milwaukee, but also raising Vatican issues and how cases were handled there. It has been important to say that these films serve as an examination of conscience for the Church.

One of the areas in which Church representatives have been found wanting is in their responses to the media. Journalists have their job to do and they do it. Sometimes, they reveal an agenda, which can be for or against the Church which can be crusading. They are not always on the wavelength, don't have information, find difficulties with the technical language that the Church uses. Despite the urgings of Pope John Paul II that media are gifts of God, media is often seen by Catholics as the enemy.

I have found that the media respect those whom they perceive to be honest. Too many of our spokesperson don't communicate their honesty because of their aggression or their apprehensiveness or because they befuddle issues with 'inside' talk and terminology. And this happens despite so many diocesan or Catholic communications offices being set up to deal with the media and the abuse scandals. There is a continual need for training as well as selection of personnel who can communicate with journalists and earn their respect.

When *The Passion of the Christ* was released, I found myself being contacted for a statement or for an interview. There was a certain amount of press hostility towards the film, towards Mel Gibson, towards the Church as well as the issues of violence on the screen and critique of anti-Semitism. An invitation came from ITV UK. You go to make-up. You are introduced to the interviewer. And the program starts. This time there was the trailer, which looked pretty bloody – and audiences had not yet seen the film, so there was a certain amount of shock. Then there was an interview with a Jewish member of Parliament which was, to say the least, hostile to the film. What to do? Not sit there looking offended! Acknowledge the graphic tone of the film, acknowledge that the MP made some points but that you would not entirely agree. Offer an interpretation of the film discuss it with interest rather than hostility. The tone of the conversation changed. The interview went on for 13 minutes, the interviewer becoming more interested because points were made that led to discussion rather than polemic.

Further on *The Passion of the Christ*. The BBC asked me to see the Director's cut a year after the first release. They also asked me to sit in a studio at Broadcast House for two hours on a Sunday morning and be interviewed by 10 of their regional stations. All agreed to talk except BBC Belfast. Going over the same material made me realise that we are sometimes dependent on the interviewer. Most of these were stimulating with the questions they asked. A couple were either not interested or didn't have much background and asked some very lame questions. Trying to go further than this superficial agenda is very difficult, especially when the limit is three minutes.

One being-put-on-the-spot incident. The BBC Sunday program is 50 minutes (at 7.10 am) of topical religious items and interviews. I was invited on several times when there was a film of interest. The producer rang on Friday or Saturday and we worked out which questions would be of most interest to listeners. The time allotted was about three minutes. One morning, talking about *The Golden Compass* and author, Philip Pullman's hostility to churches, compere Roger Bolton suddenly asked an unprepared question, 'After all, Nicole Kidman is very beautiful?' Yes, expect the unexpected and be quick on your feet – or with your brain and your tongue! 'Well, she is an Australian, how could I say otherwise?' Much easier was pre-recording film reviews for Vatican Radio with Linda, English section, for several years.

The moral of these stories is that Church spokespersons or interviewees, no matter how apprehensive they feel on radio or television or with a press journalist, the interviewer can usually sense honesty and detect cover-up. Honesty and directness and admitting one does not have all the answers leads to being reported more fairly.

I am not sure whether all that just now was what I intended to write as I began this reflection, but there it is.

Now.

The ever-widening screen had not quite widened in the way expected

46. 'IT'S CANCER'

SOMEHOW or other, I had never thought that I would ever have cancer. Something else. Heart? In fact, I had never given any thought to the phrase 'renal carcinoma', though 'renal' was often a handy standby for those puzzles with letters for the nine letter word and other words.

Perhaps best to tell the story as it unfolded. Skip at will – or share mine with ER, Chicago Hope or All Saints experiences.

Always noticing the symbolic, I realise that the initial aches and nausea came on the first Sunday of the Passion, March 2012. In Dad's tradition of grin and bear it, that seemed to the best (allowing for a Panadol or two!). The community urged me on Holy Thursday to try to get an appointment with Denis Rebic, our longtime doctor. Providence, a vacancy that afternoon. As I explained how I felt, he immediately diagnosed a kidney stone. Never had one of those before and listening to subsequent stories of all those who felt they should vouchsafe their stories of stone pain (agony), mine seemed minor in comparison. Denis suggested a scan, so a hurried drive (and search for a parking spot), blood test and imaging in Prahran. One scan was done but they told me better to come back on Tuesday, after the Easter holiday, for another.

Tuesday. Imaging said that they needed something more for the scan and best to consult my GP. Denis suggested I come over to see him. Uh-ho, ominous. Premonitions! While I have just written this lightly, I was aware that there was something wrong – confirmed when I came out from Denis' office because I had inadvertently parked in a local permit zone ($72.00 fine) and, for the first time, had locked the keys in the car. I went into Denis, known him for years. He looked across his desk, reached out for my arm, clasped it, and simply said, 'it's cancer'. There's something to be said for no preparation for this news. And he added, 'weeks in hospital'. Not only that, I was to go to Cabrini Hospital Emergency that afternoon for the stone.

My parking errors and waiting for the RACV to come and unlock the car door for me were something of a gift. Time. As I waited and walked up and down Wellington Street, I had quite some time to contemplate: between the extremes of benign and malignant, to appreciate that I had had a wonderful life even if it was to end. That providence had guided my life – and would now.

Into Cabrini Emergency, where you also have plenty of opportunity to contemplate while they examine, test and do the formalities and as you sit for quite some time in a wheelchair. Let me spare you some details while giving others: general surgery with Mr. Ross Snow, the surgeon Denis recommended. Coming to consciousness in the recovery room, where everybody seemed to be chatting loudly and incessantly, I almost immediately worked out the nine-letter word from the morning's *Age*. I had mistakenly been thinking 'ch' words, whereas the correct word was 'hurricane'! Then the news from Mr. Snow that he could not reach the stone, too high up in the kidney. He had put in a stent – which, I must say offers a great relief, except when, excuse the detail, one is passing water. 'And it shall come to pass ...!' Then the aching tension lets you know the stone is still there. Come back in a fortnight for a lithotripsy! That is a day procedure, needing general anaesthetic, where the stone is laser-smashed. Recovery room again, but I had already worked out the nine-letter-word for that day.

We are now at the end of April. There are still four months or so before the surgery.

You would have to be detachment personified not to be at least a little concerned about how one really was healthwise and what was going to happen. Maybe it's surgeon tradition, but the next three months called for some stoic patience in uncertainty. And, the trouble was that I felt perfectly well and continued life as normal. I Googled, of course, but am not sure what I learnt about the growths themselves. What I did find was that most kidney growths are discovered through scans. One could be living with them without any realisation or pain whatsoever.

The next step, after a fortnight, was a scan to check on the stone and its removal. Then another fortnight or so before the interview with Mr. Snow. I was to realise that every step was in fortnightly scans, biopsies, interviews. When I was wheeled at last into the operating theatre, Mr. Snow did actually say, 'finally'. He had also mentioned that the process had dragged out over the months when we had the final pre-op meeting. Indeed.

This is where it gets a bit dire. The initial scan from imaging and a subsequent scan for Mr. Snow had revealed a large lump in the left kidney. That was the alarm for Denis. But the new scan revealed another lump, this time in the right kidney. It had been hidden in previous scans by the stone. Verdict. Malignant lumps in each kidney. Two operations needed (and no keyhole surgery shortcuts). One on the right kidney first (in case the left kidney had to be removed entirely), then, after a month or so, the operation on the left kidney.

Of all things, after the stent placement, I was tidying my room and looking at various folders. What should I find but the death certificate of my mother's father, the grandfather from Dunedin? Glancing down, as one does, I noted 'Cause of death': left kidney carcinoma! Mr. Snow was not always forthcoming. But he did ask what age my grandfather had died and seemed happier that it was 81 (and that was in 1953 before a lot of medical developments).

Any authority can be intimidating, but the community prevailed on me to phone him as there was nothing definite forthcoming. He told me the urology group met each Thursday and were discussing what was best to do in my case. Surgery could be either 11 July or 18 July. I was bold enough to ask whether the lumps were benign or malignant. The answer, 'malignant, but 'good malignant'. Which I presumed meant that they were not aggressive. It transpired that Mr. Snow was about to go on annual leave and would return for the 11th.

June. A surprise message to go for a biopsy on the left kidney. The doctor in charge of biopsies, Dr. Alain Lavoirpierre, was a genial humourist who had grown up in Mauritius, a devout Catholic who enjoyed talk about the Church, and Church jokes. I hardly felt a thing. The inevitable two weeks, but I was to see Mr. Snow's associate, Mr. Grummet. He was a pleasant man. As he got the x-rays in order, I thought I heard him say 'good news' but, since that was the last thing I was expecting, I wasn't sure whether I had heard correctly. He said it again. What possible good news?

It appeared that the large lump in the left kidney, the one that alarmed Denis, was benign. No need for an operation. Regular surveillance, scan or ultrasound would be sufficient to check whether it had grown. It was an Oncocytoma (and back to Googling). Only one operation needed, an extraordinary relief, an extraordinary grace.

Speeding up now. Why not a biopsy of the right kidney? Still the cheerful doctor (who, when the nurse missed my vein for the injection, suggested she be excommunicated!) but this lump was more difficult to reach, but really minimal discomfort. Then the wait for an interview. Best to do another scan to make sure the stone was completely gone and that the growth had not migrated to the lungs or chest. Fortnight. Mr. Snow was back. Yes, surgery needed. How about 15 August? Better than on 8 August, my birthday.

Since one is unconscious during the surgery, little to tell. Except that I was told afterwards that I had to be opened a second time on the 15th. The team was unsure about internal bleeding (and Mr. Snow had warned that this kind of surgery could lead to extensive bleeding and the need to remove the entire kidney). Apparently I was given another general anaesthetic. Not blood inside, only ooze from the operation. OK.

Since the two operations took most of the day, I woke up in intensive care (the HD, high dependency ward). Just as noisy as the recovery room. Then to the ward. The previous visits to Cabrini were in a shared ward. Now I was given, without asking, a private room. No complaints.

Mr Snow came each morning. Each morning he looked at 'the wound'. 'Looking good.' So, a week of gradual recovery, fluid diet for four days, concern about passing wind (a lot of the pain would eventually be gone with the wind!), sitting up, washing, then showers, little walks. I had come prepared with books and DVDs but had no inclination for them really. Radio is a great standby. But, if you have had surgery or visited family or friends, you know about this. Then home – where I am writing this. Therapy? Perhaps.

A word about the wound. When I saw it in the mirror, I realised it was a gash, a GASH, about 30 centimetres. From the back down to the front of the stomach. The thought came of Jesus saying to Thomas, put your hand in my side. By the look of the length of this one, no problem. Staples not stitches, 24 of them. (And now the scar is scarcely visible.)

The problem is that, except for the soreness on my right side and some distention, I feel all right. Eat whatever you like! But, Mr. Snow did promise that after a month or so I would be back to normal. So, quiet, patience, no stretching, being waited on (and wondering when I can go reviewing again!).

While I was in hospital, news came that director Tony Scott (*Top Gun*, *Unstoppable*) had leapt from an LA bridge. There was mention of a note citing 'inoperable cancer'. This was later denied. But, there was the phrase. I had had an operable cancer. That really brought home to me – or, at least, I pray that it has, that this is what I had experienced. (And I could start my own gallery with all the x-rays I have collected.)

In January, 2012 was never going to be like this. We make decisions and God laughs, though this time, with the stone, he gave me a head start. When I realised that the growths came to light because of the experience of the stone, I knew that prayers can be answered beforehand, so to speak. Had there been no stone, who knows how the growths might have developed and what threat would have eventually been revealed? The promise of prayers from so many, the supportive concern of confreres and friends, was overwhelming. The success of the surgery, no excess blood, 'looking good' each day, seem a wonderful testimony to the prayer of petition. I am full of wonder.

The other thing I realised is that the kindness and concern of everyone, phone calls, visits, cards and messages, Peter Curry taking me to surgery and staying all day even with the extra operation (and bossing me about afterwards with commands to rest!) also made me full of wonder. The many facets of love, tenderness, genial humour and people putting themselves out for my sake made me aware that these were the facets of God's love, tenderness, humour.

So, no matter what happens now, health or illness, I have been given graced time to contemplate what life has meant, what it means, and to appreciate it as a gift – which now must be shared even more.

47. AND ...

TIME TO BRING this book to a conclusion. I need to tell you that I travelled to Europe for a conference in Poland two months after the surgery and, almost immediately after that, to Israel for another conference on Peace and Reconciliation. And visits to the surgeon are sixth-monthly. Again, a sense of gratitude and grace.

I forget whether I actually explained why I have called the book *An Ever-widening Screen*. It comes from an image of the early 1950s. In 1953, at MGM theatres like the Regal at Bondi Junction, the main feature began with the box screen format we were used to. I am remembering Jane Powell in *Small Town Girl*. After the director credit faded, the curtains opened just that little wider on to a broader screen. Seemed a little movie magic at that time (but more than a touch prosaic as I type this). Oh well, it's an image. But ... six months later or so, Philip and I were sitting in the Regent Theatre in George Street for the first Cinemascope film, *The Robe*. And the curtains opened, opened, opened, opened, revealing an ever-widening screen. So you see what I mean.

Looking at my life on this ever-widening screen, I see my Australian setting, my Catholic background, no, foreground. I see education, religious formation, commitment by vows in a religious order with its spirituality of the heart. There are theological studies, ANU studies, studies in Rome and a literal opening to the world at large, let alone the impact of the Second Vatican Council. And always the pictures until they turned into films, to cinema and (I write with a touch of anti-American sentiment and distaste) the movies. I see teaching in school in the turbulence of the mid- to late-1960s. Teaching as well to young seminarians, sharing in their formation in the uncertain, disrupted late 1960s and the 1970s.

Then, the pace of life on the screen picks up. Years go by. Exhilarating experiences of formulating curricula for the MCD, different adult education programs, personal formation work with students in those not so easy, uneasy, times of 1968 to 1983. Another opening to the world with a sabbatical in Berkeley, California. Moving into a small house in the suburban streets and housekeeping. Even more adult education and a longer sabbatical in New York City.

And, all this time, reviewing films, writing, teaching, learning.

Then 20 plus unpredicted and unpredictable years of the Catholic Church's cinema and audiovisual organisations. The screen is world-widening. Australia, the Pacific, world responsibility. What is an Australian Catholic priest doing in this cinema world? What should he be doing? What did he do?

In the *Golden Years of Hollywood*, the film came to its conclusion with 'The End' up there on the screen. In more recent decades, that ending has lapsed. The film goes on with acknowledgement of all those who have contributed with craft, skills and imaginative creativity. The first credit is usually for the director. For my ever-widening screen, to start using God-language might seem pompous, pious or twee. But I have always been most comfortable in using the language of Providence. Looking back, God's Providence has been a creative, hands-on director. I won't go through all the credits, from family, religious confreres, friends, many members of religious orders, teaching colleagues, spiritual listeners and advisers, OCIC and SIGNIS collaborators – and the surgeon and Cabrini hospital staff for deft surgery and care.

After that last sentence with credits that could have been expanded, you will realise why so many audiences feel the compulsion (wrongly) to exit the theatre as instantly as possible.

But, during those credits, the story sometimes continues, or the makers and cast offer us funny out-takes of filming boo-boos. Sometimes there is more after the credits come to an end, some funny after-images – and even something mysterious that indicates there can be more, a sequel. Life consists of sequels, so the final word has to be (providentially): And ...

AFTERWORDS: MY MOTHER, EILEEN, MY FATHER, JOE

EILEEN

Eileen. Eileen Grace. Lovely names.

Dying. An ordinary ward, clean, light. Standard iron bedstead, hospital white linen, trolleys, pans, table, chairs. She was dying. She had been dying for months now. Our last visit.

We had brought flowers. Two little boys with flowers for their mother, for their last visit with their father.

'They're lovely.' Not her last words to us, but the last words I remember.

What happened during the visit so long ago? So long ago that the medical expertise of the day could not save her. Could help her, not save her. Pregnant, in the Royal Women's Hospital, Paddington, with many other pregnant 30-year-old mothers. But ill, terminally ill, her blood clotted, a tumour on the brain.

What happened during the visit so long ago? What did the two little boys know? Quite a lot at seven-and-a-half. A little less at just turned five. But not enough to know what dying was like. Name it, yes but not know. And what about feelings? Crying would come soon. But, why? Why tears for dying? End? Absence? Love? Loss? Bewilderment?

'They're lovely.' Gentle words from a young woman everyone said was gentle. And it's still there in the photos, those snapped so joyfully and skilfully by her brother-in-law. It's still there in the photos nicely, reverentially, displayed in the albums: the wedding, the lace and veil of the times, the graceful stoop and the gathered train to step into the car, the downward glance and glimmer of inner smile in the more formal groupings, bridesmaid sisters who would become aunts, bald-domed

father standing stately and prosperous, mother-in-law a touch severe in her joy, but proud of her son, standing, posed, but a good-looking, strong, friendly man whose day of happiness it was.

Quickly turning the album pages now, you can see the certainly expected, but delightful glimpses of a loving couple, new parents and baby and even a goo-goo shot in Centennial Park. Baby baptised, held by mother, by father, by grandmother, by aunts, by uncle, no doubting the Christian family community. Baby at play, a spade and shovel, the beach, plumptoddling, wearing mummy's hat. And then new parents again. New baby: ditto. And two little boys take over the photos, hardly any of the parents.

I suppose the memories of relatives and friends are like the photographs. Glimpses, moments of life coming alive in the spoken word: 'Your mother never let you wear shoes in the backyard. Better for your feet.'

'Bananas witl their skins on, orange peel. You ate the skins and the peels. Natural health. Eileen let you eat them.' 'Do you remember the time you went up to Our Lady's altar in the Maroubra Junction church? Everyone else took up flowers. You took up fruit.' 'Your mother was very patient and trained you well. The time you crawled into a cupboard and she spent 20 minutes explaining to you why you shouldn't do it.'

Glimpses: In fact, there are some glimpses, but blurred.

A green overcoat. Going to Charles E Blank's studios in Pitt Street to be photographed for an advertisement. Going to the Sydney radio station to the recording of *The Quiz Kids*. 'And don't sing. You haven't got a good voice.'

Going to the Children's Hospital in Camperdown. The younger boy was two but had to have a serious eye operation. One eye stronger than the other. He had to have it out and put back. Waiting to visit him. But wonderful meals at Grace Bros. cafeteria.

Going to visit friends with a palatial home at Balmoral (the bathroom and the bath were green with green dolphin taps). But the paralysis was starting and the steep flight of steps up from the harbour was too much. She had to sit and rest.

An irrational outburst of tumour temper, a clock thrown, the mediation of her sister.

Coming home from the First Communion Party. She was too sick, too bedridden to be there.

Being taken out by Mrs. Adams who had to look after us in the last months to her numberless sons' and daughters' homes all over Sydney, to the pictures.

And that's all. Memory albums with only a few snaps.

'They're lovely', and, now, I think 'Goodbye', or am I imagining her? I do see her waving as we leave, awkwardly, paralysis constricting her arm. Oh yes, and the little trickle of specked spittle dribbling slowly, helplessly from the corner of her mouth.

'They're lovely.' 'Goodbye.'

Little boys don't go to funerals. Mrs. Adams took us to one of her daughter's homes at Hammondville, until it was all over. Sheltered. But we were brought up in a piety of hope. Dying was perfectly natural. 'Your mother is in Heaven now.' Of course, she was. Looking down on us lovingly, looking after us. Every year, her anniversary was a saint's feast day, a time of happiness, 23 February. She was in Heaven. There's an enormous reserve of strength and comfort in that piety, though there are regrets in retrospect that we weren't at the funeral. It wasn't a fact. And the crowded-in, neglected grave in Botany cemetery seems unreal.

Eileen Grace. Lovely names. Memories of memories.

JOE

This is not so much a story about Joe but a tribute to a man whose father drove a tram for 30 years, who left school at the age of 12 after evading an education that scarcely met his natural intelligence (where he was frequently caned for mucking up), who survived the Depression by playing cricket with Bradman and tle greats and touring country New South Vales playing half-back in Rugby League, whose 30-year-old wife died when he was 36 leaving him with two small boys, who never married again (though he claims there were a couple of near missesnear-missus), who re-shaped his life interstate working as a wardsman until he was over 50, who kept and cared for bowling greens meticulously and became a bowls champion (and an apostle for the sport) – who has an innate savvy about the stock exchange that would astonish the professionals, who keeps honing his media talents developed when he worked in advertising and radio and sport in the 1940s and jots down and then telephones in to columnists the sports commentators' 'Boot in Mouth' faux pas, who used to prepare the Chelsea parish altar for Mass, but in later years has prepared it for the Eucharist, who loves people (and not just en masse but individuals and is tolerance personified (well, except for a couple of sportsmen and a Victorian premier named Kennett), who delights flirtatiously in the presence and company of women, enjoying being called 'Joseph' and who did not hesitate for a moment in saying 'yes' to his two sons' decisions to become priests, never hesitating to let everyone know how much he enjoys their lives and ministry, which take place in academic circles he never moved in, beyond the shores of the country he never left, and who always signs his letters, 'Your proud Dad.'

You have to begin with a joke, not necessarily a pun (that usually leads to half a dozen more, minimum), but a joke. Joe always enjoys telling a joke. This one is from the Scottish assistant priest who was always ready with a selection and Joe always says that if there's nothing else in the Mass homily, at least you've got the joke to take home. It's this one:

Did you hear about the priest who was having a nightmare.

He dreamed he was giving a sermon.

But then he woke up...

... and he was.

(To gain the best effect for this joke, you need to perfect your timing for pauses between lines and it's a great gimmick to test whether people are actually paying attention to what you say).

But how to tell the Joe story? You can't really. It's been a quietly eventful life, though the pain came earlier rather than later. In so many ways, there's so much to tell. But then again, there's nothing particularly spectacular. I think a photo album might do more justice to Joe's life, but not the predictable photos, rather the unexpected snapshots, the snaps that you might not put into the album.

The first would definitely be that First Communion morning. He's standing at the door of the school hall after Mass. It's communion breakfast time and the boys and girls are being treated to sweets. Joe is smiling, giving out the ice-creams. That shows you how long ago that was just after the war. But he stands there, always smiling. And, half a century later, he has not lost his genial smile.

The next snapshot is something of a glimpse as well. He had had to make a hard decision after Eileen died so young. And the two boys were so young. To stay living in the family home that he had built and where they were still staying, more or less as boarders, because he had invited cousins in with their large family? or to move away?

First of all, he arranged for the boys to go to boarding school, away in the country, where they would be looked after, have women's influence in their growing up, and be taught by the nuns. He himself would change his life completely and move from Sydney to Melbourne. The boys knew he had gone but did not know when he would be coming back. This is the glimpse. Visiting day at the college, the boys all in the large dining room. For no real reason, one of the boys looks up and sees two nuns guiding a man along the linoleum from one door to the other through the centre of the hall-like room. But the man's head is turned away from where the boys are sitting. But it's Joe. He and the nuns had kept his coming a secret, to be a wonderful surprise. It was.

Now for a real photo. Joe is standing with his two sons, one still at school, the other looking particularly gaunt and solemn in a religious habit on his profession day. Joe looks marvellous. He is 47, dapper in his smart suit, healthy and fit (though he has a pipe which does not seem to have had any lasting effect on him). His is proud of his sons.

You would need an album or more for the bowls photos. Joe played bowls professionally and religiously, in several clubs along the eastern bay side of the Mornington Peninsula. He was a frequent pennant winner and won an extraordinary number of trophies, not for the mantelpiece but, in the tradition of the edifying Victorian (at times, mid-Victorian) bowling club ethos, there were grocery vouchers, table glasses, fruit bowls. Joe also became the official green-keeper at Carrum and never has a green been so pampered, watered, re-seeded, shaved, from earliest morning to late evening. There he is bending over the lawn, picking out the smallest of weeds. There he is, in the compulsory immaculate whites, checking the kitty and eye-lining for the curve and the bias. He started as a disciple, but then became an apostle for bowls. It offers sporting spirit and exercise; it offers a community for the elderly and the lonely; it is an equalising experience. And Joe, when he was a member of the more affluent Beaumaris club, was happy that he could park his little Hyundai with the BMWs and the Mercedes.

While we are still outside, we can look at a photo of Joe in his garden. Joe loved his garden, flowers, yes, but principally vegetables. A very early riser, he liked to walk to buy *The Age*, and along the Chelsea beach, the amateur beachcomber par excellence. The amount of money he has found in the sand, along with biros and cigarette-lighters, is much much more than you are thinking. And then to the vegetables, with soil, manure and seaweed: lettuces, cabbages, broccoli, carrots, potatoes and tomato vines. Joe believes in healthy, simple food and he doesn't believe in doctors.

Speaking of doctors suggests another glimpse. At the age of 82, Joe eventually found himself in hospital, in need of a hernia operation. It took several false alarms, offers of a free bed being withdrawn on the day he was supposed to go in. The hospital system was in chaos that year. But early in Christmas week they admitted him. The operation was a success. When the ward sister came to the phone to answer enquiries about how he was, she said that he was awake and saying how wonderful it was to be surrounded by such lovely nurses. He was all right.

But, there he is in a ward of six. Within hours, he had the life story of each patient, especially the hefty bloke in the bed opposite who had been bashed at his front door. Joe sat up in bed chatting, but his eyes were darting around the ward and out into the corridor, not missing anything that was going on. Should he need to have to go to hospital again, this was a great (and entertaining) rehearsal.

But he won't want to go. He is of the stoic old brigade. You put up with the pain. If you fall or if you strain your ribs, then you live with it. If it's cold, then you fill up your water-bottles and know that it will eventually get warmer.

A few snaps of Joe with his many friends: Margot whom he met when she was a TB patient in the '50s, Joan who was his matron when he worked at the War Vets hospital. And the various nun friends whom he likes ringing and having long chats with when they have the time. He heartily approves of the changes in religious life and the chance for nuns to be women. (He enjoys going with Sister Patricia, the parish assistant, to lunch at Sizzler). And the men and women he has got to know over the years, saying hello spontaneously, caring for them although he would never put it that way himself. But he does. In fact, while he has lived for almost half a century by himself, and away from most of his family, he loves people.

Writers who comment on the basic stories that shape all our lives tell us that our final life issue is 'freedom'. The stories they associate with that deepest freedom are the stories of the 'sage', the stories of experience and wisdom, and the 'fool' (not as silly as it might sound), the stories of delight and being oneself and not beholden to anyone. Joe has an engaging and infectious smile. It is the smile of a human sage and a divine fool.

Joe, after a few days of pain and frustration, quietly stopped breathing in the early morning of 12 December 1997. His most constant companion at home and at Cluny Hostel, his water bottle, held a prominent place on his coffin during his co-celebrated requiem. He is buried in the lawn at Cheltenham Cemetery facing a busy road where a lot is going on a touch of extrovert's Heaven for him.

Joe and Eileen, wedding, 1938

Three generations, 1947

With Nana and Aunty Sheila

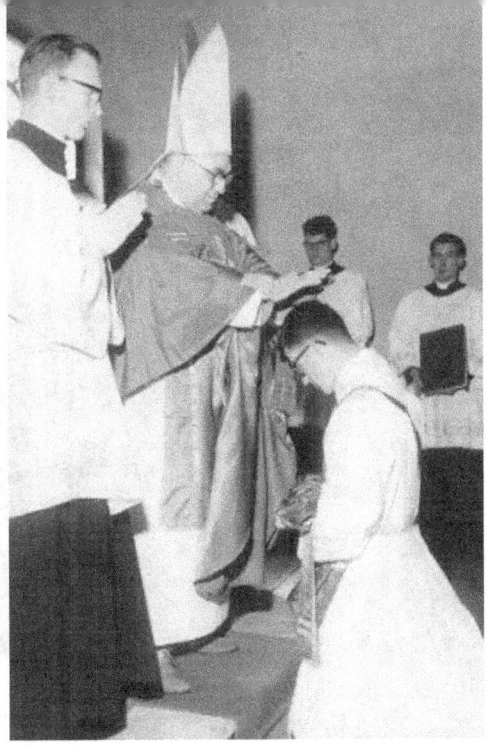
Ordained by Archbishop Pericle Felici, Rome, 1965

Profession Day, 1958

Graduation, Australian National University, 1968

Fr Fred Chamberlin, mentor

Croydon Community, 1975

Media workshop with Peter Thomas, Cook Islands, 1987

St Elizabeth's in Washington Heights, 1989

Dad, 'the real Father Malone', Philip and Peter, 1990

Malone family gathering, Philip's Silver Jubilee, 1991

Nazareth House, Hammersmith

OCIC award to Rolf de Heer, Venice, 1993

Presenting OCIC members to John Paul II

SIGNIS Asia meeting, Manila, 2002

With Ken Loach, Cannes, 2004

SIGNIS Board, Strasbourg, 2004

Visiting MSC, Vietnam, 2005

With Rose Pacatte FSP, Los Angeles, 2006

Discussion panel, Dhaka, 2006

Presenting SIGNIS awards, Fajr Festival, Tehran

Maggie Roux, Trinity University, Leeds

Friends and support, Jan Epstein and Phyl Coffey

An honorary doctorate, Melbourne, University of Divinity

Guido Convents, Cinema desk, SIGNIS, 2010

Robert Molhant, Secretary General, OCIC and SIGNIS, 2003

MSC Victoria-Tasmania Community, 2013

www.ingramcontent.com/pod-product-compliance
Lightning Source LLC
Chambersburg PA
CBHW071231300426
44116CB00008B/995